PRACTICING ORGANIZATION DEVELOPMENT

WILLIAM J. ROTHWELL
JACQUELINE M. STAVROS
ROLAND L. SULLIVAN
EDITORS

PRACTICING ORGANIZATION DEVELOPMENT

LEADING TRANSFORMATION AND CHANGE

FOURTH EDITION

WILEY

Published by John Wiley & Sons, Inc., Hoboken, New Jersey
Published simultaneously in Canada

Library of Congress Cataloging-in-Publication Data is Available:

ISBN 978-1-118-94-770-8 (hardback)
ISBN 978-1-118-94-772-2 (ePDF)
ISBN 978-1-118-94-771-5 (ePub)

Cover Design: Wiley
Cover Image: ©iStockphoto/Squaredpixels

Printed in the United States of America

SKY10021235_091520

*William J. Rothwell dedicates this book
to his wife Marcelina, his son Froilan, his daughter Candice,
and his grandsons Aden and Gabriel.*

*Jacqueline M. Stavros dedicates this book to her husband Paul,
her children Ally and Adam, her parents, students, her colleagues
in the Appreciative Inquiry field, and her Lawrence Tech family,
who provide unconditional support and guidance.*

*Roland L. Sullivan dedicates this book to his daughter Arielle, his
brother Thomas, and centric mentors: Dr. Sivananda of Rishikesh,
Dr. Jack Gibb, Richard Beckhard, Dr. Bob Tannenbaum,
Ms. Kathleen Dannemiller, and Dr. David Cooperrider.*

CONTENTS

LIST OF FIGURES, TABLES, AND EXHIBITS

Exhibits

ACKNOWLEDGMENTS

No book is the product of its editor or authors alone. This book is no different. Creating a fourth edition takes a great deal of time, effort, depth of conversations, and flurries of emails with many people. Accordingly, we would especially like to thank the editorial, design, and production team at John Wiley & Sons for their support of this project, especially Matt Davis (Acquiring Editor), who has provided direction and answered our questions for each and every edition. We also enjoyed working with Heather Brosius and Tiffany Colon (Editorial Assistants), Abirami Srikandan (Production Editor), Becky Morgan (Manufacturing Manager), and Paul McCarthy (Cover Designer) on this edition.

We are tremendously grateful to our contributing authors for their willingness to write their chapters and respond to our repeated requests for revisions and proper citations with references. The array of authors provides a wealth of history, present moments, and future possibilities of OD since the 1950s. It has been an honor to work with them! Thank you to Lou Carter, who has made many contributions to the field of OD and took the time to write the Foreword for the fourth edition, capturing the success, changes, and challenges of the field especially in this edition as it relates to transformation.

A special thank you to family and friends who provided backup reviews and edits to our chapter reviews as the deadline came to a close. These include Jae Young Lee, Paul Stavros, and Aileen Zaballero. We would also like to give special thanks to Ally Stavros, who once again provided devoted assistance to double-checking citations, formatting, and references for each chapter.

And, we thank our families and friends for their support and patience during the long writing and editing hours especially during the holidays.

FOREWORD

ORGANIZATION DEVELOPMENT: TRANSFORMING THE WHOLE ORGANIZATION TO THRIVE, PERFORM, ACHIEVE GOALS, AND GROW SUSTAINABLY

Louis Carter
Founder and CEO
Best Practice Institute
www.bestpracticeinstitute.org
West Palm Beach, FL

Since 1998, Best Practice Institute has released its top best practice organization development (OD) programs highlighting the most admired and innovative companies around the world. Topping the 2014 best practice leaders are the global brands of Bristol-Myers Squibb, Kimberly-Clark Corporation, Cigna, Hilton Worldwide, QBE, Baxalta, Tyco, MasterCard, Thomson Reuters, and BlackRock, among others. These are all globally recognized leaders in their respective industries and represent organizations whose employees report high levels of job satisfaction, are convinced of their management's credibility, and enjoy strong ties to their companies' culture, goals, vision, and operating philosophy.

Each of these companies have created both a corporate culture of transforming and thriving through their strong sense of community and loyalty among their workforce that extends to their business and community partners, customers, and shareholders. Their employees have become partners with their companies, and as such, are invested in their companies' ongoing success and empowered to be innovative and forward-thinking. Furthermore, the companies' enthusiasm and dedication are recognized by potential stakeholders who desire to partner with thriving companies.

A defining factor in the accomplishments of these companies is their focus on *development*—the ongoing process of innovation and improvement—whether it be a product, process, policy, or person. Today's business strategists must be mindful not just of product growth, but of the importance of planned, careful OD, transformation, and change.

While the concepts of OD and change are not new, it has become even more important in today's globalized, competitive environment as organizations are required to quickly adapt to evolving marketplace pressures, streamline global supply chain processes, adopt technological advances, and compete for the best and brightest talent to perform and sustain themselves.

Unfortunately, many business executives still do not take full advantage of OD and fail to understand how to make a positive impact for every stakeholder. By understanding the foundation, theories, practices, and processes of successful OD, internal and external OD practitioners can help their companies to identify avenues for successful transformation; this planned process ultimately results in the very successes identified by the employees, partners, and customers of Best Practice Institute's best practice organizations.

In exploring various models of OD and frameworks for effecting improved organizational performance, *Practicing Organization Development* has been a strategic resource for business leaders, HR professionals, process consultants, trainers, and researchers since the first edition was first published in 1995. The new, fourth edition of the book continues this tradition, providing insight into exciting new voices in the field of OD and change. The new edition also introduces the concept of transformation, because many organizations are looking for those who fundamentally understand and can lead transformation.

The enduring popularity of *Practicing Organization Development* among OD practitioners and scholars owes to its reach beyond the typical business casebook; it is designed from proven OD theories and practical application as well as focused on current and future challenges and implications of the OD field.

Over 50 internationally recognized OD practitioners and scholars have contributed their knowledge and expertise to the fourth edition. This new edition signals a period of the importance of transformational change and leadership that has been recognized in today's global environment. For the fourth edition, new contributors bring relevant insights on their research and practices that apply specifically to the twenty-first-century challenges that OD professionals face today. This new edition will help the readers:

- Understand new and classic theories and practices of transformation
- Examine diversity and inclusive whole system dynamics to impact change
- Identify contemporary themes in OD, such as positive organizational scholarship, sustainability, Appreciative Inquiry, social media, coaching, dialogue, well-being theory, strengths-revolution, social networks in heterarchical organizations, and more
- Elevate and extend their practices with new theories and models for positive transformational change
- Understand the different OD cultures
- Utilize the concept of behavioral change to promote and sustain individual development
- Create innovative teams
- Build the ethical strength of a firm
- Leverage diversity and create a common language to increase collaboration
- Understand how power and politics affect OD

The fourth edition also includes a comprehensive consideration of practical applications and special issues such as:

- Understanding how to implement transformational change, its complexities, and how transformation change drives business results
- Using a model for change as a compass to direct the change process
- Harnessing the power of T-groups to achieve personal and professional development
- Develop transformational leaders
- Applying OD practices for large systems and global environment
- Using SOAR framework to build strategic capacity
- Learning how environmental sustainability calls for new competencies
- Leveraging the relationship between organization design and OD
- Predicting performance and assessing competency
- Marketing your OD skill set
- Understanding the engagement and launch phase of OD
- Navigating the countless number of evaluation tools and how to assess the effectiveness of OD interventions (i.e., mergers and acquisitions)

- Measuring change management to determine and demonstrate the value of change

The final section of this new edition takes an in-depth look into dialogic OD, a review of five future implications for the practices of OD, transformation, and change, and wraps up with a contributor survey of the most critical elements of OD issues today. Also new for this edition is the inclusion of online resources and a set of discussion questions located at the end of each chapter.

Readers of this new edition will note the focus on transformation. Transformation poses unique challenges for OD leaders in that we must now find ways to transfer this new knowledge and development to the workplace so that we can develop specific goals and measure results. We must redefine our role to include stewarding the process of metrics and measurements—all measurements and metrics—including sales, customer service, profit margin, and growth metrics. Our goals should be tied to these metrics and lead change in the areas of sales, operations, and customer service departments, and connect directly to what each is responsible for.

Indeed, this is no easy task, but without these linkages, there are no measurable results. Without measurable results, there can be no OD. We must create and achieve a common mental model and understanding of how we connect to these results.

I would like to recognize the editors' visionary contributions to amass in one book the best as well as the most complete and practical set of materials for anyone wanting to learn more about OD and how to lead change. This latest edition continues to serve as the best primer for OD, defining what it is, what to do, how to do it, and why it should be done—in addition to offering more contributions and applications with meaningful and measurable impacts, more evidence of positive impacts of transformational change, and new insights. The resources provided are a rich companion to anyone engaged or wanting to become engaged in OD. The discussion questions at the end of each chapter allow you to reflect and discuss how to understand and move forward with this wealth of information.

No matter what your experience in OD, I expect that you will want to reference this book again and again. Armed with this resource, you can work with your organizations to create systemic approaches to whole system planned change that truly leaves the organization stronger and healthier to embrace and anticipate the future. As the future unfolds in our global complex environment, the focus of OD is on human values and potential in organizational life.

I wish you great health, strength, and courage to connect to business goals as you continue your practice in OD, transformation, and change.

Introduction

Getting the Most from This Book

William J. Rothwell, Jacqueline M. Stavros, and Roland L. Sullivan

In the third edition of *Practicing Organization Development*, the focus was on using organization development (OD) as a guide for leading change initiatives. Change continues to be a major dynamic in organization life. What we have heard and seen since the last edition is the word *transformation*. That is when an organization goes through a planned process of profound and dynamic change that takes the organization to the next level—a new direction for its stakeholders. The fourth edition integrates transformation because many organizations are looking for leaders who can understand, lead, and support organizational transformation. According to Don Warrick, "There is an urgent need in organizations of all types and sizes for transformational leaders who have the courage and skills to reinvent and build organizations capable of succeeding in today's times of dynamic change and scarce resources" (2011, 11). This new edition has many contributions to get at the heart of transformational change at the individual, team, department, and/or organizational level.

To embrace transformational change, organizations and their leaders must take innovative strategic paths by applying organization development (OD) and change efforts that foster dialogue around strategic conversations of what is (purpose) and what could be (future). Results from these strengths-based conversations are more healthy, vibrant, productive, and high-performance workplaces. New theories, methods, technologies, and approaches must be embraced and designed specifically to prepare for the changing future, ranging from engaging multiple classes of stakeholders to strengths-based, whole system approaches to OD. To make the leap, we need to change the way we think,

1

plan, implement, and evaluate OD. An emphasis must be placed on creating dialogues around understanding the purpose of the system and also moving a system forward while engaging the "mindset, skill set, and heart-set" of the stakeholders involved in the change process (Peters and Grenny 2013, 486). An organization's most valued resources is its people, and if thoughtfully and carefully taken care of—it is people who can make the positive impact to produce positive results for themselves, their teams, organizations, and industries.

Practicing Organization Development: Leading Transformation and Change is now both about facilitating transformational and incremental changes. This new edition recognizes that OD is both a field and profession, and there are a diversity of frameworks, models, and approaches to handle organization issues. The book is about the power and possibilities of OD that puts human conversation and behaviors at the heart of the change to "achieved enhanced performance and human fulfillment (Van Nistelrooij and Sminia 2010, 408). There are several definitions of OD, our favorite is from the tenth edition of *Organization Development and Change*, two great OD practitioner-scholars—that is, Tom Cummins and Chris Worley—who define OD as "a system-wide application and transfer of behavioral science to the planned, development, improvement, and reinforcement of the strategies, structures, and process that leads to organization effectiveness" (Cummings and Worley 2015, 2). Their definition incorporates most of the view of our contributors.

THE AUDIENCE FOR THE BOOK

Practicing Organization Development: Leading Transformation and Change (fourth edition) is written for existing and new OD practitioners (that is, internal to the organization or external, which is an OD consultant) and scholars and line managers who wish to broaden their understanding of OD and stay current knowing the field and profession. Those who are new to the field will find the entire book useful from the foundations to the process and applications. Those experienced business leaders, practitioners, and scholars will find the book as a most comprehensive organization change resource compendium to embrace and plan for change at any level.

At the broadest level, this book is designed for those interested in planned change and unplanned change. This is evidenced by the increase in memberships by international, national, and local OD networks, the expansion of the Appreciative Inquiry (AI), positive psychology, and positive organizational scholarship (POS) communities, Society for Human Resource Management (SHRM), the Academy of Management divisions on OD and Change, Strategy, Management Consulting, and Social Issues in Management and the expanding

Asian, African, Indian, and Middle-Eastern OD networks. This book has several intended audiences beyond internal OD practitioners and external OD consultants to workplace learning and performance professionals, human resource and strategic management, and managers and executives.

The primary audience is OD professionals who need to stay updated to guide, facilitate, and support change. For those OD professionals new to the book, there are chapters focused in Part One on formal grounding in OD theory and practice and even the historical T-groups. This handbook can be used for students enrolled in programs or courses on OD, organizational behavior, and change management. Undergraduate programs will find the book can span one or two courses. Master practitioners and doctoral students will also find this book valuable as a guide to OD literature, new theories and applications, and as a resource to help them orient, train, and mentor other OD professionals.

Our second audience includes human resource (HR) generalists and talent development practitioners, previously called human resource development (HRD) practitioners. Some talent development practitioners specifically train employees. They devote their attention largely to increasing employees' job knowledge and to improving individual performance in organizational settings. But many talent development practitioners go beyond training to ensure that identified training needs take organization and work-group cultures into account. In addition, results-oriented talent development knows that individual performance improvement can only occur when the surrounding work environment supports it. The theory and practice of changing organization and work-group cultures are OD topics. To do their jobs and achieve results, talent development practitioners often apply competencies associated with OD.

Our third audience comprises managers, executives, management consultants, social entrepreneurs, and leaders looking for ways to transform whole organizations and communities to thrive in the twenty-first century. In today's dynamic business environment, they must know how to introduce and consolidate change successfully if they are to realize their visions for improved organizational performance. Executives or managers who lack competence in OD, transformation, and change theory will have trouble seeing their visions realized and ultimately serving the stakeholders through its mission (present purpose).

THE PURPOSE AND OBJECTIVES
OF THE BOOK

The purpose of *Practicing Organization Development: Leading Transformation and Change* (fourth edition) is to build the reader's competencies in assessing the need for change, managing change, and facilitating the implementation of *transformational* change in organization settings. After finishing this book, the reader should be able to:

1. Define OD, transformation, and change and how these relate to each other
2. Understand a variety of models of planned change, its key attributes and phases
3. Describe and apply the competencies needed to conduct planned change
4. Understand the phases of OD work and levels of change and how to make the new change "stick"
5. Facilitate the contracting of an OD project and work successfully with key stakeholders to plan and implement the change
6. Define a variety of OD interventions as used in the OD field
7. Learn the importance of strengthening and shaping the organization's culture and design
8. Understand the impact of special issues to OD, such as globalization, sustainability, whole system approaches, large-scale transformation, complex adaptive systems, mergers and acquisitions, ethics, diversity and inclusion, social networks, and constructive use of power

This handbook supports the ongoing development of leaders, managers, practitioners, and consultants with its coverage of the foundations, key theories, concepts, methodologies, models, and applications as they apply to improving the performance of individuals, teams, organizations, and industries. The book has been designed so each major section and chapter can stand alone and can also serve as a reference to other chapters.

What's New in the Fourth Edition

The convergence of OD with transformation, change management, organizational behavior, ethics, and human resource management are more prevalent today than it ever has been before given the changes in our global business environment. *Practicing Organization Development: Leading Transformation and Change* (fourth edition) expands and dramatically updates the third edition to reflect the current and future states of OD and change as it also relates now to transformational change and leadership. The fourth edition is comprehensive and provides the essentials: foundations and principles, OD phases, current state and future challenges, and implications of the OD field with the latest and most widely used models, frameworks, strategies, and methods to improve human and organization health and performance.

Readers will note unique similarities and differences between the third and fourth editions of this book. The editions are similar in that both share the foundations and phases of planned change in OD. The fourth edition is different because it has been wholly rewritten and updated from the previous authors from the third edition, and it includes 24 new contributors. These new contributors bring OD frameworks and approaches into leading, managing, consulting, and coaching, while also increasing the sensitivity to transformation and positive change, and their aptitudes in facilitating generative dialogues and learning exchanges.

The fourth edition includes 33 *new* chapters and 49 contributors chosen from a wide variety of leading OD scholars and practitioners who share theory and practices of OD as it relates to whole system, strengths-based, and positive change methods, transformation, and the importance of practicing OD at five levels: individual, organizational, interorganizational, transorganizational, and global. Each chapter has a set of discussion questions and additional online resources for you to review. This new edition of *Practicing Organization Development* will help any organization build its capacity and capabilities to operate efficiently and effectively to improve its whole system while operating in its current environment.

To stay current and relevant, this growth and development must continue and that is why there will be an accompanying website to support the book. The book's website (www.wiley.com/go/practiceod) contains:

- PowerPoint presentations
- Sample syllabi for an Introduction to OD course
- Videos supporting the materials in the book
- Interviews from the founders and elders of the OD field
- OD and change websites
- Archives of significant chapters and studies from the earlier editions of *Practicing Organization Development*

Based on the contributions in this fourth edition, we realize that OD has been transitioning from being primarily focused on "organizations" to more inclusive of how the "human systems" transforms the organization. Over the past several years, communication on OD and change-related LinkedIn groups and Facebook along with articles in leading OD, human resources, strategy, and change management, journals are moving in this direction.

Theoretical and Practical Foundation of the Book

This book's contributors are both OD practitioners and scholars whose research activities include creating, validating, and applying OD theories, methods, and tools. There is a new chapter on OD competencies. A *competency* is defined as any "personal quality" that contributes to the successful practice of OD. It includes who one is (*being*), from what theory one acts (*knowing*), and how one performs (*doing*). The concept of self-as-instrument is provided in Chapter Five on how to self-assess one's leadership style and competencies to plan and lead transformational change.

The book also emphasizes practice in several senses. As Kinnunen (1992, 6) points out, *to practice* can mean any or all of:

- To do frequently or by force of habit
- To use knowledge and skill in a profession or occupation
- To adhere to a set of beliefs or ideals
- To do repeatedly to become proficient
- To drill to give proficiency

The meanings of practice listed above apply to the editors' intentions in assembling this book: to emphasize the need for development as a practitioner through a focus on the knowledge and skills—and the beliefs and ideals—that are important to be proficient in the practice of OD. As you will see, the practice of OD is embedded with a deep connection to the human endeavor involved in both personal and organization transformation and change: OD practitioners must have the competencies to be effective. To be competent means to have "an underlying characteristic of an employee (that is, motive, trait, skill, aspects of one's self-image, social role, or a body of knowledge), which results in effective and/or superior performance in a job" (Boyatzis 1982, 20). To be competent is associated with an individual's characteristics in performing work and includes *anything* that leads to successful performance and results. All five sections of this book emphasize competence and developing your competencies and the characteristics that define successful performance of the practitioner: who one needs to be, what one needs to know, and what one must be capable of doing.

The Structure of the Book

Practicing Organization Development: Leading Transformation and Change brings together a rich collection of theories, concepts, models, case applications, innovations, and historical and postmodern expansions in OD, transformation, and change. This book is structured in five parts:

- Part One (Chapters One–Seven), *Foundations*, provides essential background information and origins about OD, change process and models, what it takes to transform organizations, OD competencies for success, transformational leadership development, and Appreciative Inquiry (the strengths-based revolution).
- Part Two (Chapters Eight–Fourteen), *Organization Development Process to Guide Transformation and Change,* includes seven chapters that focus

on the OD process. Chapters in Part Two address marketing and positioning OD, engaging the client system (front-end work), assessment, planning, launch, implementation, evaluation (with a focus on return on investment) and measurement, separation (closure), and shaping the organization's culture.

- Part Three (Chapters Fifteen–Eighteen), *Levels and Types of Change*, covers different levels of change interventions from individual, team, and organization to whole system and strengths-based interventions in large-scale and strategic change.

- Part Four (Chapters Nineteen–Thirty), *Special Issues in Organization Development, Transformation, and Change*, has material on positive states of organizing, ethics, sustainability, organization design, mergers and acquisitions, the T-groups, diversity and inclusion, global OD, and understanding the relationships between OD and HRM and OD and change management. This section ends with a piece of constructive use of power in OD and a new piece of research into understanding how to leverage social networks in OD.

- Part Five (Chapters Thirty-One and Thirty-Three), *The Future of Organization Development: Embracing Transformation and New Directions for Change*, explores future perspectives in the field and includes a survey completed by our contributors in Chapter Thirty-Three. The results represent an excellent cross-section of scholars and practitioners in the field. This part addresses three critical questions: How relevant is OD for today's organizations? What is the purpose of OD? What are the major challenges facing OD?

Change is constant and fundamental to human systems at all levels from individual to global. By learning to anticipate and plan for change, you can strategically build strong, flexible, capable, and healthy people and organizations that perform in humane, sustainable, and profitable ways to achieve ethical, moral, value-laden success. More than any other time in history, our organizations must be able to master enterprise-wide ongoing transformation and change. This book provides the conceptual frameworks and approaches to help our organizations' leaders and members become transformational agents of change.

References

Boyatzis, R. E. 1982. *The Competent Manager: A Model for Effective Performance.* New York: John Wiley & Sons.

Cummings, T. G., and C. G. Worley. 2015. *Organization Development and Change.* 10th ed. Cincinnati, OH: South-Western.

Kinnunen, G. 1992. "The Practice of Practice." *NSPI Insight* 6 (November).

Peters, L., and J. Grenny. 2013. "Crucial Conversations, Transformational Moments, and Real Organizational Change." In *The Change Champion's Field Guide*, edited by L. Carter, R. Sullivan, M. Goldsmith, D. Ulrich, and N. Smallwood, 480–493. San Francisco: John Wiley & Sons.

Van Nistelrooij, A., and H. Sminia. 2010. "Organization Development: What's Actually Happening?" *Journal of Change Management* 10 (4): 407–420.

Warrick, D. D. 2011. "The Urgent Need for Skilled Transformational Leaders: Integrating Transformational Leadership and Organization Development." *Journal of Leadership, Accountability, and Ethics* 8 (5): 11–26.

PART ONE

FOUNDATIONS

CHAPTER ONE

Organization Development, Transformation, and Change

William J. Rothwell, Jacqueline M. Stavros, and Roland L. Sullivan

W hat are organization development (OD), transformation, and change? Why should you care about them? What key terms are associated with OD, transformation, and change? What is systems thinking, and why is it important to OD practitioners? This first chapter addresses these concepts and related questions.

WHAT ARE ORGANIZATION DEVELOPMENT, TRANSFORMATION, AND CHANGE?

Organization development (OD) helps people in organizations plan how to deal with changes in their environment. Before we define it more precisely, try the following exercise. Get paper and write down the first thing that comes to your mind in response to each question:

1. *Who* should be involved in an organization change effort, and how should they be involved?

2. *Who* should decide about how a change effort of any kind is launched? Implemented continually? Evaluated?

3. *What* do you believe about change in the world and today's organizations?

4. *What* does transformation mean to you?

5. *What* do you believe are the biggest challenges facing decision makers in organization change efforts?

6. *What* do you believe are your strengths and developmental needs in enacting the role of helper to others in a change effort? What do you do especially well? What do you wish to develop to become a more effective change agent? On what basis do you believe as you do?

7. *When* do you believe that a group of people might need an external facilitator in a change effort?

8. *Why* should OD, transformation, and change be a focus for managers? Other groups?

9. *How* should change be defined? Marketed? Launched? Implemented? Evaluated?

10. *How* have you reacted or felt in the past to change in an organization in which you have been employed or to which you have been a consultant?

Now identify a few professional peers or colleagues and pose these questions to them. Use this activity as a warm-up exercise to focus your thinking and understanding about OD, transformation, and change. When you finish, continue reading because many of your answers may *change*.

Organization Development Defined

Over the years, OD has been defined by many scholars, and each definition has a different emphasis. A few definitions are presented chronologically as follows:

Organization development is "an effort (1) planned, (2) organization-wide, and (3) managed from the top, to (4) increase organization effectiveness and health through (5) planned interventions in the organization's 'processes,' using behavioral-science knowledge" (Beckhard 1969, 9).

Warner Burke said, "Most people in the field agree that OD involves consultants who work to help clients improve their organizations by applying knowledge from the behavioral sciences—psychology, sociology, cultural anthropology, and other related disciplines. Most would also agree that OD implies change; and, if we accept that shifts in the way an organization functions suggest that change has occurred, then, broadly defined, OD is analogous to organizational change" (Burke 1982, 3).

Organization development is "a system-wide application and transfer of behavioral science knowledge to the planned development, improvement, and reinforcement of the strategies, structures, and process that lead to organization effectiveness" (Cummings and Worley 2015, 2).

These definitions imply several key themes. First, OD is long-range in perspective. Second, OD works best when supported by senior leadership. Third,

OD effects change primarily, although not exclusively, through education. Fourth, OD emphasizes employee participation in assessing the current state and in planning for a positive future state; making free and collaborative choices on how implementation should proceed; and, empowering the system to take responsibility for creating and evaluating results.

What Organization Development Is Not

OD is not a toolkit filled with canned tricks, piecemeal programs, gimmicks, techniques, and methodologies. As Cummings and Worley (2015) write, "The human resource function tends to provide change management skills through traditional training programs, not through a learning-by-doing process that has been so effective in OD" (145). OD involves people in change and does not coerce them into doing that which they vehemently oppose. Ideas for what and how to change come from everyone and not just managers.

OD is not a mindless application of someone else's best practice. It uses one's whole self, encountering the full and quantum living system. Living systems comprise vibrant communities and changing networks (formal and informal) that practice feedback, self-organization, continuous change, and learning. OD is not about short-term manipulation to achieve immediate financial gains. Instead, OD is interactive, relational, participative, and engaging.

Effective trainers are often understood to be in control of a management development effort. But facilitators of organization change are not in control of the change effort. Instead, they *facilitate* collaboration with internal partners. Facilitators learn, shift, and change with the organization. Successful change efforts require an ebb and flow.

Transformation and Change Management Defined

Transformation means to transcend from a static state. The translation of *trans* means to transcend or rise above. When an organization transforms, it is going through a transformation process that is "primarily the performance of the organization that is mediated via the performance of both groups and individuals" (Palmer, Dunford, and Akin 2009, 128). Noel Tichy and Mary Anne Devanna, in their classic work of 1986, outline a three-step process for transforming organizations: (1) revitalize, (2) create a new vision, and (3) institutionalize the change. Transformation brings about dynamic change in an organization. Hence, there is a connection to OD and transformation. Transformation is viewed in more detail in Chapters 4 and 5.

Change is part of organizational life, and the sustainability and growth of an organization depends on change and transformation. *Change management* means the process of helping individuals, groups, or organizations change.

The word "management" implies an effort to best manage and implement the change. Warner Burke (2008) believes, "The change that occurs in organization is, for the most part, unplanned and gradual" (1).

Burke further states, "Planned organization change, especially on a large scale, affecting the entire system, is unusual; not exactly an everyday occurrence" (1). Planned change has always been a key component of OD (Marshak 2006). Change can happen at any level, and this is examined in Part Three of this book. Many of the most popular OD interventions, techniques, and methods involving the whole system are presented throughout this book.

WHY CARE ABOUT OD AND CHANGE?

According to the Greek philosopher Heraclitus, "There is nothing permanent but change." By that he meant that everything is always in flux.

The recent radical changes in global markets and national economies show that the world is becoming more interconnected and economies and industries are global. We will likely experience more change during the next few decades than has been experienced since the beginning of civilization. We can expect more confusion in our organizations attempting to cope with change than at any other time in history.

Why Is Change Occurring So Fast?

The challenge of the future is to help people learn to ride the waves of transformation and change in real-time and as events unfold. Time has become important precisely because changing technology provides strategic advantages to organizations that understand the importance of timely action. Today, the organization that makes it to market first often seizes the lion's share of the market and is likely to keep it. And, organizations that miss technological innovations that increase production speed or improve quality lose out to global competitors who function in a world where differences in labor costs can easily be taken advantage of because of the relative ease of international travel and communication.

Changing technology is also a driver for the information explosion—and vice versa. Consider the sheer magnitude and pace of the information explosion stimulated by technological change. The quantity of information is increasing so fast that no one can keep pace with it. The information created and consumed over the past 30 years are far greater than what was produced over the previous 5,000 years. "Researchers estimate that global information consumption exceeds 9,570,000,000,000,000,000,000 bytes (or 9.57 zetabytes) per year.

In other words, if this information were a stack of books, it would measure 5.6 billion miles and would stretch from Earth to Neptune 20 times over" (Smith 2011, para. 2). The information stored on the Internet is huge because it is not on one computer but on a network comprising millions of computers. No one, not even Google or MSN, has successfully indexed or cataloged the entire Internet because it is so vast (see www.barbarafeldman.com, *Where Is All the Data Stored?*).

People have different ways of responding to information overload and change. One approach is to give up. Another approach is to multitask. But efforts to cope with the effects of change by trying to do more than one thing at a time are causing additional problems. Multitasking can reduce productivity because it may take as much as 50 percent longer to process two tasks performed simultaneously than it takes to do them one after the other (Rubinstein, Meyer, and Evans 2001).

What Effects Are Those Changes Having?

There are many effects of change.

One effect is that change begets more change. As organization leaders struggle to meet competitive challenges, they search for ways to slash cycle times for product development, chase fads to discover new ways to gain advantage, and struggle with efforts to manage too many simultaneously implemented initiatives and improvement programs.

A second effect is that the turbulent changes in the environment (political, economic, technological, and social) have prompted increasing cynicism about change, an emerging theme in the literature about change management (Bruhn et al. 2001; Stanley, Meyer, and Topolnytsky 2005). Cynicism about change means that workers and managers increasingly question the motives of those who sponsor, champion, or drive change. Cynicism about the motives of other people erodes trust and confidence in organizational leaders. A growing number of scandals in business, government, education, the media, and the church only reinforce that cynicism. Conspiracy theorists also intensify that cynicism about why events happen and what motives are behind them.

A third effect is growing stress on individuals and their families. As the rate and magnitude of change increase, individuals struggle to keep up emotionally and cognitively. Their stressed-out feelings about change, if expressed, occasionally erupt in increased alcohol abuse, drug abuse, workplace violence, domestic violence, suicide rates, heart disease, and even cancer (Magyar 2003). Stress may also prompt increasing instances of "desk rage" (Wulfhorst 2008), create pushback through growing interest in work/life balance programs, and encourage people to seek innovative ways to work that distance them from others.

So Why Should Anyone Care?

The field of OD can help an organization anticipate, adapt, and respond to trans-formation and change at any level: individual, team, department, organization, and even society. According to Cummings and Worley (2015), "OD is both a professional field of social action and an area of scientific inquiry" (p. 1) that we feel can positively impact human and organizational effectiveness and per-formance. So people should care about OD because it is rapidly emerging as the leading business topic—if not *the* key business topic—on how to handle transformation and change effectively.

The ability to lead and manage transformation and change successfully sets leaders apart from followers. A study by the Center for Creative Leadership on "Essential Leadership Skills for Leading Change" (2006) found the ability to lead employees is number one, and the ability to manage change is number two (whereas they were number 1 and 7, respectively, in the 2002 study) as requirements for continued success and competent change leadership. As the pace increases, the field of OD is experimenting with the idea that "transfor-mational leadership" skills will be essential at every level of the organization. OD processes create ways to empower all levels and categories of workers to become leaders and innovators within their own spheres of influence to positively impact others and the organization's performance.

WHAT SPECIAL TERMS ARE USED IN ORGANIZATION DEVELOPMENT?

As in every other field of endeavor, OD has its own special terms. Although these terms can create barriers to understanding and may be sources of suspi-cion for those not versed in them, the following terms are useful to know in communicating with others.

Organization Change

Change is a departure from the status quo. It implies movement toward a goal, an idealized state, or a vision of what should be, and movement away from present conditions, beliefs, or attitudes. Different degrees of change exist. In a classic discussion on that topic, Golembiewski (1990) distinguished among three levels of change:

1. *Alpha change* implies constant progress, a shift from a prechange state to a postchange state in which variables and measurement remain constant. It is sometimes associated with incremental change.

2. *Beta change* implies variable progress, a shift from a prechange state to a postchange state in which variables and measurement methods

themselves change. As members of an organization participate in a change effort, they learn of emerging issues that were unknown to them at the outset. The members change their vision of what should be and alter the course of the change effort itself.

3. *Gamma change* implies, besides beta change, a radical shift from what was originally defined as a prechange state and a postchange state. It is sometimes called transformational change, a radical alteration from the status quo, a quantum leap or paradigm shift. It involves a complete revolution in "how we do things" or "what results we strive to achieve."

Anderson and Anderson (2010) provide another classic perspective on levels or types of change. They distinguish among:

Developmental change: "[It] represents the improvement of an existing skill, method, performance standard, or condition that for some reason does not measure up to current or future needs" (34).

Transitional change: "Rather than simply improve what is, transitional change replaces what is with something entirely different" (35).

Transformational change: It is the "most complex type of change facing organizations today. Simply said, transformation is the radical shift from one state of being to another, so significant that it requires a shift of culture, behavior, and mindset to implement successfully and sustain over time" (39).

Change Agent

In the 1950s, the National Training Laboratories (NTL) founders were in Europe collaborating with the Tavistock Institute. Someone from Tavistock used the phrase "change agent" to describe a person who facilitates change by intervening in groups and organizations. The NTL group used it, and now it is a common phrase among change makers and leaders. OD practitioners are agents who facilitate positive learning, change, and development.

A change agent attempts to facilitate change in an aspect of an organization or an environment. Change agents "are often OD practitioners who assist through their process and OD expertise" (Jones and Brazzel 2014, 117). These practitioners may be internal or external to the organization. A major impact of this new age of continuous change on the field of OD is on the role and tasks of the "change agents" themselves. While OD practitioners have most often been defined as "facilitators" of change (rather than "leaders"), the complexity of every individual environment in which OD practitioners work demands a more "facilitative" and even "educational" approach to helping the system identify and plan for new ways of functioning and relating. The major reason for this shift is that people internal to any organization must learn how to cope with the changing rate of change. Without this approach of imbedding the OD skills in the system itself, we see high rates of "failure" reported.

In response to this reality, it is interesting to note that Drucker took the term "change agent" to a new level. As the classic definition above states, the phrase traditionally refers to a *person*. But management pundit Drucker (2004) challenges us now to see the *organization* as change agent. In his conscious shifting of meaning we attach to the work "change," Drucker tapped into the emerging idea in OD that "change" is not an event, but the constant state in which we live. While the rate of change may vary as in any living system from the human body to the universe, once change ends, the living system is dead! Change is the water we swim in. OD is a process for enabling human systems to embrace and continuously build upon the changes that are an inevitable part of a living system.

Client. The *client* is the organization, group, or individuals whose interests the change agent primarily serves. Although OD practitioners often think of the client as the one who authorized the change effort and pays their bills, they are not always certain whose purposes are to be served. A key question for any OD practitioner to consider is "Who is the client?" (Varney 1977). Occasionally, the "client" may not be the one who originally sponsored or participated in the change effort. Again, in this new era, the potential exists for the whole system to be the client.

Culture. One focal point of OD is changing an organization's *culture*. Prior to the early 1980s, culture was restricted to anthropology and OD circles, but culture became a popular buzzword after the publication of *Corporate Cultures: The Rites and Rituals of Corporate Life* by Deal and Kennedy (1982) and *In Search of Excellence: Lessons from America's Best-Run Companies* by Peters and Waterman (1982). Peters and Waterman provided numerous examples demonstrating the importance of culture in many of the best-known and best-run companies in the United States. Corporate culture means: "Basic assumptions and beliefs that are shared by members of an organization, that operate unconsciously, and that define in a basic 'taken-for-granted' fashion an organization's view of itself and its environment. These assumptions and beliefs are learned responses to a group's problems. They come to be taken for granted because they solve those problems repeatedly and reliably" (Schein 1985, 6).

Intervention. In the nomenclature of OD, an *intervention* is a change effort or a change process. It implies an intentional entry into an ongoing system. Cummings and Worley (2015) define intervention as "a sequence of activities, actions, and events intended to help an organization improve its performance and effectiveness" (157). It is the implementation or execution phases of a change effort.

Sponsor. A *sponsor* underwrites, legitimizes, and champions a change effort or OD intervention. Sponsor tactics can include listening, supporting, developing, empowering, or promoting a person or group as capable. It can include verbalizing positive impressions and images regarding performance, expression of feelings of goodwill, or promoting acceptance, or making statements of capability, or the likeability of a person or group. Of necessity, sponsorship is not a one-time gesture.

Stakeholder. A *stakeholder* is anyone who has a stake in an OD intervention. Stakeholders are the people who maintain an interest in the organization's success or failure. Stakeholders may be employees, board members, customers, suppliers, distributors, and government regulators.

WHAT IS SYSTEMS THINKING AND WHY IS IT IMPORTANT?

In the simplest sense, a *system* comprises interdependent components (Burke 1980). Organizations may be viewed as social systems because they depend on interactions among people (Katz and Kahn 1978). In addition, any organization that gives and takes information from the environment is an *open system*. Organizations take in *inputs* (customer requirements, raw materials, capital, information, or people), appreciate value through the input of a *transformation process* (production or service-delivery methods), and release them into the environment as *outputs* (finished goods, services, information, or people; see Figure 1.1). This transformation cycle must continue to add value in producing desired results if an organization is to survive.

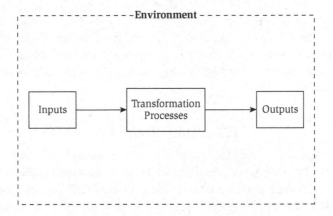

Figure 1.1. A Model of a System

A *subsystem* is part of a larger system. In one sense, subsystems of an organization (a system) may include work units, departments, or divisions. In another sense, subsystems may cut across an organization and encompass activities, processes, or structures. It is possible to focus on an organization's maintenance, adaptive, or managerial subsystems (Katz and Kahn 1978).

Facilitating collaboration with clients is a key competency for OD practitioners. The identity of a system shifts when it creates a new collective and common understanding. The shift creates a culture where many ideas for action will bubble up. Helping the system distill "B" (suboptimal) ideas from "A" (best) ideas is a role much needed today. And, as OD practitioners experiment with whole system processes, the trend is toward "trying out" ideas in multiple experimental processes rather than trying to sort ideas with pre-experimental judgments. It is sometimes the idea we might label "suboptimal" that turns out to be the solution!

Systems thinking is also important to OD because a change in any part of a system inevitably changes other parts of the system. The implications of this simple statement are profound. The change process in any part of a system creates change in all parts of the system. Any change in a system will have both predictable and unpredictable consequences. Mitigating the unpredictable consequences best occurs if all parts of the system are in collaboration throughout the change effort.

WHAT ARE THE PHILOSOPHICAL FOUNDATIONS OF ORGANIZATION DEVELOPMENT, AND WHY ARE THEY IMPORTANT?

One way to view the history of OD stresses its emergence from four separate but related behavioral-science applications: (1) laboratory training, (2) survey research and feedback, (3) Tavistock sociotechnical systems, and (4) process consultation. It is worthwhile here to offer a brief view of historical influences to provide readers with essential background information at the start of this handbook.

Laboratory Training

An early precursor of thinking about OD and change, laboratory training is associated with unstructured, small-group sessions in which participants share their experiences and learn from their interactions. Bradford, Gibb, and Benne (1964) explain this application in the following way: "The term 'laboratory' was not idly chosen. A training laboratory is a community dedicated to the stimulation and support of experimental learning and change. New patterns of behavior are invented and tested in a climate supporting change and protected for the time from the full practical consequences of innovative action in ongoing associations" (3).

Unlike employee-training sessions, which focus on increasing individual knowledge or skill in conformance with the participant's job requirements, laboratory-training sessions focus on group processes and group dynamics. The first laboratory-training sessions were carried out in the 1940s, the work of the New Britain Workshop in 1946, under the direction of such major social scientists as Kurt Lewin, Kenneth Benne, Leland Bradford, and Ronald Lippitt, stimulated much interest in laboratory training. The leaders and members of the workshop accidentally discovered that providing feedback to groups and individuals at the *end of each day* produced more real learning about group dynamics than did lectures. The groundbreaking work of the New Britain Workshop led to the founding of the National Training Laboratories (NTL Institute for Applied Behavioral Science).

Early laboratory-training sessions were usually composed of participants from different organizations, a fact that led such groups to be called "stranger T-groups." (The term *T-group* is an abbreviation of "training group.") Bradford, Gibb, and Benne (1964) define a T-group as relatively unstructured where individuals participate as learners. The data for learning are not outside these individuals or removed from their immediate experience within the T-group. The data are transactions among members' behaviors in the group, as they work to create a productive and viable organization and support one another's learning within that society.

Behavioral scientists later discovered that the participants had difficulty transferring insights and behavioral changes to their work lives. This transfer-of-learning problem increased interest in conducting such sessions in a single organization, a technique that has evolved into what is now called *team building*. Laboratory training was an important forerunner of OD because it focused attention on the dynamics of group or team interaction.

Survey Research and Feedback

Survey research and feedback also contributed to the evolution of OD. This approach to change was developed and refined by the Survey Research Center at the University of Michigan under the direction of Rensis Likert. Likert directed the Survey Research Center from 1950 to 1970. He became widely recognized for his innovative use of written survey questionnaires to collect information about an organization and its problems, provide feedback to survey respondents, and stimulate joint planning for improvement. This technique is called *survey research and feedback* or *survey-guided development*.

Likert's method evolved when he observed that many organizations seldom used the results from attitude surveys to guide their change efforts. Managers authorized the surveys but did not always act on the results. This "ask-but-don't-act" approach produced greater frustration among employees than not asking for their opinions.

The centerpiece of Likert's approach was a technique called the *interlocking conference*. Survey results were given to top managers during the first conference, and then other conferences were held to inform the organization's successively lower levels. In each conference, group members worked together to establish an action plan to address problems or weaknesses revealed by the survey. This top-down strategy of feedback and performance planning ensured that the action plan devised by each group was tied to those at higher levels.

Likert's views, described in his two seminal books, *New Patterns of Management* (1961) and *The Human Organization* (1967), had a profound influence on OD. He demonstrated how information can be collected from members of an organization and used as the basis for participative problem solving and action planning. In addition, he advocated pursuit of a norm for organizational functioning that has since prompted others to pursue similar norms for organizations.

Tavistock Sociotechnical Systems

Another major contributor to the evolution of OD is Tavistock Sociotechnical Systems. Tavistock, founded in 1920, is a clinic in England. Its earliest work was devoted to family therapy in which both child and parents received simultaneous treatment.

A team of Tavistock researchers experimented in work redesign for coal miners at about the same time that laboratory training was introduced in the United States. Before the experiment, coal miners worked closely in teams of six. They maintained control over who was placed on a team and were rewarded for team production. New technology was introduced to the mine, changing work methods from a team to an individual orientation. The result was a decrease in productivity and an increase in absenteeism. The Tavistock researchers then recommended that the new technology could be used by miners grouped into teams. The researchers' advice, when implemented, improved productivity and restored absenteeism rates to historically low levels in the organization.

Tavistock sociotechnical systems' key contribution to OD was an emphasis on both the social and the technical subsystems. Tavistock researchers believed that organizations are systems composed of key subsystems. One such subsystem is the people in an organization. The other is the nonhuman subsystem. Both must be considered if a change is to succeed.

Process Consultation

A more recent influence on the OD field has been Edgar Schein's (1999) process consultation. *Process consultation* can be defined as the creation of a relationship that permits both the consultant and the client to perceive, understand, and act on the process events that occur in the client's internal and external environment to improve the situation as defined by the client. It involves intervening to improve the ways groups of people work together to achieve results.

SUMMARY

In this chapter, we explore the meaning of OD, transformation, and change, with the primary focus on OD. We discuss what OD is and what it is not and define terms that are specific to OD. With these topics and others, it has been our goal to give you a foundation to understanding what OD is, and how OD relates to transformation and change to prepare you for what comes next in this book.

Discussion Questions

1. What are transformation and change management (CM) key components of organization development (OD)?

2. What organizational functions are impacted by OD?

3. What is systems thinking, and why is it important to OD?

Resources

Mind-Blender, from *Psychology Today* website: "Why Is the World Changing So Fast?": www.psychologytoday.com/blog/mind-blender/201403/why-is-the-world-changing-so-fast

Valerie Keller, "Fit for Purpose: Changing in a Changing World," on the *Huffington Post* website: www.huffingtonpost.com/valerie-keller/fit-for-purpose-changing-_b_3697932.html

References

Anderson, L. A., and D. Anderson. 2010. *The Change Leader's Roadmap: How to Navigate Your Organization's Transformation*. 2nd ed. San Francisco: Pfeiffer.

Beckhard, R. 1969. *Organization Development: Strategies and Models*. Reading, MA: Addison-Wesley.

Bradford, L., J. Gibb, and K. Benne. 1964. *T-Group Theory and Laboratory Method: Innovation in Re-Education*. Hoboken, NJ: John Wiley & Sons.

Bruhn, J. G., G. Zajac, and A. A. Al-Kazemi. 2001. "Ethical Perspectives on Employee Participation in Planned Organizational Change: A Survey of Two State Public Welfare Agencies." *Public Performance & Management Review* 25 (2): 208.

Burke, W. W. 1980. "Systems Theory, Gestalt Therapy, and Organization Development." In *Systems Theory for Organization Development*, edited by T. Cummings, 209–222. Chichester, UK: John Wiley & Sons.

Burke, W. W. 1982. *Organization Development: Principles and Practices*. New York: Little, Brown.

Burke, W. W. 2008. *Organization Change Theory and Practice*. Thousand Oaks, CA: Sage.

Cummings, T. G., and C. G. Worley. 2015. *Organization Development and Change*. 10th ed. Cincinnati, OH: South-Western College Publishing.

Deal, T., and A. Kennedy. 1982. *Corporate Cultures: The Rites and Rituals of Corporate Life*. Reading, MA: Addison-Wesley.

Drucker, P. 2004. "The Way Ahead: Get Ready for What Is Next." *Executive Excellence* 21 (5): 3.

"Essential Leadership Skills for Leading Change." *Leading Effectively* (January 2006). www.ccl.org.

Golembiewski, R. 1990. *Ironies in Organization Development*. New Brunswick, NJ: Transaction.

Jones, B. B., and M. Brazzel. 2014. *The NTL Handbook of Organization Development and Change: Principles, Practices, and Perspectives*. 2nd ed. San Francisco: John Wiley & Sons.

Katz, D., and R. Kahn. 1978. *The Social Psychology of Organizations*. 2nd ed. Hoboken, NJ: John Wiley & Sons.

Likert, R. 1961. *New Patterns of Management*. New York: McGraw-Hill.

Likert, R. 1967. *The Human Organization: Its Management and Value*. New York: McGraw-Hill.

Magyar, S. V. 2003. "Preventing Workplace Violence." *Occupational Health and Safety* 72 (6): 64.

Marshak, R.J. 2006. "Organization Development as a Profession and a Field." In *The NTL Handbook of Organization Development Organization Change: Principles, Practices, and Perspectives*, edited by B. B. Jones and M. Brazzel, 13–27. San Francisco: Pfeiffer.

Palmer, I., R. Dunford, and G. Akin. 2009. *Managing Organizational Change: A Multiple Perspectives Approach*. 2nd ed. San Francisco: McGraw-Hill.

Peters, T. J., and R. H. Waterman, Jr. 1982. *In Search of Excellence: Lessons from America's Best-Run Companies*. New York: Harper & Row.

Rubinstein, J. S., D. E. Meyer, and J. E. Evans. 2001. "Executive Control of Cognitive Processes in Task Switching." *Journal of Experimental Psychology: Human Perception and Performance* 27 (4): 763–797.

Schein, E. 1985. *Organizational Culture and Leadership*. San Francisco: Jossey-Bass.

Schein, E. 1999. *Process Consultation Revisited: Building the Helping Relationship*. Reading, MA: Addison-Wesley.

Smith, C. 2011. "This Is How Much Information the World Consumes Each Year." *Huffington Post*, April 7. www.huffingtonpost.com/2011/04/06/world-information-consumption_n_845806.html.

Stanley, D. J., J. P. Meyer, and L. Topolnytsky. 2005. "Employee Cynicism and Resistance to Organizational Change." *Journal of Business and Psychology* 19 (4): 429–459.

Tichy, N. M., and M. A. Devanna. 1986. *The Transformational Leader*. New York: John Wiley & Sons.

Varney, G. 1977. *Organization Development for Managers*. Reading, MA: Addison-Wesley.

Wulfhorst, E. 2008. "Do You Suffer from Desk Rage?" *Huffington Post*, July 11. www.huffingtonpost.com/2008/07/11/do-you-suffer-from-desk-r_n_112238.html.

CHAPTER TWO

The Origins of Organization Development

John J. Scherer, Billie Alban, and Marvin Weisbord

The organization development (OD) profession was born from pioneer research studies, theories, models, and practices developed by a handful of applied social scientists shortly before, during, and after World War II. These included Kurt Lewin (1890–1947), a German refugee; Wilfred Bion (1897–1979), a British psychiatrist; Bion's wartime collaborator, Eric Trist (1909–1993); Fred Emery (1925–1997), an Australian psychologist who came to Britain to work with Trist; and Douglas McGregor (1906–1964), an MIT psychology professor who developed many of their ideas into a seminal management book, *The Human Side of Enterprise* (McGregor 1960).

We begin with three giants on whose shoulders we OD practitioners are standing: Kurt Lewin, Wilfred Bion, and Douglas McGregor, each of whom contributed significantly to the fundamentals of OD still used today. Who named "Organization Development" and what the correct name for the field actually *is* comes next, followed by Billie Alban's Timeline of OD, showing in graphic form the major events and people shaping our evolution. We close with a closer look into several of OD's more significant fundamental principles and elements that flowed from our origins.

KURT LEWIN—THE GRANDFATHER OF ORGANIZATION DEVELOPMENT (1939)

No one was more crucial to OD's evolution than Kurt Lewin, "the grandfather of applied behavioral science." Lewin, a Berlin-educated Polish Jew, pioneered an innovative social psychology before leaving Nazi Germany for the United States in 1933. "I will not teach in a country where my daughter cannot be a student," he said. This kind of principled stand informed everything he did while creating revolutionary conceptual models for human behavior. Coupled with this commitment to principles was Lewin's belief that valid knowledge could be demonstrated only by applying it to real-world situations. "There is nothing so practical as a good theory," he said, highlighting that the word "theory" (from the Greek *theorein*, "to see") enables one to *see* what is happening in new ways.

Many of Lewin's new ways of seeing things were put to work in the single, well-documented Harwood Manufacturing Company project that began in 1939. Harwood, a new pajama-making facility, was losing money rapidly, with very high turnover and absenteeism, in spite of wages and other benefits greater than workers could make elsewhere. When the Lewin-oriented consultants arrived, they initiated what was then a radically different process, one that you will recognize as standard practice for OD practitioners today. First, they interviewed the plant manager, then the other managers and supervisors, and finally a representative group of front-line employees. After observing the system in action for a while, they made recommendations to the management team. The gist of their proposal: begin an experiment with the front-line people, to learn what might make a difference in their productivity. It is hard for us to understand how revolutionary this was in 1939.

Employee Involvement (ca. 1939)

The consultants also held informal weekly meetings with a cross-functional collection of high-producing workers to discuss what difficulties they encountered and how they might be overcome, using one of Lewin's models called "Force Field Analysis" to understand what was happening. The consultants hypothesized that motivation alone does not suffice to lead to change, and that a simple process like decision making in a group, which takes only a few moments, is able to "freeze" workers' conduct for a long time.

$$B = F(P,E)$$

One of Lewin's most significant contributions to OD thinking is this one: individual behavior (B) is a function (f) of personal factors (p), multiplied by the impact of the current social environment (e). This model explains why some training-oriented change efforts aimed at the individual often fail. Like the alcoholic treated alone and then sent back to an unchanged family system, change efforts that do not take into account making changes in the (social) environment as well will not "take."

The Birth of the T-Group

The OD profession in the United States grew out of a leadership training program in the summer of 1946. The Connecticut State Inter-Racial Commission invited Kurt Lewin to conduct a race relations training program for community leaders. He proposed a program to train leaders (action) and conduct a change experiment (research) at the same time. His team included Ron Lippitt, once his graduate student at Iowa, Lee Bradford, and Kenneth Benne, soon to be the founder of NTL Institute. The team led discussions during the day about the roots and impact on communities of interethnic prejudice (primarily between Polish, Irish, and Italian immigrants). As Ron Lippitt described what happened (personal communication to John Scherer): Each evening the staff met in a basement room at the training site to discuss the day's progress. Several participants wandering by looking for a lost jacket heard a snatch of the conversation and asked if they could sit in. Some staffers, afraid the participants' presence would bias the researchers' "neutral" observations, said, "No, this is a staff meeting." Lewin, always open to learning, said, "Ya, Ya, come in and join us!" When a participant disputed one researcher's observation, a heated debate began. It was "like an electric shock," Bradford said later. From talking about prejudice, the group plunged into an experience of prejudice-in-action. Lewin, obviously excited, saw that they spontaneously had created a temporary community, acting out the forces that create prejudice. The next evening, more participants joined the debriefing session. It had become the program's most energized session! They had discovered the power of the exchange of "feedback," a mutual experience of differing perceptions. Lewin for the first time saw the power of what he dubbed "here-and-now" interactions. He suggested that the next year's program be planned to *feature* such conversations. Hence the seeds were planted for a wholly new profession (for more details see Bradford 1964).

The pioneers called these small group sessions "sensitivity training," intended to sensitize participants to the group dynamics energized by exploring the formation of attitudes and prejudices in daily life. The method spread rapidly. It later was adopted as a vehicle for personal growth by the Western

Behavioral Science Institute, where the name was shortened to "T (for Training)-group." Today, National Training Laboratories (NTL) Institute calls its T-groups "Human Interaction Laboratories," and focuses on self-awareness and personal growth.

How the T-Group Led to Organization Development

Lewin died suddenly at age 57 of a heart attack in February of 1947, as his followers were on the verge of founding NTL to continue his work. Other practitioners, such as Carl Rogers, Jack Gibb, Will Schutz, and Matt Miles, began using the unstructured T-group format for individual development in workplaces and public workshops. Consultants and researchers soon found that people changed themselves dramatically, but they had difficulties at work trying to practice new norms in traditional systems, which changed not at all. To carry out the original intent of improving community and organizational life, a new profession arose, created by consultants, faithful to action research, and seasoned by T-groups. The next generation included such names as Herb Shepard, Tony Petrella, Peter Block, Marvin Weisbord, Billie Alban, Bob Golembiewski, Stuart Atkins, Allan Katcher, and John Scherer. They created training variations, retaining the power of small group dynamics while reducing unnecessary personal exposure and risk. Roger Harrison's "role negotiation" was a major programmatic step in reducing the threat of team building. John and Joyce Weir's invention of "percept language" made it possible for people to provide feedback to *themselves* while using others as projection screens (http://reology.org/about/john-weir-and-joyce-weir). John Scherer created the Leadership Development Intensive (LDI) that integrates personal, team, and organization transformation in the context of the larger system (www.scherercenter.com/LDI).

These and similar workshop designs focused on real-life applications and led directly to the invention of a new form of practice: OD. Even now, the power of small groups as the basic unit of organizational change cannot be overemphasized.

WILFRED BION—THE TAVISTOCK METHOD

While Lewin was working in America, Wilfred Bion, a British psychiatrist, was responding to a request from London's Tavistock Institute to help shell-shocked soldiers from World War II battlefields. There were so many that Bion and his collaborator, Eric Trist, treated them in groups, intending to work with one veteran at a time, while the other patients observed. Like Lewin, they too discovered the power of "The Group," as soldiers spontaneously shared their experiences, reaching out to their buddies. Participants both helped and learned from each other, and not just from authority figures. Bion (1940) came to see that the way leaders conducted themselves created predictable responses from those they were leading. This discovery paralleled the findings of Lewin, Lippitt, and White's authority-democracy studies with boys clubs at the University of Iowa in 1938–39.

Bion's observation was that when the leader took sole responsibility, participants reacted to the authority figure with one of three behaviors:

1. **Fight**—resisting or doing the opposite of whatever the leader suggests
2. **Flight**—finding a way to leave, physically or emotionally, or going along with whatever the authority suggests in a subservient way
3. **Pairing**—forming coalitions with one or two others in the group as a safe haven

When the leader simply raised awareness of the group's functioning, participants were more likely to respond with what Bion called *work*, a fourth option. A participant engaged in work stayed aware of what was happening in themselves and in the group, and worked through whatever conflicts emerged. Bion discovered how a leader can empower a group to take responsibility for its own work and learning.

The Origin of Socio-Technical Consulting and Self-Managed Work Teams

Marvin Weisbord (2012) recounts a marvelous anecdote, told to him by his friend and mentor, Eric Trist, that led to insights into how people can work together more effectively to produce more. Immediately after World War II, in the coal mines of England, miners tried desperately to recover from the devastation of the war. Kenneth Bamforth, a Tavistock student of Trist's and a long-time unionized coal miner himself, went back to visit the South Yorkshire mine where he had worked before the war.

What Bamforth saw stunned him. His former miner colleagues had been experimenting with new ways to make extracting the ore continuous, having thrown out the older, traditional "long wall" approach, where groups of miners were organized into teams that performed a single task (think Taylor). Instead, the unionized miners and general manager had gotten together and planned a new system in which miners were multiskilled and performed all jobs—an old way of doing things that had died under the influence of the industrial revolution. The result was that they could now mine coal 24 hours a day, not having to wait for an earlier shift to complete a task. Bamforth went back to Tavistock and invited his favorite professor, Eric Trist, to come down into the mine with him to see if this might not be useful to the country's business recovery.

As Trist said later, "I came up a different man," (Sashkin 1980, 145). He realized the connection between England's business recovery and what he had just seen, putting together the therapeutic work Bion and he had done with shared leadership in groups, and Lewin's work in small group dynamics. If given the proper supports and resources, Trist hypothesized, teams could redesign how they plan, manage, and do their work—and produce at higher levels. Because of our 50 years of OD hindsight, it is hard for us to realize the dramatic impact of this discovery!

Bion and the Tavistock Institute recognized in the late 1940s and early 1950s the relationship of the larger social network to the work structure and the technical system, setting the stage for the naming and exploration of today's "systems thinking." Their finding: It was not enough to focus on individuals or groups internally; you had to look at the structures and systems that surrounded them. These approaches recognized that an employee's productivity and creativity have more to do with the way the job was designed and the system around that employee than with the characteristics of the person, something the Tavistock Institute had seen and highlighted in their earlier coal mine studies.

DOUGLAS MCGREGOR—THEORY X AND THEORY Y

It was Douglas McGregor, a young faculty member in psychology at MIT, who enticed Lewin to come to MIT in 1946 to create the Research Center for Group Dynamics. McGregor, a young industrial relations manager during World War II, found in Lewin's work the theoretical base for his research in solving labor-management problems. Like Lewin, McGregor liked the rough-and-tumble world of the workplace and, by attaching the Center to the School of Engineering, the two of them were able to avoid many of the constrictions and traditional paradigms they would have faced had they joined the school of academic psychology. Due to little turns in the road like this, OD's birth took place in the laboratory of work—money, machines, information, and people—and not in the laboratory of pigeons or rats such as in classical psychology.

McGregor is best known for his Theory X and Theory Y management model, which asserts that there are two diametrically opposed worldviews available to managers that result in completely different workplace results. McGregor's theories had their roots in his family of origin. His father was an authoritative lay minister. The elder McGregor ran a shelter for men who had lost their jobs, and carried the pain of his clients heavily in his heart. Douglas McGregor's Theory X model has an uncanny resemblance to his father's and grandfather's "hard" and largely negative view of human nature as dominated by sin and fallenness (Bennis 1969). Young Doug, it could be asserted, strived for his whole life to choose another path, one with a more "positive" view of human nature, his Theory Y.

Theory X managers hold that people are, by nature, lazy, greedy, self-centered, and must be tightly watched and managed (controlled) from the outside in order to get the best work out of them. Theory Y managers believe that people are, by nature, predisposed to want to do well, to make a contribution, to learn and grow, and only need a sense of direction and support in the form of feedback and coaching to manage themselves to do their best.

One caveat here, from Marvin Weisbord: Most of us need to learn democratic management practices, as was shown in the classic research study that opened the door to the "leadership style" industry (Lewin et al., 1939). We are born helpless and dependent, and grow up in authoritarian systems such as family, school, church, or the military. We have little in our repertoire on the continuum between authoritarian and laissez-faire behavior. Nobody is born practicing Theory Y assumptions.

McGregor's 1960 book, *The Human Side of Enterprise*, took the workplace world by storm. It offered a rational explanation, with supporting evidence, for what could be counted on when it came to motivating people. OD owes a great deal of its positive stance regarding human beings and the potential of teams and organizations to Douglas McGregor. People like Frederick Herzberg took McGregor's theories to the next level (Herzberg, Mausner, and Snyderman 1959) and made the distinction between "satisfiers" (pay, benefits, working conditions), which can never motivate—only dissatisfy if they are not sufficiently present—and true "motivators" (recognition, achievement, responsibility, learning), similar to Maslow's hierarchy of needs.

As Weisbord (2012) notes, McGregor grounded his work in values strikingly similar to those of Frederick Taylor (1856–1915), the "Father of Scientific Management" (1911). Taylor consulted full-time to Bethlehem Steel Corporation from 1898 to 1901, where he simplified jobs, reduced stress, raised wages, and upped production. Eighty years later, Bethlehem hired Block, Petrella, and Weisbord, an OD firm, to help it recover from the mindless repetition of Taylor's time-and-motion studies. The legacy turned out to be bitter labor-management relations and losses of $80 million a month. Reading Taylor's magnum opus, *The Principles of Scientific Management*, for clues, Weisbord was astonished to find parallels in McGregor's *The Human Side of Enterprise* to Taylor's values, publishing nearly identical quotes from both authors on the centrality of teamwork, training, and labor-management cooperation. Those who admired Taylor, as Weisbord puts it, divorced his values and married his techniques. He considers this a useful warning to OD practitioners who trace their ancestry to Kurt Lewin (Weisbord 2012).

WHAT IS DIFFERENT ABOUT ORGANIZATION DEVELOPMENT?

OD's founders, above all, valued principles on which they conceived research studies and methods to put their values into action. They were curious, wanting to learn what was happening with people at work and why. Our OD "Grandparents" Lewin, Bion, Emery, Trist, and McGregor, handed these fundamental truths down to us, each in his own way. In Scherer's words, they hypothesized that finding out what is actually happening and why with stakeholders (research), then getting all that data "on the table" where it is seen and discussed in a safe environment with people who are empowered to act, has the power to change people and systems (action). Every subsequent OD theoretical model, exercise, and/or practice, to be valid, must engage clients in participative reflection on the processes governing what is happening.

WHO NAMED ORGANIZATION DEVELOPMENT?

In 1974, Larry Porter, long-time editor of *The OD Practitioner*, asked Richard (Dick) Beckhard and Herb Shepard, "Who named OD?" As Larry explained to one of the authors, "Both Herb Shepard and Dick Beckhard are OD consultants of the external persuasion. After some discussion among the three of us as to who did what, we agreed that I (Larry) would identify them as follows in the article: Dick Beckhard, while consulting at General Electric in 1957, invented the term organization development. Herb Shepard, while consulting at Esso in 1957, invented the term organization development," (Porter 1974, 1).

The originators of the name intended it to be "organization development" and not "organizational development." As Peter Vaill puts it, "Organizational development means *any kind of development as long as it occurs* in *the organization*. This could conceivably include the VP's potted plant. Organization development means *the development* of *the organization*," (Peter Vaill, personal correspondence). Please, everyone, from now on call our field organization development. Please drop the "al," okay?

THE ORIGINS OF ORGANIZATION DEVELOPMENT TIMELINE

Billie Alban has done everyone who practices OD a huge service by creating "The Origins of OD Timeline." (See Figure 2.1.) Using a process she and her colleagues pioneered in the now well-established practice of "Large Scale Change" (Bunker and Alban 1997; Weisbord and Janoff 2010), the timeline

History of Organization Development and the Environment
The Environment

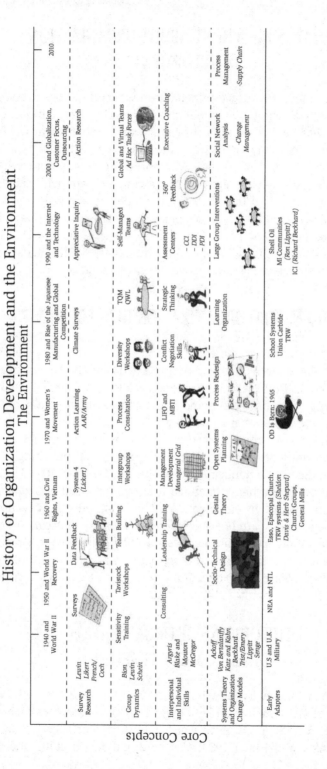

	1940 and World War II	1950 and World War II Recovery	1960 and Civil Rights, Vietnam	1970 and Women's Movement	1980 and Rise of the Japanese Manufacturing and Global Competition	1990 and the Internet and Technology	2000 and Globalization, Customer Focus, Outsourcing	2010
Survey Research	Surveys	Data Feedback	System 4 *(Lickert)*	Action Learning AAR/Army	Climate Surveys	Appreciative Inquiry	Action Research	
Levin Likert French/ Coch								
Group Dynamics	Sensitivity Training	Tavistock Workshops	Team Building	Process Consultation	Diversity Workshops	TQM QWL	Self-Managed Teams	Global and Virtual Teams *Ad Hoc Task Forces*
Bion Levin Schein								
Interpersonal and Individual Skills	Consulting	Leadership Training	Management Development *Managerial Grid*	LIFO and MBTI	Conflict Negotiation Skills	Strategic Thinking	Assessment Centers – CCI – DDI – PDI	360° Feedback	Executive Coaching
Argyris Blake and Mouton McGregor								
Systems Theory and Organization Change Models	Socio-Technical Design		Gestalt Theory	Open Systems Planning	Process Redesign	Learning Organization	Large Group Interventions	Social Network Analysis *Change Management*	Process Management *Supply Chain*
Ackoff Von Bertalanffy Katz and Kahn Beckhard Trist/Emery Lippitt Senge								
Early Adapters	U.S and U.K Military	NEA and NTL	Esso, Episcopal Church, TRW systems *(Sheldon Davis & Herb Shepard)* Church Groups, General Mills	OD Is Born: 1965	School Systems Union Carbide TRW	Shell Oil MI Communities *(Ron Lippitt)* ICI *(Richard Beckhard)*		

Core Concepts

Figure 2.1. Origins of OD Timeline

shows what was happening as OD came into being, the core concepts and when they emerged, major contributors, significant external forces and events that paralleled and impacted things, and OD's early-adapter institutions.

The horizontal axis is Time, and shown vertically are Core Concepts. Even though they run across the page as discreet elements, in real life they merged and blended with each other. For instance, data feedback is also used in team building, and systems theory is applied in many of the core concepts. We have gone into a little more detail with several of the more significant elements: action research, Appreciative Inquiry, group dynamics, early adopters, instrument-based and skill development, systems theory, and open systems.

Action Research

Lewin's now-classic postulate, "No research without action; no action without research," defines this element on the chart. One of OD's fundamental principles is the use of data-gathering as the basis for planning subsequent interventions. Survey feedback, initially used by industrial psychologists, pioneered in the early 1960s at the University of Michigan's Center for Research in the Utilization of Scientific Knowledge (CRUSK) and the Institute for Social Research (ISR), is a staple in many OD practitioners' repertoire today. Survey feedback has been part of the OD field from the beginning, the difference being that, in OD, we involve stakeholders in the process.

While at ISR, Rensis Likert developed what would become a widely used approach to action research using a scale of responses, allowing people to indicate how strongly they held a particular position on some item, thus quantifying "soft" data. He also graphed people's responses so they could visualize the extent to which their unit, or division, or whole organization was authoritarian, participative, or in between.

It will be interesting to see over time the impact of the Internet on action research and the use of surveys. Many organizations are now surveying their employees in real time using social media, providing for the first time virtually instantaneous feedback on whatever elements need to be researched. One such survey of organizational culture, developed in 1980 by a Dutch consultant Gert Hofstede (2005), was a study of 130,000 IBM employees in 40 different countries, and online platforms like SurveyMonkey allow for the creation of custom-designed surveys.

Appreciative Inquiry

An interesting new approach to action research, based on several early OD models, has been the development of Appreciative Inquiry (AI), pioneered by David Cooperrider and others (Cooperrider and Srivastva 1987). In brief, rather than focusing on what is *not* working and needs to be fixed, it looks at the positive aspects of "what is working" and "what do we need more of" now that can be enhanced (for more information on AI, see Chapter Six).

Group Dynamics

It is important to note that in Lewin's model, receiving and giving feedback on individual behavior was only one of the elements of group dynamics training. Lewin was very interested that people learn about the dynamics of groups as models of larger social systems, what helped them function effectively, and what helped them make decisions that the group would willingly commit to. Lewin and his students saw small group work as having a political aspect—a kind of *training for democracy*. What we know now as "team development" evolved in the mid-1960s at places like TRW Systems in Redondo Beach, California, an on-the-job "laboratory" for a brilliant OD pioneer, Shel Davis, and one of the first matrix organizations.

Early Adopters

Organizations had come out of World War II with a need to increase production and improve human relationships within work groups. More managers started asking, "How could we make a group of people working together on a task more effective?" If you look at the bottom of the OD Timeline, you will see some of the early adopters, usually led by internal industrial or labor relations people and/or human resource staff working with external consultants. Esso, now Exxon, was one of the companies to experiment, with Herb Shepard being one of the consultant pioneers. Shepard also started a project with Syncrude in Alberta, Canada, inserting a then-26-year-old Jonno Hanafin to consult with the 56-year-old president. General Mills had a similar project, led by Douglas McGregor, and TRW Systems initiated a long-term OD effort, led internally by Stan Herman.

People embracing the newly emerging field of OD came from surprising places. The Episcopal Church began sending selected clergy and lay leaders to NTL laboratories in the early 1950s. Their enthusiasm spun off several organizations dedicated to spreading OD and the applied behavioral sciences into religious settings. Early NTL-trained Episcopal movers and shakers were Dick Byrd, David Jones, Bill Yon, and Mary Beth Peters, who came together with Lutherans Otto Kroeger, Roy Oswald, and John Scherer; Methodists Ken Mitchell, Jack Tesmer, and Bob Crosby; and Presbyterians Newt Fink, Del Poling, Mike Murray, and Arnie Nakajima to launch the Association for Religion and Applied Behavioral Science (ARABS) in 1969, which morphed into the Association for Creative Change in Religious and Other Social Systems (ACCROSS).

A handful of U.S. Army chaplains attended early NTL programs and brought back what they had learned about OD to their colleagues. As a follow-up, NTL members Rad Wilson, Otto Kruger, and Denny Gallagher trained and consulted with the Army chaplains for 11 years. That effort, one of the first long-term OD applications in the military, evolved into the Army's unique Organization Effectiveness Staff Officer (OESO) program, which resulted in the placing of highly trained internal consultants on Army bases around the world. The 18-week OESO curriculum started with a T-group with Will Schutz (imagine a group of hardened Vietnam veterans learning to see group process and expressing their feelings), and went on to things like Consulting Skills with Jack Sherwood, and Conflict Management with John Scherer.

As the civil rights movement took off, groups were being used to sensitize people to deal with issues related to race and gender. As the United States found itself in a far more competitive market after World War II, groups were formed to study some of the methods being used in Scandinavia and Japan, such as Quality of Work Life and Total Quality Management. Proctor and Gamble, in several of their plants, began experiments in self-managed teams. Team building continues today as one of the most-used OD interventions (see Chapter Sixteen on team building).

The dramatic increase in the number of global, matrix, and multicultural teams of individuals from around the world has presented the field with some interesting challenges, including not only the distance factor but also the meshing of deep-seated differences. There is also the pioneering "global OD" work of Allon Shevat (www.gr2010.com), who points out that the most widely used OD principles and processes were developed for the most part by white males from the United Kingdom and the United States in the 1940s and 1950s. Some of those principles will work anywhere, but many will not. How a manager from Indonesia, China, or Mexico handles conflict or communicates a problem to a superior will be very different from how an American or a German manager will do it. Chapter Twenty-Seven offers more insight into global OD.

The Internet has facilitated the birth of "virtual teams" as a way of managing globally dispersed people who have a common task or project (Lipnack and Stamps 1997). It is important to note that these teams are found to perform better when they start out with a real face-to-face experience, another testimony to the fundamental nature of the small group in human effectiveness.

Instrument-Based Skill Development

As a number of early OD practitioners modeled, different types of individually oriented surveys were used to gather responses from a manager and also from their subordinates and peers, providing feedback on some aspect of their managerial style. Current data feedback surveys such as last in, first out (LIFO), Myers-Briggs Type Inventory (MBTI), Dominance, Influence, Steadiness, and Conscientiousness (DISC) Profile and other 360° feedback instruments, are examples. It was recognized that people at work need additional skills like conflict resolution, systems thinking, and coaching.

Systems Theory and Organization Change

Although the concept of systems theory was familiar to some of the founders of the field, much of the early work was done in small groups. There was a general belief that by working with groups of people in an organization you would change the larger culture. From 1958 to 1959, an interesting event took place at General Mills that provided a caveat: Richard Beckhard, the external consultant, and Cy Levi, the internal, went to work "sensitizing" the first-line supervisors on the shop floor to give them better interpersonal skills in managing the hourly work force and to encourage more participative ways of managing. After the workshop was over, research was conducted on a wide basis to see if the desired behavioral change had taken place. The numbers showed that there had been a definite shift in the culture.

However, several months later, the researchers returned, and to their surprise the situation was now worse than it had been before the workshops had occurred! What came to light was that nothing had been done with the mangers who supervised the first level. A clear system theory message emerged: If you want to change an entire system, you must address the whole system. Marvin Weisbord and Sandra Janoff's Future Search Conferences and Roland Sullivan's Whole System Transformation are built on the principle of "getting the whole system in the room."

A seminal book appeared during this time, Katz and Kahn's (1966) *The Social Psychology of Organizations*, which took the system theory of the biologist, Ludvig von Bertalanffy, and applied it to organizations. Bertalanffy had written that living organisms survive by their ability to work out a meaningful relationship with their environment. For OD, organizations survive to the degree that they can adapt to a changing internal and external environment.

Open System Planning

After the end of World War II, there was such a need for consumer goods that companies focused simply on quantity, meeting the demand. It was a while before the Japanese and German emphasis on quality, initially in automobiles and then in other imports, began to capture market share from U.S. and U.K. companies. In addition, the rapid and inexorable growth of the global economy has put enormous pressures on both for-profit and nonprofit sectors to innovate or die. Billie Alban and her colleague, Barbara Bunker, have been pioneers in Large Group Interventions, an effective way of addressing large-scale problems in complex organizations and systems (Bunker and Alban 1997; and see Chapter Seventeen for more on Large Group Interventions).

OD started with social scientists conducting action research in small groups as a means for creating organizational change. This was followed by a more psychological emphasis on changing the individual, especially managers and leaders. Finally, there has been a recognition that change has to do with taking the whole system into account both internally and externally. Today, OD presents itself as embracing all of the above.

SUMMARY

The pioneers of OD, those who shaped and gave form and direction to our practice, were all about research, discovering the principles that govern what happens to people at work. The next generation took those principles and put them to work in creating what is, in effect, a profession. It is now up to us, their descendants, to do what they did so many years ago: discover *new* principles and methods of assisting leaders, members, and their organizations to be as effective as they can be in a world that is changing at the speed of light.

These are some of the classic "big books" that helped shape and define our field, in chronological order:

1911	*The Principles of Scientific Management*, by Frederick Taylor
1948	*Resolving Social Conflicts: Selected Papers on Group Dynamics*, by Kurt Lewin *Field Theory in Social Science*, by Kurt Lewin *The Dynamics of Planned Change*, by Ron Lippitt, Jeanne Watson, and Bruce Westley
1960	*The Human Side of Enterprise*, by Douglas McGregor
1961	*Experience in Groups*, by Wilfred Bion *The Planning of Change*, edited by Warren Bennis, Kenneth Benne, and Bob Chin *T-Group Theory and Laboratory Method*, edited by Leland Bradford *Interpersonal Dynamics*, by Warren Bennis, Ed Schein, Fred Steele, and David Berlew *Organization and Environment*, by Paul R. Lawrence and Jay W. Lorsch
1969	*The Practical Theorist: The Life and Work of Kurt Lewin*, by Alfred Marrow *New Technologies in OD*, by Warner Burke
1973	*Organization Development: Behavioral Science Interventions for Organizational Improvement*, by Wendell French and Chip Bell

Discussion Questions

1. What did each of these four contribute to the development of the field of OD: Taylor, Lewin, Bion, and McGregor? How much of what they "discovered" is still in use today by OD practitioners?

2. How did "group development" expand to become "organization development"? What was the role of the T-group in that evolution?

3. What stands out for you as you study Alban's OD Timeline? What are some examples of how what was happening in the larger world contributed the context and/or the stimulus for something that happened in the evolution of OD?

Resources

Free tools and information for effective leader of change: www.change-management-coach.com

NTL Institute: www.ntl.org

Training Development Solutions: Classic OD Theories: www.trainanddevelop.co.uk/article/frederick-herzberg-theory-of-motivation-a78

Marvin Weisbord resources and video clip on the founding principles of OD: www .organizationaldynamics.upenn.edu/weisbord

FutureSearch Network: www.futuresearch.net

Action Research by John Scherer: www.wiseratwork.com/videos/action-research

Global OD blog by Allon Shevat: www.blog.gr2010.com

References

Bion, W. 1940. "The War of Nerves." In *The Neuroses in War*, edited by E. Miller and H. Crichton-Miller, 35–42. London: Macmillan.

Bennis, W. G. 1969. *Organization Development: Its Nature, Origins, and Prospects*. Reading, MA: Addison-Wesley.

Bradford, L. P. 1964. *T-Group Theory and Laboratory Method: Innovation in Re-Education*. New York: John Wiley & Sons.

Bunker, B., and B. Alban. 1997. *Large Group Interventions: Engaging the Whole System for Rapid Change*. San Francisco: Jossey-Bass.

Cooperrider, D. L., and S. Srivastva. 1987. "Appreciative Inquiry in Organizational Life." In *Research in Organizational Change and Development, Vol. 1*, edited by R. W. Woodman and W. A. Pasmore, 129–169. Stamford, CT: JAI Press.

Herzberg, F., B. Mausner, and B. Snyderman. 1959. *The Motivation to Work*. 2nd ed. New York: John Wiley & Sons.

Hofstede, G., and G. J. Hofstede. 2005. *Cultures and Organizations: Software of the Mind*. 2nd ed. New York: McGraw-Hill.

Katz, D., and R. L. Kahn. 1966. *The Social Psychology of Organizations*. New York: John Wiley & Sons.

Lewin, K., R. Lippitt, and R. K. White. 1939. "Patterns of Aggressive Behavior in Experimentally Created 'Social Climates.'" *Journal of Social Psychology* 10: 271–299.

Lipnack, J., and J. Stamps. 1997. *Virtual Teams: Reaching across Space, Time, and Organizations with Technology*. New York: John Wiley & Sons.

McGregor, D. 1960. *The Human Side of Enterprise*. New York: McGraw-Hill.

Porter, L. 1974. "OD: Some Questions, Some Answers." *The OD Practitioner* 6 (3): 1–8.

Sashkin, M. 1980. "Interview with Eric Trist, British Interdisciplinarian." *Group and Organization Studies* 5 (3): 144–166.

Taylor, F. 1911. *The Principles of Scientific Management*. New York and London: Harper & Brothers.

Weisbord, M. R. 2012. *Productive Workplaces: Dignity, Meaning and Community in the 21st Century*. 3rd ed. San Francisco: Jossey-Bass Wiley.

Weisbord, M., and S. Janoff. 2010. *Future Search*. 3rd ed. San Francisco: Berrett-Koehler.

CHAPTER THREE

Change Process and Models

William J. Rothwell, Roland L. Sullivan, Taesung Kim,
Jong Gyu Park, and Wesley E. Donahue

A model for change is a simplified representation of the general steps in initiating and carrying out a change process. It is rooted in solid research and theory. Managers and consultants, when demonstrating the competencies of an OD practitioner, are well-advised to rely on a model for change as a compass to show them the direction in which to lead the change effort and change process. In this chapter, we review numerous models to guide the change process.

AN OVERVIEW OF KEY MODELS FOR ORGANIZATIONAL CHANGE

The change models we share rely primarily on a normative, reeducative, and innovative approach to behavioral change. They are (1) the traditional action research model, (2) Appreciative Inquiry, and (3) an evolving view of the action research model.

The Traditional Action Research Model

Action research has long been the foundation for many change efforts. It is properly regarded as a philosophy, a model, and a process. Like any change model, action research is a simplified representation of the complex activities that should occur in a change effort if it is to be participative, engaging, and empowering for those affected by it. The model serves as a compass to consultants facilitating change. While it does not tell consultants, managers, or workers exactly what to do in a paint-by-the-numbers fashion, it provides a process whereby the consultant and client can jointly inquire and decide what change is required. It helps consultants track where they are and where they are going. While the action research model has been depicted in different ways, the depictions of it share common characteristics. Figure 3.1 illustrates a general model of action research.

Action research may also be understood as a process of continuing events and actions. In a classic description, French and Bell (1990) defined this interpretation of action research as "The process of systematically collecting research data about an ongoing system relative to some objective, goal, or need of that system; feeding these data back into the system; taking actions by altering selected variables within the system based both on the data and on hypotheses; and evaluating the results of actions by collecting more data" (99).

One way to think about the traditional action research model is to depict it as a necessary step in any change effort (see Figure 3.1). This traditional depiction is based on the steps originally presented in Burke (1982) and in "Essential Competencies of Internal and External OD Consultants" (McLean and Sullivan 1989).

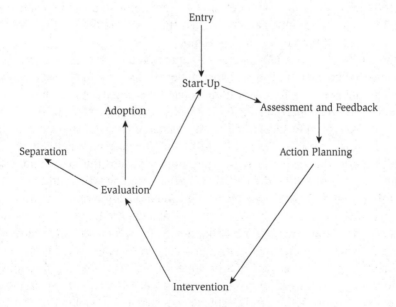

Figure 3.1. The Traditional Action Research Model

Although the length and depth of each step may vary across change efforts, the steps are usually present in one form or another. In long-term change efforts—as many are—each step in the model may actually turn into the whole model in miniature. For example, when it is time for action planning, the consultant may use all or some of the generic action research model phases. In other words, that step alone may call for a start-up phase, followed by assessment, action planning, and an evaluation component once or several times during the action planning process. The steps will be discussed in Part Two of the book.

Appreciative Inquiry (AI)

Appreciative Inquiry (AI) is the most exciting development in thinking about change in recent years. In one of the last conversations with the authors, Dick Beckhard, the person who coined the phrase "managing change" in the 1950s, told the authors of this chapter that he believed AI held within it the most promising future for OD. Like the action research model, AI is a way of being, a model, conceptual framework, and a process to guide change. Originally conceptualized by Case Western Reserve professor David Cooperrider (see Cooperrider and Srivastva 1987), it has captured much attention in recent years (see, for instance, Cooperrider 1990; Cooperrider 1995; Cooperrider, Whitney, and Stavros 2008; Watkins and Mohr 2001; Watkins, Mohr, and Kelly 2011). If the action research model can be comparable to the chip inside the OD computer that drives change efforts, then the Appreciative Inquiry model can be a different—but complementary—chip.

Appreciative Inquiry (AI) is an OD approach and process to change management that grows out of social constructionist thought. AI is the "cooperative co-evolutionary search for the best in people, their organizations, and the world around them" (Cooperrider et al. 2008, 3). Instead of starting out to solve problems—a typical focus of traditionally trained managers, steeped in a philosophy of Management by Exception (MBE)—AI focuses on what is going right, what is motivating, what is energizing, and what are the key strengths of a setting. Instead of asking the question, "What is going wrong and how do we solve that problem?" AI begins by asking, "What is going right and how do we leverage that strength to achieve quantum leaps in productivity improvement?"

Applying AI thus requires a paradigm shift from focusing on what is going wrong to what is going right and then trying to leverage what is going right into new, higher-level visions of a positive future. AI is both a philosophy and an approach to change, often represented as a 4-D method for application: Discovery, Dream, Design, and Destiny. See the AI 4-D model in Figure 3.2. The addition of Define, the initial "contracting" phase, to the 4-D model results in the AI 5-D model (Watkins et al. 2011).

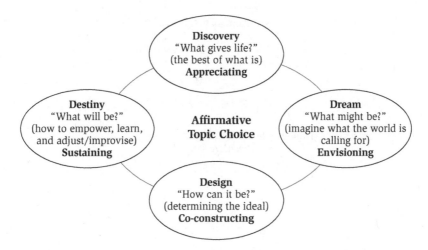

Figure 3.2. AI 4-D Model

THE EVOLVING VIEW OF THE ACTION RESEARCH MODEL

Burke (2002, 2014) reviewed the change process. In doing so, he posited what might be regarded as the seeds for evolving the action research model. What is exciting about this new view is that it gets away from the traditional action research model, which implicitly describes any change process as functioning as a drawn out and somewhat simplistic process.

Unfortunately, recent experience suggests that so many change efforts are going on at the same time in many organizations that a linear change approach no longer works. One reason is that so many concurrent change efforts lead to a crowding out effect. They burn people out and drive people crazy because it is not possible to remember all the change efforts going on at once. Against that backdrop of too many simultaneous change "projects," a single-minded project-based approach to change is no longer workable. What is needed is a new model to guide change that does not assume a beginning, middle, and end to a change effort. Instead, change efforts are continuing and are regarded from a whole systems standpoint.

Burke (2014) describes the phases of change as pre-launch, launch, and post-launch. The model is written as a guide for change leaders. Change efforts are regarded as proceeding like spirals rather than circles to depict their ongoing chaotic nature—and the view that what is learned from each phase of a change effort can be rolled into subsequent phases. In this way, organizations are transformed into learning organizations that "learn" from experience, and

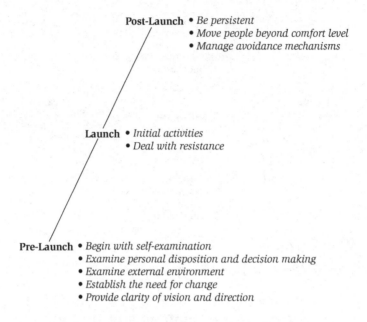

Post-Launch
• *Be persistent*
• *Move people beyond comfort level*
• *Manage avoidance mechanisms*

Launch
• *Initial activities*
• *Deal with resistance*

Pre-Launch
• *Begin with self-examination*
• *Examine personal disposition and decision making*
• *Examine external environment*
• *Establish the need for change*
• *Provide clarity of vision and direction*

Figure 3.3. Action Research Model

the spirals represent sequential learning curves of change. The new view of the action research model is depicted in Figure 3.3 and briefly summarized below. As Burke (2014) notes, "An interesting paradox about organization change is that we plan as if the process is linear when, in reality, it is anything but linear" (303).

Pre-Launch. The pre-launch phase occurs before the change effort begins. It establishes the foundation for a successful change effort. Without it, a change effort is likely to fail—or be short-lived—as other, more pressing daily crises demand attention. Pre-launch begins effectively when leaders follow the famous advice of Socrates to "know thyself" and start with self-examination. Burke (2014) suggests considering several additional issues during the pre-launch phase:

• Scanning the external environment

• Establishing the need for change

• Providing clarity of vision and direction

Launch. The launch phase is the beginning of the change effort. It begins with communication to key stakeholders inside and outside the organization about the need for change. This is what some leaders call "making the business case," and the case for change must be made by credible people who will be believed. According to Burke (2014), the key to the launch phase is creating initial activities that will seize attention and deal with resistance.

A major challenge in a long-term intervention is to create a sustained communication strategy about the change effort. Stakeholders must be reminded what is being changed, why it is being changed, how the change effort is proceeding, and what benefits are being realized from the change effort (Rothwell 2001).

Post-Launch. Post-launch involves sustaining a change effort over time. That can be particularly frustrating. The reason is that events in a change effort, even when successful, may appear to spiral out of control.

Burke (2014) recommends that CEOs follow the advice of Heifetz (1994). He has three suggestions. First, be persistent. Second, help people in the organization move beyond their comfort levels while keeping stress to a minimum. And third, be prepared to manage during the change effort the predictable "avoidance mechanisms" that can surface such as "blaming, scapegoating, and appealing to authority figures for answers" (Burke 2014, 318).

NEW ACTION RESEARCH CHANGE MODEL: PERPETUAL AND INSTANTANEOUS POSITIVE CHANGE

Change consulting in the twenty-first century requires a new model—a model that works in an environment of rapid, chaotic change. Many consultants and managers today are frustrated by the time required for the traditional action research model, but it should not be abandoned. The response in our practice has been to create a model that responds more adroitly to the growing complexity of the consulting world but is based on the founding principles of the OD field.

We reviewed hundreds of models being used in the field. One we particularly liked was Warner Burke's. It seemed to supply a foundational framework to integrate into our traditional eight-phase model. Using his framework of pre-launch, launch, and post-launch, we came up with the model depicted in Figure 3.4.

The model reflects the most current research around change agent competencies. It provides architecture to frame what change technologists do. The model is not a cookbook technique to be followed mindlessly but a change framework that drives what OD consultants do. This framework becomes a philosophical foundation that comes alive only with personal and creative application, since you (as OD consultant) are the instrument of change.

Each phase of our new change model is discussed in this book. Here we will provide a brief overview of each phase. We call them phases because, unlike steps, different elements blend with others in myriad ways. As we have noted

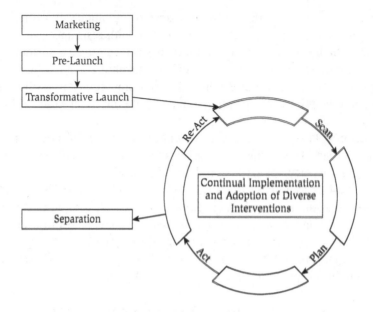

Figure 3.4. Sullivan Rothwell Change Process Model

above, change efforts are seldom sequential, so keeping the overall framework in mind is important.

Marketing

OD practitioners often stumble over themselves for marketing and selling. Internal change agents must also attend to marketing. Often they do not publicize their successes in their own enterprises and are thereby robbed of the credit they so richly deserve. All organizations want a present better than the past and a future better than the present. OD is all about doing just that. So the need for OD services exists.

Pre-Launch

Pre-launch begins when consultants clearly have clients committed to work with them. The marketing, selling, and entry issues are complete. It ends when the psychological and nonpsychological contract, relationship connecting, and clarification of expectations are completed. An old adage in the field says that if anything goes awry in the change effort, it can usually be traced back to mistakes made in this phase.

Peter Block has had much to say about the importance of relationships in the early phases of a change effort. He says that the core competency in consulting is how to contract with clients. This is the heart of his most popular book, *Flawless Consulting* (Block 2011). For Block, contracting is about treating the relationship as significant and central. He believes one must continually process and reset the relationship. Modeling competency in relationship development will also help the client deal with key relationships. We intend to transfer our competence to the client system. Our research over the years has led us to believe that the ability to initiate and maintain excellent interpersonal relationships is paramount to success in the pre-launch phase and is essential to a successful engagement.

Transformative Launch

This phase starts the change process by assessing the situation and planning for action in order to launch a long-term, ongoing effort. Sometimes, it's a good idea to start with a striking catharsis or a euphoric liftoff! In other cases, a quiet start can be more effective as a team searches for early, quick wins in a sensitive situation. Ideally, the top team starts with itself. In either case, a flawless beginning can do much to commit the entire top team to supporting engagement and involvement of all parts of the organization.

Some situations require *transformative change,* the dramatic shift in focus and priorities that can occur when conditions are just right. Transformative change is more than step improvement or incremental change. Freeing a caterpillar from an enclosed jar improves its situation but doesn't change its nature. In transformation, the caterpillar becomes a butterfly. For transformative changes, the launch phase should be a striking and dramatically positive jump into a brilliant future.

Today, we see the change cycle requiring a process and philosophy built in for constant reaction and continual planning efforts. It is not a phase of a long-term effort, but rather an ongoing implementation of a myriad of interventions, an endless loop (or spiral) of short-cycle change.

In Figure 3.4, you can see the launch phase broken out into a submodel, which we call SPAR: Scan, Plan, Act, and Re-Act. Each phase or each session within a phase may include all four elements of SPAR. That is the Chinese box phenomenon—the famous puzzle consisting of a series of progressively smaller boxes inside a large box—which may typify many change efforts. In other words, when a change effort is big enough and long-term enough, the assessment and feedback moment or experience (for instance) may itself have an entry component, a start-up component, and so forth.

Scan. Diagnosis traditionally is the phrase used to describe the major function of the Scan phase. Our quantitative research over the years involving almost four thousand change agents has produced many heated arguments over whether to use assessment or diagnosis. We have been won over to the assessment side of the street because diagnosis comes more from a medical model looking for something sick. Assessment is typically known as a classification of someone or something regarding its worth. When a change process is positive, conversations are energizing. The process entropies when conversations are about problems, negativity, and blamestorming.

This is the phase where valid information is central. Common sense and classic research agree. Too often we see people in organizations jump right into the end-state planning without generating an accurate picture of where they are now and a clear view of a desired destiny.

Asking the right questions is key. David Cooperrider (founder of Appreciative Inquiry, which depends heavily on crafting the right questions) says that he spent days of intense concentration determining the exact questions he would use in breakout groups while he facilitated leaders of all the major world religions in a summit. Asking the right questions has much to do with where the client system lands in the next phase of planning. Usually we like to co-create scanning questions with the client. They know better than we do what is important. Often they need help rephrasing questions that could elicit negative, and perhaps unhelpful, responses.

In sum, the scan phase is about helping the client system get a comprehensive view from individuals or small groups about where they are and wish to be. Creating a system-wide synthesis and common-ground intelligence base comes in the next phase.

Plan. There is a wide assortment of techniques and methods that can be used to plan what you will act on. What approach should you use? It all depends. It may depend on the scope of the effort, the style of leadership, or the nature of the data-collection methodology. Here are some practical tips for the Plan phase:

- Feed back the data in a distilled manner
- Spend some time validating the data collected
- Do allow the system to disturb itself
- Be sensitive in confrontation
- Work together to create compelling propositions
- Ensure that clients are able to freely choose their plan
- Anticipate and name the resistance that may arise
- Create a simple, elegant master plan format

Act. Acting the plan is the heart and soul of what we do in OD, where the interventions we have planned with clients are carried out. The Act phase is where we get the results and where we add value. When we do it well, performance improves. If we have done all previous phases and subphases competently, success should spontaneously occur.

Chris Argyris (2004) offers a clear, simple, and profound statement around "Act." He writes, "In order to act, human beings diagnose problems, invent solutions, and evaluate the effectiveness of what they have produced" (p. 2). These are indeed the same steps we are describing in SPAR. A key competency of an OD practitioner is to facilitate client conversation to help these effective change actions happen.

Argyris continues by noting that "productive reasoning (1) produces valid knowledge, (2) creates informed choices, and (3) makes personal reasoning transparent in order for the claims to be tested robustly. The core of productive reasoning is that the parties involved are vigilant about striving to avoid unknowingly deceiving themselves and others" (2004, 3).

The following are some practical tips for the Act phase:

- Increase the quality of the conversation
- Facilitate high-performing relationships
- Establish a climate of trust and openness
- Empower all to "act" through engagement
- Ensure that the people in the organization are prepared to support the action
- Engage the leaders
- Help internal change agents

Re-Act. The Re-Act phase occurs in more than one way. Planning renewal is a must. Re-action is necessary as the organization responds to the implementation of the plan. The action plan always evolves differently than you might have expected, so your plan must be updated and adjusted. Reaction feeds corrective action. Now is also the time to extract the learning from the previous three phases and to be prepared for the next cycle of SPAR.

The following section highlights issues related to this phase:

- Obtain information on which to base reaction
- Deal with challenges
- Avoid slippage to old ways
- Celebrate success
- Apply lessons learned

Every year or so, depending on how much people in an organization thirst for positive change, the change effort may start back at the launch phase when a deep dive transformation lift is needed. For one of our clients, the largest financial system in South Africa, launching transformative change has become a way of life. They are known to do a dozen summits per year. The summits are designed where the system boundaries are open to customers and events in the larger culture. That keeps them close to their customers and has made them one of the most loved brands in Africa.

So we see that the SPAR model can be a cycle within a cycle—a Chinese box within a box—an endless loop of response to the ongoing change in today's organizations. Leaving the SPAR model, we come back to our larger change frame and conclude.

Separation

When we search the literature, we find little on consultant separation or closure. Yet we know from our learning on the dynamics of small groups that saying good-bye and endings are very important.

Separation is already treated in this book, so we only wish to add one story. We know of a well-known and respected OD consultant who establishes up-front ground rules for separation. One key ground rule is this: Either the consultant or the client can call a separation meeting at any time. The clients and the consultant commit to a full-day session offsite in an environment free from distractions. At that time they can process the engagement with openness, trusting that a mutual decision about how and when to separate will evolve. A heart-to-heart conversation will start movement for additional external help or a termination that can be settled on in a manner that is agreeable to everyone.

ORGANIZATION DEVELOPMENT EFFECTIVENESS MODEL

Given all the insightful approaches and their relentless applications to practices, it is interesting to realize that a recent argument by IBM that organizational change strategies fail about 60 percent does not differ from Druckman and Bjork's (1991) assertion over 20 years ago. While reminded again of the complex and difficult nature of change efforts, we felt compelled to present another model that would help increase the success rate of the efforts.

The new model's approach is threefold: (a) building on well-rounded wisdom, (b) incorporating constructive feedback, and (c) learning from other disciplines, particularly innovation diffusion research. The new model, illustrated in Figure 3.5, offers additional and complementary considerations to the existing models for more effective organization development and change.

The OD Effectiveness Model emphasizes the individual's approach to change and the crucial role of interpersonal and technological communication networks. Many change models take a normative/reeducative approach to

Figure 3.5. Organization Development Effectiveness Model™

- Sustaining and revitalizing the change
- Evaluating the effort
- Continuing to view the present with an eye to the future

- Developing an operational effectiveness roadmap
- Establishing communication plans and roles
- Establishing feedback systems

- Viewing the present
- Appraising goals, capabilities, and cultures
- Understanding communication practices and structures

- Sharing knowledge about the change
- Maintaining the momentum while being flexible
- Managing distortive communications and resistance

- Envisioning the future
- Reviewing the change options and top leaders' commitment
- Identifying scenarios with potential benefits and costs

PEOPLE

TRANSFORMATION
REVITALIZING
DOING
PLANNING
STRATEGIZING
INQUIRING

individuals' behavior change, as mentioned earlier in this chapter, when people are empirical/rational and act on self-interest (Duck 2001). In other words, these models imply authority-driven, top-down approaches to managing change when individuals seek for trustworthy communications to help with their independent and voluntary change decisions (Smollan 2013; Zhou 2008). This new model, therefore, complements the existing change models by emphasizing the importance of the change process on the individual's side as well as the organization's side.

What follows is a summary of the phases.

Inquiring

Living systems, whether organizations or individuals, are continuously changing and challenged with the impetus to view and appraise the present in pursuit of a better future.

Previous change models have relied mainly on either of two representative approaches to understanding the present: (a) examining data that represent value-neutral reality and (b) engaging in communications that disclose people's perceived reality. Considering that objective/subjective goals, capabilities, and cultures coexist in an organization, the present needs to be viewed using the two approaches simultaneously and interpreted from both perspectives of initiators and adopters of change. Again, there is no "one best way" to manage change.

Unless an organization is in a complete dysfunction, issues or opportunities identified from the appraisal cannot be let go without being addressed. A seminal activity, before coming up with a strategy to address these, is to inquire into how the organization's communication practices and structures look like. The comprehensive understanding of decision-making practices, formal/informal communication networks, and information technology systems should be a key to establishing robust strategies for any changes to come. Success of change efforts depends on whether and how well these are inquired and explored.

Strategizing

As a next step in change efforts beyond inquiring, a desirable future is envisioned for change efforts, and the options that could drive the present to or beyond the future are reviewed. This process is called strategizing.

Referring to the future as if it is something concrete is misleading. Rather, the future is really an organic moving target. A caveat, therefore, is that envisioning the future is an activity that should involve recursive redefinitions aided by the feedback systems in place. As a story unfolds and people engage, it constantly changes.

In reviewing change options, multiple aspects should be assessed, including the attributes of each option, its fitness with the target groups and individuals, their readiness for change, and the organizational communication network. Top leaders' commitment should also be discussed as they are the primary change agent and cheerleader who would accept of the premise that change must happen at all levels and that it is part of their job.

It is a desired practice to put change options into scenarios with potential benefits and costs. Scenarios with potential crises, plausible possibilities, and predicted communication patterns and responses among the target people will help make a sound decision about change options and plan on solutions.

Planning

Once selected, the change options need to be crafted into the form of organizational change initiatives—a visionary implementation plan with anticipated consequences.

A major consideration in this phase, in addition to planning the time frame and resources, is to design a communication scheme consisting of two core components: (a) framing messages to help people pay more attention to certain facets of the change initiative and shape perspectives, and (b) formulating communication networks to engage messengers and technologies in communicating the initiative in the framed manner. For example, information and messages need to be framed in an understandable, advantageous, and compatible way; executives, middle managers, opinion leaders, target individuals, and even potential resisters, along with communication technologies, need to be assigned to a proper role. The communication scheme should also continue to be revisited throughout the change process.

Undesirable consequences, such as instability of the organization and members' resistance to change, may arise before, during, and after implementation of a change initiative and should be discussed in this phase and on-the-go. Since it is impossible to anticipate all the possibilities, the importance of having the feedback systems work is emphasized here again. The feedback systems will help vibrant communications and appropriate/timely adjustments take place along the way, while enabling a substantive evaluation at the end.

Doing

Once the implementation plan is in full swing, the change initiative transforms from an organization's blueprint to vivid reality that members and related stakeholders face, respond to, and co-create.

In this phase, effective knowledge sharing should occur to help the target adopters be informed of and interested in the proposed change (Rogers 2003). As planned, the capacity, effectiveness, and efficiency of communication technologies should be harnessed for informing people; the communicators should fulfill their assigned job in influencing them. Especially, the impact and contribution of formal/informal opinion leaders must be vitalized because they are those who can move people's minds. Knowing is one thing, and doing is another.

Once the change is welcomed by early adopters, it is more likely to appeal to a broader audience (Centola 2013) through the interactions that the communication networks, opinion leaders, and already-adopters have with not-yet others. As diffusing, the change initiative continues to develop in a certain way hopefully similar to or possibly different from what was originally planned. Required of change leaders, therefore, is to maintain the momentum and keep approximating the anticipated outcome by being flexible and creative rather than trying to stick to the predetermined details. Meantime, negative reactions to and evolving characteristics of the change initiative need to be monitored and discussed by the relentlessly working feedback systems. A poorly managed process might result in not only the initiative's failure but also the organization's failure.

Revitalizing

In the midst of change, living systems keep self-organizing and sense-making. Even after making a change decision, they engage in the activities to try it, to confirm or revoke it, and to revitalize the change to inspire whole new possibilities.

This phase consists of three major components: (a) helping sustain the change, (b) evaluating the effort, and (c) inspiring people to keep renewing and transforming. While the efforts to offer reinforcements and foster an organizational ecology conducive to change are being made, the evaluation of the change initiative should be conducted according to the established plan. In particular, top leaders are encouraged to celebrate the new practice and to keep engaging in the constructive feedback, as well as to champion the final phase of a thorough evaluation about the processes, consequences, and lessons learned; all with an eye to the future.

If formative evaluations have been conducted to get ongoing feedback as things unfold (Ashley 2009) and proactively used for modification of the strategies throughout the process, this phase would be more robust and rewarding with its outcomes. A follow-through evaluation is also recommended to see if continuous improvements are being made in the organization with its people, strategy, process, and structure, and if there is another change opportunity. As one innovative product is not an end to change, just an end to a phase of the change cycle that keeps going on, specific change initiatives may come to a certain conclusion, yet change in organizations is constant and must continue.

SUMMARY

A model for change serves as a compass to guide managers and consultants as they lead or facilitate change efforts. These models are best understood as simplified representations of the general steps in initiating and carrying out a change process. This chapter reviewed numerous models for change … some old, some evolving.

The traditional action research was the first model examined in this chapter. It was used as a foundation for many change efforts. It is properly regarded as both a model and a process. A typical way to view it is that change is managed as a project and encompasses eight key steps.

A second model examined in this chapter was Appreciative Inquiry (AI). AI is a philosophy and an approach to change. It "invites us to choose consciously to seek out and inquire into that which is generative and life-enriching, both in our own lives and in the lives of others, and to explore our hopes and dreams for the future" (Watkins and Mohr 2001, 58).

A new view of action research was a third model examined in this chapter. It is in response to recent research that indicates that the old linear models are not working. It reinvents the traditional action research model based on the assumption that change efforts should not be managed as projects but instead as a process.

The final section of the chapter reviewed a new change model. A large section of this book is based on the evolving view of action research. The reader will therefore find chapters in the rest of the book that address these methods in more detail.

Discussion Questions

1. What criticisms might you expect to hear from operating managers about the traditional action research model, and how might you answer them?
2. Why is Appreciative Inquiry often regarded as a revolutionary approach to change?
3. How are Burke's pre-launch, launch, and post-launch unique and different from other approaches to change?
4. What is the difference between *incremental* and *transformational* change?
5. How does action research compare to Appreciative Inquiry?

Resources

Change management models: www.scrumalliance.org/community/articles/2014/march/change-management-models

Kotter's 8-Step Change Model: www.mindtools.com/pages/article/newPPM_82.htm

Kurt Lewin 3-Phase Change Model: www.change-management-consultant.com/kurt-lewin.html

References

Argyris, C. 2004. *Reasons and Rationalizations: The Limits to Organizational Knowledge*. New York: Oxford University Press.

Ashley, S. R. 2009. "Innovation Diffusion: Implications for Evaluation." *New Directions for Evaluation* 124: 35–45.

Block, P. 2011. *Flawless Consulting: A Guide to Getting Your Expertise Used*. 3rd ed. San Francisco: Pfeiffer.

Burke, W. W. 1982. *Organization Development: Principles and Practices*. Boston: Little, Brown.

Burke, W. W. 2002. *Organization Change: Theory and Practice*. Thousand Oaks, CA: Sage.

Burke, W. W. 2014. *Organization Change: Theory and Practice*. 4th ed. Thousand Oaks, CA: Sage.

Centola, D. M. 2013. "Homophily, Networks, and Critical Mass: Solving the Start-Up Problem in Large Group Collective Action." *Rationality and Society* 25 (1): 3–40.

Cooperrider, D. L. 1990. "Positive Image, Positive Action: The Affirmative Basis of Organizing." In *Appreciative Management and Leadership*, edited by S. Srivastva and D. L. Cooperrider, 91–125. San Francisco: Jossey-Bass.

Cooperrider, D. L. 1995. *Introduction to Appreciative Inquiry: Organization Development*. 5th ed. Upper Saddle River, NJ: Prentice-Hall.

Cooperrider, D. L., and S. Srivastva. 1987. "Appreciative Inquiry in Organizational Life." In *Research in Organizational Change and Development, Vol. 1*, edited by R. W. Woodman and W. A. Pasmore, 129–169. Greenwich, CT: JAI Press.

Cooperrider, D. L., D. Whitney, and J. M. Stavros. 2008. *Appreciative Inquiry Handbook: For Leaders of Change*. 2nd ed. Brunswick, OH: Crown Custom.

Druckman, D., and R. A. Bjork. 1991. *In the Mind's Eye: Enhancing Human Performance*. Washington, DC: National Academies Press.

Duck, J. D. 2001. *The Change Monster: The Human Forces That Fuel or Foil Corporate Transformation and Change*. New York: Crown Business.

French, W. L., and C. H. Bell. 1990. *Organization Development: Behavioral Science Interventions for Organization Improvement*. 4th ed. Englewood Cliffs, NJ: Prentice-Hall.

Heifetz, R. 1994. *Leadership Without Easy Answers*. Cambridge, MA: Belknap Press.

McLean, G., and R. Sullivan. 1989. *Essential Competencies of Internal and External OD Consultants*. Unpublished manuscript.

Rogers, E. M. 2003. *Diffusion of Innovations*. 5th ed. New York: Free Press.

Rothwell, W. J. 2001. *The Manager and Change Leader*. Alexandria, VA: The American Society for Training and Development.

Smollan, R. K. 2013. "Trust in Change Managers: The Role of Affect." *Journal of Organizational Change Management* 26 (4): 725–747.

Watkins, J. M., and B. J. Mohr. 2001. *Appreciative Inquiry: Change at the Speed of Imagination*. San Francisco: Pfeiffer.

Watkins, J. M., B. J. Mohr, and R. Kelly. 2011. *Appreciative Inquiry: Change at the Speed of Imagination*. 2nd ed. Hoboken, NJ: John Wiley & Sons.

Zhou, Y. 2008. "Voluntary Adopters versus Forced Adopters: Integrating the Diffusion of Innovation Theory and the Technology Acceptance Model to Study Intra-Organizational Adoption." *New Media & Society* 10 (3): 475–496.

CHAPTER FOUR

Organization Development and Transformation

What It Takes

Linda Ackerman Anderson

My OD practice in "planned change" evolved significantly over a 37-year career as an internal and external practitioner. It started with meeting facilitation, event design, organization assessment, and performance systems, and evolved to focus solely on large-scale strategic change consulting. I realized that my understanding of organizational change had to expand in order to achieve outcomes and business benefits at scale that, heretofore, my colleagues and I were not able to attain. Was the shortcoming in the way we were practicing OD, or was it that the nature of the changes we were attempting to guide was different, more complex, and unable to be "planned" or controlled as we had been taught?

It was both. This recognition gave rise to the identification of a unique type of change—*transformation*—that was far more complex than our OD practices were originally designed to serve. Transformation is defined below, and its unique requirements outlined. OD is now optimally positioned to take on the challenge of consulting to transformational change as a primary focus of our practice.

Note: All figures in this chapter are from *Beyond Change Management*, Copyright © 2010 by Dean Anderson and Linda Ackerman Anderson or *The Change Leader's Roadmap* © 2010 by Linda Ackerman Anderson and Dean Anderson, with permission of the publisher, John Wiley & Sons.

This chapter starts with a description of how transformation came to be named. Then, considerations are offered for how the field of OD might expand its approaches to large-scale change to better serve organizational results. To ground this discussion, conscious change leadership is introduced, the method Dean Anderson and I have co-developed over the past 35 years to guide consultants, leaders, and senior executives through successful transformation. My opinions about the practice of OD are based largely on my observations of the practitioners within my client systems and are not reflective of the written guidance of the field.

HOW ORGANIZATION
TRANSFORMATION EMERGED

Until the mid-1990s, OD, quality (process improvement), and project management were the primary fields addressing change in organizations. During that time, transformational change became more prevalent, and it is my opinion that none were able to adequately address its complexities. Executives, wanting more help with project implementation and overcoming people's resistance, gave rise to the field of change management. Over the past decade, this field has grown, establishing standards and practices through the Association of Change Management Professionals. However, this field is also not designed to handle the complexities of transformation. What's missing? Will OD evolve itself to fill the gap? Let's look at history for some clues.

In the early 1980s, a group of OD practitioners gathered at a regional OD network conference to explore some emerging questions and patterns we were seeing about change in the organizations we served. John Adams, Harrison Owen, Linda Nelson, Frank Burns, Laury DeBivort, myself, and others started a conversation that resulted in the conclusion that there was a "new" type of change afoot that was very different than what we were used to seeing. We shared common challenges: We couldn't plan for everything that was happening or needed as things were emerging and shifting by the day; change was underway without a clear picture of an end state; leaders were unsettled and without clear plans; people were deeply affected by how much disruption the change was causing them; and there were cultural barriers to making progress. These dynamics of change were nothing like the theory we had learned and practiced of "unfreeze, change, and refreeze."

We sponsored a symposium to gather other organizational consultants who also recognized these unique dynamics to attempt to define transformation and how to approach it. We sent out 50 invitations, and 170 people showed up! This was the first of many annual gatherings over the next two decades, and the field of organization transformation (OT) was born.

Perhaps describing OT as a field was a naive misnomer. Many of our OD colleagues immediately reacted and a debate ensued. Was it OD or OT? Which do you do? Which is better, right, and more important? While heated at the time, these questions were off the mark. We realize now that OD is a practice performed by both internal and external practitioners, and transformation is a type of change, one that OD practitioners (and change consultants from other fields) can and should be able to support, since I see it as the most prevalent type of change in our organizations today.

The conferences and the debate led me to publish an article (Ackerman 1986) to define transformational change by contrasting it with two other types of organizational change—developmental and transitional change. These definitions are explored in the next section. Defining transformation began a several-decade journey of determining how to lead it, consult to it, and support it to succeed. This work continues today.

THREE TYPES OF CHANGE

The following descriptions define the three types of change. OD practitioners can and should be positioned and capable of consulting to all of these types, start to finish.

Developmental Change

Developmental change represents the *improvement* of an existing skill, process, performance standard, or condition that for some reason does not meet current or future needs. Metaphorically, they are enhancements "within the box" of what is already known or practiced (see Figure 4.1). Such improvements are often logical adjustments to current ways of working with the goal to do "better than" or "more of" what is already being done. The key focus is to strengthen or correct what exists in the organization, thus ensuring better numbers, improved performance, reduced cost from mistakes, and greater satisfaction. Developmental change is best designed to motivate people to grow and stretch to attain new and meaningful performance levels.

Developmental change is the simplest of the three types. The focus of the new state—its content—is a prescribed enhancement of the old state, rather than a radical or experimental solution requiring profound change. The impact on people is relatively mild, usually calling for new knowledge or skills. It is the least threatening type as most people understand the need to improve over time. Traditional project management and training approaches suffice, as the variables are predictable and can be managed against time and budget. Developmental change applies to individuals, groups, or the whole organization and

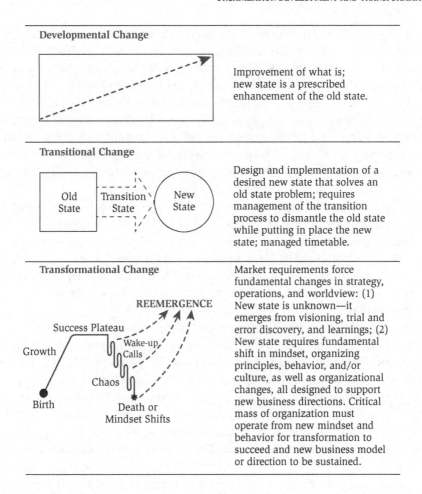

Developmental Change

Improvement of what is; new state is a prescribed enhancement of the old state.

Transitional Change

Old State — Transition State — New State

Design and implementation of a desired new state that solves an old state problem; requires management of the transition process to dismantle the old state while putting in place the new state; managed timetable.

Transformational Change

Birth — Growth — Success Plateau — Chaos — Wake-up Calls — Death or Mindset Shifts — REEMERGENCE

Market requirements force fundamental changes in strategy, operations, and worldview: (1) New state is unknown—it emerges from visioning, trial and error discovery, and learnings; (2) New state requires fundamental shift in mindset, organizing principles, behavior, and/or culture, as well as organizational changes, all designed to support new business directions. Critical mass of organization must operate from new mindset and behavior for transformation to succeed and new business model or direction to be sustained.

Figure 4.1. Three Types of Change

Source: From D. Anderson and L. Ackerman Anderson, *Beyond Change Management: How to Achieve Breakthrough Results Through Conscious Change Leadership,* 2nd ed. (San Francisco: Pfeiffer, 2010), 53.

is evident in changes such as training (both technical and personal), increasing sales or production, process or quality improvement, or team building.

Transitional Change

Transitional change is more complex. It is triggered by the need to respond to more significant shifts in environmental forces or marketplace requirements for success. Rather than simply *improve what is*, transitional change *replaces what is with something different*. It begins when leaders recognize a problem or see an opportunity not being pursued. Therefore, something in the existing operation must change or be created to better serve current and/or future demands. The process of addressing transitional change involves an assessment of the need and opportunity against current reality, and then the design of a better future state to satisfy new requirements. To achieve the new state, the organization must simultaneously dismantle and emotionally let go of old ways of operating while the new state is put into place. This process, while tricky, can be managed against a fairly rigorous budget and timeline since the solution is clearly defined in advance. Project management is usually effective for transitional change, especially when the people impacted by the change are engaged in it and are committed and supported to make it happen.

OD and change management help in addressing these human dynamics. Along with acquiring new knowledge and skills, people can be supported to change or develop new behaviors and practices. Significant problems occur, however, if executives view their organization's transitional changes as purely technical, operational, or structural and do not provide adequate OD and change management support to the people affected, especially when people are overworked.

We must note that William Bridges's (2004) well-known work on transitions is different from the transitional change to which we refer. Bridges's work addresses understanding how people go through change psychologically and emotionally and how to help people get through their personal process in effective ways (in other words, make the emotional "transition"). Since all organizational change, regardless of type, impacts people, Bridges's work can be used in all types. The variable that affects the people strategies is the degree and depth of the impact. Prosci's ADKAR model (Hiatt 2006) supports all types of change as well.

Examples of transitional change include reorganizations; simple mergers or consolidations; new technology that does not require major changes in culture, behavior, or mindset; and the creation of new products, services, systems, processes, policies, or procedures that simply replace old ones.

Transformational Change

Transformation is one of the most challenging yet potentially rewarding undertakings for leaders. It holds the greatest possibility for breakthrough results. The transformational process is triggered by a profound shift in worldview, with leaders realizing that the organization cannot continue to function or produce what the future demands and must undergo a radical shift to meet the requirements of its changing marketplace. It begins with the overt recognition that the status quo must fundamentally change.

The first challenge in transformation is that the future state is largely uncertain at the beginning. It is known that something very different must be done, but it is unclear about exactly what that needs to be. For example, it may be known that the organization wants to be fully digitized, but it is unclear what that entails. Therefore, both the future state design and the process to figure it out and implement it are often emergent. Things are discovered along the way that could never have been known without first launching the journey. No plan stays in place for long. Through responding quickly to what shows up, clarity emerges. As events proceed, leaders (and practitioners) must have acute awareness of what they are trying to accomplish, how they are trying to get there, how they respond to what shows up, and how to make adjustments. Therefore, the change process is nonlinear, with numerous course corrections. These requirements are generally not comfortable for leaders, and less so for middle management and the workforce waiting for direction and clarity. Figure 4.2 shows the journey, emphasizing the need for active and continuous course correction of both the outcome and the change process.

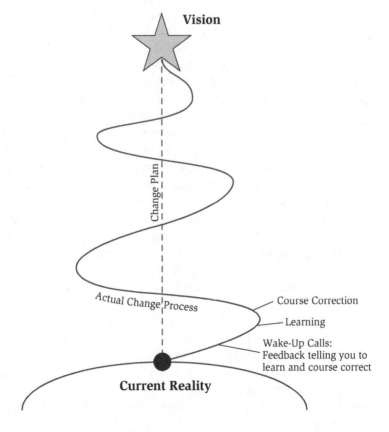

Figure 4.2. The Journey of Transformation

Source: From D. Anderson and L. Ackerman Anderson, *Beyond Change Management: How to Achieve Breakthrough Results Through Conscious Change Leadership*, 2nd ed. (San Francisco: Pfeiffer, 2010), 66.

To complete the picture, while addressing a radical change in the way the organization works, transformation also triggers profound human dynamics. Beyond managing the uncertainty, it requires a shift in people's awareness, mindsets, ways of relating across boundaries, and culture that significantly alters how they see the marketplace, what their customers need from them, their work, their peers, and themselves. Leaders must lead differently, managers must manage differently, and the workforce must operate differently. How? The process needs to make the expectation for deep personal change up front. The need for personal change must be integrated into the plan and be supported over the life of the effort. Given these dynamics, you can appreciate why even the best application of project management or change management, alone or in tandem, does not suffice. Leading this process is not about minimizing variance from the plan; it is about maximizing intelligent adjustments to it as rapidly as possible.

Since leaders do not have all the answers they are accustomed to having, and they need to support rapid course correction, they must lead in new ways. And, without answers from leaders, or seeing things change so often, people are typically more uncertain and afraid. If the workforce is accustomed to being told what to do and how, they will not like being "kept in the dark," feeling yanked around, or thinking leadership is not telling them the whole truth. Succeeding at transformation requires engaging the people who must make changes in the field or on the ground in the challenge of finding the best solutions and ways of working. Early and ongoing stakeholder engagement, especially in identifying potential course corrections, is key to every transformational strategy. It is one of the central cultural shifts that can drive successful transformation and produce breakthrough results. It is the best strategy for leaders to demonstrate their seriousness about the transformation being owned by the organization and therefore, sustainable.

The people dynamics are so significant that without leaders overtly addressing them, the transformation will fail. Leading developmental change is comparatively easy. Leading transitional change is more demanding, but manageable. Leading transformational change requires leaders to develop themselves, from the inside out. They need to walk the talk of what they are asking of the organization. This development is core to the change process and must be a part of the OD practitioner's required services. Leaders have brought the organization to its current reality with their existing set of skills, strategies, and mindsets. Transformation demands a change in all of these, so that leaders can actually guide the organization through the complexities of change with the inspiration and capability to succeed in its new reality.

You can determine whether your change effort is transformational by answering three questions:

1. Does the change require your organization's strategy, structure, systems, operations, products, services, or technology to change radically to meet the needs of customers and the marketplace?

2. Does your organization need to begin its change process before the destination is fully known and defined?

3. Is the scope of the change so significant that it requires the organization's culture and people's behaviors and mindsets to shift fundamentally in order to implement the changes successfully and sustain the benefits of the new state?

If the answer is "yes" to any two of these questions, then you are likely undergoing transformation. If the answer is "yes" to all three, then you are definitely facing transformation.

REQUIREMENTS FOR TRANSFORMATION TO SUCCEED

Transformation is the dominant type of change in organizations today. Change management, project management, and others each have valuable practices to contribute, but all are partial, and most are set up to compete or function in piecemeal fashion on major initiatives. None provide the entire breadth and depth of what is needed in an integrated way. OD can step into this void. The following describes key requirements for success.

Take a Conscious Approach to Change Leadership

For the past 30 years, we have been developing the approach of *conscious change leadership*. This type of leadership is essential to support successful transformation, outlining the awareness, knowledge, methods, and skills OD needs to serve leaders in transformational journeys. This approach is both the practice of consciously designing the process of change and a personal way of being.

Leaders who embody conscious change leadership are actively aware of both the organizational dynamics they are dealing with, and their internal states that are impacting the status of the change and the people involved. Simply said, it entails simultaneous attention to the external factors at play in the organization undergoing the change and the inner factors of the leader's mindset and reactions. Leaders engage in personal development to produce the highest outcomes from the change, keeping the best interests of the organization and stakeholders in mind.

Conscious change leaders demonstrate an advanced level of ego development in how they think and operate. William Torbert, in *Action Inquiry* (2004), has articulated a hierarchy of adult stages of ego development that indicate predictive impacts on leaders' ability to be successful in complex circumstances, which is true of transformation. Based on Torbert's work and our 30 years of observation, transformational efforts succeed or fail in direct proportion to the level of ego development of the leaders. The more self-aware—conscious—the leaders are, the more they can see beyond their traditional worldviews and "get perspective on their perspectives." They have the ability to objectively assess if what they are seeing and doing is working. If not, they proactively consider what else they, and their stakeholders, might generate that will work better in their current circumstances. The conscious change leadership of transformation requires a greater depth and breadth of perspective to see how best to address its complexity and volatile demands. It requires leaders to be willing and able to adapt their mindsets, behavior, and subsequent decisions.

Contrast taking a conscious approach with taking a reactive approach. The reactive approach refers to leaders who operate on autopilot, simply doing what they have always done as if the transformational playing field is the same as "running the business." Reactive leaders orient only to their external reality and approach it as they always have, applying habitual methods without awareness of the fact that a different approach might be needed. Conscious leaders understand that their "mindset is causative," that how they see the world heavily influences what they see in the world. They can better identify when they are stuck "in the box" rather than "getting out of the box." They know their internal reality is at play, so they consciously innovate, learn, and course correct. They see people and change process dynamics that reactive leaders miss. Consequently, they can proactively plan and mitigate those dynamics rather than be blindsided by them. Their awareness gives them far greater insight into how to design and implement transformational change processes that effectively address people's needs so they engage in and commit to change, rather than resist it.

Conscious leaders set their change efforts up for success from the beginning; reactive leaders never take this time, typically being too busy or moving too fast. Conscious leaders stay involved and give the attention required on a regular basis, separate from running operations. Reactive leaders "bless and delegate to a project team" and disappear until things go awry.

Taking a conscious approach requires providing leaders with significant self-awareness training, development, and coaching. In the book *Beyond Change Management* (Anderson and Ackerman Anderson 2010), the nuances and power of taking a conscious approach are described and explored. Leaders must learn to move beyond their head-level understanding of how to lead change and fully engage in the personal development work to discover how they need to think, act, and relate differently for the transformation to succeed. This personal work must be built into the change strategy for the transformation.

Take a Process Approach and Use a Process Methodology

The next requirement for transformation to succeed is to take a process approach and use a change process methodology to guide the transformational journey with all of its unpredictable dynamics. A process approach plans for and adjusts to the action required to get the organization—and its people—from where they are to where they need to go. Because the specifics of the future state are unclear until they emerge during the process, leaders must rely on shaping a process that enables them to observe, assess, learn, and course correct continuously and rapidly. As leaders expand their awareness, they see and understand change process dynamics they previously missed. This is true of both the change plan and the desired outcome. Taking a process approach requires a conscious leader *and* a conscious OD practitioner to be in full alignment.

Most change models are dashboard and toolkit-based. They have myriad tools that generate data about the current status of change that gets fed into a project dashboard. Leaders are given periodic status reports, such as the balanced scorecard "Red-Amber-Green" status where green is positive and red is negative. While the snapshot is momentarily useful, leaders need to take time to understand and use the data to consciously course correct the process. It is my experience that executive time is typically not spent to explore data to realign strategy and action. For conscious leaders, data are most useful when they drive new insight and action in the change process, whereas reactive leaders put the data first and then assume others will fix it.

Conscious leaders design a comprehensive flow of activity to handle both the tangible organizational changes as well as the human dynamics at play. Reactive leaders orient to isolated events and checklists, reacting against things going wrong. Conscious leaders understand where the effort is in its process and drive it at a strategic level. Reactive leaders bounce from event to event, trying to mitigate red issues rather than proactively design a process that minimizes their occurrence from the beginning.

Transformation requires a process methodology as its guidance system, one that integrates the organizational changes with the people changes and enables rapid course correction. Many organizations use project management, Six Sigma, and change management to generate separate and distinct plans. Transformation requires one integrated plan. A process model fit for transformation is Being First's nine-phase Change Leader's Roadmap (CLR; Ackerman Anderson and Anderson 2010) shown in Figure 4.3.

Figure 4.4 shows the CLR model at its next level of detail, the activity level (Ackerman Anderson and Anderson 2010). As the activities show, the CLR is robust, addressing launch, case for change, the creation of a change strategy, and the design and implementation of organizational changes as well as the human dynamics and culture change from start to finish. It supports taking a conscious approach and enables leaders to generate breakthrough results. More detail on the Change Leader's Roadmap is available in a book by the same title (Ackerman Anderson and Anderson 2010).

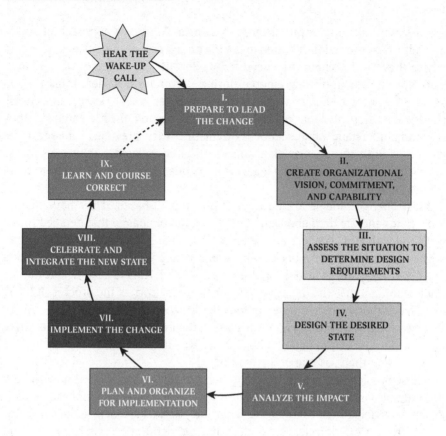

Figure 4.3. The Change Leader's Roadmap (CLR)

Source: From L. Ackerman Anderson and D. Anderson, *The Change Leader's Roadmap: How to Navigate Your Organization's Transformation*, 2nd ed. (San Francisco: Pfeiffer, 2010), 23.

Align on Vision and Design Requirements for the Future State

The next requirement is to align the vision and design requirements for the future state. While the specifics of the desired solution for the organization and its people may not be clear at the outset, the "aha" that triggers the change typically includes information that is essential to figure out what that future needs to be in reality. Getting leaders aligned to what they are trying to accomplish, and what their vision is for their new state is an essential step during launch. They must articulate the factors and principles that are guiding their decision to transform, their design requirements for what the future needs to produce or accommodate, and even their boundary conditions for what cannot change.

Given that leaders do not yet have all the information or insight to determine a tangible outcome, they can begin to model a more conscious leadership style

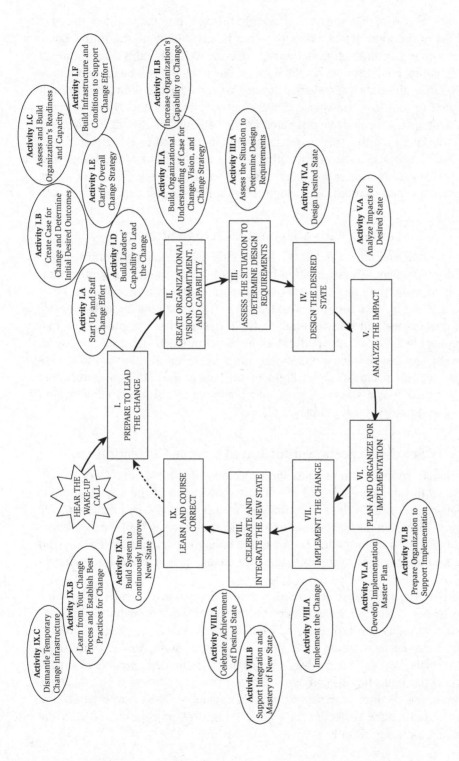

Figure 4.4. The Change Leader's Roadmap Activity Level

Source: From L. Ackerman Anderson and D. Anderson, *The Change Leader's Roadmap: How to Navigate Your Organization's Transformation,* 2nd ed. (San Francisco: Pfeiffer, 2010), 27.

by sponsoring a highly engaging visioning process, one that gathers the best thinking of their key stakeholders for what is possible, what the future holds that is compelling and exciting. This type of early engagement is a core strategy for generating breakthrough results because stakeholders will begin to own the change from the outset. Leaders will need to consider the input, but are not obligated to follow it. However, just asking stakeholders and giving genuine consideration to their ideas generates greater energy for the transformation, as Appreciative Inquiry (AI) practices have demonstrated (see Chapter Six on AI). It can also accelerate the creation of the actual future state design and enable rapid course correction. Note how different this strategy is from hiring an external expert to produce a design solution *for* you, not *with* you.

Launch with a Dynamic Change Strategy

Transformation requires a dynamic change strategy. Most change efforts begin with a project plan. Transformation begins with the creation of a strategy that then guides the planning process over the life of the effort. A change strategy aligns the leaders about how to lead the effort, enabling an agile process, good governance and decision-making, and a scope that integrates the organizational, behavioral, and cultural changes required. It declares the use of early engagement, inspiring communications, adequate resources and capacity, and realistic pacing. Chapter Eighteen introduces the SOAR framework and its 5-I approach as a way to engage stakeholders into a strategic conversation to create a strategy and/or strategic plan.

Set the Expectation for Rapid Course Correction

The change strategy also enables the expectation for rapid course correction. The need to stay acutely aware of what is showing up in the organization as it changes is critical to the transformation's success. Many organizations have norms in place that inhibit risk-taking and mistakes, such as "Kill the messenger of bad news!" Transformation is dependent on getting smarter by the day, and incorporating changes to the outcome, the change process, and leadership as required.

Leaders must establish and model course correction to demonstrate how important it is that all stakeholders be on the lookout for what is happening that supports the future state, what is still needed, and what is blocking it. There needs to be an overt process for establishing and accomplishing course correction—a strategy, way of engaging stakeholders, process of surfacing potential indicators of course correction, ways to address the data, make changes, and communicate how things have shifted. Once the organization believes that course correction is a good thing, this process can enliven the transformation significantly.

Ensure Early and Ongoing Stakeholder Engagement

The case has already been made for the benefit of engaging stakeholders in the change process from launch. When seeking new information for what the future needs to be and how the process can work most effectively, those undergoing the change will likely have a lot to say if they feel safe to speak. They live in the "trenches" and have a keen eye for the reality on the front lines. They may even have a good sense for strategy and design requirements. Your resistors may be the very people who have valuable ideas you have not considered. In the conscious leadership approach, their input is treated as "friendly data" and given attention.

Engagement goes far beyond calling people into a large hall and informing them via an extensive slide deck about what is about to occur. Good engagement is task-driven, where any action in your change process may be designed to engage appropriate stakeholders. Obvious tasks for high engagement include making the case for change and visioning, generating design requirements, solution design, impact analysis and resolution, and input on course corrections.

Attend to Mindset, Behavior, and Culture

Perhaps the most important requirement of successful transformation is to overtly attend to leadership and employee mindset, behavior, and culture. Transformation means a shift in worldview, seeing through new eyes. Leadership development is essential to address how to alter leaders' mindsets and behavior in the context of the business' needs. This work starts with the executives and typically cascades to the managers and workforce depending on the nature of the transformation affecting them. If leaders do not change their mindsets, and do not walk the talk they are asking of the organization, the transformation will not sustain. There is more on leadership development for leading transformation in Chapter Six.

Mindset is to the individual as culture is to the organization. A strategy to change culture is also required, one that assesses which aspects of the current culture already support the desired future, which block it, and what may need to be created to better serve it. Leaders must design their desired culture and consciously clarify how it serves the specific needs of the future they aspire to create. Every initiative within the transformation, even technology, impacts culture. The integrated change plan must identify the indicators in the current organization that inhibit the future—including leadership norms. Then, it must clarify how to recreate, reinforce, and reward new indicators or norms so that both leaders and stakeholders learn to act in ways that contribute to the adoption and sustainment of the future. A typical desired cultural indicator is the willingness of leaders to share information across boundaries instead of working in silos. While making organizational changes takes a significant amount of time, culture change—which is people-dependent—takes longer. Again, sustainment strategies must account for this, following go-live.

Ensure Adequate Capacity for Change

One of the biggest factors that inhibits transformation is the lack of adequate capacity for change. Many leaders assume that change work can happen on top of people's already excessive workloads. However, change takes time, attention, and resources. Space must be made on people's calendars to participate, input, learn, and adjust to what is being asked of them. If the organization is already experiencing change fatigue (a clear symptom of this issue), conscious leadership attention needs to be given to how to generate adequate capacity for the transformation. This is not a nice-to-have; it is a must, and a clear indicator of taking a conscious approach.

Align with the Rest of the Organization

Lastly, it is critical to align the transformational outcomes with the rest of the organization. A transformation in a portion of the organization must be designed so that it can achieve its outcomes in the context of what is best for the larger organization. The change process and scope will inevitably interact with what is not changing around it. In a conscious approach, the interface needs to be raised, addressed appropriately by senior leadership, and conditions set up in advance to ensure that the transformation can make its contribution to the larger organization.

Secondly, the outcome of the transformation must be aligned with the rest of the organization, or its scope increased to address additional changes. We often see the need to change the reward system, talent management strategies, shared services, and supply chain. Any aspect of the organization may come under scrutiny when it becomes evident that it is blocking the possibility of the transformation happening or sustaining. Many large organizations run in functional or business unit silos, even if they share infrastructure and protocols. It may become obvious that the prime cultural shift required is to dismantle the silo orientation and create a cross-boundary, collaborative way of leading and working. The conscious leadership approach does what is best for the overall organization, not just a piece of it.

IMPLICATIONS FOR THE ORGANIZATION DEVELOPMENT PRACTITIONER

There are many opportunities for OD practitioners to support projects as well as create services for enterprise-level transformational change efforts.

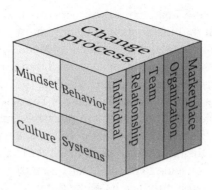

Figure 4.5. Conscious Change Leader Accountability Model

Source: From D. Anderson and L. Ackerman Anderson, *Beyond Change Management: How to Achieve Breakthrough Results Through Conscious Change Leadership*, 2nd ed. (San Francisco: Pfeiffer, 2010), 5.

A consolidated way to summarize what goes into an integrated strategy for transformation is shown in Figure 4.5, the Conscious Change Leader Accountability Model (Anderson and Ackerman Anderson 2010, 5). The model names the areas requiring conscious attention when consulting on, or leading, transformational projects. It is adapted from the AQAL Model by Ken Wilber, author of *A Theory of Everything* (Wilber 2000).

The left-hand quadrants on the front face describe *internal* people dynamics at the individual and collective levels—mindset at the individual level and culture for the collective. The right-hand quadrants depict *external* dynamics—behavior for the individual (what people are doing and how they are going about their work), and systems for the collective. "Systems" is a broad label that refers to all organizational elements that we can see, work with, and change, such as structure, business processes, work practices, strategy, plans, IT, training, and so on. When consulting on transformation, all of the quadrants must be accounted for, integrating the internal people dynamics and the external organizational requirements. Most leaders only think and care about the external quadrants. Project management is designed for the external quadrants. Both the internal and the external are essential to transformation, which is why an integrated strategy and process plan are essential.

The right-side face of the cube lists the levels of the system that may need attention: individual, relationship, team, organization, and marketplace. Marketplace includes customers, vendors, regulators, and so on. When the transformation has been scoped, you will know which of these levels needs attention. Many OD practitioners work at the individual, relationship, or team levels. Large-scale change work involves all levels.

The top face of the model refers to the process of change, which infers the need to handle all elements in the model, as well as those that show up along the way. The Change Leader's Roadmap is the process methodology that enables the leader and consultant to think about and incorporate all aspects of the model.

The Conscious Change Leader Accountability Model also helps describe the set of competencies that consulting on successful transformation requires. The first of these is *conscious process design*, which is the competency for taking the conscious process approach described above. The design of the transformational strategy and plan, both of which are processes, must take into account what has gone before, what is happening now, what is near-term, and what is likely to be needed in the future. Staying on top of the change process is critical, going much beyond managing to the plan. Each step in the process will need to be consciously designed to produce its optimal impact. Most OD practitioners have been trained in meeting and event design. That is a great foundation for up-leveling these same skills to design large-scale multilevel change processes.

The second competency is *systems thinking*—taking into account all of the distinct elements of a situation that interact to impact the collective whole (Senge 2006). This is not new to OD, but combined with conscious process design, accounting for both the internal and external dynamics inherent in transformation, and addressing all levels of the system transforming, it takes on a whole new magnitude. OD practitioners can hone their systems thinking skills in the context of supporting transformation.

SUMMARY

Transformational change is everywhere and needs competent support. Imagine working at the large-system scale and helping to deliver lasting breakthrough results. Imagine working in close partnership with other change resources in your organization to do this, as all have value to contribute to transformational change. Take a conscious leadership approach; use a process methodology that integrates both the content of the change and the people and cultural dimensions of it. Set up the expectation for leadership to transform themselves to be able to transform their organizations. And, support them to engage the organization in the compelling challenge to generate breakthrough results. There is huge gratification in bringing the conscious change leadership approach to our organizations so that they can excel at the inevitable transformational journey.

Discussion Questions

1. What types of change are you consulting on? Are any of these changes transformational?

2. How well do your clients understand the unique requirements of transformational change and how to lead them?

3. How could you get better positioned to consult on large-scale change efforts from their launch, especially those that are transformational?

4. What large-system change methodologies do you or can you use? How well do they address the requirements of transformational change?

5. How well are you positioned to provide executive coaching to leaders who aspire to lead their change efforts in conscious ways?

Resource

To access the following resources from Being First, Inc., please go to: www.beingfirst .com/practicing-od-chp4-resources/

Articles

"A Candid Message to Senior Leaders: Ten Ways to Dramatically Increase the Success of Your Change Efforts"

"Awake at the Wheel: Moving Beyond Change Management to Conscious Change Leadership"

"Which Will Be Most Successful for Your Current Change Effort: A Change Process Approach or a Change Tool Approach?"

"Why Leading Transformation Requires a Shift in Leadership Mindset"

Overview of the Change Leader's Roadmap Model presented by Linda Ackerman Anderson

References

Ackerman, L. 1986. "Development, Transition, or Transformation: The Question of Change in Organizations." *OD Practitioner* 18 (4): 1–8.

Ackerman Anderson, L., and D. Anderson. 2010. *The Change Leader's Roadmap: How to Navigate Your Organization's Transformation*. 2nd ed. San Francisco: Pfeiffer.

Anderson, D., and L. Ackerman Anderson. 2010. *Beyond Change Management: How to Achieve Breakthrough Results Through Conscious Change Leadership*. 2nd ed. San Francisco: Pfeiffer.

Bridges, W. 2004. *Managing Transitions: Making the Most of Change*. 2nd ed. Cambridge, MA: Da Capo Press.

Hiatt, J. M. 2006. *ADKAR: A Model for Change in Business, Government, and Our Community*. Houston: Brown Book Shop.

Senge, P. M. 2006. *The Fifth Discipline: The Art & Practice of the Learning Organization*. New York: Doubleday.

Torbert, W. R. 2004. *Action Inquiry: The Secret of Timely and Transforming Leadership*. San Francisco: Berrett-Koehler.

Wilber, K. 2000. *A Theory of Everything*. Boston: Shambala.

CHAPTER FIVE

Transformational Leadership Development

Jacqueline M. Stavros and Jane Seiling

While the idea of transformational leadership has a rich and well researched history, few leaders are familiar with the term, few organizations are developing transformational leaders, and very few leaders have any idea how to be a transformational leader.
—Warrick 2011, 11

There is a huge need for revolutionary transformation change in organizations of all types—yet, unfortunately, Warrick's statement above is most definitely true. Among scholars, organization development (OD) practitioners, and knowledgeable organizational leaders, fortunately, there has been an expansion of interest in transformational leadership behaviors and their role in group and organizational performance beyond individual and small-group dynamics and their role in organizational change behaviors. Krishnan (2012, 551) quotes Burns (1978), noting that transformational leadership "occurs when one or more persons engage with others in such a way that leaders and followers raise one another to higher levels of motivation and morality" (20). Krishnan notes these efforts result in "transforming effects on both leaders and followers" (551).

Of interest are the *transforming effects* experienced by parties engaged in these transformational relationships—especially during change. It has become evident that newer OD practices are perceived as important in engaging strategic issues and interpersonal matters (Van Nistelrooij and Sminia 2010). Transformation leadership behaviors are recognized as having a central role in achieving the transforming effect in these processes. Learning and practicing transformational leadership is important for today's leaders. A question of importance is: How do my leadership abilities become a transforming factor during change?

It is relevant that the focus moves to the development of those leaders charged with leading change. This chapter starts with defining transformational leadership and two key components: (1) self-awareness and mindfulness and (2) what transformation means in a dynamic environment. Then, we provide a leadership self-assessment process to discover how one can best aspire to understand and lead one's self and others effectively.

UNDERSTANDING TRANSFORMATIONAL LEADERSHIP

Transformational leadership is defined by Mitchell et al. (2014, 2) as "a style of leadership that transforms followers to rise above their self-interest and challenges them to move beyond their current assumptions (Bass and Riggio 2006; Pieterse et al. 2010)." They encourage followers to move beyond their own self-interest and to transform their "perspective from [solely their] own goals to group or collective goals" (Effelsberg, Solga, and Gurt 2014, 131). Relevant to the transforming effect of focusing on others instead of total self-interest is the need for organizational members to be willing to engage in self-sacrificing, group-oriented behavior of their own that benefits their organization (Effelsberg et al. 2014).

Research in OD has identified a mixture of personality traits, experiences, knowledge, consulting skills, relational skills, competencies, and so on, important to leading change (Burke 2008). In addition, the psychological aspects of leading change (influencing skills, intrapersonal skills, and interpersonal skills) and building competency skills (abilities in managing the consulting process, general consultation skills, and knowledge of OD theory) are necessary. The sense of obligation to "do no harm" during leadership efforts and OD consulting activities is also important. This obligation calls the OD person to focus first on self as an instrument—to first look at oneself from the standpoint of change and development in order to effectively lead.

TRANSFORMATIONAL LEADERSHIP DEVELOPMENT—TWO COMPONENTS

This section emphasizes the importance of transformational leadership development (TFLD) through initiation of a self-focus (Taylor 2010) on seeking self-awareness and the practice of mindfulness. Assessment of self begins with becoming more aware of issues and changes essential to leading self and others. Baumeister's (2005) comprehensive review of literature by psychology researchers concludes that self-awareness is "anticipating how others perceive you, evaluating yourself and your actions according to collective beliefs and values, and caring about how others evaluate you" (7). Hall (2004) notes two components of self-awareness: "The internal (recognizing one's own inner state) and the external (recognizing one's impact on others)" (155).

Mindfulness is also a significant part of the process. Without being mindful of self—and seeking the input of respected others—it is difficult to believe the need for change brought forward by concerned others. "Fundamental organizational change is difficult," state Reger, Mullane, Gustafson, and DeMarie (1994, 31). This is assumed as an appropriate statement because of the long list of failed change efforts—even when touted as successful. Perhaps the number of successes would have grown if change leaders had started with a dedication to self-change—transformation of self involves a dedication to transformational leadership development—change of self.

Self-Awareness

Leader self-awareness and purposeful development are essential to *knowing thyself* in order to effectively lead others (Taylor 2010). Although it is not clear how to define, detect, and measure self-awareness, scholars and leaders are becoming more aware of the need to better understand their personal strengths and identify where expanded development is needed (Ilies, Morgeson, and Nahrgang 2005; Taylor 2010). Being "other-oriented" is a key element of transformational leadership (Quinn and Quinn 2009). A key to this recognition is transformational leadership development (TFLD). TFLD is reliant on relatedness and the development and exchange of trust during the change process. Self-awareness has been a topic of research and interest for decades, ultimately identifying it as fundamental to psychological functioning—and the emergence of social relations and personal well-being (Miller 2003). The ideal place to expand self-awareness and approach its rewards is in the process of TFLD.

According to Krishnan (2012), "Transformational leadership is a mutually stimulating and engaging relationship between leaders and followers," (550). He also notes, "According to Burns (1978), transformational leadership 'occurs *when one or more persons engage with others* in such a way that leaders and followers raise one another in such a higher level of motivation and morality' (20), and results in a transforming effect on both leaders and followers" (251, emphasis added). This engagement with others in the process of learning through awareness will be evident in the transforming effect experienced through the process of development offered later in this chapter.

Mindfulness

Weick and Sutcliffe's (2001) writings on mindfulness (as related to aircraft carriers) suggest "a preoccupation with updating" (44), that can be adapted to the practitioner's need for updating personal understandings and skills in preparation for planning and leading change. According to Weick and Sutcliffe, one must reexamine discarded information by refining, differentiating, updating, and replacing misinformation with information that is relevant to the situation. They define mindfulness as "The combination of ongoing scrutiny of existing expectations, continuous refinement and differentiation of expectations based on newer experiences, willingness and capability to invent new expectations that make sense of unprecedented events, a more nuanced appreciation of context and ways to deal with it, and identification of new dimensions of context that improve foresight and current function" (Weick and Sutcliffe 2001, 42).

Weick and Sutcliffe's definition verifies Langer's (1997) suggestion that "When we are mindful, we implicitly or explicitly: (1) View a situation from several perspectives, (2) See information presented in the situation as novel, and (3) Attend to the context in which we perceive the information, and eventually create new categories through which this information may be understood" (111).

In the following section, we pay attention to the mindfulness that the OD practitioner commits to when examining and reworking self prior to leading change. This includes attention to the practitioner's values, vision, and mission pertaining to work and how they impact client performance as an OD practitioner. The self-assessment process is discussed regarding how it supports the growth of the OD practitioner's ability to lead and the expansion of their practices of "leading with" and influencing others during change. Unless noted, the terms "leader" and "practitioner" are interchangeable for this writing.

TRANSFORMATION IN A DYNAMIC ENVIRONMENT

Dynamic environments are not unusual; it is often part of the normal environment of working in fast-paced, growth-oriented, and innovative organizations. Dynamic environments benefit from the presence of transformational leaders for many reasons. For example, dynamic relationships are benefactors of transformational leaders throwing themselves into strong relationships with organizational members who then respond with active and responsive engagement. There are also transformational leaders who provide opportunities to be together in an *appreciative paradigm* of beneficial relatedness (Stavros and Torres 2005). These efforts create dynamic environments of possibility for the present and the future. It is this environment that designs the usual and unusual context within which people work productively. Note the following example of a dynamic environment as it relates to performance.

Weick and Sutcliffe (2001) studied people on aircraft carriers. This group was chosen because the dynamic nature of their work requires them to operate at a very high level of performance. In a constant state of high complexity and a high need for precision, carriers offer a unique environment for the study of change. The study concluded that this combination of complexity and precision required a high level of mindfulness.

First, Weick and Sutcliffe (2001) found that people working on aircraft carriers are *"preoccupied with failure"* (47, italics in text); the workers focused on working to avoid failure while always accomplishing their goal(s). For practitioners leading change, preoccupation with identifying what needs to be done (and not done) to lead a successful change is essential. To avoid failure, preoccupation is an attribute the OD practitioner sorely needs.

Second, people on carriers are *"reluctant to simplify,"* while taking nothing for granted (47, italics in text). OD practitioners know that to simplify can be a barrier to accomplishment of change. Simplification can lower the level of belief in need for change and lessen the intensity of purpose by the participants to move toward accomplishment of the targeted change.

Third, people on carriers *"maintain continuous sensitivity to operation"* (47, italics in text). They have an ongoing concern with the normal and the unexpected. Practitioners pay attention to process and know that development of a flexible process encourages a focus on the goal while knowing outcomes are unpredictable. Change is significant to growth and survival for the organization. Practitioner efforts for continual mindfulness are a top priority in order to maintain sensitivity to the interventions needed to accomplish change.

Fourth, the people on carriers have a *"commitment to resilience"* (48, italics in text). Resilience is defined as the ability to demonstrate both strength and flexibility in the face of change (Barrett 2004). Practitioners strive for resilience, recognizing that there will be times the process appears out of control and that good and bad surprises will occur. Comfort with chaos, disorder, and uncertainty is important. Resilience is key to psychological fitness to lead others (Seligman 2011).

And fifth, people on carriers *"maintain deference to expertise"* (48, italics in text). Listening to and acknowledging those with a deep knowledge of technologies, people, and potential organizational capacities are important to a successful change process (while being merged with the avoidance of failure). The act of giving these potential hidden contributors a "voice of expertise" can influence them and others to expand their support and contribute extra efforts for change.

This section emphasized the importance of transformational leadership, recognizing self-awareness and mindfulness as essential to *knowing thyself* to effectively lead others through change using relatedness and development of trust. The remaining part of this chapter provides a leadership self-assessment process to discover how one can aspire to lead change effectively for transformation.

CREATING SELF-AWARENESS

The OD practitioner's ability to create meaning (the creation of understanding mindfulness around a particular change process) and get things done are filtered through choices made by people doing something the leader/practitioner may have requested or discussed. These choices include (1) which decisions are to be made, (2) the choice to make decisions happen—or not, and (3) the generation of personal responsibility and accountability to and with others regarding "what we have to do together to make things work."

Quinn (1996) offers a set of questions about how to empower oneself for generating personal deep change and change in others. As practitioners, we (the authors) often use an adaptation of these questions to support leaders in becoming mindful of personal development needs, specifically about leading change:

1. How can I *become aware* of my own sense of meaning and task-alignment?
2. How can I *become aware* of my own sense of impact, influence, and power?
3. How can I *become aware* of my own sense of competence and confidence to rally efforts toward change in others?
4. How can I *become aware* of my own sense of self-determination and choice? (228, adapted)

Quinn's original questions used the verb *increase*; we changed it to "become aware of" to make the question more reflective. Taking the time to write out the answers to these questions, specifically for yourself, can "shift the responsibility for our own empowerment from someone else to ourselves" (Quinn 1996, 228), ultimately increasing task-alignment, impact competence, and confidence, as well as efforts toward change, self-determination, and choice.

Warner Burke (2008) believes there are as many diverse definitions of leadership as there are of love. One's personal definition of leadership, he adds, will probably depend on past experiences with and/or observations of leaders and whom one is talking to at the moment of definition. Burke offers the following explanation (not definition) of leadership: "Power is the capacity to influence others; leadership is the exercise of that capacity." He adds, "[L]eadership [is] the act of making something happen that would not otherwise occur" (228). Our challenge to this definition is: Leaders cannot *make* things happen. What a leader *can* do is rally a group of stakeholders around a shared vision (direction), provide leadership and resources attuned to a purpose (mission), and demonstrate a presence of personal values and motivation (inspiration) to get things done. Warren Bennis (1991) said it well, "A leader creates meaning. You start with a vision. You build Trust. And you create meaning" (5).

The ability and opportunity to rally a group requires being aware of one's *personal direction-setting capabilities*—your believed-in vision, which, according to Boyatzis and Akrivou (2006, 625), is based on the *ideal self* ("a core mechanism for self-regulation and intrinsic motivation") as an envisioned self in the future.

KNOW THYSELF

The most basic competence of the change leader and/or practitioner is identifying his or her ability to *know thyself* before leading others. Knowledge of the processes for change is located in the *head*. Self-awareness of one's role and capabilities in addressing the emotions involved with loss, concern for the member, and authentic caring for the people involved in the change is located in the *heart*.

In order to legitimately and authentically lead, a leader must start first with looking at his or her self. At the end of the day, the leader should consider three questions:

1. Why would anyone want me to lead him or her?
2. How well did I lead today?
3. How can I lead better tomorrow?

As noted by Hesselbein (2002, 4), "Just as leaders are responsible for understanding their organization's strengths and preparing for its future, we must assess our personal strengths and take responsibility for planning our own development." This requires the leader to do the hard assessment and retrospective thinking required to make necessary personal changes. They must step back and examine their basic understandings regarding their own values, vision (direction), and mission (purpose), and how they might impact their ability to lead others.

Leaders of change must understand their leadership style, including their personal strengths, weaknesses, and aspirations, and then be willing to make changes to develop their personal model for leadership further. To take steps to improve their leadership style continually shows others that being mindful of personal development is ongoing—especially as it pertains to leading others. While emphasizing personal development and change, every leader can build trust, confidence, and rapport with those he or she serves in his organization. Achievement of transformational personal change, as described in this chapter, involves deep thinking and reflection, interviews, and writing about it to bring clarity.

The process first starts with focusing on the self as the foundation for change; the journey begins with identifying your values. Second, you will write your vision and mission statements. You should identify your vision and mission in all four domains of life—self, work, home, and community—to create alignment among them. Third, you will identify your leadership competencies and leadership style—being honest and forthright with yourself.

Once you have identified your values, vision, mission, and leadership competencies and style, you will have conversations with *trusted advisors*. The role of your advisors is to offer guiding information for learning and growth. You must be open to their feedback and insights. Reflect deeply on the feedback of your trusted advisors. This takes the form of a contemplative, honest, and forthright *written* leadership self-assessment.

Last, in the same assessment, identify a continuation of development that moves through specific areas of need for improvement, making commitments that stretch to strengthen one's leadership in years to come. If there are no stretches to strengthen, you will have fallen short of the opportunity for transformational leadership development.

THE SELF-ASSESSMENT PROCESS

Transformation is change that can be seen, in this case, in a person's leadership behavior. *Change* is a departure from the status quo. Thus, significant *transformational change* by a leader can transform the nature of the organization and its members (Palmer, Dunford, and Akin 2009).

As noted above, for personal and organization transformation to happen, leaders must first examine themselves. Self-assessment requires time, dedication, and a willingness to learn about *yourself* from others. And, it is a futile effort unless there is a willingness to believe what has been heard and a desire exists to act on the assessment by taking steps toward change. The following expands on the above described components of the self-assessment process.

Values

While Meglino and Ravlin (1998, 354) characterized values as "oughtness" (how one ought to behave), Feather (2003, 34) conceived of values as "general beliefs about desirable ways of behaving or about desirable general goals." Identifying your values provides the foundation for writing your vision and mission statements. Values identification helps to answer the following questions:

- What do I want to live and work by each and every day?
- How do I want to treat others?
- What do I stand for?
- What do I care about?
- How do I show I care about others?

Values are only "good intentions" unless you take the time to reflect on their impact on your actions each day—especially when making key decisions. Satisfaction with decisions comes with deciding while being mindful of your core values. In identifying your values, you should be able to locate your top ten-to-fifteen values without much thought or hesitation. Then, narrow the listing down to five or six core values. It is in reflection on why you have selected these values that you identify what is important to you and where to focus in the future. A *Values Exercise* is posted on this book's website.

Table 5.1 offers an example of a leader's value set. Later in this chapter, we present how her values connect to her vision and mission, plus the values, vision, and mission of her boss and organization. She feels her values are based on her history and experiences so these are also provided. Her values

Table 5.1. Values Listing

Her History	I grew up in a family of six in Detroit. We lived a simple life. There was plenty of love, a lot of sibling rivalry, and lessons learned while growing up. We lived in a flat above Grandma near a large automotive plant and next to a Union 76 gas station until my parents had enough money to move to the suburbs so we could attend public schools. Now my family and extended family provide unconditional love and support.
Family	In my values, "family" includes close friends. For a family to be strong, it includes connection and belonging, feelings of acceptance and feeling like my presence matters to those I care about.
Integrity	Integrity provides the basis for living. Each of us has a purpose in life. We need to model our purpose through being genuine and honest in our relations with self and others to gain trust and respect. Living with integrity makes it easy to sleep at night!
Respectful-Kindness	I strive to see a "sense of worth" in people and situations. In doing so, I strive to use consideration and kindness no matter how tough or frustrating the situation may get. This allows me to be honest with people and help them grow.
Energy	I value the energy that I awaken with each morning and the opportunity to renew it when I go to sleep at night. In order to live my values and take care of my family and career, I need a balance of physical, emotional, mental, and spiritual energy. If you find your passion and define your vision based on what you are passionate about, energy is fueled. You need energy to go after your dreams! I live my life trying to make sure that I have a full energy source.
Humor, Health, and Humility	Mental health (along with the field that I work in) requires that I live with the presence of ambiguity and uncertainty. My life never fails to give ample opportunities to encounter ambiguity. Laughter is healthy, and I use it to diffuse situations. I try to bring humor and laughter into my life every day.

are bolded. The additional information is her description of the meanings of her values.

In this case, her organization's values are teamwork, integrity, excellence, respect, and sustainability. There is a connection between the core values of "integrity" and "respect," plus, although not an exact word connection, the values of "teamwork" and "family" connect. She sees an alignment of her values with her organization's values. Ideally, there should be an opportunity for the leader to share her values with others in her organization and to have them do the same. The result can be a significant increase in respect, communication, patience, understanding—and accountability, over time.

Vision

Leading scholars and practitioners have stated that *vision* is a key differentiating factor when comparing leaders to managers (Buckingham 2005; Kotter 1996). Vision is based on a person's values. We study values because they enable one's vision to happen—how we create our futures and they also impact the futures of those we lead in our organizations. The following questions should be considered in preparation for writing your vision:

- Think of a future you feel strongly about. What do you want your "ideal self" to be experiencing in this future? What is your vision as it relates to that future?
- What is your organization's vision? Is there alignment?
- Do you act as a symbol of your vision?
- How does your vision reflect your values?
- How could you communicate this vision to others?

Having a vision is about providing the power to take action toward reaching that future. Leaders use this mental image as power (energy) to fulfill their leadership roles and responsibilities and to inspire others. According to Kotter, "The direction setting aspect of leadership does not produce plans; it creates a vision and strategies ... it is ... simply a description of something (an organization, a corporate culture, a business, a technology or an activity) in the future, often the distant future, in terms of the essence of what it should become" (1990, 36).

The impact of a powerful vision provides a clear direction that *motivates movement forward*. This view is also supported by Tichy and Devanna (1986), "The vision is the ideal to strive for. It releases the energy needed to motivate the organization to action. It provides an overarching framework to guide day-to-day decisions and priorities and provides the parameters for playful opportunism" (123).

At work, leadership is about aligning people, which includes getting the people behind an organization's vision (Kotter 2002; Kotter and Cohen 2002). The way the leader-change agent communicates the vision serves as a symbol of the authenticity of the vision. The leader is the central advocate for the vision. Leaders must also work diligently to ensure that the stakeholders know where this vision is going and how it affects them. This includes asking for their insights and engaging them in dialogue about the vision so the vision is real to them.

People (and organizations) can have multiple visions that overlap. For example, a leader can have both a personal and professional vision—and, as noted, they must be aligned to achieve the two visions successfully. Within an organization, different divisions that make different products may have different visions, but the *overriding* vision is the vision of the parent company—the dominant vision that must be shared and adhered to.

In an organization, visioning is a process of creating and communicating the direction of the organization as it impacts every stakeholder, especially the employees and customers. A process of education, training, questioning, and communicating must be used to bring the vision to life for each organizational member. The vision statement found in the strategic plan, a website, or on the wall must find a way into the behavior, attitudes, purpose, and heart of the people as well as to the goals, strategies, and tasks to be achieved for the organization.

Returning to our example, the leader who presented her values above, her organization's vision is "To take a leadership role in preparing our students to be life-long learners while making a difference in a global environment." The president's vision is "To create a more humane and sustainable world community by developing global learners and leaders." There is alignment of the president's vision with the organization's shared vision. Her vision is "To strive for authentic simplicity and engage in learningful relationships with a meaningful and sustainable purpose." Like her values, her vision aligns with the president's and with the organization's vision. There is a shared direction.

As noted, a person can have visions for different parts of his or her life, but a person's dominant vision can change or adjust other visions at any given time. Be aware of the connections between them. Having a meaningful personal vision provides "the ideal to strive for." It also provides a basis for action and provides the motivation for creating and committing to one's direction. Being mindful of one's vision is crucial for it to have an impact on one's work and life.

Identification and communication of a set of core values and a vision (both personally and organizationally) is a strong start. Yet, a vision is only effective if purposeful action is taken reflecting the meaning of the vision. The next step is to identify one's personal mission that stimulates action.

Mission

Mission is purpose. It is what you do each and every day to *live* by your values. Also, a mission statement will support taking you where you want to go, to reaching your vision. A mission statement helps you to focus on what should be done. It can energize the highest and most creative energies to attain set goals. This suggests the benefits of writing a good *personal* and *professional* mission statement. Mission statements, like vision statements, take time to write and require deep reflection to achieve connection across one's values, vision, and mission. Consider the following example as a place to start in writing a personal mission statement.

My *mission* is _____ _____ _____ (use action verbs) for what: _____ (principle or cause) to/with or for (whom) _____ .

The question to be considered: What is the guiding purpose that pulls you closer to realizing your vision? Continuing with the above leader illustration, the organization's mission is "Developing leaders through innovative and agile programs that focus on the sustainability and entrepreneurial issues for organizations." We define sustainability as including the whole system to collectively consider human, financial, and environmental capital as it relates to profit that can result in a better world for this generation and generations to come.

The president's mission is "Developing and delivering distinctive and innovative management programs that maximize students' potential." The organization's member wrote a mission that is simple yet significant to the organization's and president's mission. Because she is a faculty member that serves students, her mission is "Facilitating learning and serving with others to create a sustainable future for the students, myself, and my organization." There is alignment of her mission to both the president's and the organization's mission.

As noted above, the mission statements for both the leader and his or her organization are at the center of the process of knowing what you, as the leader of change, should be doing today as a leader of change. There are practical implications for writing a meaningful personal mission statement. Being fully engaged is essential to commitment to one's mission and the quest to fulfill goals.

In order to go beyond just writing the words to design what Quinn (1996) calls "rules of operation," one must be able to closely identify with and be continually mindful of the behaviors and actions that are reflected in the written statements. Because change, for our purposes, includes hearing challenges, resistance, and agreements, writing your mission statement can be a challenging activity—especially as it relates to personal change. Yet, according to Quinn, "Knowledge accumulates, assumptions are made, values formulate, competencies develop, and rules of operation are established" (1996, 9). Importantly, a person's rules-of-operation are best based on *written* vision and mission statements that gain full commitment by a determined writer. Next, you will think about leadership competencies. Many of your competencies have been influenced and made possible the formation of your values, vision, mission, and the ability to lead effectively.

Transformational Leadership Competencies

It is no mystery that a leader's competencies will manifest themselves in demonstrated actions. The areas in which a leader is strong will receive more attention and show through—whether or not they are beneficial competencies. A study by Stavros (1998) shows that outstanding capabilities of a leader come to the surface as the leader functions with organizational members. Skills, such as oral communications, networking, self-confidence, initiative, and attention to detail, may be the hallmark of a particular leader's activities. Also in Stavros' studies of leaders, the ability to take the initiative in creating a new vision, communicating the vision to others, giving attention to detail, presenting feedback, and having the confidence to move forward demonstrates the essence of effective leadership skills. These are noted as the competencies required in an organization for leadership of transformational change to happen. For identifying your leadership *core competencies*, Table 5.2, based on Boyatzis (1998), provides terms and definitions.

Taylor (2006) notes that the key to self-development is the *real self* being identified through the accurate knowledge the person has of self and then through gaining input from others that adds to self-knowledge. "This is because the individual and others have unique insights into the individual's real self, making their joint observations a more complete assessment than either assessment would be alone" (644). Therefore, after identifying leadership competencies, these competencies can also be used in an interview process with three to four of your *trusted advisors*. These are people you respect and admire, people who have known you for a good while, and people you have worked with in the past. Trusted advisors also may include a personal acquaintance such as a family member or close friend whom you request to be honest as well as people who genuinely want the best for you.

Prior to your conversations with your trusted advisors, you will ask them to identify your core values. Then, you will share your values, vision, and mission and compare their perceptions with yours. This conversation will help you best understand your trusted advisors' perceptions of you and your leadership style and whether your actions reflect their understanding of your values, vision, and mission. The goal is to learn what *they* believe are your leadership competencies and then compare their list with yours. Seek trusted advisors who are willing to give straightforward answers regarding what leadership competencies they see you demonstrate in your personal and work environment and to be honest about where improvement is needed. The openness of the trusted advisors will

Table 5.2. Leadership Competencies to Effectively Lead Change

Competency	Competency Define
Efficiency Orientation	The ability to perceive input/output relationships and the concern for increasing the efficiency of action.
Planning	The ability to define goals/objectives, strategy, tactics, and resources to be used to meet the purpose (mission).
Initiative	The ability to take action to accomplish something and to do so before being asked, forced, or provoked into it.
Attention to Detail	The ability to seek order and predictability by reducing uncertainty.
Flexibility	The ability to adapt to changing circumstance, or alter one's behavior to fit the situation better.
Networking	The ability to build relationships, whether they are one-to-one relations, a coalition, an alliance, or a complex set of relationships among a group of people.
Self-Confidence	The ability to consistently display decisiveness or presence.
Group Management	The ability to stimulate members of a group to work together effectively.
Developing Others	The ability to stimulate someone to develop his abilities or improve his performance toward an objective.
Oral Communication	The ability to explain, describe, or tell something to others through a personal presentation.
Pattern Recognition	The ability to identify a pattern in an assortment of unorganized or seemingly random data or information.
Social Objectivity	The ability to perceive another person's beliefs, emotions, and perspectives, particularly when they are different from the observer's own beliefs, emotions, and perspectives.

Source: Adapted from Boyatzis (1998) and (2007).

support future development efforts. It is helpful to rank these competencies listed as outstanding, above average, average, or needs improvement.

Writing Your Leadership Self-Assessment

An important step in the journey to awareness is to write your findings regarding each step in this journey. Write it down. Don't miss anything, and make it a comprehensive journey of leadership development.

The findings include putting your values, vision, and mission at the beginning and writing a narrative that is *a personal message to yourself* and then comparing it to the organization's values, vision, and mission. The following are some questions to consider:

1. Why is the journey occurring (including why you are doing the assessment)? What do you hope to accomplish? Does it matter?

2. What have you done in the past in developing leadership capacity? How do you expect to accomplish growth through this effort?

3. What are your values, vision, and mission statements? It could include why you chose the five values. Write comments from your trusted advisors perceptions of your values, vision, and mission. What is the true reality identified? Is it yours, theirs, or something new?

4. What is the outcome of the assessment? How do you expect to use these results? Write a report and commentary on your interviews regarding your leadership competencies and the evidence provided to support these competencies (the matrix). What competencies surprised you? Which ones do you need to further develop? What are your thoughts on what was said about your leadership competencies? (This is the larger part of your report.)

5. What will you do as a result of what was learned? What must you be mindful of regarding performance as a leader? Write a commitment describing how you will *specifically* use the information from the interviews and the collected materials from the process. What *specifically* will you do in the next weeks and months to achieve your vision and mission? How will you expand your leadership capabilities for your performance as a transformational leader?

6. Make a commitment to developing yourself in identified areas and how often you will revisit the materials to stay on track. Stay focused on your values, vision, and mission and their alignment with your work and your organization.

The goal in writing this self-assessment is to *make sense* of the possibilities that can and do arise from the learnings achieved from the assessment. The final question above is linked to the essence of this learning process.

SUMMARY

This chapter provides the materials to support a leader's developmental journey, whether they are active OD practitioners or organizational leaders. Effective transformational leadership development requires a self-organized assessment process. We acknowledge there are many ways to move through deep, personal transformational change. Living an effective life requires us to listen to the messages of "shoulds" offered by experiences, thinking, reflections, and personal learnings (Buckingham and Clifton 2001). It also requires us to be mindful of how to successfully utilize those messages. According to Sethi (2009, p. 7), "Mindfulness at work is a key leadership competency, and leaders now more than ever need to live and lead mindfully, coach others to be mindful, and create a mindful organization."

Transformational leaders can transform organizations because, by knowing themselves and their organizations, visionary leadership can be the outcome, while also resulting in "new ways of thinking about strategy, structure, and people, as well as about change innovations, and having an entrepreneurial perspective" (Warrick 2011, 13). This is a leadership style that can be learned and nurtured through mindfulness and self-awareness.

Discussion Questions

1. How can transformational leadership help transform organizations?
2. What OD competencies help to strengthen a transformational leader?
3. Do your personal values, vision, and mission align with your organization's values, vision, and mission? If so, how and why? If not, what can be done?
4. How can you as a transformational leader stay aware of internal and external factors of your organization and its environment before and during an organization's transformation?

Resources

Center for Creative Leadership Development: www.ccl.org

Brian Tracy's Leadership Blog on successful leadership: www.briantracy.com/blog/leadership-success/great-leadership-leadership-traits-types-of-leadership/

"How Good Are Your Leadership Skills?" assessment by Mindtools: www.mindtools.com/pages/article/newLDR_50.htm

The Frances Hesselbein Leadership Institute, formerly the Drucker Foundation:www.hesselbeininstitute.org

References

Barrett, F. 2004. "Coaching for Resilience." *Organization Development Journal* 22 (1): 93–96.

Bass, B. M., and R. E. Riggio. 2006. *Transformational Leadership*. Mahwah, NJ: Lawrence Erlbaum Associates.

Baumeister, R. F. 2005. *The Cultural Animal: Human Nature, Meaning, and Social Life.* New York: Oxford University Press.

Bennis, W. 1991. "Creative Leadership." *Executive Excellence* (August): 5–6.

Boyatzis, R. E. 1998. *Transforming Qualitative Information: Thematic Analysis and Code Development*. Thousand Oaks, CA: Sage.

Boyatzis, R. E. 2007. "ORBH450: Executive Leadership Notes for Class 1." Executive Doctorate in Management Program. Case Western Reserve University, Cleveland, Ohio (August 21).

Boyatzis, R. E., and K. Akrivou. 2006. "The Ideal Self as the Driver of Intentional Change." *Journal of Management* 25 (4): 624–642.

Buckingham, M. 2005. *The One Thing You Need to Know: … About Great Managing, Great Leading, and Sustained Individual Success*. New York: Free Press.

Buckingham, M., and D. O. Clifton. 2001. *Now, Discover Your Strengths*. New York: Free Press.

Burke, W. W. 2008. *Organization Change: Theory and Practice*. 2nd ed. Thousand Oaks, CA: Sage.

Burns, J. M. 1978. *Leadership*. New York: Harper.

Effelsberg, D., M. Solga, and J. Gurt. 2014. "Getting Followers to Transcend Their Self-Interest for the Benefit of Their Company: Testing a Core Assumption of Transformational Leadership Theory." *Journal of Business Psychology* 29: 131–143.

Feather, N. T. 2003. "Values and Deservingness in the Context of Organizations." In *Emerging Perspectives on Values in Organizations*, edited by S. W. Gilliland, D. D. Steiner, and D. P. Skarlicki, 33–66. Greenwich, CT: Information Age.

Hall, D. T. 2004. "Self-Awareness, Identity, and Leader Development." In *Leader Development for Transforming Organizations: Growing Leaders for Tomorrow* edited by D. V. Day, S. J. Zacarro, and S. M. Halpin, 153–176. Mahwah, NJ: Lawrence Erlbaum Associates.

Hesselbein, F. 2002. "Putting One's House in Order." In *On High-Performance Organizations*, edited by F. Hesselbein and R. Johnston, 1–5. San Francisco: Jossey-Bass.

Ilies, R., F. P. Morgeson, and J. D. Nahrgang. 2005. "Authentic Leadership and Eudaemonic Well-Being: Understanding Leader-Follower Outcomes." *Leadership Quarterly* 16: 373–394.

Kotter, J. P. 1990. *A Force for Change: How Leadership Differs from Management*. New York: The Free Press.

Kotter, J. P. 1996. *Leading Change*. Boston: Harvard Business School Press.

Kotter, J. P. 2002. "The Marketing of Leadership." In *On High-Performance Organizations*, edited by F. Hesselbein and R. Johnston, 19–29. San Francisco: Jossey-Bass.

Kotter, J. P., and D. S. Cohen. 2002. *The Heart of Change*. Boston, MA: Harvard Business School Press.

Krishnan, V. R. 2012. "Transformational Leadership and Personal Outcomes: Empowerment as Mediator." *Leadership & Organization Development Journal* 33 (6): 550–563.

Langer, E. J. 1997. *The Power of Mindful Learning*. Cambridge, MA: Perseus Books.

Meglino, B. M., and E. C. Ravlin. 1998. "Individual Values in Organizations: Concepts, Controversies, and Research." *Journal of Management* 71: 492–499.

Miller, J. G. 2003. "The Cultural Grounding of Social Psychological Theory." In *Blackwell Handbook of Social Psychology: Intraindividual Process*, edited by A. Tesser and N. Schwarz, 22–43. Malden, MA: Blackwell Publishing.

Mitchell, R., B. Boyle, V. Parker, M. Giles, P. Joyce, and V. Chiang. 2014. "Transformation Through Tension: The Moderating Impact of Negative Effect on Transformational Leadership in Teams." *Human Relations*, 1–27.

Palmer, I., R. Dunford, and G. Akin. 2009. *Managing Organizational Change: A Multiple Perspectives Approach*. New York: McGraw-Hill/Irwin.

Pieterse, A. N., D. Van Knippenberg, M. Schippers, and D. Stam. 2010. "Transformational and Transactive Behavior: The Moderating Role of Psychological Empowerment." *Journal of Organizational Behavior* 31 (4): 609–623.

Quinn, R. E. 1996. *Deep Change: Discovering the Leader Within*. San Francisco: Jossey-Bass.

Quinn, R. W., and R. E. Quinn. 2009. *Lift: Becoming a Positive Force in Any Situation*. San Francisco: Berrett-Koehler.

Reger, R. K., J. V. Mullane, L. T. Gustafson, and S. M. DeMarie. 1994. "Creating Earthquakes to Change Organizational Mindsets." *Academy of Management Executive* 8: 31–43.

Seligman, M. E. 2011. *Flourish: A Visionary New Understanding of Happiness and Well-Being*. New York: Atria.

Sethi, D. 2009. "Mindful Leadership." *Leader to Leader* 51 (Winter): 7–11.

Stavros, J. M. 1998. *"Capacity Building: A Relational Process of Building Your Organization's Future."* Dissertation, Weatherhead School of Management, Case Western Reserve University, Cleveland, Ohio.

Stavros, J. M., and C. B. Torres. 2005. *Dynamic Relationships: Unleashing the Power of Appreciative Inquiry in Daily Living*. Chagrin Falls, OH: Taos Institute.

Taylor, S. N. 2006. "Why the Real Self Is Fundamental to Intentional Change." *Journal of Management Development* 25 (7): 643–656.

Taylor, S. N. 2010. "Redefining Leader Self-Awareness by Integrating the Second Component of Self-Awareness." *Journal of Leadership Studies* 3 (4): 57–68.

Tichy, N. M., and M. A. Devanna. 1986. *The Transformational Leader*. Hoboken, NJ: John Wiley & Sons.

Van Nistelrooij, A., and H. Sminia. 2010. "Organization Development: What's Actually Happening?" *Journal of Change Management* 10 (4): 407–420.

Warrick, D. D. 2011. "The Urgent Need for Skilled Transformational Leaders: Integrating Transformational Leadership and Organizational Development." *Journal of Leadership, Accountability, and Ethics* 8 (5): 11–26.

Weick, K. E., and K. M. Sutcliffe. 2001. *Managing the Unexpected*. San Francisco: Jossey-Bass.

CHAPTER SIX

Appreciative Inquiry

Organization Development and the Strengths Revolution

Jacqueline M. Stavros, Lindsey N. Godwin, and David L. Cooperrider

Appreciative Inquiry (AI) is a theory and practice of inquiry-and-change that shifts the perspective of organization development (OD) methods by suggesting that the very act of asking generative questions has profound impact in organizational systems. Inquiry and change are not separate moments. Our questions focus our attention on what is "there" to be noticed. Reflecting its social constructionist roots (Cooperrider, Barrett, and Srivastva 1995; Gergen 1995), which suggest that *words create worlds*, AI offers a new change imperative by suggesting that we be aware of the negativity bias that pervades our investigations into organizational life and instead shift our focus to the good, the better, and the possibilities that often go undernoticed in our systems. Building on Gergen (1995) and Cooperrider and Avital (2003), Cooperrider and Godwin (2012) summarize, "AI posits that human systems move in the direction of the questions they most frequently and authentically ask; knowledge and organizational destiny are intimately interwoven; what we know and how we study it has a direct impact on where we end up" (740).

Leveraging the power of generative questions, AI changes the focus of what we typically study in organizational life, questioning the prevailing mindset that "organizations are problems to be solved," (Cooperrider and Srivastva 1987). Instead, AI suggests that "organizations are mysteries and miracles of human relatedness; they are living systems, alive and embedded in ever-widening webs of infinite strength and limitless human imagination. Organizations, as centers of human connectivity and collaboration, are 'universes of strengths,'"

(Cooperrider and Godwin 2010, 10). AI invites change agents to look into their organizations with "appreciative eyes"—scanning the system for things for which to be grateful, seeking out what is next and what is possible, and focusing on *valuing those things of value worth valuing*. AI theorists posit that such a shift in our approach to organizational change is needed if we are to inspire our imaginative capacities to their fullest potential.

An entirely different approach to organization inquiry, transformation, and change emerges when such an appreciative approach is applied to OD work. Transforming our underlying metaphor of organizations transforms how we approach them as agents of change. If organizations are not problems to be solved but instead are conceptualized as alive—as living systems—then the fundamental question of change also shifts. Instead of seeking to answer *What is wrong here and how do we fix it?* We instead search for *What gives life to the living system when it is most alive? What is the positive core of this system—including all past, present and future capacity—and how do we magnify and engage this positive core with constructive, transformational intent?*

At its heart, AI is about the search for the best in people, their organizations, and the strengths-filled, opportunity-rich world around them. AI is not so much a shift in the methods and models of organizational change, but a fundamental shift in the overall perspective taken throughout the entire change process to "see" the wholeness of the human system and to "inquire" into that system's strengths, possibilities, and successes. The *appreciative paradigm* has emerged as a way to describe any OD change approach that attends to the *positive core* of relationships and organizations. It is a *causative theory* applicable to OD, transformation, and change methods. Examples of interventions with an appreciative perspective are discussed throughout this book.

AI practitioners discover that applying such an appreciative perspective increases the power, effectiveness, and sustainability of any classical OD intervention, from strategic planning and organization redesign, to team building and diversity, to coaching and personal growth approaches. AI is being used worldwide in both small- and large-scale change initiatives across every type of organizational sector (case studies, podcasts, and video clips are available at http://appreciativeinquiry.cwru.edu). Given the vast usage of AI across the globe, Ken Gergen, a thought leader in social constructionism, reflects that, "The growth and application of Appreciative Inquiry over the past two decades has been nothing short of phenomenal. It is arguably the most powerful process of positive organizational change ever devised" (in Whitney, Trosten-Bloom, and Rader 2010, x).

This chapter begins by further defining AI, followed by a brief history of AI, and an overview of both the classic and emergent principles of AI. The AI 5-D model is then briefly reviewed, and AI is situated within the emerging field of positive organization development (POD). The chapter concludes with a discussion of how AI is providing the grounding philosophy for the emerging three circles of the strengths revolution within the field.

DEFINING APPRECIATIVE INQUIRY

To begin understanding Appreciative Inquiry (AI), it is important to first examine the very words themselves that is what it means to *appreciate* and *inquire*.

> ap-pre-ci-ate, v., 1. to recognize and like a favorable critical judgment or opinion; to perceive those things that give life (health, vitality, excellence) to living systems 2. to feel or express gratitude 3. to increase in value (e.g., the economy has *appreciated* in value) 4. to fully know of; realize fully. *Synonyms*: value, prize, esteem, honor.
>
> in-quire, v., 1. to explore and discover 2. to question 3. to be open to seeing new potentials and possibilities. *Synonyms*: discover, search, systematically explore, and study (Cooperrider, Whitney, and Stavros, 2008, 1).

Over the years, AI has been defined in many ways. It has been called a philosophy, an approach, a method, a process, and a way-of-being for engaging all levels of an organizational system in an inquiry into its *positive core*. The positive core is that which makes up the best of an organization and its people and all of its relationships. This positive approach leads to changes in the organization based on images of the best possible future as articulated and visualized by the people and stakeholders who make up the human system of the organization. The most commonly cited practitioner definition says:

> AI is the cooperative co-evolutionary search for the best in people, their organizations, and the world around them. It involves the discovery of what gives *life* to a living system when it is most effective, alive, and constructively capable in economic, ecological, and human terms. AI involves the art and practice of asking unconditional positive questions that strengthen a system's capacity to apprehend, anticipate, and heighten its potential. AI interventions focus on the speed of imagination and innovation instead of the negative, critical, and spiraling diagnoses commonly used in organizations. The discovery, dream, design, and destiny model links the energy of the positive core to changes never thought possible. (Cooperrider, Whitney, and Stavros 2008, 3)

Many articles, book chapters, and books have defined AI as an approach to organization dialogue, development, design, and learning. No matter how AI is defined, it is deliberate in its *life-giving search* to help organizational systems discover their positive core of what gives life to their system. The 5-D Process (described later in this chapter) for applying AI in organization systems is, like the classical OD process, dramatically transforms Kurt Lewin's action research model. The major difference is in the *appreciative* perspective and the role of the OD practitioner. Rather than the practitioner working to identify problems and deficits in an organization, AI involves the whole system in dialogues among members (including external stakeholders) of the organization. These conversations focus on lifting up all of the "life giving factors" inside and outside of a system, and are narrative rich. Instead of analysis of the information being done only by the OD practitioner, AI encourages narrative process and dialogue to learn about the best of the past to understand what relevant stakeholders want more of, and to use that as a basis for imagining the most preferred future for their organization. It is not a top-down approach, nor is it bottom-up; rather the approach is "whole," with all voices in the system working in concert during each phase. When the whole organization aligns with a positive image of the future based on discoveries from the storytelling, dialogue of strengths and opportunities, and images of the future, multiple projects are designed, agreed on, and implemented to create that future.

BRIEF HISTORY OF APPRECIATIVE INQUIRY

The birth of AI came in 1980 via the coauthorship, thought leadership, and collaboration between Dr. David Cooperrider and his advisor, Dr. Suresh Srivastva. As a doctoral student, David was involved with a group from Case Western Reserve University working with the Cleveland Clinic in a conventional diagnostic organizational analysis in search of "What is wrong within this organization?" In gathering his data, David was amazed by the level of positive cooperation, innovation, and egalitarian governance he was finding in the organization. Suresh noticed David's excitement and suggested he follow his fascination and excitement and make it the focus of his inquiry.

David obtained permission from the Clinic's chairman, Dr. William Kiser, to reverse the diagnostic organizational focus and instead take a life-centric stance in his analysis of the Clinic. This analysis focused on the factors contributing to the most highly effective functioning of the Clinic when it was at its best in every way. The Cleveland clinic became the first large organizational site where a conscious decision to use an inquiry focusing on life-giving factors formed the basis for an organizational analysis. The term *Appreciative Inquiry* (AI) was first introduced and written as a footnote in the feedback report of "emergent themes" by David and Suresh for the board of governors of the Cleveland Clinic. The report created such a powerful and positive stir that the board called for ways to use this method with the whole group practice. The momentum set the stage for David's seminal dissertation and AI's first theoretical articulation in a journal article calling for an appreciative paradigm shift for the field of organization and management thought (Cooperrider 1986; Cooperrider and Srivastva 1987).

The research, in brief, demonstrated a Heisenberg "observer effect" on steroids, how just the mere act of inquiry in human systems can change a whole organization. That realities shift as we put our attention on something, asking questions, gathering information, and paying attention to someone, is so commonplace by now that we forget that it might just be the most important first principle for a field devoted to human systems development and change. For some, this simultaneity between inquiry and change is an incidental phenomenon. It has a name. It has been dubbed "the mere measurement effect." However, as it relates to the generative task of AI, there is nothing at all minor about it. The Cleveland Clinic—under the leadership of Dr. William Kiser, who saw the power of AI to bring out the best in human beings—became one of the finest medical systems in the world. As Dr. Kiser later commented, AI created the goodwill, the collaborative mindset, and the positive practice environment to inspire an entirely new generation of extraordinary achievement at the Cleveland Clinic (see Cooperrider 1986).

AI was articulated first as a method for building generative theory. It was a call for "a scholarship of the positive," focusing our attention on "what gives life" to human and ecological systems when they are most alive (Cooperrider 2013). Quickly—beyond its use as a positive organizational scholarship and theory-building method—the applied power of AI was discovered, and soon it spread to many domains such as organization development, strengths-based management, applied positive psychology, evaluation studies, change management, coaching and counseling, corporate strategy, sustainable development, social constructionism, design thinking, organizational behavior, biomimicry, and learning theory. In his *New York Times* best-selling book, *Go Put Your Strengths to Work*, Marcus Buckingham (2006) points to the theory of AI was one of the important academic catalysts for the "strengths revolution" in management. Beyond the work of Cooperrider and Srivastva, the other two foundational sources of the strengths revolution in management included Peter Drucker's *The Effective Executive* (1966) and Martin Seligman's call for positive psychology (Seligman 1999). Together, AI, Drucker's management theory, and positive psychology have created a society-wide, positive-strengths movement, argued Marcus Buckingham, "because it works."

Now, nearly 30 years since that seminal work at the Cleveland Clinic occurred, AI has spread to become a global phenomenon. Today, many OD practitioners and scholars are advancing the theory and practice of AI as part of a historical shift in the social sciences toward more constructionist, strengths-based, and positive approaches to research, OD, transformation, and change. Thousands of organizations are embracing this positive OD revolution by applying AI in for-profit, nonprofit, government, and social sectors. These range from global and government agencies, nongovernmental agencies, Fortune 100 organizations, nonprofits, and school systems to community planning organizations. World conferences on AI have been held in the United States, Nepal, Belgium, and South Africa.

Given the impact from almost three decades of practice in every corner of the world, we can assert with confidence that AI is both a way of being with a process that respects and affirms both the differences and similarities in gender, culture, and nationality. It is a way to talk generatively across differences and to find ways forward no matter how challenging the path. AI is an approach to OD that is highly culturally sensitive and adaptable across a wide variety of national cultures (Yaeger, Head, and Sorensen 2006). Whenever an appreciative approach is used, though, it is grounded in the fundamental principles of AI—to which we now turn our attention.

APPRECIATIVE INQUIRY PRINCIPLES

Appreciative Inquiry (AI), in whatever form it takes, rests on a set of five principles originally articulated by David Cooperrider (1986): constructionist, simultaneity, poetic, anticipatory, and positive. These five original principles are central to AI's theoretical basis and practice for OD work that is generative and strengths-based. The defining article that first outlined these principles is "Appreciative Inquiry into Organizational Life" (Cooperrider and Srivastva 1987). Besides these original principles, there are also five emergent principles, which include: wholeness, enactment, free choice, awareness, and narrative. Knowing these 10 principles facilitates the application and adaptation of the original AI 4-D cycle to any organization, from the interpersonal to the whole system level. Organizations that work to embed the AI principles into their culture have been shown to become generative and creative, leading to even more innovation in the use and form of AI itself.

The Five Original Principles

The five original principles detail the underlying beliefs that connect AI from theory to practice. Besides using these principles to guide organizational change efforts, applying these principles in one's life leads the OD practitioner to experience their relevance in creating strengths-based relationships and success in organizations and communities (Stavros and Torres 2005).

Constructionist Principle. Reflecting a social constructionist stance toward reality and knowledge creation (Gergen 1995), this principle states that knowledge about an organization and the destiny of that organization are interwoven. Rather than assuming one absolute truth, this stance suggests that truth is local, meaning that organizational members are continually co-constructing their own realities (Gergen 2001). Therefore, what we believe to be true about an organization, how we "know" it, will affect the way we act and the way we approach change in that system. It reminds us that organizational systems are never static entities; rather they are continually evolving and products of our collective co-constructions through our conversations and interactions. These constructionist dialogues predict the next moment.

Simultaneity Principle. Working in concert with the Constructionist Principle, this principle proposes that *inquiry is intervention*. This means that change begins simultaneously at the moment we first pose a question in a human system, not after we find an answer. Questions, whether positive or negative, become fateful because they are the catalytic force that sets the stage for the areas on which we focus our attention and energy. Therefore, one of the most impactful things an OD practitioner does is to ask questions. The questions we ask set the stage for what we "discover," and what we "dream" creates the narratives that lead to conversations about how the organization lives in the present moment and will construct its future, which is "design" and "destiny." Just as Heisenberg's (1949) principle holds true for the physical world, so it is true for our social systems; we create new realities during the process of inquiry. What we focus on appreciates, or grows, in value.

As Cooperrider and Godwin (2012) describe, an organization-wide survey on low morale produces ripple effects through the mere act of asking: "What are the causes of low morale?" This question concentrates attention on what or who is causing the low morale; it provides a more precise language for speaking about low morale, and provides a presumptive assurance if we "figure out the problem," then we can apply the "right" intervention to help the system return to a more normal state. However, one more expensive low-morale survey, even with all the good intentions, will not tell us how to create a supercharged, highly engaged workforce. If we want to learn about how to create an engaged workforce, we must ask questions about when people have felt most engaged and what engagement looks like to them.

Poetic Principle. The Poetic Principle acknowledges that human organizations are like open books to be interpreted. An organization's story is constantly coauthored by the people within the organization and those outside who interact with it. The organization's past, present, and future are endless sources of learning, inspiration, and interpretation, just as a good poem is open to endless interpretations. We can study *any* topic related to human experience in *any* human system. We can inquire into stress or the nature of positive emotions.

We can study moments of innovation or moments of failures. We have a choice because all aspects of humanity exist in every system.

Anticipatory Principle. This principle suggests that human beings act based on their "anticipation" of future events, and this anticipation affects themselves, the people, and systems in the organization. Leveraging the Simultaneity Principle with the power of questions and the Constructionist Principle with the power of co-construction, the Anticipatory Principle invites organization systems to ask questions that help them generate a collective understanding of the present and vision for a desired future. This image of a better tomorrow guides the current behavior of any person or organization. If we act from our expectations and we move toward what we anticipate, an important task for change agents is to help organizations articulate a powerful image of their ideal state, which becomes a beacon for the realization of that vision.

Positive Principle. This principle's premise is that the more positive and affirmative the images we carry, the more likely we are to move into these images. The Positive Principle supports the other four principles. Positive questions lead to positive images of the future, and positive images lead to positive, long-lasting actions (Cooperrider 1999). Taking an appreciative stance in organizational change helps positively impact the affective side of transformation by creating upward spirals of positive emotions in organizations (Fredrickson 2009). The positive emotions of hope, optimism, compassion, and awe generated by appreciative work literally strengthen a person or organization's ability to bring their positive images of the future into fruition (Fredrickson 2003).

The Five Emergent Principles

The five original principles have since been augmented by the principles of wholeness, enactment, free choice (Whitney and Trosten-Bloom 2010), awareness (Stavros and Torres 2005), and narrative (Barrett and Fry 2005). A summary of these are presented in Table 6.1. These emergent principles have elevated and extended the original principles, further helping OD practitioners apply an appreciative stance when leading organizational change work.

THE APPRECIATIVE INQUIRY 5-D CYCLE

If these principles represent the overarching gestalt of Appreciative Inquiry (AI) work, the 5-D cycle offers generative yet practical scaffolding upon which AI work is often built, as illustrated in Figure 6.1. Each of the Ds represents different activities and generative dialogues happening in a systematic manner throughout the organizational system. Regardless of the level of work within the system, from one-on-one coaching, to team building, to system-wide change, the 5-D model can be leveraged as a guide for creating positive change.

Table 6.1. Five Emergent AI Principles

Principle	Meaning
Wholeness (Whitney and Trosten-Bloom 2010)	To include all parts of a system in creating the future. Important to recognize that an organization is a "whole" and all parts are interrelated.
Enactment (Whitney and Trosten-Bloom 2010)	When we act as if something is true in our organization, then it becomes true. If we want a more egalitarian organization, then use an egalitarian process to create it.
Free Choice (Whitney and Trosten-Bloom 2010)	People can choose how to engage and contribute in the change process; they then perform better and are more committed to the change.
Awareness (Stavros and Torres 2005)	Self-reflective awareness of the connectivity of original principles is needed to apply AI in daily living. Being aware of your thoughts, habits, and actions allows you to operate in an appreciative paradigm.
Narrative (Barrett and Fry 2005)	Stories have a transformative power in organizational life. Stories should be told and written to reflect the best realities and to live into these stories.

Figure 6.1. AI 5-D Cycle

Each phase is summarized briefly below, but many resources further articulate the details of these phases depending on the OD work one is leading. We recommend that you visit the AI Commons (www.appreciativeinquiry.case.edu) and the *AI Practitioner: The International Journal of Appreciative Inquiry* website (www.aipractitioner.com) that combined has hundreds of illustrations of AI in action.

The Defining Phase—What Is the Topic of Inquiry?

While the AI 4-D (Discovery, Dream, Design, and Delivery) cycle remains the simplest and the most often-used visual when describing the appreciative process, in OD work there should always be a conversation on *defining* the purpose of how and why AI will be used. Many OD practitioners have concretized this process by adding this fifth D, *Define*, to center the model to cover what OD practitioners typically call the "contracting" phase of the process. In this phase, the guiding question is, "What generative topic do we want to focus on together?" This phase often involves reframing or clarifying a pressing organizational issue into opportunity areas for further inquiry.

For example, when British Airways launched a change initiative that became the largest customer responsiveness program in the company's history (Cooperrider and Whitney 2005), the first step in the process was to define the generative topic in which they wanted to invest. While the topic initially presented as a problem of "How do we deal with *excessive baggage loss*," it ultimately evolved into "How do we create *outstanding arrival experiences*." The generative reframing of the topic was fateful, as it helped launch a discovery process into the existing moments of outstanding arrival experiences and a dreaming process of what outstanding arrival looks like, and so on. Ultimately, it became one of the most successful and well-documented change programs ever done at British Airways (Whitney and Trosten-Bloom 2010).

The Discovery Phase—What Gives Life?

In the *Discovery* phase, the goal is to inquire, learn about, and appreciate the best of "what is" in a person or organizational system via appreciative one-on-one interviews. The ability to collect strengths-based, life-giving (i.e., the Positive Principle), and future-oriented data (i.e., the Anticipatory Principle) is key to the Discovery phase. The guiding question for this phase is, "When we have been at our best, what were we doing?" The assumption is that every person or system has strengths, high-points, and positive things to be discovered (i.e., the Poetic Principle) and leveraged for the future.

The Discovery phase has several important aspects. First is the importance of lifting up individuals' stories (i.e., the Narrative Principle). Through sharing stories, the organization's members get in touch with their ideas and beliefs about what makes a peak experience and understand how to create more of these positive experiences (i.e., the Constructionist Principle). According to research on the human brain, stories have the power of connecting the *left brain*, where reason and language reside, with our *right brain*, where our artistic nature, innovation, and creativity reside (Dew 1996). By tapping into the whole brain (i.e., the Wholeness Principle), we access our full range of ideas and emotions, giving a powerful base to our images of an ideal state. Five classic appreciative questions are:

1. *Reflecting on History and High Point Moments*: What is a peak experience of "x" or at "y" (customized to the focus of the inquiry)?

2. *Learning from Others/Search for Inspirational Practices*: What are best practices from others regarding "x" and how can we learn from what has worked elsewhere to inform what we want to do?

3. *Building on What We Value Most/Continuity*: No matter what changes about "y," what do we value most about ourselves, our colleagues, and our organization?

4. *Images of the Future*: Imagine it is five years in the future and the organization has become what you most want it to be, what does it look like?

5. *Three Wishes*: If you had three wishes for your organization, what would they be?

The "x" refers to a topic of inquiry such as a high-performing team and "y" could refer to the organization. AI interviews can go deep when interview partners are coached to listen with curiosity and probe their partners to share details about their experiences and visions for the future. The insights from this phase are typically culled and themed (often by a facilitator in collaboration with members of the organization) and then shared back to participants to help set the stage for the Dream phase.

The Dream Phase—What Might Be?

The *Dream* phase is an invitation for the participants to amplify the positive core of the system by imagining possibilities for the future (i.e., the Positive and Anticipatory Principles). For example, the conversation may center on what a high-performing team might look like, based on the list of themes created from the interviews in the Discovery phase. The guiding question for this phase is, "When we achieve our ideal state of success, what will it look like?" The Dream phase seeks to expand the organization's true potential and begins to "shift" the current status quo toward a desired future reality. This phase creates momentum, synergy, and excitement among the participants of "what can be." Dreaming is a significant activity that leads to higher levels of creativity, commitment, and enthusiasm for the organization's future. It is in these higher levels that participants access the ideas and energy for identifying and articulating tasks and actions in the Design phase.

How data are gathered in this phase depends on the size of the organizational system. Typically, teams across the organization will engage in this process and then share their collective visions with the wider system. There is no methodological recipe to do this, you just have to decide how to work the process and what you want to discover in the Dream phase. For example, in the British Airways example, they "wanted to uncover and transport from station to station all the best practices that would support British Airways' world-class service" (Whitney and Trosten-Bloom 2010, 130).

The Design Phase—What Should Be the Ideal?

The *Design* phase focuses on leveraging the best of the past as discovered in the stories (continuity) to help move the system toward action steps for achieving (transition) their desired state as articulated in the Dream phase. The design steps vary depending on the complexity of the project, but include a two-step process: (1) brainstorming and (2) rapid-prototyping. First, the team, group, or organization brainstorms a list of activities and ideas of things they want to create in their ideal organization. These are activities and processes that can be planned and implemented in alignment with the dreams created in the previous Dream phase. A guiding question for this process is often, "How might we make our vision a reality?"

Once the brainstorming ideas are synthesized and prioritized, the focus then becomes on exploring the question, "What will these ideas look like in action?" While there are a variety of models and processes within the purview of OD practice that can be blended with an AI perspective to help answer this question, one of the most promising approaches has come from the field of design. As detailed by Coughlan, Suri, and Canales (2008), prototyping helps an organizational system concretize their ideas into tangible artifacts. Prototyping represents the Constructionist Principle in action, where an idea such as "We need a new employee-orientation program" gets co-created into an initial iteration of what that would look like (i.e., the elements of the program are sketched out, communication templates are mocked up, a calendar for the program is drawn out, etc.) for further evolution in the Destiny phase.

The Destiny Phase—How to Empower, Learn, and Improvise?

In this phase, the organizational members discuss how to *deliver* the dream and design by leveraging the strengths and resources lifted up during the discovery dialogues. Like the previous three phases, the *Destiny* phase (sometimes it is also referred to as the *Delivery* phase) continues with a whole system dialogue. The guiding question now becomes, "How do we continue to leverage our strengths to deliver on the promise dreams and ensure our system flourishes in the future?"

While there are many forms of the Destiny phase, this phase will depend on the complexity of the system and what are the expected outcomes of the 5-D application. Many systems will create an interval process where the 5-Ds are continuously used to access how projects are proceeding and update plans for the future. This review involves asking the system/group another discovery question: "Tell a story about the best things that have happened in this project since we began." This is followed by a dream question that refocuses them on creating an updated image of success; that is, "Imagine it is three months from now and the project has become wildly successful, what does that look like?" This can be followed by another *Design* process to continue moving the project forward with new iterations. Ultimately, the *Destiny* phase transforms the organizational culture into an appreciative learning culture and the cycle continues.

While these phases for applying AI are fairly concrete and understandable—whether 4 or 5 Ds—the way those steps are carried out makes all the difference. In traditional OD processes, large-group planning often aims to produce a list of things that the group wants done expecting some senior-level people will make it happen. The AI process, however, must be "owned" by the "whole" of the organization so any external facilitator/consultant functions as coach or advisor. Of major importance in all of these phases is that some configuration of the whole is working together to bring about the lasting change they have identified as desirable. This might literally be the whole system of thousands of people coming together as in an AI Summit (see examples in Cooperrider, Godwin, Boland, and Avital 2012), or it may be representative members from across the system collaborating on behalf of the whole.

APPRECIATIVE INQUIRY AND THE ORGANIZATION DEVELOPMENT STRENGTHS REVOLUTION

Compared to the deficit-based management culture that dominates much of our organizational life, it is perhaps no surprise that the strengths-based movement that has emerged within the field of OD is being called a revolution. Since the 1940s, organizations have used the traditional deficit-based approach to solving problems. Traditionally, it starts with identifying problems, then diagnosing and analyzing the problems and ends with a plan to fix the problems. As detailed above, Appreciative Inquiry (AI) provides an alternative to this approach and challenges the traditional approach to a more affirmative, strengths-based way to look for what is working well in the organization and what the organization wants more of in its future.

Strengths-based Principles

AI posits that organizations need not be fixed. Instead, they need constant reaffirmation and opportunities to be solution-seeking. More precisely, organizations as heliotropic systems grow toward the direction of what they most focus on, or put more precisely, what they most persistently ask questions about. Whereas traditional OD work has aimed at asking questions to identify problems, diagnose the underlying causes of those problems, analyze possible solutions, and plan how to lessen those problems, the appreciative approach starts the change process from a different paradigm, with a different set of questions. AI invites people to appreciate and ask about the best of what exists within their system, envision what might become in the future, dialogue about what should evolve, and innovate together to make their highest hopes become realities. Cooperrider and Godwin (2012) created a set of strengths-based principles, which are summarized in the left-side column of Table 6.2. We present the implications for OD practitioners in the right-side column.

Table 6.2. Principles of Strengths-based Approaches and Implications for Positive OD

Strengths-based Principle	Implications for Positive OD Practitioners
1. We live in worlds our inquiries create.	Be aware of the questions being asked within organizations as well as the ones you pose. The ROI on change initiatives is dependent upon what we inquire into: deficiencies or the best in life.
2. We excel only by amplifying strengths, never by simply fixing weaknesses.	Pay attention to the initial framing of your work and beware of the negativity bias inherent in our traditional OD approaches because excellence is not the opposite of failure.
3. Small shifts make seismic differences; strengths-based change obeys a tipping point.	Instead of focusing 80 percent on what's not working and 20 percent on strengths, it is important to put this 80/20 rule in reverse to harness the transformative power of the "positivity ratio."
4. Strengths do more than perform, they transform.	It is important to help organizations and the individuals within them to uncover the best within themselves and imagine "what is next" in order for them to create upward spirals.
5. We live in a universe of strengths; what we appreciate (see as having value) appreciates (increases in value).	Focus your attention and the attention of the organization on what they want to become more of, not less of. There are unlimited strengths in any organizational system to be found and amplified if we seek them out, including success, vitality, and flourishing.

These principles are informing a new epoch in our work as leaders of organizational change. Building on the strengths revolution (Buckingham 2006; Rath 2007) and fueled by AI, positive OD work entails three main stages: (1) the elevation of strengths, (2) the alignment or connected magnification of strengths, and (3) the creation of strengths-based organizations to become positive institutions—vehicles for elevating, magnifying, and refracting our highest human strengths outward to the world (Cooperrider and Godwin 2012; Cooperrider et al. 2008). As illustrated in Figure 6.2, these three circles of work are undergirded by the appreciative paradigm—the capacity to see beyond problems and see possibility and inquire into what gives life to a system when it is. These three circles, while not exhaustive, provide a framework for the many streams of scholarship informing the strengths-based approaches we are seeing gain traction today in OD.

Three Circles of the Strengths-Based Revolution for Positive OD

The focus of the first circle—Elevation of Strengths—leverages the theories and methodologies in domains such as positive psychology (Seligman

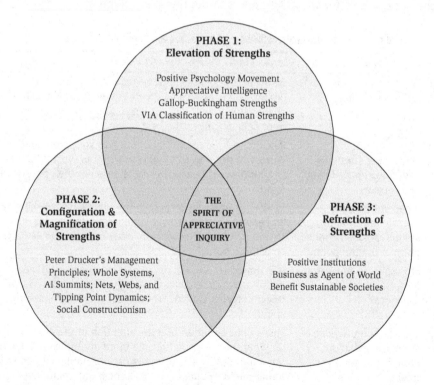

Figure 6.2. Strengths-Based Revolution for Positive OD

Source: From D. Cooperrider, "The 3-Circles of the Strengths Revolution," *AI Practitioner: International Journal of Appreciative Inquiry* (November 2008, 8), with permission.

2011; Seligman, Steen, Park, and Peterson 2005), appreciative intelligence (Thatchenkery and Metzker 2006), positive organizational scholarship (Cameron, Dutton, and Quinn 2003; Cameron and Spreitzer 2012), emotional intelligence (Boyatzis and McKee 2005), and strengths-based management (Buckingham 2006; Rath 2007). The guiding question of this level of work is: "What are the strengths of individuals within this system?"

To help answer this question, OD practitioners are benefiting from the growing array of tools being developed that lift up strengths and talents of individuals, small groups, and teams. From strengths-finders such as the Values in Action (VIA) (Peterson and Seligman 2004) and Strengths-Finder 2.0 (Rath 2007), to tools such as the Best Self Analysis (Roberts, Dutton, Spreitzer, Heaphy, and Quinn 2005), the SOAR Profile (Stavros 2013), to appreciative coaching methodologies (Orem, Binket, and Clancy 2007), there are a wide assortment of instruments, frameworks, and processes at the modern OD practitioner's disposal to discover and lift up the individual strengths and assets that have often gone unnoticed, unlabeled, and underappreciated.

Elevating strengths lays the foundation for the work of the second circle, which involves creating an alignment and magnification of individual's strengths. The guiding question for this level of work is: "How do we take isolated strengths and amplify them to a new level?" The domains of work informing this circle of work include the anthropological power of narrative from the social constructionist realm (Miller, Potts, Fung, Hoogstra, and Mintz 1990), the Drucker-esque management philosophy that emphasizes the importance of the *alignments of strengths* (Drucker 1966), and investigations into high quality connections (Dutton and Heaphy 2003). One of the most powerful tools used in this sphere of work is the classic AI Summit methodology, which has been used to convene whole systems of hundreds to thousands of individuals (see examples in Cooperrider, Godwin, Boland, and Avital 2012). New technologies are making it even easier for the AI Summit to truly become a macro-management tool that aligns disparate parts of complex systems across time and space (Godwin, Bodiford, and Kaplan 2012). Other tools for aligning and magnifying strengths include the World Café model (visit: www.theworldcafe.com), Asset-Based Community Development (Kretzmann and McKnight 1994), Future Search (Weisbord and Janoff 1995), and SOAR (strengths, opportunities, aspirations, and results; Stavros 2013)—the appreciative alternative that leverages and amplifies the "S" and "O" of SWOT.

The lifting up, magnifying, and aligning of strengths become the building blocks for the third circle—the creation of positive institutions, which "not only elevate and connect human strengths (internally) but serve to refract and magnify our highest human strengths into society" (Cooperrider and Godwin 2010, 738). This circle is perhaps the greatest realm of work affecting the future of OD, as it asks: "How do we co-create institutions that support both the creation and reflection of our best selves outward to the world?"

A myriad of terms have emerged to describe the work being done in this domain—sustainability, eco-efficiency, social entrepreneurship, social responsibility, triple bottom-line, and sustainable development, to name a few. Theoretical frameworks informing this work include stakeholder theory (Freeman 1984), the call for sustainable value (Laszlo 2008), and the search for business to act as an agent of world benefit (BAWB; Piderit, Fry, and Cooperrider 2007). From advances in biomimicry (Benyus 2002), to the BAWB world inquiry (see www.worldbenefit.cwru.edu/inquiry), tools for accomplishing these lofty aims include the bottom of the pyramid protocol (see www.bop-protocol.org) and the next generation AI Summit, or "the sustainable design factory" (Cooperrider 2008).

These circles are not necessarily linear. As detailed by Cooperrider and Fry (2012), organizations can also cultivate what they refer to as "mirror flourishing" by committing to sustainability and other initiatives that help to bring out the best of the individuals within them. They define mirror flourishing as "The consonant flourishing or growing together that happens naturally and reciprocally to us when we actively engage in or witness the acts that help nature flourish, others flourish, or the world as a whole to flourish" (8). When people see positive outcomes happening within their organizational system, it helps inspire them to bring their best selves to their work and their world. Positive institutions can lift up and align individuals' strengths, just as individuals' strengths can be aligned to create positive institutions.

SUMMARY

Appreciative Inquiry (AI) was originally intended and used first as a qualitative research process—an appreciative way of exploring what is going right in a system to build future-oriented prospective theory (Cooperrider 1986). Over the years, AI has evolved to become part of the OD discipline as a philosophy and process that engages individuals across the organizational whole system in processes that create renewal and positive transformational change.

Today, AI is a global phenomenon that offers a way of being and a framework for organizational inquiry from an appreciative, strengths-based lens. Anchored in its principles, AI can be embedded into all levels of an organization, from an individual's life, to team dynamics, to entire systemic change initiatives. There are several ways to apply AI (via its 4-D or 5-D cycle). The AI 5-D cycle operates on the belief that the responsibility for transformation and change resides with the people. The shift begins with individuals within the organization taking responsibility for the process through story sharing and dialogue that is generative.

The impact of AI across organizations has been felt around the globe. A recent empirical study by Verleysen, Lambrechts, and Van Acker (2014) suggests that "leaders of change would be well advised to help enact and sustain the principles of AI and 4-D cycle of AI" and that "AI is an effective way to increase psychological capital ... which are conditions for co-creating new possibilities and effective systematic change" (21). There are many possibilities to transforming and creating a positive future for you, your department, organization, or industry. The probability that any of these comes into reality depends on how you embrace the possibilities; ask yourself: *What kind of future should we live into?*

Discussion Questions

1. Take a negative situation; using the AI philosophy and principles, how would you reframe the situation into a positive situation—something that you wish to learn about and have more of?

2. How are you seeing the three circles of the strengths revolution affecting the field of OD today? How are you working to lift up, magnify, and refract strengths in yourself and others through your work?

3. Reflect on how you might experiment with the impact of inquiry—how much do you track the impacts of different types of questions you ask? How does a deficit-based question lead to a different dialogue than an appreciative question?

4. How can you integrate the principles of AI with other OD methodologies to experiment with new approaches for creating positive organizational change?

Resources

AI History and Timeline: http://appreciativeinquiry.case.edu/intro/timeline.cfm

AI Video Clips and Interview Guides: http://appreciativeinquiry.case.edu/practice/video.cfm

Appreciative Inquiry: A Conversation with David Cooperrider: www.youtube.com/watch?v = 3JDfr6KGV-k

David L. Cooperrider Center for Appreciative Inquiry in the Stiller School of Business, Champlain College: www.champlain.edu/appreciativeinquiry

Appreciative Inquiry Practitioner—The International Journal of AI: www.aipractitioner.com/

References

Barrett, F., and R. E. Fry. 2005. *Appreciative Inquiry: A Positive Approach to Building Cooperative Capacity*. Chagrin Fall, OH: Taos Institute.

Benyus, J. 2002. *Biomimicry: Innovation Inspired by Nature*. New York: Harper Collins.

Boyatzis, R. E., and A. McKee. 2005. *Resonant Leadership: Renewing Yourself and Connecting with Others Through Mindfulness, Hope and Compassion*. Boston, MA: Harvard Business School Press.

Buckingham, M. 2006. *Go Put Your Strengths to Work*. New York: Free Press.

Cameron, K. S., J. E. Dutton, and R. E. Quinn. 2003. *Positive Organizational Scholarship*. San Francisco: Berrett-Koehler.

Cameron, K. S., and G. M. Spreitzer. 2012. *The Oxford Handbook of Positive Organizational Scholarship*. New York: Oxford University Press.

Cooperrider, D. L. 1986. "Appreciative Inquiry: Toward a Methodology for Understanding and Enhancing Organizational Innovation." Unpublished dissertation at Case Western Reserve University in Cleveland, Ohio.

Cooperrider, D. L. 1999. "Positive Images, Positive Action: The Affirmative Basis of Organizing." In *Appreciative Management and Leadership*, edited by S. Srivastva and D. L. Cooperrider, 91–125. Euclid, OH: Lakeshore Communications.

Cooperrider, D. L. 2008. "*The 3-Circles of the Strengths Revolution.*" AI Practitioner: International Journal of Appreciative Inquiry (November): 8–11.

Cooperrider, D. L. 2013. "A Contemporary Commentary on Appreciative Inquiry in Organizational Life." In *Advances in Appreciative Inquiry*, 4th ed., edited by D. L. Cooperrider, D. Zandee, L. Godwin, M. Avital, and R. Boland, 3–67. Bingley, UK: Emerald Group.

Cooperrider, D. L. 2013. www.davidcooperrider.com/?s = romney&search-but = .

Cooperrider, D. L., and M. Avital. 2003. *Constructive Discourse and Human Organization*, Vol. 1 of *Advances in Appreciative Inquiry*. San Diego, CA: Elsevier.

Cooperrider, D. L., F. J. Barrett, and S. Srivastva. 1995. "Social Construction and Appreciative Inquiry: A Journey in Organizational Theory." In *Management and Organization: Relational Alternatives to Individualism*, edited by D. M. Hosking, H. P. Dachler, and K. J. Gergen, 157–200. Aldershot, UK: Avebury.

Cooperrider, D. L., and R. Fry. 2012. "Mirror Flourishing and the Positive Psychology of Sustainability." *Journal of Corporate Citizenship* 46 (Summer): 3–12.

Cooperrider, D. L., and L. Godwin. 2010. "Current Commentary on AI and Positive Change." *Appreciative Inquiry Commons*. Retrieved from http://appreciativeinquiry .case.edu/intro/comment.cfm.

Cooperrider, D. L., and L. Godwin. 2012. "Positive Organization Development: Innovation-Inspired Change in an Economy and Ecology of Strengths." In *The Oxford Handbook of Positive Organizational Scholarship*, edited by K. S. Cameron and G. M. Spreitzer, 737–750. New York: Oxford University Press.

Cooperrider, D. L., L. Godwin, B. Boland, and M. Avital. 2012. "The Appreciative Inquiry Summit: Explorations into the Magic of Macro-Management and Crowdsourcing." *AI Practitioner: International Journal of Appreciative Inquiry* 14 (1): 4–9.

Cooperrider, D. L., and S. Srivastva. 1987. "Appreciative Inquiry in Organizational Life." In *Research in Organization Change and Development*, edited by W. A. Pasmore and R. Woodman, 129–169. Greenwich, CT: JAI Press.

Cooperrider, D. L., and D. Whitney. 2005. *Appreciative Inquiry: A Positive Revolution in Change*. San Francisco: Berrett-Koehler.

Cooperrider, D. L., D. Whitney, and J. M. Stavros. 2008. *Appreciative Inquiry Handbook: For Leaders of Change*. San Francisco: Berrett-Koehler.

Coughlan, P., J. F. Suri, and K. Canales. 2008. "Prototypes as (Design) Tools for Behavioral and Organizational Change: A Design-Based Approach to Help Organizations Change Work Behaviors." *The Journal of Applied Behavioral Science* 43 (1): 1–13.

Dew, J. R. 1996. "Are You a Right Brain or Left Brain Thinker?" *Quality Progress Magazine* (April): *91–93*.

Drucker, P. F. 1966. *The Effective Executive*. New York: Harper Collins.

Dutton, J. E., and E. D. Heaphy. 2003. "The Power of High-Quality Connections." In *Positive Organizational Scholarship*, edited by K. S. Cameron, J. E. Dutton, and R. E. Quinn, 263–278. San Francisco: Berrett-Koehler.

Fredrickson, B. L. 2003. "The Value of Positive Emotions." *American Scientist* 91: 330–335.

Fredrickson, B. L. 2009. *Positivity: Groundbreaking Research Reveals How to Embrace the Hidden Strength of Positive Emotions, Overcome Negativity, and Thrive*. New York: Crown.

Freeman, R. E. 1984. *Strategic Management: A Stakeholder Approach*. Boston: Pitman.

Gergen, K. J. 1995. *Realities and Relationships*. Cambridge, MA: Harvard University Press.

Gergen, K. J. 2001. *Social Construction in Context*. Thousand Oaks, CA: Sage.

Godwin, L. N., K. Bodiford, and P. Kaplan. 2012. "Beyond the Room: Leveraging Collaborative Technology to Engage the Whole System." *AI Practitioner: International Journal of Appreciative Inquiry* 14 (1): 74–78.

Heisenberg, W. 1949. *The Physical Principles of Quantum Theory*. Translated by Carl Eckart and F. C. Hoyt. New York: Dover. (Original work published in 1930).

Kretzmann, J. P., and J. L. McKnight. 1994. *Building Communities from the Inside Out: A Path Toward Finding and Mobilizing a Community's Assets*. Evanston, IL: Institute for Policy Research.

Laszlo, C. 2008. *Sustainable Value: How the World's Leading Companies Are Doing Well by Doing Good*. Sheffield, UK: Greenleaf.

Miller, P. J., R. Potts, H. Fung, L. Hoogstra, and J. Mintz. 1990. "Narrative Practices and the Social Construction of Self in Childhood." *American Ethnologist* 17 (2): 292–311.

Orem, S. L., J. Binket, and A. L. Clancy. 2007. *Appreciative Coaching: A Positive Process for Change*. San Francisco: Jossey-Bass.

Peterson, C., and M. E. Seligman. 2004. *Character Strengths and Virtues: A Handbook and Classification*. Washington, DC: APA Press and Oxford University Press.

Piderit, S. K., R. Fry, and D. L. Cooperrider. 2007. *Handbook of Transformative Cooperation*. Stanford, CA: Stanford University Press.

Rath, T. 2007. *Strengths Finder 2.0*. New York: Gallup Press.

Roberts, L. M., J. E. Dutton, G. M. Spreitzer, E. D. Heaphy, and R. E. Quinn. 2005. "Composing the Reflected Best-Self Portrait: Building Pathways for Becoming Extraordinary in Work Organization." *Academy of Management* 30 (4): 712–736.

Seligman, M. E. 1999. "The President's Address." *American Psychologist* 54: 559–562.

Seligman, M. E. 2011. *Flourish: A Visionary New Understanding of Happiness and Well-Being*. New York: Atria.

Seligman, M. E., T. A. Steen, N. Park, and C. Peterson. 2005. "Positive Psychology Progress: Empirical Validation of Interventions." *American Psychologist* 60 (5): 410–421.

Stavros, J. M. (2013). "The Generative Nature of SOAR: Applications, Results, and the New SOAR Profile." *AI Practitioner: International Journal of Appreciative Inquiry* 15 (3): 6–26.

Stavros, J. M., and C. Torres. 2005. *Dynamic Relationships: Unleashing the Power of Appreciative Inquiry in Daily Living*. Chagrin Falls, OH: Taos Institute Publishers.

Thatchenkery, T., and C. Metzker. 2006. *Appreciative Intelligence: Seeing the Mighty Oak in the Acorn*. San Francisco: Berrett-Koehler.

Verleysen, B., F. Lambrechts, and F. Van Acker. 2014. "Building Psychological Capital with Appreciative Inquiry: Investigating the Mediating Role of Basic Psychological Need Satisfaction." *The Journal of Applied Behavioral Science*, 1–26. DOI: 10.1177/0021886314540209.

Weisbord, M., and S. Janoff. 1995. *Future Search*. San Francisco: Berrett-Koehler.

Whitney, D., and A. Trosten-Bloom. 2010. *The Power of Appreciative Inquiry: A Practical Guide to Positive Change*. San Francisco: Berrett-Koehler.

Whitney, D., A. Trosten-Bloom, and K. Rader. 2010. *Appreciative Leadership*. New York: McGraw-Hill.

Yaeger, T. F., T. C. Head, and P. F. Sorensen. 2006. *Global Organization Development: Managing Unprecedented Change*. Greenwich, CT: Information Age.

CHAPTER SEVEN

Competencies for Success

Steve H. Cady and Zachary D. Shoup

In the early 1970s, David McClelland (1973) wrote a groundbreaking article focused on testing for competence rather than intelligence. The reigning
paradigm of that time was to focus on intelligence testing, particularly as it
predicted grades in school. The assumption was that intelligence leads to high
performance in one's job. McClelland challenged this paradigm by first looking
at achievement motivation, then exploring what really predicts performance.
He concluded (1973), "While grade level attained seemed related to future measures of success in life, performance within grade was related only slightly. In
other words, being a high school or college graduate gave one a credential that
opened up certain higher level jobs, but the poorer students in high school or
college did as well in life as the top students." (2)

When considering what it means to be a competent professional, we look
at what is commonly referred to as KSAs—knowledge, skills, and abilities.
Knowledge generally refers to a person's education and training. Skills refer to
a person's potential to perform observable tasks related to a specific set of job
duties. Finally, abilities refer to a person's capability to exhibit certain behaviors
that lead to a predetermined result. These three provide statements of specific
requirements for effective performance in a given job position. KSA statements
guide the selection of a person for a job; and, once the person is hired, these
statements are used in a variety of personnel processes such as performance
evaluations, training, and promotion.

The purpose of this chapter is to explore the current state of competency development in organizations, provide an approach to developing a robust competency framework, and propose a way forward for competencies in the field of organization development (OD). It is important to note that the role of competencies in our field is relevant for both professionals and managers. Advancing an up-to-date competency framework that is on par with comparison fields (talent development or human resource management) will enable us to create more robust programs in education, certification, recruitment, selection, placement, employee development, and ongoing research.

COMPETENCIES AS COMPETITIVE ADVANTAGE

Competencies are applied and utilized by varying professionals across multiple disciplines, playing an integral role in overall organizational performance and growth. OD professionals and managers utilizing OD principles to improve or champion organizational change can leverage the power of competencies across multiple contexts. Competency development is quickly emerging as an opportunity for OD practitioners to stay at the forefront of organizational effectiveness as discussed next.

Recruitment and Selection

The strong connection between enacted behaviors and professional competencies creates an opportunity for organizations to identify and solicit talent using competency-based interviewing. Recent studies have further illustrated the notion that a competency framework or model provides organizational savings, primarily by improving talent selection decisions (Sutton and Watson 2013). Currently most organizations utilize a standard set of skills, behaviors, and abilities to recruit and vet potential employees. Competencies are used to establish benchmarks for prospective talent and represent indicators of applicants' fit and ability to meaningfully contribute to a given organization (Edgar 2009).

Self-Management

Professional competencies provide a target for practitioners to pursue and also guide development through an individuals' lifetime learning cycle. Professional development undertakings proliferate after the creation and implementation of professional standards and can help to advance individuals' skill levels in design, communication, or other technical area essential to work (Lattuca, Bergom, and Knight 2014). OD professionals understanding the essential competencies for the field and how they influence desirable outcomes in the workplace will provide a catalyst for increased professional development. Truly grasping the importance and impact of a robust competency model will in turn help practitioners self-manage their growth and learning within the field. Competencies as benchmarks will guide OD professionals while choosing which publications to consume and which scholastic courses to participate. A competency model in essence will act as a roadmap for increased professional capacity and learning.

Performance Evaluation

Competencies models by nature of their construction include behavioral indicators that are intended to represent actionable steps to achieve an explicit end. Because of this unique construction competencies also serve well as performance evaluation tools. Evidence exists that displays measuring either technical or behavioral focused competencies will provide indicators of overall organizational outcomes (Semeijn, Van Der Heijden, and Van Der Lee 2014). Essentially measuring expressed competencies will provide a metric for employee performance. Within any set of specific job duties the linked foundational competencies can be utilized to measure actual performance or demonstration of the key components determined as essential for the role (i.e., the competency). Often this is achieved by facilitating a comprehensive and systematic review of the employee with a focus on the previously established competency standards. Organizations can utilize varying types of 360-degree tools to illicit data in relation to the demonstration and potential related to a competency. Consequently, the adherence to the organization or the professional fields' competencies becomes the key performance metric for the employee.

Training and Development

Competency models also assist in identifying forthcoming training and development needs (Sutton and Watson 2013). Competencies include aspirational behavioral outcomes and subsequently can be utilized to generate training objectives. Competencies identified as performance musts for a specific organizational role can be incorporated into curriculum. To be assessed as competent, a person must demonstrate the ability to perform a job's specific task and developing employee training programs to teach people to understand, model, and exhibit competencies leads to competent employees.

Retention

Retention of talent is a derivative of using competencies effectively in an organizational context. As discussed above OD professionals have multiple avenues to implement competency based approaches to further any number of significant organizational pursuits. Competencies play a role in retaining people by helping clarify what role they play, how they fit in the organization, and ensuring beneficial development opportunities are presented. Competencies provide indicators for who you want to retain; and being clear about competencies, and by developing people in those competencies you can then retain the optimal talent. OD professionals can use competencies as a strategy to increase retention of the people that will make the most meaningful impacts on the organization.

DEVELOPING A COMPETENCY FRAMEWORK

Quality competency models have the most impact on the functional areas outlined above and as such are areas that professionals can continue to focus on advancing in their work with organizations and communities. A review of the literature on the professional development of competency-based approaches provides the following distinctions (Davis, Naughton, and Rothwell 2004; Elements for HR Success, 2012; Marshall and Eubanks, 1990; Richey, Fields and Foxon, 2001; Rothwell and Lindholm, 1999; Society for Industrial and Organizational Psychology 1999; Sullivan, Rothwell, and Worley 2001):

- Definition. Competencies combine KSAs into an integrated statement of what can be behaviorally observed in a person. The behavioral observations are applied to tasks that correspond to job duties, along with internal factors of the person in terms of attitudes and values.

- Standards. The competencies are focused on adding value to the organization by contributing to job performance. In addition, competencies are measured by a set of standards.

- Demonstration. While there are internal and external competencies, each statement reflects the KSAs as a demonstration; hence, it is an observable behavior. External competencies are tangible and more easily observed. Some of the observable behaviors are directly related to the gross or fine motor skills necessary to perform a job duty. Internal competencies are intangible and not directly observed. The statements, in this case, are behaviors that serve as a proxy for competencies such as mental processing, values, and attitudes.

- Understanding. It's important that competencies are clearly connected to results in that the person knows why a specific behavior is important and adds value to the organization.

- Conceptualization. Competencies are typically organized into integrated multifaceted conceptual frameworks. The frameworks tend to focus on the following: soft to hard qualities, foundations to advanced levels, and inputs to outputs for success.

- Impetus. Competency frameworks appear to be created in response to some general trends or changes being felt among most professionals in a particular field. Some of these needs include: legitimization, globalization, technology, and demographics.

- In response to the above discussion, one could argue that the distinction of competencies from KSAs is murky at best. We agree. The reason is that different aspects of a job's KSAs are represented to varying degrees in competency statements. The two are more similar than different.

Competencies and KSAs

Building on the KSA concept, and the focus of this chapter, we incorporate elements of the KSAs, yet take the "value add" aspect a step further. A competency is what a person is able to do that adds value to the organization. Richey, Fields, and Foxon (2001) define competency as, "A knowledge, skill or attitude that enables one to effectively perform the activities of a given occupation or function to the standards expected in employment" (31).

Why is the distinction between KSAs and competencies important? Because competencies are what future employers are going to be most interested in knowing in hiring decisions for employment, promotion, or specific projects. Within the field of OD, our profession is progressing to the point that managers at all levels are looking to build their OD competencies. In summary, KSAs are utilized and integrated in the creation of specific competency statements.

Competencies and Job Duties

While competencies are not the same as job duties, they are related and the success of a job is related to completing certain tasks that require certain competencies. Hence, a list of job duties set next to a list of job competencies will invariably look similar. Competencies can be thought of more broadly and generalizable to other similar functions. For example, the job duties of a labor relations specialist will be different than a recruitment specialist; the two jobs will share a set of similar competencies necessary for success, while each job will likely have a unique set of specific duties (Condrey 2010).

Writing Effective Competency Statements

A well-written competency statement provides an operational definition that makes the desired behavior accessible to the readers, particularly those required to exhibit, assess, or develop that competency. They are a clear and understandable description of the KSAs and attitudes that lead to success. So, what are the best competency statements? We draw from three important concepts as we look at a model for crafting competency statements: planned behavior and levels of specificity (Ajzen 2002; Fishbein and Ajzen 1975; Kautonen, Van Gelderen, and Tornikoski 2013), self-efficacy (Bandura 1994), and assessment centers (Arthur, Day, McNelly, and Edens 2003).

Here is the key point we wish to make. The greater the level of competence specificity provided in the statement, the more understandable, accessible, and predictable the competency will be with regard to its criterion. Our recommendation is that you explicitly consider each of the factors below and incorporate them into your competency statement. In some cases, the competency statement will be supported by two or more performance examples. Together, this hierarchy makes for a complete competency statement.

- **Target.** What is the competency impacting? In OD, it will often be at levels of analysis: individual, group, or whole. Sometimes, it may be focused on certain types within one of these levels (e.g., nonprofits, business, or government); in other instances, it may apply to more than one level.

- **Action.** What is the observable behavior involved? This is stated as a verb and can use existing concepts and terms. In some cases, the action may be related to internal mechanisms (values, thoughts, etc.). We recommend you avoid these types of statements, as they are often subject to arbitrary and capricious applications. Find a close proxy and state it clearly as the *external indicator* of that internal mechanism.

- **Context.** What is the situation or condition in which this competency takes place? This captures the circumstances and other factors in the environment that influence the target and action.

- **Time.** When does the competency need to be exhibited? This can be date, time, season, step within a process, and so on. In OD, it may be a step in the action research process.

- **Performance.** What is the desired level of performance that indicates success? Complementing the competency statement will be further defined performance criteria that describe the behavior (examples, observable, frequency, etc.) in a way that lends itself to an assessment center approach.

We developed Figure 7.1 as a concise tool for dissecting and creating effective competency statements. From this example, we offer some caveats. The phrase "During annual performance reviews" could be replaced with "In any situation and in all conversations." It is also possible to not include the statement, assuming that it is true at all times and situations. Pending the legal environment where the competencies are applied, this may need to be mentioned in the preamble to the official documentation. As a result, the phrase is not needed and could be stated as "Comprehends and learns from what another person

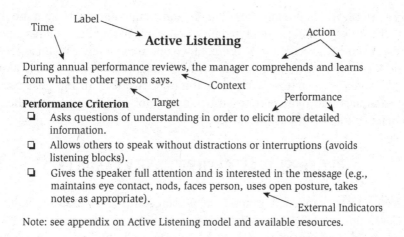

Figure 7.1. Example of Competency Statement within a Conceptual Framework

says." The key here is to explicitly consider and address the role of timing and context for the competency. In addition, notice the "Note." The purpose of this in the example is to specify that additional resources with specific required terminology may be referenced as key approved documentation connected to the competencies. That is, if you have certain models, formats, tools, procedures, or processes that need to be properly utilized, it is appropriate to reference them as a required part of the competency statement.

Conceptual Framework and Hierarchy

Taking a competency approach is more than a list of one-sentence statements. We recommend building a competency framework or model. When crafting a framework, there are three main steps. First, conduct a behavioral interview and observation study of superior performers (Berger and Berger 2003). Second, develop competency statements that are comprised of a label and basic definition supported by performance or behavioral criterion. Utilize the specificity checklist provided above to guide you in crafting the statements. The label serves as an anchor word that cues a person to the whole statement. The definition sets that stage for the supporting performance criterion. Third, build a framework or model comprised of domains, subdomains, and competency statements. For example, imagine a competency framework that is focused on management. The title is "Managerial Competencies." One of the domains is "Employee Engagement." Then, a subdomain is "Communication," and finally the competency statement is "Active Listening." The competency statement has a definition and performance criterion, described in one sentence for each concept.

The three levels of domain, subdomain, and competency statement provide a hierarchy for organizing a more dynamic or organic model that will realistically represent the holistic nature of the competency framework. Organize the key words for each of the levels into a visually integrated model. This is akin to the old saying, "A picture is worth a thousand words." In the next section, case examples will demonstrate best practices for building a comprehensive competency framework as prescribed.

PROFESSIONALIZATION: CASE EXAMPLES

In recent years, established professional organizations (e.g., Association for Talent Development [ATD] and Society for Human Resource Management [SHRM]) have tackled a similar challenge by advancing a comprehensive global competency framework for their field. Common characteristics of these initiatives include: conducting comprehensive research, involving a global community, utilizing the research-based competency framework to provide a suite of products and services, and continuously improving and validating the framework.

Industrial-Organizational Psychology

The Society for Industrial and Organizational Psychology (SIOP) began a standardized process to develop professional competencies in 1982. Their competency list is specifically tailored for doctoral level scientific-practitioners. The SIOP competency model is intended to guide curriculum planners in the creation and implementation of doctoral-level graduate programs in industrial-organizational psychology. Development of the competencies was championed by an education and training committee of experts and the most recent revision of the content was published in 1999 (Society for Industrial and Organizational Psychology 1999). SIOP defines competencies as "The skills, behaviors, and capabilities necessary to function as a new member of the profession" (Society for Industrial and Organizational Psychology, Perspective of the Guidelines, para. 6). The SIOP competency model is separated into two distinctive groups, accounting for 25 individual competencies. The first group illustrates general knowledge determined as essential to the training of industrial-organizational psychologists. This group includes six different competencies. The second group includes competencies that illustrate functional areas for the field of industrial-organizational psychology and contains 19 different competencies.

The SIOP competency model utilizes elements of the best practice competency development model process. They begin their model utilizing broad domains or competency categories and connect each to a narrative containing specific behavioral or competency statements. To illustrate, we examine the domain of "Training: Theory, Program Design, and Evaluation." This broader category of training is then connected to the competency statement, "The instructional process begins with a needs assessment, including organizational, job and task, and person analyses, to determine the goals and constraints of the organization and the characteristics of the job and trainees" (Society for Industrial and Organizational Psychology, Training: Theory, Program Design, and Evaluation, para. 1).

Instructional Design

The International Board of Standards for Training, Performance, and Instruction (IBSTPI) began a standardized process to develop competencies and performance statements in 1986. Their standards have been utilized by various professional communities and were developed specifically for instructional designers, instructors, and training managers (Richey 2002). IBSTPI has adopted and reports the standard definition of competencies are, "A knowledge, skill, or attitude that enables one to effectively perform the activities of a given occupation or function to the standards expected in employment" (Richey, Fields, and Foxon 2001, 8). Several iterations of each competency standard have been developed and work is currently being completed to further refine and improve the content.

The IBSTPI competency framework includes three distinct but interrelated components: domains, competencies, and performance statements. Domains act as broad areas that narrow into generalized competency statements, which again narrow into behaviorally based performance statements (Richey 2002). As an example, IBSTPI utilized "Design and Develop" as the broader domain, that in turn is supported by the competency statement, "Select, modify, or create a design and development model appropriate for a given project" (8). The competency statement is next linked to several different performance statements to demonstrate the behavior is enacted.

Training and Talent Development

The Association for Talent Development (ATD) began a standardized process to develop competencies in 2004. Their model was specifically developed to guide successful practice within the talent development field (Davis, Naughton, and Rothwell 2004). The most recent version of the ATD competency model has been published in 2013. This iteration of the ATD model includes a wide catalogue of topics for talent development practitioners and specific actions for achieving success. ATD defined competencies as, "Competencies encompass clusters of skills, knowledge, abilities, and behaviors required for people to succeed" (Davis et al. 2004, 19). The ATD competency model includes two hierarchical layers. The first layer includes six foundational competencies and the second layer expresses 10 specialized expertise areas (AOEs). Foundational competencies are considered essential for every practitioner within the talent development field and AOEs are specific knowledge needed for individual roles within the field (Arneson, Rothwell, and Naughton 2013).

The ATD competency model also illustrates the use of the components determined in the best practice model of developing competencies. They use the domain, subdomain, and competency statement structure. The broad to narrow structure progresses from expansive competency category to very detailed actionable statements. That is to say, ATDs "Interpersonal Skills" act as the domain, which narrows to the subdomain "Training Delivery" and is accompanied by the behavioral statement, "manages and responds to learner needs" (Arneson et al. 2013, 20).

Human Resource Management

The Society for Human Resource Management (SHRM) began the endeavor of creating a validated competency model in 2011. SHRM exists for the advancement of the human resources field and their competencies are seen as the leading human resource practitioner standards and guidelines. The SHRM model includes what they believe are essential competencies for personal and professional success in the field of human resources. SHRM defines competencies as, "Competencies are individual characteristics, including knowledge, skills, abilities, self-image, traits, mindsets, feelings, and ways of thinking, which, when used with the appropriate roles, achieve a desired result. Competencies contribute to individual exemplary performance that creates reasonable impact on business outcomes" (Elements for HR Success 2012, 5).

Their competencies are the technical and behavioral standards that HR professionals should engage in to be successful. The SHRM model includes nine different competency areas; one technical and the others behavioral. "Each area is defined with five distinctive components: (1) title, (2) definition, (3) sub-competencies, (4) behaviors, and (5) proficiency standards" (Elements for HR Success 2012, 7). The SHRM competency model has also developed differing levels to correspond with varying human resources expertise from entry to executive.

SHRM utilized the broad domain to the more specific behavioral indicator model that is seen as the benchmark of valid competency development. For example, they note, "Human Resources Technical Expertise and Practice" as a major domain, with narrowed competency and behavioral statements connecting the domain to actions. "Workforce Planning and Employment" illustrates the subdomain and is linked by the "Delivers customized human resource solutions for organizational challenges" competency statement (Elements for HR Success 2012, 10).

CURRENT STATE OF COMPETENCIES FOR THE FIELD OF ORGANIZATION DEVELOPMENT

During the 1990s, two seasoned OD practitioners from Washington developed a small but fundamental research project in an attempt to develop an empirically based competency model for the field of OD. In 1990, Julie Marshall and James Eubanks made critical steps to developing a validated research process to produce a standard list of essential OD competencies. The overall purpose of the study was to develop a competency-based model to utilize in training graduate-level OD practitioners at Washington University in Ellensburg, Washington. Marshall and Eubanks developed a model that consisted of 17 behaviorally based statements listed in three categories: (1) delivery, (2) people, and (3) data. The outcomes of the study produced broad competency domains and supporting behavioral indicators of each category (Marshall and Eubanks 1990).

Examining Marshall and Eubanks's work from the previously mentioned best practice model for developing competencies, we notice that several elements are present. They utilize domains to represent broad categories for the competency foundation and developed behavioral or competency statements to demonstrate indicators of the broader category. For example, they established "delivery" as a domain or competency category. Connected to delivery is then the behavioral indicator of "Made it clear as to what you could and could not do for the organization." Again they established "data" as the competency domain and supported it with the behavioral statement of "Used information from interviews to help the clients see how their behaviors affected the organization" (Marshall and Eubanks 1990, 9).

Many different practitioners have contributed work toward a validated competency model for the Organization Development Network (ODN). The most recent of such initiative includes the work by Roland Sullivan, Bill Rothwell, and Chris Worley in 2001. This initiative principally stems from three early research projects. Those studies included Shepard and Raia (1981); Worley and Varney's (1998) Delphi study including 70 OD practitioners; and the Worley and Feyerherm (2003) exploration of several founders of the field. Over the last 30 years, a competency list has been continuously refined by an international sample of approximately 3,500 individuals (Worley, Rothwell, and Sullivan 2010). The ODN utilizes the following definition of competencies: "An underlying characteristic of an employee (that is, motive, trait, skill, aspects of one's self-image, social role, or a body of knowledge) which results in effective and/or superior performance in a job" (Boyatzis 1982, 20–21).

The current ODN competency list includes a robust selection of competencies determined to be essential for OD practice. This list includes 17 competency domains that include 141 behavioral statements. Roland Sullivan and colleagues clearly utilize certain elements determined to be best practice component for developing competency models. They have included broad domains to capture the overall theme of the specific competency and support it by linking behavioral indicators or competency statements. For instance, they established "diagnosis" as a competency domain and link the following behavioral statement: "Utilize a solid conceptual framework based on research" (Sullivan et al. 2001, 2).

Early in the new millennium, Mary Eggers and Allan Church championed an initiative to create a more universally acknowledged and utilized set of standards for the field of OD. This competency initiative was described as the Principles of Practice. The purpose of this initiative was to provide direction for the overall practice of OD. Their principles were intended to demonstrate a standard or benchmark which OD practitioners could use for accountability and training. This professional values–laden set of standards would allow for assessment and evaluation of OD practice and practitioners. Competencies received input from a diverse sample of thought leaders and practitioners from the field of OD (Eggers and Church 2015).

One comprehensive work related to the refinement of OD competencies is a study conducted by Roland Sullivan and colleagues (Worley, Rothwell, and Sullivan, 2010). This study aimed to improve the list of OD competencies developed in 2001 by further examining the utility and structure of the content. A methodology was utilized to identify and analyze clusters of items measuring specific concepts and correlations to the overarching competency list structure. Items were examined using a section-by-section analysis and pooled-item analysis. These two analyses were next compared to further refine a final competency list (Worley, Rothwell, and Sullivan 2010). The examples in Tables 7.1 and 7.2 illustrate the section-by-section analysis and pooled-item analysis.

Table 7.1 provides a list of 32 competencies clustered around the OD process from marketing through separation. Table 7.2 provides clusters that focus on personal competencies, similar to the concept of self as instrument. The 33 clusters represented in this analysis all contained multiple correlating elements. Comparison of the two figures illustrates that the majority of the competencies clusters are present across both analysis, suggesting further validity for those specific competencies (Worley et al. 2010).

Table 7.1. The OD Process: Section-by-Section Analysis

	Competency Label	# of Items
Marketing	Ability to describe OD processes	7
	Quickly assess opportunities for change	4
	Clarify outcomes and resources	3
	Develop relationships	2
	Make good client choices	1
Start-Up	Set the conditions for change	4
	Address power	3
	Build cooperative relationships	3
	Clarify roles	2
Diagnosis/Feedback	Research methods	6
	Keep the information flowing	5
	Clarify data needs	4
	Keeping an open mind re: data	3
	Relevance	1
Action Planning	Creating an implementation plan—I	4
	Creating an implementation plan—II	3
	Facilitate the action planning process	3
	Obtain commitment from leadership	2
Intervention	Adjust implementation	4
	Transfer ownership of the change	3
Evaluation	Ability to evaluate change	5
	Use evaluation data to adjust change	4
Adoption	Manage adoption and institutionalization	9
Separation	Manage the separation	5
Other Competencies	Master self	8
	Be available to multiple stakeholders	7
	Ability to work with large-scale clients	4
	Manage diversity	3
	Be current in theory and technology	4
	Maintain a flexible focus	2
	Possess broad facilitation skills	2
	Be comfortable with ambiguity	2

Table 7.2. Self as Instrument: Pooled-Item Analysis Results

Competency Label	# of Items
Self-mastery	13
Ability to evaluate change	6
Clarify data needs	4
Manage the transition and sustain momentum	8
Keep information flowing	7
Integrate theory and practice	6
Ability to work with large systems	6
Manage the separation	3
Participatively create a good action plan	6
Apply research methods appropriately	4
Manage diversity	4
Imagination skills	2
Focus on relevant issues	5
Clarify roles	2
Address power	2
Clarify outcomes	1
Keep an open mind regarding data	2
Stay current with technology	2
Apply effective interpersonal skills	3
Set appropriate expectations	4
Let data drive action	3
Manage ownership of change	3
Be mindful of process	2
Think systemically	3
Comfort with ambiguity	3
Action plan with results in mind	1
Involve leadership	2
Be credible	2
Be a quick study	2
Monitor the environment	1
Network your services	1
Make good client choices	1
Get leadership commitment	1

SUMMARY

The field of OD is in need of a current, concise, and validated competency framework that is accessible to both professionals and managers. Why now? We are witnessing an increasing number of degree programs, job positions, and departments, all with a focus on organization development. Along with this growth, there are calls for more clarity on what the field is and what it offers, including steps to elevate the field's legitimacy in scholarship and practice (Church and Jamieson 2014).

Scholars, students, and practitioners spend significant amounts of time discussing and defining the field of OD. This ongoing discussion has been ever present and demonstrates the need for a standardized and valid set of competencies. As practitioners and scholars yearn for an answer to the question "What is OD?" we are inclined to help provide a framework for the answer. When considering the underlying need for OD competencies, three broad areas should be considered. The gap between the current state of OD competencies and the preferred future includes the components of legitimacy, relevancy, and longevity. Each of the above needs illustrates an important precipitating component and demonstrates the unique opportunities that the field of OD can improve upon.

While we have made progress as discussed above, there is an opportunity to take the work (e.g., from 2001) and build a framework that advances our field. Our contemporary professions are developing robust, continuously improving competency frameworks. We, as a field, are running the risk of getting left behind. In response, we propose implementing a process to advance the work described above and validate a framework that sets the stage for continued research, lending credibility, and encouraging learning around OD competencies. This includes bringing together an international research team in order to design and implement a long-term research project. If you wish to learn more and possibly join us on this initiative, go to www.tinyurl.com/ODcompetencies.

Discussion Questions

1. Pick a particular set of jobs (OD professionals) or roles (leadership). Create a competency framework utilizing the competency development model: domains to subdomains to the competency statement.

2. Identify existing competencies and use the model prescribed in Figure 7.1 Example of Competency Statement within a Conceptual Framework to assess how well the competency meets the specificity requirements.

3. What are the benefits of developing validated OD competencies? What are the challenges to creating a competency framework for the field of OD?

4. What role can OD practitioners play in developing and implementing competency approaches in organizations?

Resources

Organization Development Network Competency website: www.odnetwork.org/?
page = ODCompetencies

The Association for Talent Development Competency website: www.td.org/
Certification/Competency-Model

Society for Industrial and Organizational Psychology Competency website: www.siop
.org/PhDGuidelines98.aspx

References

Ajzen, I. 2002. "Perceived Behavioral Control, Self-Efficacy, Locus of Control, and
the Theory of Planned Behavior." *Journal of Applied Social Psychology* 32:
665–683.

Arneson, J., W. Rothwell, and J. Naughton. 2013. *ASTD Competency Study: The Training
& Development Profession Redefined*. Alexandria, VA: ATD Press.

Arthur, W., Jr., E. A. Day, T. L. McNelly, and P. S. Edens. 2003. "A Meta-Analysis of the
Criterion-Related Validity of Assessment Center Dimensions." *Personnel Psychology*
56 (1): 125–154.

Bandura, A. 1994. "Self-Efficacy." In *Encyclopedia of Human Behavior*, Vol. 4, edited by
V. S. Ramachaudran, 71–81. New York: Academic Press.

Berger, D., and R. Berger. 2003. *The Talent Management Handbook: Creating
Organizational Excellence*. New York: McGraw-Hill.

Boyatzis, R. 1982. *The Competent Manager: A Model for Effective Performance*. New York:
John Wiley & Sons.

Church, A., and D. Jamieson. 2014. "Current and Future State of OD Values."
OD Practitioner 2 (46): 2.

Condrey, S. E. 2010. *Handbook of Human Resource Management in Government*. San
Francisco: John Wiley & Sons.

Davis, P., J. Naughton, and W. Rothwell. 2004. *New Roles and New Competencies for the
Profession*. Alexandria, VA: The American Society for Training and Development.

Davis, P., J. Naughton, W. Rothwell, and R. Wellins. 2004. *Mapping the Future: Shaping New Workplace Learning and Performance Competencies*. Alexandria, VA:
The American Society for Training and Development.

Edgar, S. 2009. "Guidance on Writing Competency Statements for a Job Application. Occupational Division of the Employment Service: Version 2." www.gov.uk/
government/uploads/system/uploads/attachment_data/file/128968/competency-
guidance.pdf.

Eggers, M., and A. Church. 2015. "Principles of OD Practice. Organization Development
Network." www.odnetwork.org/?page = PrinciplesOfODPractiElements.

Fishbein, M., and I. Ajzen. 1975. *Belief, Attitude, Intention, and Behavior: An Introduction to Theory and Research*. Reading, MA: Addison-Wesley.

Kautonen, T., M. Van Gelderen, and E. T. Tornikoski. 2013. "Predicting Entrepreneurial Behaviour: A Test of the Theory of Planned Behaviour." *Applied Economics* 45 (6): 697–707.

Lattuca, L. R., I. Bergom, and D. B. Knight. 2014. "Professional Development, Departmental Contexts, and Use of Instructional Strategies." *Journal of Engineering Education* 103 (4): 549–572.

Marshall, J., and J. Eubanks. 1990. "Establishing a Competency Model for OD Practitioner." *OD Practitioner* 2 (22): 8–9.

McClelland, D. C. 1973. "Testing for Competence Rather than for 'Intelligence.'" *American Psychologist* 28 (1): 1–14.

Richey, R. 2002. "The IBSTPI Competency Standards: Development, Definition and Use." In *Educational Media and Technology Yearbook*, Vol. 27, edited by M. A. Fitzgerald, M. Orey, and R. M. Branch, 111–119. Englewood, CO: Greenwood.

Richey, R., D. Fields, and M. Foxon. 2001. *Instructional Design Competencies: The Standards*. 3rd ed. Syracuse, NY: ERIC Clearinghouse on Information & Technology.

Rothwell, W. J., and J. E. Lindholm. 1999. "Competency Identification, Modelling and Assessment in the USA." *International Journal of Training and Development* 3 (2): 90–105.

Semeijn, J. H., B. I. J. M. Van Der Heijden, and A. Van Der Lee. 2014. "Multisource Ratings of Managerial Competencies and Their Predictive Value for Managerial and Organizational Effectiveness." *Human Resource Management* 53 (5): 773–794.

Shepard, K., and A. Raia. 1981. "The OD Training Challenge." *Training & Development Journal* 77: 30–33.

Society for Human Resources Management. 2012. "SHRM's Elements for HR Success: Competency Model." www.shrm.org/hrcompetencies/documents/competency %20model%208%200.pdf.

Society for Industrial and Organizational Psychology. 1999. "Guidelines for Education and Training at the Doctoral Level in Industrial/Organizational Psychology." www .siop.org/PhDGuidelines98.aspx.

Sullivan, R., W. Rothwell, and C. Worley. 2001. "20th Edition of the Organization Change and Development Competency Effort." www.odnetwork.org/?page = competencies.

Sutton, A., and S. Watson. 2013. "Can Competencies at Selection Predict Performance and Development Needs?" *The Journal of Management Development* 32 (9): 1023–1035.

Worley, C., and A. Feyerherm. 2003. "Reflections on the Future of Organization Development." *Journal of Applied Behavioral Science* 39 (1): 97–115.

Worley, C., W. Rothwell, and R. Sullivan. 2010. "Competencies of OD Practitioners." In *Practicing Organization Development: A Guide for Leading Change*, 3rd ed., edited by W. Rothwell, J. Stavros, R. Sullivan, and A. Sullivan, 107–135. San Francisco: John Wiley & Sons.

Worley, C., and G. Varney. 1998. "A Search for a Common Body of Knowledge for Master's Level Organization Development and Change Programs: An Invitation to Join the Discussion." *Academy of Management ODC Newsletter* (Winter): 1–3.

PART TWO

ORGANIZATION DEVELOPMENT PROCESS TO GUIDE TRANSFORMATION AND CHANGE

CHAPTER EIGHT

Entry

Marketing and Positioning Organization Development

Alan Weiss

Most organization development (OD) practitioners fail to realize that they are in the marketing business. Consultants cannot get work because they believe marketing is not required. Average OD consultants are doing well because they recognize the importance of marketing and can do it. Consultants who are great marketers can name their fee. Which group would you rather be in?

Even when you work internally, you should not sit back and wait for employee line areas to call you. You must analyze the organization from a business perspective and proactively recommend to executives what can be done to improve productivity. This chapter will enable you to: determine your value proposition, identify your buyer, establish routes to reach that buyer, achieve conceptual agreement, and create a proposal to close business.

DETERMINING YOUR VALUE PROPOSITION

There are three critical factors to embrace when attempting to market professional services: (1) What is the market need? (2) What are your competencies? and (3) What is your passion?

What Is the Market Need?

This is the essence of marketing. There may be a preexisting need—for example, sales development or leadership improvement is typically needed. Or, you can create a need, such as satisfying employees before satisfying the customer. Since OD is an often nebulous and inexact concept, it is vital to create a clear value proposition.

A value proposition is always a benefit for the potential client and never a description of your methodology. Here are good and poor value propositions:

Good	Poor
• Improve retention of core talent	• Perform exit interviews
• Decrease time-to-market of new products	• Assess marketing/sales relations
• Merge acquisition and parent cultures	• Run focus groups for new people
• Improve customer response time	• Create customer survey

You can embrace existing market need or create a new market need. Apple is adept at "jumping on the next big thing," in Steve Jobs's words, and creating recombined new needs, the iPhone being an example.

You must become proficient in articulating your value proposition as a client outcome. Here is mine: "We improve individual and organizational productivity and performance." (The only legitimate response to this rather vague statement is, "What does that mean?" I reply: "Well, tell me something about your business, and I will be more specific." You cannot learn while you are talking, and the more you talk, the more the other person will tend to "deselect" you.)

One other point: You can anticipate need. In your organization or a client organization, is there an emerging need to manage virtual teams that never see each other, or to change recruiting practices to hire different types of skills, or use an internal social networking medium? These are key OD marketing competencies.

What Are Your Competencies?

Competencies are skills, experiences, and behaviors that make you proficient. Your competencies cannot come from "store bought" materials from training vendors. Believe me, if they were sufficient, the company wouldn't need you.

Exhibit 8.1. The Rainmaker Attributes

Strategies for Marketing

- Intellectual breadth
  — Able to discuss a wide variety of issues
- Sense of humor
  — Able to ease tension, maintain perspective
- Industry conversancy
  — Able to relate to and identify situational issues
- Superb communication skills
  — Able to command a room or a meeting
- Presence: *Sogomi*
  — Able to be accepted as a peer of the buyer
- Framing skills
  — Able to quickly describe problems and opportunities
- Innovation
  — Able and willing to raise the bar, seek new paths
- Resilience
  — Able to accept rejection and reject acceptance
- Life balance
  — Able to view life holistically

If you do not have sufficient competencies, then the good news is that you can always acquire more. But what are you good at, and what would you like to become good at? Exhibit 8.1 lists the marketing traits for a "rainmaker" (namely business developer/marketer) that I have discerned over the years.

What Is Your Passion?

Market need and competency must be fueled by passion. Isolate those competencies and needs you most favor and are most passionate about, and focus on them. I will not do any "downsizing" work, because I am against it, since I consider downsizing to be a heinous act implemented to compensate for executive error. I am passionate about developing leadership, so I actively seek that work. If you refer to Figure 8.1, you will see four possibilities:

1. Need and capability without passion create drudgery. You become a hired hand with little motivation and no "ownership" of outcomes.
2. Market need and passion without competency makes you a snake oil seller, hawking your potions but without the real medicine needed to cure the ills.

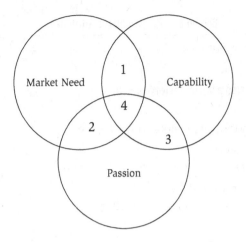

Figure 8.1. Three Areas and Four Conditions for Value

3. Capability and passion without market need make you a dilettante, offering aesthetic solutions to problems no one cares about unless you can convince them otherwise.

4. The combination of these elements makes you an effective marketer.

If you have these elements in place, then you need only respond to the following questions—and the good news is that marketing is difficult but not complex—to arrive at your marketing strategy:

1. *What is my value proposition?*
   What outcomes do you provide for the client? Consider another way to ask this question: After you walk away, how is the client better off? How has the client's condition been improved?

2. *Who is likely to write a check for that value?*
   I call this the "economic buyer" or the "true buyer." He or she has the budget to authorize, approve, and launch your project. In large organizations there are scores (or even hundreds) of economic buyers. In small organizations, there may be just one or two. If your contact must go elsewhere for approval or to "seek budget," you are not talking to an economic buyer.

3. *How do I reach that buyer?*
   A key problem in marketing is that too many consultants go directly to point 3 without understanding the first two points. But the only way to arrive at point 3 is after establishing the first two realities.

IDENTIFYING AND REACHING
THE ECONOMIC BUYER

There are two types of "buyers" in organizational settings:

1. *Economic buyer*: Possesses the power and authority to approve a check for your services and to fund the project.

2. *Feasibility buyer*: Provides opinion and analysis of the project's appropriateness in terms of culture, scope, credentials, content, and other relative clients.

Most consultants fail at marketing because they spend too much time with feasibility buyers—who cannot say "yes" but can say "no"—and not enough time (or no time at all) with economic buyers who can say "yes." That is why the attributes mentioned above are so important. You must be able to relate to economic buyers on a peer basis. Your content and OD skills are not sufficient for that. You must have business acumen and conversancy.

When you encounter feasibility buyers—"gatekeepers" and "filters"—you must endeavor to go around or through them to the economic buyer. You can do this in three ways.

1. *Appeals to rational self-interest*. Try to convince the feasibility buyer it would be dangerous to proceed even with a tentative plan or preliminary proposal without hearing from the true buyer's lips exactly what he or she expects. Explain that your experience about this is unequivocal: The economic buyer must be brought into the discussion, however briefly, early when creating a proposal. Attempt to form a partnership with the feasibility buyer to accomplish this.

2. *Guile*. Use some device to get past the feasibility buyer. Here is my favorite, and honest, alternative: "Ethically, I must see the person who has the fiduciary responsibility for the project, since I need to understand exactly what his or her expectations are before deciding whether to bid on this work." Another: "It is unfair of me to expect you to market on my behalf, especially if there may be adverse reactions. Let me take that responsibility."

3. *Power*. Ignore, circumvent, or blast through the gatekeeper. Although this will create bad relations, you will not get the business in any other way. Send a letter, email, fax, or phone message informing the economic buyer you have enjoyed working with the gatekeeper but must have 20 minutes of his or her time before submitting a proposal. Provide your contact information and hope for the best.

If you content yourself with people who will see you but cannot help you (cannot say "yes"), you will fail as a marketer (and as an effective OD practitioner). A strong value proposition will capture the attention of an economic buyer if you can reach that person. When people are empowered only to say "no," that is what they will inevitably say. Find the person who can say "yes" or "no," which at least gives you a fighting chance.

ESTABLISHING THE ROUTES TO THE ECONOMIC BUYER

The best way to market is to create a "gravity" that draws people to you. This changes the entire buying dynamic. Instead of having to prove how good you are, you instead engage people interested in what you can do for them. This is why branding, reputation, and word-of-mouth are so important. No one enters a McDonald's to browse. The buying decision has already been made before entering the store. Figure 8.2 lists a variety of ways to create gravity, and these are discussed in the following sections in more detail. Internally, you can build powerful brands. It's not unusual to hear an executive request, "Get Jane Hudson on this, we need her to help us find the right solution."

Figure 8.2. The "Gravity" Concept of Marketing OD Services

Pro Bono Work

Pro bono work for marketing should have the following characteristics:

- A cause or objective in which you believe and wish to support
- Relatively high-profile nonprofit or charity
- Public events and media coverage
- Significant potential buyers or influencers are volunteers and/or key exhibitors (the editor of the local newspaper, the general manager of the electric company, the senior vice president of a major bank)
- Involvement will be interactive, and not individual

Seek a leadership position or fill a difficult position in the organization. Typically, fund-raising, managing volunteers, and publicity are vitally needed and tough to do well. You want a high-visibility position and one in which you can rub elbows with your potential buyers and influencers. Take on the difficult jobs, but do them well. Make the reports at the meetings, give interviews to the media, and shower credit on your colleagues.

When the time is right, suggest to the executive you have worked with or the publisher you have supported that it might make sense to have lunch and compare notes about your two organizations. Pro bono work like this automatically builds relationships and allows others to see your abilities on neutral turf. That is why you should do the tough jobs and do them well. Excellent organization ability, strategies, management of others, fiscal prudence, and similar traits translate well into the needs of your pro bono colleagues.

Pro bono work is especially powerful for those living in fairly major markets and who wish to reduce their travel and work closer to home. I have done work for everyone from the League of Women Voters to a shelter for battered women to local theater groups.

Basic Rule. Engage in at least one pro bono activity each quarter.

Commercial Publishing

A commercially published book can provide a strong credibility statement. For successful consultants endeavoring to reach the next level, this may be the shortest route. Early in my career, I published books that addressed the issues I wanted to be hired to consult about: innovation, behavior and motivation, and strategy. Later in my career, I published books that capitalized on my established expertise: marketing, consulting, and speaking professionally. An entirely new career was launched for me when I published *Million Dollar Consulting*, which established me as a "consultant to consultants."

Writing a business book is not like writing a novel. You need a topic, 10 or 12 chapters, and a half dozen key points supported by facts, stories, and anecdotes in each chapter. If you do not believe this, pull any 10 random business books off the shelf and look.

Another aspect of commercial publishing involves articles and interviews in the popular and trade press. Circulate article query letters and manuscripts regularly. Successful consultants, with a raft of client experiences and case studies, should be able to create powerful, vivid pieces that will draw interested readers to want to know more.

Try to include an offer to contact you in your articles of research studies, visits to your website, email responses to questions, and so on, enabling readers to continue to connect with you in more personal ways.

Basic Rule. Set a goal to publish one article per quarter, meaning you should propose four articles per quarter in different publications.

Position Papers

I often refer to these as "white papers." These are powerful tools that can be used for:

- Content in your press kit
- The basis for an article or booklets to be published
- Web page content
- Handouts at speeches
- Giveaways for inquiries

Position papers are two-to-six-page discussions of your philosophy, beliefs, findings, experiences, and/or approaches. They should never be self-promotional. Instead, they should build credibility through the impact of their ideas and the applicability of their techniques. Try to provide as many immediately useful ideas as possible. The best position papers can be used. The reader should come away from them saying, "I would like to apply this, and I would like to hear more from the author."

Position papers are one of the most economical, high-impact, and versatile aspects of the gravitational field. You probably have sufficient experience and ideas to create several dozen. Create short ones that are "plain vanilla" and straightforward and some longer ones with graphs and charts.

Basic Rule. Create one white paper every month.

Radio and Television Interviews

Do radio and even television appearances at any point in your career. They are relatively easy to do, since there is a constant need for fresh voices and faces to provide expert commentary on issues ranging from management fads to business etiquette to how to retain key talent.

As with the entire gravitational field, do not evaluate media interviews by number of "hits" or new business. Regard them strategically as an ongoing part of your major thrust to create recognition and higher levels of credibility. Some radio appearances may seem worthless in terms of short-term business, but you never know who will hear you and pass your name on or what other media professional might then invite you to a more appropriate setting.

Radio interviews should be done, with rare exception (such as National Public Radio and some major syndicated shows), from your home and over the phone. Television shots are done in the nearest local affiliate. For a memorable interview (most TV shots are only five to eight minutes, while some radio interviews can last for an hour), follow these rules:

- Provide the interviewer and/or segment producer with detailed background about you, including pronunciation of your name, and key "talking points" or questions to ask.

- Research the topic so you can quote a few dramatic statistics and anecdotes. The media love pithy sound bites. Practice short responses to all questions so more questions can be accommodated.

- Always have two or three points in mind that promote that you can work into responses no matter what the question. Do not rely on the host to promote you, no matter what the promises. Example: If the question is, "Alan, what is your opinion of large-scale downsizing and its impact on our society?" then answer this way: "One of the reasons I am asked to work with executives from top-performing organizations is that they want me to help them retain key talent, not throw it away. So let me answer from their perspective ... " If you have written a book, then say, "As I point out in Chapter Four of my newest book, *Good Enough Isn't Enough ...* "

- Obtain an MP3 download or other recording. Usually, asking the station in advance will do it, but always back it up with another taken from the actual airing by a friend. Splice these recordings/downloads together for a "highlights" reel of your media work, which will sell more sophisticated media outlets and just might get you on national TV. A recording is also impressive with prospects.

Radio and television work requires a promotional investment for ads and listing, but it is well worth it when you have reached the stage where your experience and accomplishments make you an "authority."

Basic Rule. Appear in a minimum of one major listing source with at least a half-page ad annually.

Electronic Sources and Social Media

Aside from your website, you have the potential to use blogs, Facebook, LinkedIn, and other social media to contact people, network, and show your capabilities. You're best off if you already have a brand, because people will follow you. Also consider a well-done (not generic or formulaic) blog to convey your intellectual property, ideas, reactions, and guest commentary. Use social media to keep people informed of what you're doing and why.

Basic Rule. Spend a little time with social media. Executives do not explore the web to find consultants; they rely on peer referrals and more public visibility.

Speaking

Early in people's consulting careers, I advocate they speak wherever and whenever they can to improve credibility and visibility. However, for the experienced consultant, professional speaking is not only a key gravitational pull but is also lucrative.

Audiences must be captivated and even entertained if they are to accept any message. The keynote spot at major conferences or in-house company meetings provides a terrific platform to reach hundreds (and sometimes thousands) of potential buyers and recommenders to establish the beginnings of a relationship with you at one time. This is not the place to go into the details of developing a professional speaking career, but we can examine a few key steps to consider.

- As a keynote speaker or concurrent session speaker, continually cite your experience and other organizations with which you have worked so the audience can think about how you might be helpful to them. *Always clarify that you are a consultant who speaks at such meetings and not a speaker who also consults.*

- Provide handouts with your company's name and full contact information.

- Obtain a participant list of everyone in your session.

- Come early and stay late so you can network with the organizers, senior management, participants, exhibitors, and others.

- Charge a high fee for your speaking, just as you would for your consulting. I suggest a three-part fee of increasing amounts for keynotes, half-days, and full-days.

I used to speak for free as a method to publicize what I do. Then, I realized that not only were others being paid, but that the speakers doing the most important spots were always the highest paid. Today, it is not unusual for a client to say, "I would like you to address our annual meeting, and then let us explore how you can work with us to implement the theme."

National Trade and Professional Associations of the United States (Columbia Books; www.columbiabooks.com) is an excellent resource if you want to find out which associations are holding meetings, the executive director, what the themes will be, who will be in the audience, and what the budget is.

Basic Rule. Speaking at least once a month in front of groups that include potential buyers.

Website and Electronic Newsletters

Your website should be state of the art and up to date from a marketing stand-point, not necessarily a technical one. It is not the bells and whistles that matter but the "draw" and appeal for potential customers. I often tell prospects to "be sure to visit my website" only to hear, "That is where I just came from." A high-powered website should follow these tenets:

- Sufficient search engine presence using generic and key words to drive people to the site
- A user-friendly initial page—with immediate appeal and options for the visitor
- Easy navigation and no "traps" that force visitors to hear more about your methodology than they would ever need to hear
- Immediate value in articles to download; links to related, high-quality sites; tools and techniques; and so forth
- An opportunity to contact you easily
- A compelling reason to return and to tell others about the site

By posting an article each month (still more utility provided by the position papers discussed earlier), new lists of techniques, and other value-added additions, you create a useful site. Develop and upgrade your site with the potential buyer in mind.

Electronic newsletters are a wonderful means by which to reach more buyers, since readers routinely pass excellent newsletters along to colleagues as a favor. Start with your current database, create a sign-up spot on your website, and offer the newsletter in your signature file on your email. An excellent electronic newsletter should:

- Be brief—on average, no longer than a single screen
- Be nonpromotional—and carry your contact information at the bottom
- Enable people to subscribe and unsubscribe easily (which is also required by law)
- Contain high-value content immediately applicable for most readers
- Go out at least monthly and regularly on the same day

- Be consistent and constant; consistency is everything
- Be copyrighted
- Use an ISSN number to protect your newsletter (the equivalent of an ISBN number on books): www.issn.org/.

One person in my mentoring program began with a modest list and soon had thousands of subscribers to his sales skills newsletter, which addressed "sales acceleration." He closed a piece of business with a bank in Toronto he never would have even spoken to without someone in the bank finding the newsletter and realizing that the bank's loan officers needed this sales help. Commercial list servers can automatically deliver the newsletter and add and delete subscribers for less than $50 per month.

Basic Rule. Consider a newsletter—either a monthly electronic one or at least a quarterly print version.

Word of Mouth, Referrals, and Third-Party Endorsements

All of us need to keep fueling the "buzz" that surrounds our names and our approaches. I have found that consultants become blasé about endorsements and testimonials after a while, but they are our stock-in-trade.

In every engagement, ask the client for a referral, a blurb for a product you are creating, to serve as a reference, and to provide a testimonial letter. If you do not ask, they rarely happen.

Write letters to magazines, newspapers, and electronic sources that rely on your credibility for the point you make, pro or con, relative to a recent article. Stand up at business, social, civic, and professional meetings to make your point. Take controversial and "contrarian" stands if you must.

Once you have an established reputation, it is far easier to maintain the momentum of word of mouth, which is a powerful lead source. But we rarely bother any longer, which is ironic, since it is now easier than ever. And this leads into other parts of the gravitation field. It is likely that some of your high-level buyers can place you in front of the trade associations to which they belong as a featured speaker at the next convention or meeting. Are you pursuing these connections?

Basic Rule. Active clients should provide a minimum of one testimonial and three highly qualified referrals every month. Ask for these very reasonable resources.

Trade Association Leadership

At this point in your career, when you may feel you are not getting anything out of professional associations and trade associations (and justifiably so, since most members will be at a lower level), it is time to use them differently. It is time to take a leadership position.

In the first case, the association and its membership can use your expertise and experience. In the second, it is a good way to "pay back" the profession that is so kind to us. And third, the visibility will be a tremendous source of gravity.

You do not have to take on time-consuming national duties. You can serve as an officer at the local or chapter level, head a committee, organize an event, or sponsor an initiative. Whatever it is, your status within the industry will be enriched. I find that many of my referrals come from other consultants who feel they cannot handle the assignment and hope I will either reciprocate time or involve them in the project, both of which I am happy to do. Since few capable people ever seek these offices, it is almost guaranteed that you can be as responsible and as visible as you choose.

Basic Rule. Belong to the Institute of Management Consultants (IMC; www .imcusa.org/), or the Society for Advancement of Consulting® (SAC; www .consultingsociety.com) and be known to your local membership, presenting a session at least once a year at a scheduled meeting.

Teaching

You will establish an entirely new circle of references and contacts through teaching part-time at a university, college, or extension program. You can earn the title of "adjunct professor" usually and teach one evening a week. The ideal is to teach at the graduate level, where you will be challenged by students and receive a diversity of opinions you might not experience in business life. These positions add immeasurably to your ability to become published, gain higher levels of credibility, and receive references from the university (and, sometimes, from the students).

You can almost always find a junior college or trade school to start out with if you are uncertain and want to test the waters—or do not possess the requisite doctorate for work at a senior institution.

Basic Rule. Teach as a guest lecturer three or four times a year at local institutions or by contract at national sites.

Alliances and Networking

I have placed these two together for discussion since alliances are often the result of effective networking. Interestingly, and short-sightedly, experienced consultants sometimes feel that their networking days are behind them. But that is only if you see networking as a tactic instead of a marketing strategy—and a strong aspect of gravitation. Among those who constitute networking potential for you are

- Buyers
- Media people
- Key vendors
- Mentors
- Endorsers
- Meeting planners
- Recommenders to buyers
- Bankers
- Key advisors
- High-profile individuals in your business
- Trade association executives
- Community leaders

Networking is far easier than ever, utilizing email, voice mail, instant messaging, social networking, and other communication alternatives, but nothing is as effective as the face-to-face interaction that allows for personal chemistry to develop. If possible, networking should be done in person. It should then be followed up or reinforced through other communications avenues.

Basic Rule. Network at some event at least twice a month and establish at least one useful contact from each one.

ESTABLISHING CONCEPTUAL AGREEMENT

Whether you contact people or they approach you due to "gravitational pull," you must achieve conceptual agreement on three basic issues prior to submitting a proposal. Most practitioners submit too many proposals too soon in the marketing process. Conceptual agreement means you and the economic buyer agree on:

1. *Objectives.* What are the outcome-based business objectives to be achieved through this project? There are usually only a handful in a cogent project. Keeping them tightly described avoids "scope creep" (the gradual enlargement of projects as clients keep asking for more tasks to be accomplished) through the focus on specific, mutually agreed-on goals.

2. *Measures of success.* What are the metrics that will indicate that you have made progress and/or reached the goals? Agreeing on these means that your proper contribution will be noted and the proper time to disengage has arrived.

3. *Value to the client.* What is the worth and impact of what you are accomplishing, *and is it annualized*? By stipulating to the value of the project, the client is focused on value and not fee and can make an appropriate ROI determination. If you are discussing fees and not value, you have lost control of the discussion.

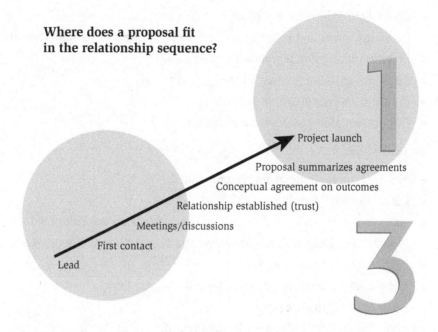

**Where does a proposal fit
in the relationship sequence?**

Project launch

Proposal summarizes agreements

Conceptual agreement on outcomes

Relationship established (trust)

Meetings/discussions

First contact

Lead

Figure 8.3. Conceptual Agreement as the Key to Closing New Business

Figure 8.3 shows the role of conceptual agreement in the overall marketing process. You can see two factors in Figure 8.3. First, conceptual agreement is the heart of the process. Second, the proposal should not be submitted until after conceptual agreement is gained, since it is merely a summation and not an exploration. Let us conclude by considering powerful proposals.

CREATING PROPOSALS THAT CLOSE BUSINESS

Let us begin with the parameters of what proposals can legitimately and pragmatically do and not do. Proposals should:

- Stipulate the outcomes of the project
- Describe how progress will be measured
- Establish accountabilities
- Set the intended start and stop dates
- Provide methodologies to be employed
- Explain options available to the client

- Convey the value of the project
- Detail the terms and conditions of payment of fees and reimbursements
- Serve as an ongoing template for the project
- Establish boundaries to avoid "scope creep"
- Protect both consultant and client
- Offer reasonable guarantees and assurances

Proposals should not:

- Sell the interventions being recommended
- Create the relationship
- Serve as a commodity against which other proposals are compared
- Provide the legitimacy and/or credentials of your firm and approaches
- Validate the proposed intervention
- Make a sale to a buyer you have not met
- Serve as a negotiating position
- Allow for unilateral changes during the project
- Protect one party at the expense of the other
- Position approaches so vaguely as to be immeasurable and unenforceable

There are nine steps to a great proposal which you can find in my work, *How to Write A Proposal that Can Be Accepted Every Time*, or you can find the steps on this book's website.

SUMMARY

We have discussed how to: (1) determine your value proposition; (2) identify your buyer; (3) establish routes to reach that buyer; (4) achieve conceptual agreement; and (5) create a proposal that will close business.

Marketing is the first of the OD phases to plan and facilitate change. The following chapters will take you through the pre-launch and launch phases of an OD intervention and beyond. However, unless you market effectively there will be no projects.

Discussion Questions

1. Do you find market needs changing for your expertise?
2. Are you periodically asking if your passions are changing?
3. Are you spending time on ideal or less-than-ideal buyers?

4. Are you meeting an average of two ideal buyers weekly?

5. What book topics would find appeal among your ideal buyers?

6. What events can you host that will attract buyers/recommenders?

Resources

Free articles, podcasts, and videos: www.summitconsulting.com www
.contrarianconsulting.com

Discussion groups: www.alansforums.com/

Speech at Harvard on consulting: www.youtube.com/watch?v = 9ztFJmapypw

CHAPTER NINE

Front-End Work

Engaging the Client System

David W. Jamieson and Rachael L. Narel

Engaging the client system is the front-end work critical in all service, consultation, and helping roles. It establishes the platform for success with sustainable outcomes as the quality of the relationship and contract drive your influence and the capability of the client to sustain and follow through. When an organization development (OD) practitioner initially enters a client system to facilitate change, several early outcomes must go well as the front-end phase serves as the platform for subsequent OD work. The quality and clarity of the foundation established at the outset will help or hinder subsequent work phases. Often, challenges encountered later in change work can be traced to missed or flawed outcomes during this initial intervention phase.

All OD practitioner relationships require a sound beginning regardless of philosophical orientation, style, or approach. Any helper must contract for the work, create relationships, build rapport, establish credibility, and validate the issues and needs within the organization. This will help clarify what the OD practitioner must do, who they will need to work with, how they will conduct the process, how fast it will need to occur, and what the results should look like.

This phase rarely falls neatly, distinctly, or sequentially between the marketing and closing activities and the assessment and diagnosis work. Because of this complexity, some elements can occur while obtaining the work and continue throughout the engagement. For this chapter, front-end work begins when an OD practitioner has a client with a desire to work, and when the activities associated with marketing, selling, and closing have been completed.

It concludes when the OD practitioner and client have clarified the change effort, their working relationships, their expectations, and their contract; and when they are ready to proceed with more extensive diagnosis or other initial activities. However, front-end work is, in reality, a series of outcomes that comprise an ongoing effort as the cyclical nature of organization development requires entry and contracting throughout the engagement.

In business today, front-end work requires even more iterative action (Burke 2010). In the early years of OD, the concept of planned change was useful in that one was intervening using a systematic approach to effect some desired change and the environment was relatively placid. The inherent complexities, uncontrollable variables, unanticipated events, and speed of environmental change will undoubtedly affect modifications in outcomes and any change plans (Jamieson 2003). Some front-end activities ordinarily create some "unfreezing," but most organizations today experience rapid, continuous change, chaos, and uncertainty, and are quite "unfrozen" (Weisbord 2012; Worley and Lawler 2010).

As Burke (2014) has emphasized, much of the work of implementing change today is about managing reactions of people and organizations, balancing multiple interventions simultaneously, handling complex variables, and adapting. A consultant cannot plan change or work in sequential phases, yet still must accomplish certain outcomes involving entry and contracting at the beginning and throughout the engagement. This is the dilemma of front-end work that OD practitioners face today. This chapter explores the critical elements of front-end work and illustrates how to engage with a client system to achieve sustainable change.

THE ESSENCE OF THE FRONT END

The essence of the front-end phase is to enter the client's world, build a platform for engaging in change work, and contract for work, methods, relationships, and exchanges. Everything done to obtain these early outcomes is an intervention, affecting the client system (Bruce and Wyman 1998) from first contact, early questions, discussions, and gathering diagnostic information (Schein 2010). These help consultants understand the organization (values, vision, and needs); identify initial clients and sponsors; preliminarily assess helps or hindrances of change; agree on work tasks and methods; and establish relationships characterized by mutual openness, trust, and influence. Achieving these outcomes is critical to the success of the change effort and ensures a client-focused project on the "right" path, with the right relationships, using the correct methods, working within the specified time, and eliciting the proper support. Since resources such as time and money are valuable, it is the responsibility of both the OD practitioner and client to conduct sound front-end work.

Front-end work is relevant for both internal and external OD practitioners. While internal practitioners may know the client and the organization, they can also be enmeshed in the culture and see the world as the clients do. They should not make early assumptions about what needs to be done or what has to be clarified. External OD practitioners (i.e., consultants) must do more to become familiar with the organization and contract financial arrangements. However, both must establish a sound platform during front-end work.

In building the foundation for working together on change, certain issues must be addressed and certain agreements must be made. Seven key elements must be realized at the outset and at other key junctures during the engagement:

1. Identifying the client(s) and sponsor(s).
2. Becoming oriented to the client's world.
3. Establishing competence and credibility.
4. Developing an open, trusting, and aligned relationship.
5. Completing a preliminary diagnostic scan.
6. Contracting for the work, working relations, and exchange.
7. Introducing the engagement and consultant(s) to the larger organization.

IDENTIFYING THE CLIENT(S) AND SPONSOR(S)

It is not always possible to know immediately who all the players in the client organization will be or who will be involved, but those who are known and who are possible key players should be the early focus of attention (French and Bell 1999) whether an individual, a group, or even multiple clients. Sometimes the client at the outset is replaced by subsequent clients as the intervention progresses (Cummings and Worley 2014). There may be a primary client directly involved and secondary clients influenced by the results. Also there are differences in sponsors, who initiate and often pay for the work but have minor participation, and clients, who have direct or indirect participation and impact. It's important to clarify client(s) and sponsor(s) because it requires contracts with each, and their involvement, responsibility, and perspective are critical for success.

Burke (1994) offers another perspective on identifying clients. He suggests the relationship and/or interface between individuals or units comprise the client. Identifying interactions and interrelationships in the issues or central focus of a desired future identifies the players. This concept is supported from the classic work on consulting as intervention by Argyris (1970): "To intervene is to enter into the ongoing system of relationships, to come between or among persons, groups, or objects for the purpose of helping them" (15).

The importance of client identification is further illustrated by Schein (1997), who defined six basic clients in complex systems:

1. Contact clients: Individual(s) who make first contact with a request, question, or issue.

2. Intermediate clients: Individuals or groups involved in various interviews, meetings, and other activities as the project evolves.

3. Primary clients: Individual(s) who ultimately "own(s)" the issue being worked on or the desired future being developed; typically also own(s) budget.

4. Unwitting clients: Members of the organization or client system above, below, and laterally related to primary clients who are affected by interventions but are not aware of it.

5. Indirect clients: Members who know that they will be affected but who are unknown.

6. Ultimate clients: The community, total organization, or any other group whose welfare must be considered in any intervention (202–203).

For many in OD, the health and vitality of the whole organization, its various subsystems, and its individual members define "client" in the broadest sense.

While each project is unique, initially there is a discussion with one person from the organization that is then broadened to a group of key sponsors, management, or employees. These group members may continue as clients or become engagement sponsors. Depending on the interventions, a new group, such as a design team, may become the client. The consultant may also be asked to work as a co-consultant with others from inside or outside the organization or department. These co-relationships can become problematic and careful clarification is required, however, as roles can range from being helper, to equal partner, to the "real" client.

Clients and sponsors can have different perspectives, work styles, and levels of influence. Sometimes the OD practitioner may need to work with people who cannot make necessary intervention-related decisions, requiring the involvement of other decision makers or may sometimes listen too much to one group over others. Direct clients may not agree on a key sponsor. All viewpoints should be included; if (unknowingly) the OD practitioner is not in contact with all key players, inappropriate courses of action may happen or work derailed by powerful players excluded. It is important at the front end to identify and create alignment in contracting among all clients and sponsors.

BECOMING ORIENTED TO THE CLIENT'S WORLD

People in organizations operate from perceptions of reality influenced by their experiences, their organization's history and culture, work technology and processes, beliefs and assumptions about their organization, industry, and competitors, and how work should be performed. The OD practitioner must understand and appreciate how the clients perceive their world; this involves questioning, observing, and reading.

OD practitioners should also familiarize themselves with characteristics of the client system, including work, structure, technology, culture, and people. This is a significant part of what Margulies and Raia (1978) called "mapping." Because organizations are systems, parts and interconnections must be understood and change must be viewed in its largest context. When becoming familiar with the client's world, the consultant must know what else the organization is doing, working on, or changing to integrate and coordinate the change effort appropriately.

This provides the OD practitioner a foundation; a way of understanding language, fears, desires, frustrations, and present state. It provides a basis for relating, introducing alternative thinking, different frameworks, and new ideas. It also demonstrates the OD practitioner cares, is credible, and connects with people through their reality. This connection can be powerful because it's important to start where the system is (Shepard 1985). This foundation can also help the consultant talk about change or desired future states grounded in current reality.

ESTABLISHING THE CONSULTANT'S COMPETENCE AND CREDIBILITY

The competence and credibility of the OD practitioner rest in the eye of the beholder: the client(s). The client must perceive the OD practitioner as competent and credible *for their organization and change situation* for the OD practitioner to be influential. OD practitioners depend on influence since they have no formal power or authority. Influence derives from the social power (French and Raven 1959) they receive from clients based in part on developing competence and credibility in the clients' eyes.

Clients may have different criteria in mind when they assess an OD practitioner's competence, so they need to understand background, related experience, and values. Burke (1994) adds that clients assess competence and trustworthiness, whether they can relate well, and if previous experience applies to the present situation. Positive perception of competence and credibility can reduce client anxiety in receiving help (Lundberg 1997). Continuous and obsessive questioning of background, past experience, and credentials is often a sign of resistance, dressed as concern for competence. It needs to be addressed early so it can be dealt with appropriately.

Knowledge, skills, experience, values, and work style must fit the change intervention and client(s) needs. The OD practitioner must be appropriate for the work and client situation (Lippitt and Lippitt 1986) and is just as responsible as the client in determining a match (Greiner and Metzger 1983). Few clients are sophisticated enough to understand differences in expertise and specialties. It is ineffective and unethical for an OD practitioner to work on a project for which he or she lacks competence. Engaging guidance of someone more experienced or creating a team arrangement provides requisite skills and the OD practitioner can learn and build competence.

Competence comes from various areas. It may result from expertise in a particular content area required for the intervention, such as work-process redesign. Competence also may result from the OD practitioner's expertise in process design and facilitation, such as ability to involve people, run large groups, generate new ideas, or reach consensus. It also may be based on outcomes of previous work, understanding of the situation, or their writings or teachings.

Credibility is associated with more than just the right knowledge and competencies; authenticity, honesty, and confidence contribute. It is enhanced when strengths and limitations are discussed, concerns are voiced, and confidence or enthusiasm is expressed. Credibility grows from ability to organize action, such as next steps and sequencing. Ultimately, the success of an intervention depends both on what is done and the effectiveness of the client-OD practitioner relationship.

Competence and credibility can easily be underplayed or overplayed. If too much time is devoted to displaying credentials, discussing successes, or naming bigger clients, some clients may become intimidated or put off. Demonstrate expertise, establish credibility, and share experience to gain confidence and comfort without giving a sales pitch, creating dependence, or setting expectations of solving the client's problem (Lippitt and Lippitt 1986).

DEVELOPING AN OPEN, TRUSTING, AND ALIGNED RELATIONSHIP

Developing an effective working relationship is essential for gaining client trust, building support from power brokers, and ensuring influence (Jamieson and Armstrong 2010). The client-consultant relationship provides an understanding of culture and continual data on progress of the work (Schein 2010). Through relationships much of the consultation occurs (Jamieson 1998), and Old (1995) describes the nature of this relationship as "partnering." It must be built on a foundation of mutual openness, confidence, and trust (French and Bell 1999). Confidence comes from perception of competence and credibility. Openness is important because all information must be shared, including important information about organizational and personal concerns, fears, and everyone's opinions.

Trust is essential, especially since the OD practitioner and client must rely on each other for an unimpeded flow of information to decide. The OD practitioner must feel his or her skills are being used properly with the right motives; clients must feel that their confidential information will be properly handled and the OD practitioner is working for their best interests. They do not have to agree on everything but have to be candid, discuss differences, and clarify how to proceed.

Major barriers to openness and trust can stem from a client's negative past experiences with other consultants, organization culture, or vulnerability. OD practitioners, as role models, have to take initiative showing support, sharing realistic concerns, expressing reservations or optimism, modeling openness and authenticity, talking honestly about what has worked and what has not, and discussing their working relationship. However, barriers can also stem from "who" the OD practitioner is and his or her "self" strengths and issues (Eisen 2010; Jamieson 2003; Jamieson, Auron, and Shechtman 2010; Keister and Paranjpey 2012). Fears, personal needs, values, and unresolved emotional issues all translate into what one can see, understand, and do.

Openness and trust also emanate from a foundation of alignment, honesty, and authenticity. To establish such a foundation, all must maintain a continuing dialogue about what is meaningful, significant, compelling, or frightening; addressing issues as they arise. They must discuss what forces support and hinder the success of the intervention, motivations underlying the change effort, and what they find exciting about the desired future (Jamieson and Armstrong 2010).

Values are also an important part of achieving alignment; everyone operates with desired methods and results in mind. OD practitioners often bring to a change effort perspectives that contain such principles as a high regard for employee involvement, empowerment, and respect for human dignity. The OD practitioner must know which of the client's values relate to the change effort, what the client is changing for or changing to, and how compatible these values are with those of the OD practitioner (Jamieson and Gellermann 2014).

Mixed feelings about a change effort can lead to resistance on contracting closure. Additional barriers are created if clients find it difficult to understand or work with the OD practitioner. Satisfaction and comfort during change work are affected by how clients are included, informed, and what is asked of them.

Often, the consultant experiences a mix of support and resistance from clients throughout the work; elation after a discussion of intended end states but discomfort after reviewing a methodology that differs from preferences. Without contracting, readiness checking, and commitment testing throughout early interactions, many forms of passivity, discomfort, or sparring may show up.

Margulies and Raia (1978) stressed the importance of consultant-client "fit" and described the quality of the relationship as dependent on value systems, competency, and ability to "help" with the perceived challenge, experience with other consultants, expectations about the OD practitioner's role and process, personalities and interpersonal styles, and compatibility with needs and objectives. Massarik and Pei-Carpenter (2002) describe this relationship as interconnecting "selves" with the overlay defining congruence of styles, needs, objectives, and values. Mitchell (2010) also discusses the importance of alignment of client and OD practitioner preferences on approaches.

In developing open, trusting, and aligned OD practitioner-client relationships, the OD practitioner's ultimate value is in maintaining a boundary position (Cummings and Worley 2014) with marginality and objectivity (Margulies and Raia 1978). Becoming intimately involved with the culture yet remaining apart from it provides detachment and objectivity required for effective work. It involves an ability to understand and empathize with the system while avoiding becoming so acculturated that one mirrors the same biases and subjectivity. Ability to not be absorbed by culture (French and Bell 1999) and remain free from organizational forces that might distort the OD practitioner's view of the organization and its issues should not be compromised in developing a quality client–OD practitioner relationship.

COMPLETING A PRELIMINARY DIAGNOSTIC SCAN

In a preliminary diagnostic scan, OD practitioner and client are "scouting" (Kolb and Frohman 1970), which involves developing a general understanding of:

- Current state (presenting issues and needs, culture, vision);
- Potential sources of resistance and support;
- Apparent power and political system; and
- Perception of the organization's readiness, commitment, and capability.

The Current State

At the front end, the OD practitioner attempts to learn enough about client and change desires to contract effectively for initial work. One must approach this aspect with a spirit of inquiry and neutrality, accessing one's ignorance (Schein 1997), and avoiding inappropriate assumptions or premature conclusions about the situation and treating hunches as hypotheses. It is also important to know of and control diagnostic orientation and biases to avoid creating self-fulfilling prophecies (Lippitt, Watson, and Westley 1958).

In a preliminary scan, OD practitioners should not strive to obtain great detail; rather, they look to understand issues, possibilities, and relationships among them. In part, OD practitioners are trying to achieve clarity and elevate confidence about what to work on and how, while serving as an organization mirror (Bruce and Wyman 1998), sharpening clients' understanding. OD practitioners are also trying to establish the validity of current state (Cummings and Worley 2014) and determine commonality of perceptions or distinctions among viewpoints; they should seek information from multiple parties.

Sometimes OD practitioners are trying to scope the situation to design a diagnostic approach, and at other times gauging the possibilities and strength of resources to plan an appreciative process. They want enough knowledge of the issue(s), resources, and desires to enable informed choices about proceeding with the engagement (Cummings and Worley 2014). OD practitioners may have to facilitate discussions to surface real strengths, issues, and challenge beliefs, and review studies, memos, or other documents that relate to the issues, needs, and viewpoints. It may be helpful to observe regular meetings or tour work areas to see the operations, interactions, and culture at work. A preliminary scan will help contract for, and place the change on, the right path.

Support, Resistance, Power, and Politics

When performing the scan, OD practitioners should also note who appears to support or resist and why to help crystallize motives and personal agendas. Supporters and resisters may dramatize real hurdles ahead or identify key considerations in designing content and process. Resistance provides valuable data and can be an indicator of missing information, lack of understanding, poor prior involvement, and disagreement with some aspect of what's planned, power assertions, or violation of existing norms.

It is also important to identify potential leverage points for change (Burke 1994) by understanding the power system and political dynamics (Greiner and Schein 1988). Knowledge of the power structure can positively help leverage change (Cobb 1986; Cobb and Margulies 1981; Greiner and Schein 1988). Who has significant influence, how decisions are made, and who has expertise are all pertinent to the change effort. It is imperative to learn about the motives, perspectives, and values of those in power in the organization to understand political dynamics inherent in its culture. Greiner and Metzger (1983) refer to this aspect of consulting as "meeting the power structure."

Readiness, Commitment, and Capability

When performing the preliminary scan, OD practitioners should assess organizational readiness, level of commitment, capability of members, and extent of resources available to support the effort (Burke 1994), including commitment of key stakeholders. People can be against change direction, neutral about letting it happen, passively for it, or wanting to make it happen (Beckhard and Harris 1987). Assessing commitment to change by those involved helps ascertain the strength of change champions and how much readiness building is needed.

The capability of organizational members is measured by knowledge and experience with change, change processes, and level of required skills, including ability to participate, work productively in groups, function openly, think creatively, and flexibility. In some organizations, this could be new, counter-cultural, and people may be highly rigid. Others may be accustomed to change, having learning cultures (Senge 2006; Worley and Lawler 2010), with employees who seek variety and innovation. Being familiar with an organization's change competence can help determine how much education or skill building should be included in the intervention strategy and how to use the organization's human resources during the change.

A preliminary diagnostic scan will often move the client from wanting a simple training solution to desiring a more complex reexamination of the organization's work structure or culture or a participative assessment/planning process. Alternatively, when present-state descriptions are presented by the client, they may be full of attributions and can be seen more accurately only by surfacing real causes. Skipping or short-cutting preliminary diagnostic scanning can be disastrous. Without a good understanding of "reality," subsequent work can be off-target, designed too narrowly, or end up as "a hammer looking for a nail." If an OD practitioner hurries to begin intervention, resistance may be elevated, necessitating unnecessary remedial work. The OD practitioner must help pinpoint real needs and intentions. Only then is it possible to contract appropriately and design diagnostic and action strategies effectively.

CONTRACTING THE WORK, WORKING RELATIONSHIPS, AND EXCHANGE

The information learned so far provides a foundation for the contracting process and data for identifying content of work and contracts (Boss 1985). The term "contracting" is appropriate given its original roots; tractus: to draw something along; con: with someone else (Bruce and Wyman, 1998). In consulting, contracting means establishing and clarifying expectations about the change effort, working relationship(s), consulting support needs, and financial or other arrangements. Contracting is a focus during the front end, but will be continuous in some respects and reopened as conditions change.

Block (2011) refers to contracting as an explicit agreement about what all parties should expect and how they should work together. This can be a formal document or verbal agreement where wants, offers, and concerns of everyone are clarified and agreement is reached through negotiation. Weisbord (1973) defines contracting as an explicit exchange of expectations, clarifying what all parties expect to obtain from the relationship, time invested, when, and at what cost, and basic ground rules.

Contracting allows good decisions to be made about how to carry out the change process (Beer 1980) and sets the tone for the entire intervention (Block 2011), establishing clarity needed to have effective working relationships and avoiding subsequent surprises or problems that derail projects. The organizations or persons with whom OD practitioners should contract will depend on who is identified as different client(s), sponsor(s), and other key player(s). OD practitioners may sometimes need to perform primary contracting for all aspects of a change effort and working relationships with some client(s), but auxiliary contracting for parts of the change effort or limited relationship needs with others.

Contracting for the Work

The OD practitioner should begin by gaining agreement about desired results, intended outcomes, value proposition(s), and options, methods, timing, and accountabilities anticipated. They should establish critical success factors or organizational effectiveness criteria that can later be used in evaluating success (Smither, Houston, and McIntire 1996). These can include objective, measurable outcomes, such as reduced turnover or quality improvements, and/or more subjective attitude or behavior outcomes, such as improved morale or positive group dynamics. However, there is no guarantee of improvement in human systems work. Often, it is impossible to directly correlate changes to the intervention and there are external, uncontrollable factors that can negatively affect change, such as an economic downturn. Regardless, there can be no change or improvement without full support and committed participation of the organization, hence the mutual nature of contracting process and change. Boss (1985), Lippitt and Lippitt (1986), and Schein (1988) have all stressed the importance of joint responsibility of clients and OD practitioners during contracting.

Developing consensus on strategy and methods will produce more detailed information on project boundaries, work tasks, and data requirements; which people are involved and how; where work occurs; sequencing; timing and pace; how technology will be used in data collection or ongoing communication; deliverables; and approximate duration. Flexibility should be included in contractual language because there are still many unknowns. Even though there may not be a separate assessment or diagnosis phase, contracting for how data will be generated and used as effective interventions requires valid and useful data, free and informed choice, and internal commitment (Argyris 1970) leading to action taking.

The result of contracting is often a plan that is more specific and detailed for immediate next steps, such as diagnosis, and more general for subsequent cycles of design, intervention, and implementation. Sometimes contracting is broken into phases, such as education, diagnosis, design, and implementation work, or preparation, design, and execution of a large-scale event. It is helpful to include key decision points in the change plan for review.

Contracting for Working Relations

The most in-depth relationship contracting occurs with the direct client(s) addressing the full range of relationship issues and developing a working relationship. In developing working relations, OD practitioner and client are contracting primarily for psychosocial aspects of the relationship and creating an interpersonal relationship for changing the organization (Bruce and Wyman 1998). Trust and openness are of central importance. In addition, OD practitioners will find it essential to clarify their roles, client roles, and expectations from each other, how they should work and plan together, and how they should reach critical decisions (Jamieson and Armstrong 2010).

Unless there is mutual understanding and agreement about the process, there is significant risk that one or both parties' expectations will not be met (Bellman 1990). It is reasonable to expect that roles and needs will change during the project; contracting requires recycling, the OD practitioner and client asking for what they want or need (Block 2011; Boss 1985), and each having self-awareness and clarity of individual motives and values (Smither et al. 1996). "Self as an instrument of change" (Eisen 2010; Jamieson 2003; Jamieson et.al. 2010) is particularly accentuated in contracting since outcomes depend on what each person can put on the table, knowing what's personally important to stand firm on, and how each honors agreements.

OD practitioners have numerous orientation, role, and style choices based on who they are and what the system requires (Jamieson 1998) which are a part of establishing expectations and "fit." They might position themselves in the foreground, central in change work and highly visible, or in the background, working through the client(s), educating and building their capability through transferring knowledge and skills, being task or process oriented (Margulies and Raia 1978), or relying more on the client's knowledge and experiences than their own. OD practitioners can be more or less directive, supportive, confrontive, or facilitative (Jamieson 1998; Lippitt and Lippitt 1986), serving as experts, pairs of hands, or collaborators (Block 2011). These choices create different dynamics in the client-consultant relationship and meet different client system change needs and parties' personal needs.

Harvey and Brown (2001) identified five consultant styles based on the emphasis on effectiveness or goal accomplishment, relationships, morale, and participant satisfaction:

1. Stabilizer: Low on effectiveness and satisfaction; keep from rocking the boat; low profile.

2. Cheerleader: High on satisfaction and morale; smoothes differences, maintains harmony; nonconfrontational.

3. Analyzer: High on goal accomplishment; rational problem solving; operates from expertise.

4. Persuader: Focus on both dimensions; optimizes neither; low risk; motivated to satisfy differing forces.

5. Pathfinder: Seeks high effectiveness and satisfaction; collaborative problem solving; challenges organization.

An insightful study identified the client's profile of the ideal consultant: listens, but does not sell; fits into the organization, embracing its mission and culture; teaches internal staff, helping them achieve independence; provides good customer service; protects confidentiality; challenges assumptions; recognized expert; provides perspective and objectivity; and celebrates with the organization (Bader and Stich 1983).

There are critical implications to clarifying if the primary client's role includes project manager, co-consultant, or decision maker. The more OD practitioners act as experts on substantive content issues, the less effective they will be on managing process (French and Bell 1999) and the more they intrude on a needed client role. If the client(s) acts in a co-consultant role, they lose power and context of being the decision maker (Jamieson and Armstrong 2010).

Sponsors and key power players also want different levels of involvement; some joining in, others observing; all need to be informed and provide input. Contracting here involves determining level of participation, contributions, and updates and faith in the OD practitioner's ability to pursue their objectives. If others will be involved later, it may be helpful to brief them on the project, determine communication mechanisms, estimate timing and level of impact, and discuss, if appropriate, preparation for participating.

Once roles have been discussed, working processes and expectations such as meeting frequency, planning, and facilitation, and communications and accessibility can be clarified. Work styles also must be considered as some people require very detailed designs and discussions; others work well with general outlines. Some require everything to be data-based; others work well from intuition, a concept, value, or vision. Other issues include how quickly people learn and work; preferences for working alone or collaboratively; and tolerance for ambiguity, flexibility, and risk taking. Sometimes, these are compatible and relationship contracting is easy. When they are not compatible, clarity and compromise may be necessary to minimize tension and frustration.

Ground rules often originate from work styles, involvement, and information-sharing discussions. Agreements such as "It's okay to call me at home" or "We will share everything and avoid surprises" provide everyone with understanding of what is acceptable and effective. These might relate to anticipating problems, listening, equality, timeliness, logistics, or how each party grows and develops. All must clarify and agree on how they will work together in a trusting, productive, and rewarding manner.

The OD practitioner should also discuss termination options during contracting, including planned termination and transfer of expertise, circumstances causing breach of contract, who can terminate, and penalties for premature termination.

Organization Development Practitioner Support Needs

Sometimes OD practitioners need help to see the change effort through to a successful conclusion, including administrative assistance and other support services. These services may be supplied by either the client or the OD practitioner. Frequent on-sites may require office space, clerical help or travel, and lodging arrangements. Many interventions require members of the organization to supply and/or analyze data. Which party is responsible for the expenses associated with these items? If questions about support are left unanswered, they may cause misunderstandings or lead to a situation in which support tasks are not carried out and aspects of the engagement are handled poorly.

Organization Development Practitioner-Client Exchange

The last aspect of contracting involves the "what" and "how" of the exchange. Most involve financial payments, but it is possible to barter for using developed materials, exchange of services, or OD practitioner learning, for equity. When financial arrangements are used, client and OD practitioner must agree on rates, expenses, and billable time definitions, and provide estimate of effort and cost up front. Invoice processes including recipient, level of detail, payment terms, and fees should be clarified. There are often sensitivities and misunderstandings related to money; be clear about billing and payment procedures and document them.

Both parties should discuss any changes affecting the financial arrangement, such as utilizing the budget faster than anticipated or unanticipated cuts in funding. They should also discuss, periodically, change effort progress in relation to expenditures. When cost-benefit relationship does not seem correlated, everyone's concerns should grow: People do not want to spend substantial sums of money without witnessing visible progress toward goals!

Throughout contracting, the OD practitioner must pay attention to ethical issues to establish the right boundaries, relationship, and work methods. White and Wooten (1983) summarized ethical dilemmas in OD: misrepresentation and collusion, misuse of data, manipulation and coercion, value and goal conflicts, and technical ineptness. Page (1998) added client dependency. It is common in OD to ensure that participation is voluntary; protection from harm, confidentiality of information, individual data are owned by individuals; and the organization owns nonconfidential and nonanonymous data (Smither et al. 1996). OD practitioners should not misrepresent their abilities, require clients to overly depend on them, or collude with one part of an organization against another part. Gellermann and Egan (2010) suggest ethical dilemmas in OD are created through conflict between competing rights, obligations, and interests. Remembering these will help improve the quality of OD contracting and practice.

Each situation is unique; contracting must be customized to meet individual and mutual needs of both parties. It should enhance rather than interfere with the working relationship. Contracting is a complex, human-interactive process requiring sensitivity, skill, and flexibility.

INTRODUCING THE ENGAGEMENT TO THE ORGANIZATION

Introducing the OD engagement and OD practitioner(s) can be difficult. The OD practitioner must know culture and systems to present the intervention properly. If people are not informed before the OD practitioner arrives, they might resist. The "who" and "how" of the introduction affects credibility, and the wrong person or method of communication could begin the intervention poorly.

Involvement of key members in the introduction helps others to see the work as important, cross-organizational, and not "owned" by one person, group, or faction; the OD practitioner, client, and sponsors can all have roles. Part of the introduction should be in writing to have a clear statement without multiple interpretations (Greiner and Metzger 1983) providing rationale for what is being started and why. More than one medium, such as email notification followed by a small group session, can be beneficial. Today, technology can be used posting this information on the company website or intranet for review and response.

OD practitioners can also meet key people informally before the introduction to build comfort and rapport while minimizing feelings of concern. Providing personal and professional information about themselves can also help build credibility and the larger client's confidence.

How various parts of the organization will be involved or affected should determine how much time and effort should be devoted to the introduction. Some people should just be informed; others should be involved in two-way forums to ensure they understand the intervention and what to expect. The OD practitioner should know how information is usually introduced, but may want to differentiate the change effort with a new process if its method is ineffective.

SUMMARY

Numerous difficulties arising in OD interventions can be traced to flaws in the front-end phase. Difficulties can stem from misunderstanding the organization, ignoring issues associated with power structure, disagreeing about work methods, not reaching agreements on rates or time commitments, or clashing work styles. Setbacks and issues can be avoided if a consultant takes care to address them early on.

Consultants must work carefully in surfacing organizational issues or starting down a new path with a client; working to instill trust and matching their personal styles to expectations of multiple players. Starting OD projects takes on great significance because change is inherently risky and both parties also face uncertainty and ambiguity. OD practitioners can be lured by feelings of competence, unworthiness, or dependency to engage in inappropriate agreements or ones not in their best interest. Change can engender feelings of vulnerability, guilt, or inadequacy in clients, intensifying emotions in ways that complicate helping relationships.

The concept of "self as instrument" (Eisen 2010; Jamieson 2003; Jamieson et. al. 2010; Keister and Paranjpey 2012) is central to understanding OD work. OD practitioners are change agents who have to rely on thoughts, feelings, strengths, and weaknesses throughout their work. Quade and Brown (2002) take this concept to a new level discussing the importance of being "conscious consultants" who enlarge awareness of who they are, their styles and ways of thinking, working, and interacting, and who actively track and change implicit models and assumptions in their work. In each engagement, one is using self and growing self.

Authenticity and skills are central to establishing effective working relationships that contribute to successful change. OD practitioners cannot be too needy or too greedy, too passive or too controlling. They have to remain marginal to the system yet remain close enough to the change effort and the people to obtain valid data and to instill trust and confidence.

Work that OD practitioners do is affected by how quick they are to judge, criticize, or conclude. Communicating, listening, and probing effectively will increase understanding and ease client fears. Confronting others appropriately and giving timely and effective feedback will increase clients' clarity about issues and authenticity in approaching problems and solutions. How well OD practitioners adapt to cultures may determine the success of their interventions. The front-end work will be greatly improved by their ability to elicit hope, facilitate discussions, work collaboratively, empathize, and assert their points of view.

Discussion Questions

1. What have you found most challenging during front-end work?

2. What are your best practices for the front-end outcomes?

3. What have you found most critical in how your use of self shows up during this front-end work?

4. Where do you see opportunities for improving current practices?

5. Where do you see similarities or differences in opportunities and challenges for internal and external OD practitioners?

Resources

For more information on the contract and entry phase: http://organisationdevelopment .org/the-od-cycle/the-contracting-and-entry-phase/www.zeepedia.com/read.php? entering_and_contracting_clarifying_the_organizational_issue_selecting_an_od_ practitioner_organization_development&b = 52&c = 14

References

Argyris, C. 1970. *Intervention Theory and Method: A Behavioral Science View*. Reading, MA: Addison-Wesley.

Bader, G., and T. Stich. 1983. "Building the Consulting Relationship." *Training & Development Journal* 43: 55–60.

Beckhard, R., and R. Harris. 1987. *Organizational Transitions*. 2nd ed. Reading, MA: Addison-Wesley.

Beer, M. 1980. *Organization Change and Development: A Systems View*. Santa Monica, CA: Goodyear.

Bellman, G. 1990. *The Consultant's Calling*. San Francisco: Jossey-Bass.

Block, P. 2011. *Flawless Consulting: A Guide to Getting Your Expertise Used*. 3rd ed. San Francisco: Pfeiffer.

Boss, W. 1985. "The Psychological Contract: A Key to Effective Organization Development Consultation." *Consultation* 4 (4): 284–304.

Bruce, R., and S. Wyman. 1998. *Changing Organizations: Practicing Action Training and Research*. Thousand Oaks, CA: Sage.

Burke, W. 1994. *Organization Development: Learning and Changing*. 2nd ed. Reading, MA: Addison-Wesley.

Burke, W. 2010. "Consulting in the Fast Lane." In *Consultation for Organizational Change*, edited by A. Buono and D. Jamieson, 233–246. Charlotte, NC: Information Age.

Burke, W. 2014. *Organization Change: Theory and Practice*. 4th ed. Thousand Oaks, CA: Sage.

Cobb, A. 1986. "Political Diagnosis: Applications in Organization Development." *Academy of Management Review* 11: 482–496.

Cobb, A., and N. Margulies. 1981. "Organization Development: A Political Perspective." *Academy of Management Review* 6: 49–59.

Cummings, T., and C. Worley. 2014. *Organization Development and Change*. 10th ed. Cincinnati, OH: Southwestern College Publishing.

Eisen, S. 2010. "The Personhood of the OD Practitioner." In *Practicing Organization Development and Change: A Guide to Leading Change*, 3rd ed., edited by W. Rothwell, J. Stavros, and R. Sullivan, 527–535. San Francisco: Pfeiffer.

French, J., and B. Raven. 1959. The Bases of Social Power. In *Studies in Social Power*, edited by D. Cartwright, 150–167. Ann Arbor, MI: University of Michigan, Institute for Social Research.

French, W., and C. Bell. 1999. *Organization Development: Behavioral Science Interventions for Organization Improvement*. 6th ed. Englewood Cliffs, NJ: Prentice-Hall.

Gellermann, W., and T. Egan. 2010. "Values, Ethics and Expanding the Practice of OD." In *Practicing Organization Development and Change: A Guide to Leading Change*, 3rd ed., edited by W. Rothwell, J. Stavros, and R. Sullivan, 492–501. San Francisco: Pfeiffer.

Greiner, L., and R. Metzger. 1983. *Consulting to Management*. Englewood Cliffs, NJ: Prentice-Hall.

Greiner, L., and V. Schein. 1988. *Power and Organization Development*. Reading, MA: Addison-Wesley.

Harvey, D., and D. Brown. 2001. *An Experiential Approach to Organization Development*. 6th ed. Upper Saddle River, NJ: Prentice-Hall.

Jamieson, D. 1998. "Your Consulting Style." *Consulting Today* 2 (1): 1–2.

Jamieson, D. 2003. "The Heart and Mind of the Practitioner: Remembering Bob Tannenbaum." *OD Practitioner* 35 (4), 3–8.

Jamieson, D., and T. Armstrong. 2010. "Client-Consultant Engagement: What It Takes to Create Value." In *Consultation for Organization Change*, edited by A. Buono and D. Jamieson, 3–13. Charlotte, NC: Information Age.

Jamieson, D., M. Auron, and D. Shechtman. 2010. "Managing 'Use of Self' for Masterful Professional Practice." *OD Practitioner* 42: 3.

Jamieson, D., and W. Gellermann. 2014. "Values, Ethics and OD Practice." In *The NTL Handbook of Organization Development and Change*, 2nd ed., edited by M. Brazzel and B. Jones, 45–66. San Francisco: Pfeiffer.

Keister, A., and N. Paranjpey. 2012. "Self as Instrument: Dual Consulting Identities the Evaluator and the Designer." *Organization Development Journal* 30 (2): 85–97.

Kolb, D., and A. Frohman. 1970. "An Organization Development Approach to Consulting." *Sloan Management Review* 12: 51–65.

Lippitt, G., and R. Lippitt. 1986. *The Consulting Process in Action*. 2nd ed. San Francisco: Pfeiffer.

Lippitt, R., J. Watson, and B. Westley. 1958. *The Dynamics of Planned Change*. New York: Harcourt Brace Jovanovich.

Lundberg, C. 1997. "Towards a General Model of Consultancy: Foundations." *Journal of Organizational Change Management* 10 (3): 193–201.

Margulies, N., and A. Raia, 1978. *Conceptual Foundations of Organization Development*. New York: McGraw-Hill.

Massarik, F., and M. Pei-Carpenter. 2002. *Organization Development and Consulting: Perspectives and Foundations*. San Francisco: Pfeiffer.

Mitchell, M. 2010. "Whole System Consulting." In *Consultation for Organizational Change*, edited by A. Buono and D. Jamieson, 41–55. Charlotte, NC: Information Age.

Old, D. 1995. "Consulting for Real Transformation, Sustainability, and Organic Form." *Journal of Organizational Change Management* 8 (3): 6–17.

Page, M. 1998. "Ethical Dilemmas in Organization Development Consulting Practice." Unpublished master's thesis. Malibu, CA: Pepperdine University (August).

Quade, K., and R. Brown. 2002. *The Conscious Consultant: Mastering Change from the Inside Out*. San Francisco: Pfeiffer.

Schein, E. 1988. *Process Consultation. Vol. I: Role in Organization Development*. 2nd ed. Reading, MA: Addison-Wesley.

Schein, E. 1997. "The Concept of 'Client' from a Process Consultation Perspective: A Guide for Change Agents." *Journal of Organizational Change Management* 10 (3): 202–216.

Schein, E. 2010. "Taking Organization Culture Seriously." In *Practicing Organization Development: A Guide for Leading Change*, 3rd ed., edited by W. Rothwell, J. Stavros, and R. Sullivan, 301–311. San Francisco: Pfeiffer.

Senge, P. 2006. "The Leader's New Work: Building Learning Organizations." In *Organization Development: A Jossey-Bass Reader*, edited by J. Gallos, 765–792. San Francisco: Jossey-Bass.

Shepard, H. 1985. "Rules of Thumb for Change Agents." *OD Practitioner* 17 (December): 2.

Smither, R., J. Houston, and S. McIntire. 1996. *Organization Development: Strategies for Changing Environments*. New York: HarperCollins.

Weisbord, M. 1973. "The Organization Development Contract." *OD Practitioner* 5 (2): 1–4.

Weisbord, M. 2012. *Productive Workplaces: Dignity, Meaning and Community in the 21st Century*. 3rd ed. San Francisco: Pfeiffer.

White, L., and K. Wooten. 1983. "Ethical Dilemmas in Various Stages of Organization Development." *Academy of Management Review* 8: 690–697.

Worley, C. G., and E. E. Lawler III. 2010. "Agility and Organization Design: A Diagnostic Framework." *Organizational Dynamics* 39 (2): 194–204.

CHAPTER TEN

Launch

Assessment, Action Planning, and Implementation

D. D. Warrick

All phases of the organization development (OD) process are important, but the "launch" phase is the heart of the OD process. The success of OD efforts depend on it. If done well, the probability of successful change will be high. If done poorly, the aftermath can be far reaching.

The term *launch* was coined by Warner Burke (2008, 257). It is a phase of OD in which valuable information is gathered and analyzed and a collaborative approach is used to evaluate the information, plan actions around the change process, and implement changes using methods that can significantly improve the probability of successful change. While this phase of OD can make changes that address issues, the ultimate goal of the launch process is to improve the health, effectiveness, and self-renewing capabilities of an organization.

The field of OD has made valuable contributions to the knowledge and skills needed to assess reality and plan and implement changes. This chapter presents essential information for anyone interested in successfully managing change.

THE PURPOSE OF LAUNCH

While assessment and action planning may be used informally in the Pre-launch phase of OD and more formally in the launch phase, they are used variously throughout OD efforts. Likewise, implementation is a dynamic process that often requires frequent adjustments and may involve going back to the assessment and action planning phases. These three phases of OD are as interactive as all phases of the OD process. The purpose of the launch phase is:

1. To assess reality before treating what is assumed to be reality.
2. To understand the strengths, opportunities for improvement, and future possibilities of organizations, departments, teams, and other relevant groups.
3. To collect useful information for designing, managing, and monitoring the change process and improvement efforts.
4. To develop action plans based on a sound change process.
5. To know how to successfully implement change so there is a high probability for success.
6. To involve and engage people in the change process.
7. To evaluate the success of OD efforts and plan future actions.

DEVELOPING A LAUNCH PHILOSOPHY

Significant and sometimes radical changes in an organization's environment and changes in OD itself make it important to develop a sound philosophy for assessing organizations, planning actions, and implementing changes. Philosophies may run from a problem-centered philosophy focusing on what is wrong and how to fix problems, to a more positive Appreciative Inquiry (AI) philosophy that focuses on best practices and discovering the life-giving properties present when organizations are performing optimally. It is important for OD practitioners to carefully think through the philosophies they embrace as their philosophies will significantly influence how they approach the launch phase of OD.

WHAT IT TAKES TO BUILD SUCCESSFUL ORGANIZATIONS

Besides having a clear philosophy for approaching the launch phase of OD, it is also important to have an organized approach for understanding organizations and for building organizations capable of succeeding. Organizations are much like people. They have beliefs, values, attitudes, habits, strengths, and weaknesses. Like people, they can be very different. Some are exceptionally focused, healthy, productive, vital, innovative, quick to adapt to change, willing to learn and grow, and great places to work for and with. Others are confused, unhealthy, dysfunctional, rigid, slow to learn and grow, resistant to change, and great places to avoid. Understanding and assessing an organization are critical to planning and implementing changes to assure that the strategies for changing the organization fit the unique characteristics, needs, and circumstances of each organization. Otherwise, strategies are likely to fail or underachieve what is possible.

Understanding Organizations

In trying to understand organizations, it is best to rely on a model that can be used in knowing what to look for. Models can also be used in designing an assessment strategy, developing interview questions, and organizing and presenting information in a useful and understandable way. Several such models are described next.

The Diagnosing Organization Systems Model (Cummings and Worley 2014). This is perhaps the most comprehensive of the models for understanding organizations. It is a systems model that looks at inputs, design components (often called *processes* in other models), and outputs at the organization, group, and individual levels. It considers types of change, levels of intervention, and issues to consider.

The Six Box Model (Weisbord 1978). Weisbord identified six organizational components that can be used to understand organizations. The components are organizational (1) purposes, (2) structures, (3) relationships, (4) rewards, (5) leadership, and (6) helpful mechanisms. These six components influence and are influenced by the environment in which the organization functions.

The Organization Dynamics Model (Kotter 1976). Kotter's classic model focuses on seven major components for understanding organizations. These are (1) key organizational processes, (2) external environment, (3) employees and other tangible assets, (4) formal organizational arrangements, (5) social systems, (6) technology, and (7) dominant coalition (top management).

Criteria for Building Successful Organizations

In planning and implementing changes, it would make sense that OD practitioners should have a good understanding of the fundamentals of building successful organizations as a framework for everything they do. Many efforts have been made to study best-run organizations and to identify what separates these organizations from the rest. While every organization is different, there are many consistent themes in research on successful organizations. Interestingly, they focus on many of the essential targets identified early in OD for building successful organizations, such as leadership, strategy, structure, processes, systems, people, and culture while paying close attention to both organization effectiveness and health. An example of a model identifying the fundamentals of building successful organizations is shown in Exhibit 10.1.

Exhibit 10.1. Fundamentals of Building Successful Organizations

1. Lead the Way
   — Good leadership is the major key to success.
   — Top level leaders have a passion for excellence and are humble, competent, visible, approachable, trustworthy, straightforward, and skilled at providing vision, direction, and inspiration. They walk the talk.
   — Top level leaders are close to the organization and function like a united, focused, results-oriented Top Leadership Team.

2. Develop a Strategy for Succeeding and Get Everyone on the Same Play Book
   — The vision, mission, core values, and strategic goals are clear, energizing, and known throughout the organization.
   — The strategy includes a strong emphasis on both people and performance.
   — Everyone knows how they can contribute to the success of the organization and is empowered to do so.

3. Structure the Organization for Results
   — Get the right people in the right places doing the right things.
   — Align everything to support the goals and values.
   — Simple, flat, nonbureaucratic, adaptable, responsive design that is effective, efficient, and results oriented.
   — Processes, systems, technology, and practices make it easy to get things done.

4. Build a High Performance Culture
   — Values-driven culture that encourages excellence and frees people to be their best.
   — Encourages both teamwork and being self-directing.
   — Values both disciplined action and entrepreneurship.
   — Emphasis on being open, straightforward, treating people with respect, and doing what is right.
   — High level of trust.
   — Values innovative thinking.

5. Develop Value-Added Managers
   — Managers at all levels are expected to add value, get results, and make things happen.
   — Managers are empowered to get the job done and are expected to do the same with their people.
   — A strong emphasis is placed on the continuous development of the leadership and management skills of present and potential managers.

Exhibit 10.1. (*Continued*)

6. Take Care of Your People
   — Having a committed, motivated, and well-trained workforce is a top priority of the leaders.
   — People at all levels are treated with value.
   — Efforts are made to attract, retain, develop, and fully utilize committed and talented people who are a good fit with the organization.
   — Efforts are made to make working conditions and the work environment a plus rather than a minus.

7. Take Care of Your Customers
   — Being customer driven to both internal and external customers is a high priority.
   — Employees from top to bottom are encouraged to know their internal and external customers and their needs.
   — Building good relationships with present and potential customers is valued.
   — The organization has a reputation for treating customers well.

8. Build Teamwork
   — Teamwork is encouraged and developed at the top, within teams, between teams, and outside the organization with groups that are key to the success of the organization.
   — There is a one-team mentality with minimal barriers between groups.
   — Involvement and collaboration are a way of life.

9. Never Stop Learning, Improving, and Building a Great Organization
   — A strong emphasis is placed on continuous learning, improvement, and development at the individual, group, and organization levels.
   — Many opportunities are provided for people to share ideas and make improvements.
   — Complacency and maintaining the status quo are not options.

10. Keep Score and Get Results
    — Measures of excellence are simple and clear and allow the organization to know where it stands regarding performance, human resource indicators, culture, customers, and other important measures.
    — Decisive decisions are made to make needed adjustments to get the best results without damaging the culture or compromising the core values.

CONSIDERATIONS IN APPLYING THE LAUNCH PHASE OF ORGANIZATION DEVELOPMENT TO CHANGING TIMES

While the fundamental principles of OD have remained relevant, the world in which OD is applied has changed significantly and with these changes comes the need for new thinking, methods, and applications. With this in mind, in understanding the launch phase of OD, it may be helpful to keep the following in mind:

1. The potential uses of assessment, action planning, and implementation go far beyond traditional OD literature. While much of the OD literature deals primarily with existing organizations and groups, the processes may be used in forming new organizations, groups, and alliances; in preparing for and integrating merged organizations; and in working on social, political, or international issues or with geographically dispersed or culturally diverse groups.

2. Technology has opened up many new alternatives for assessing organizations, groups, and individuals, for guiding the action planning process, and for implementing change. Examples include electronic questionnaires, real-time messaging, conferencing, and action planning without geographical constraints, and many other technologically driven alternatives.

3. Efforts should be made to find ways to accelerate the change process and make change as clear, understandable, time efficient, and value added as possible. OD efforts sometimes die of their own weight because they have become too complex and time consuming.

ASSESSMENT

Assessing organizations, groups, and individuals is an important contribution and value-added aspect of the OD process. Many changes are made with little, if any, diagnosis of the realities driving the changes. This leads to potentially faulty perceptions and assumptions about needed changes and often results in treating symptoms rather than the real issues. OD has always been a data-driven approach to collecting and evaluating information that identifies present realities, future possibilities, strengths, opportunities for improvement, issues, needs, and possible solutions. The valuable information provided by the assessment can motivate change, unite key stakeholders (leaders and those involved in and impacted by change) around a common understanding of reality, and plan, track, and evaluate changes. There are four major steps in the assessment process: planning, data collection, data analysis, and data feedback (see Exhibit 10.2).

Exhibit 10.2. Organization Assessment Process

Planning

1. Involve the right people in the project.
2. Clarify the desired goals and outcomes of the assessment.
3. Agree on what and who will be assessed.
4. Choose methods.
5. Determine how to best collect data.
6. Determine how to analyze and report the data.
7. Determine how to feedback and utilize the data.
8. Agree with leaders on the process and how the results will be utilized and coach the leaders on their role in making the assessment successful.
9. Develop planning milestones.

Data Collection

10. Assure that anyone involved in performing the assessment is trained.
11. Prepare the organization for the assessment.
12. Perform the assessment.

Data Analysis

13. Develop a strategy for analyzing and presenting the assessment results in a user-friendly way.
14. Prepare a simple-to-understand presentation of the findings.

Data Feedback

15. Design a feedback strategy for determining who gets what information how and when.
16. Prepare the appropriate people on how to use the results for helpful and not harmful purposes.
17. Decide on when and how to connect the feedback to action planning.
18. Prepare people for how to understand and utilize the data in helpful and positive ways to diffuse anxiety and ensure that the process will be a beneficial and useful one.

While this chapter provides an overview of the assessment process, there are many good sources that provide the details (see Cawsey and Deszca 2012; Church and Waclawski 2007; Cooperrider, Whitney, and Stavros 2008; Kaughman and Guerra-Lopez 2013).

Planning the Assessment

A well-planned assessment can be the catalyst for breaking down resistance to change and increasing the motivation for change. A poorly planned assessment, however, can demoralize people and cause division. Therefore, it is very important that someone with expertise lead the planning process.

The size and scope of the assessment, level of expertise of the person or persons leading the assessment process, and the commitment needed to make the assessment successful will determine who and how many should be involved in the planning process. A known, trusted, and experienced internal or external OD practitioner may plan an assessment with minimal involvement. However, many efforts require considerable involvement in agreeing on who and what is assessed and how to fulfill the other steps in the planning process.

Data Collection. Technology has made it possible to collect and analyze data quickly. However, every situation must be evaluated to determine the most effective way to collect data given the realities and what leaders will do. While a wealth of information can be collected and analyzed through questionnaires, people may be more open in face-to-face interviews and communicate things that cannot be picked up in questionnaires.

The most frequently used methods of data collection are using available information (an organization's vision, mission, values, strategic goals, organization charts, turnover rates, and so forth) and using questionnaires and interviews. Ideally, both quantitative and qualitative data are preferable. *Quantifiable* data are typically collected through questionnaires; this makes it possible to know the magnitude of an issue. An average of 2.5 on a 7-point scale, with 7 being the highest favorable score, has a far different meaning than a 6.5. However, quantitative data will not tell you what is behind the numbers. *Qualitative* data are collected through one-on-one or focus group interviews and open-ended questions on questionnaires. Interviews can pick up information and impressions that explore a range of issues, including what is behind the issues.

Data Analysis

The OD practitioner leading an OD process usually compiles, analyzes, and prepares a report of the assessment results. Technology has made it possible to automate the compilation and analysis part of an assessment, and with large numbers of people being assessed, this is almost a necessity. The data go in and a report comes out, complete with attractive charts and graphs. However, no matter how dazzling the technology and resulting report may be, of much greater importance is that the analysis should provide valid and useful information presented in a brief and useful way. Some question whether this can be done solely by machine without involving an experienced OD practitioner. This part of the assessment and action-planning process is important, and a poor analysis or presentation of the results will lead to a low use and/or misuse of the assessment.

Data Feedback

Whether and how data are fed back can have a significant impact on OD efforts. Feedback properly handled can energize people, create momentum for change, and ensure that organization members trust and own the data. However, if feedback isn't properly handled and fed back in a timely manner, it can undermine OD efforts. Properly planned feedback is important to the OD process and poorly planned feedback can have many consequences such as a loss of credibility and trust in the OD process.

Although the feedback process must be designed for each unique situation, it typically includes a version of the following steps:

1. A strategy is developed by the OD practitioner in collaboration with the people about who gets what information, how, and when.

2. If appropriate, training is provided for those leading feedback sessions so there will be consistency in philosophy, methods, and outcomes in each session.

3. The top-level leader involved will usually be briefed on the findings and coached on behaviors that help or hinder the feedback process and what the feedback process comprises.

4. The feedback then is usually presented to the primary group it is intended for or cascaded down the organization, starting with top management. Each group receives the information appropriate for it to see and respond to. There are exceptions where a "bottom-up" approach is used, with recommendations eventually formulated to present to top management.

One interesting aspect of assessing organizations is that many methods can discover what is going on and what is possible (Harrison 2005). Each method has advantages and disadvantages. Interviews make it possible to collect much data, find out what is behind issues, and see and dialogue with respondents, but may suffer from interviewer bias. They also can be time-consuming and expensive if a consultant is used and many people are interviewed. Questionnaires make data quantifiable but may suffer from respondent bias and are not likely to reveal what is behind the numbers. A summary of the major advantages and disadvantages of assessment methods is shown in Exhibit 10.3.

Exhibit 10.3. Organization Assessment Methods

Method	Advantages	Disadvantages
Existing Data • Published information • Brochures • Vision, mission, values, goals statements • Organization charts • Data on profits, sales, turnover, etc.	• Information already exists • Generally easy to access • Quickly familiarizes the person doing the assessment with the organization • Efficient and inexpensive • Relatively objective	• Reality between what is stated and what is may differ • Some existing information may be difficult to access • Gives only a surface view of the organization
Interviews • Structured (specific questions designed to elicit specific responses) • Nonstructured (open-ended questions) • Individual • Group • Face-to-face • Phone or electronic	• Makes it possible to collect rich, valuable, in-depth information • Can be used for a wide range of assessment purposes • Makes it possible to probe and elaborate on information and pursue new lines of questioning • Can build empathy, trust, support for OD efforts	• Time-consuming and expensive if large number of respondents involved • Subject bias and influence • Interpreting interviews can be difficult • May not give a sense of magnitude or importance of information collected • Risks inconsistencies in interviewing style and interpretation of the results if more than one interviewer involved
Questionnaires • Used to gather data on whole organizations, groups, or individuals, or a specific focus • Quantifiable	• Make it possible to quantify and objectively analyze results • Can involve large numbers of people	• Misses qualitative data especially if open-ended questions not included • May not reveal what is behind the numbers

Exhibit 10.3. (*Continued*)

Method	Advantages	Disadvantages
Questionnaires • Open-ended questions	• Numbers can be motivators for change • Relatively inexpensive • Can compare before and after results	• Lack the flexibility of interviews • Subject to bias if respondents lack knowledge pertaining questions • Interpreting and summarizing data may require a high level of expertise
Observations • Formal (specific things to observe; information to collect) • Informal (observing, talking, attending meetings, etc.)	• Organization behavior, processes, and systems can be observed first-hand • Can obtain a better feel for the culture of the organization or group • Real-time data • Flexibility in terms of what is observed	• Not always easy to arrange and can be distracting to those being observed • Possible observer bias in interpreting what is observed • Can be expensive and time consuming for the value received • May be difficult to analyze what is observed
Live Assessments • Data collected and analyzed live at meetings and workshops • Data collected and analyzed real time electronically	• Interesting, engaging, real time, and provides fast turnaround and use of information • With skilled facilitator can be used with large groups of people • Quickly involves people and builds commitment to change	• May miss valuable information that comes from a variety of sources over time • Dependent on having key people present or commitment may be lost • Somewhat risky in the event that unforeseen things can happen that undermine the process

ACTION PLANNING

Action planning is a collaborative process of systematically planning a change effort. When done effectively, it can mobilize people, improve the impact of a change, and accelerate the time needed to achieve results. When done ineffectively, action plans will generate little commitment, have a low probability of being implemented, and produce unintended negative side effects.

Even though action planning is an integral part of any OD effort, little has been written about it. Action planning first appeared in the pre-OD days of Kurt Lewin in his action research concept and centered on gathering data, organizing and feeding it back, and using the data to explore improvements.

The Action Planning Process

Many approaches can be taken to plan change actions (Anderson 2012, 182–191). The fundamentals of the action planning process are: involve key stakeholders, evaluate and prioritize data, agree on the changes to be made, develop a change strategy, and clarify roles and follow-through on responsibilities (details are shown in Exhibit 10.4).

Action planning is a dynamic process that must be adapted to changing situations. Typically, a master strategy is developed that is then modified as needed. The degree to which strategies are changed will determine who needs to make the changes. It is assumed that an OD practitioner or change champion (a person appointed to champion the change) was appointed early in the change process to lead the change effort. If not, a person must be appointed at the latest during action planning.

Involve Key Stakeholders. Stakeholders include people at all levels of an organization that must be involved to make the change process successful. This could include an OD practitioner or person appointed to champion the change, a leader or leaders needed to support the change, and others who have influence, expertise, or experience that could be helpful in planning changes. Sometimes the stakeholders are obvious, such as in efforts involving a top leadership team or a department or team within an organization. When key stakeholders are involved in the action-planning process, voices close to the situation can be heard and those involved are likely to have a strong commitment to ensuring success. When key stakeholders are not involved, commitment may be lacking from those who can make or break changes, and the changes may make little sense to those who must carry them out.

Evaluate and Prioritize Relevant Data. It takes a skilled OD practitioner to facilitate meetings to evaluate and prioritize data and plan actions. Occasionally, the meetings to accomplish these important tasks are separate meetings, although they typically are part of the same meeting. Whether these meetings

Exhibit 10.4. Action-Planning Process

Involve Key Stakeholders

1. Involve those who are in the best position to understand and utilize the assessment and lead needed changes.
2. Ensure that someone will lead the change effort. If needed, develop a change team to plan and manage the change process.

Evaluate and Prioritize Relevant Data

3. Develop a process for evaluating, prioritizing, and making the assessment information manageable and useable.
4. Clarify the focus of change efforts (whole organization, group or intergroup, individual, structural, technological, etc.).
5. Consider the level of desired change (fine tuning, incremental, or transformational).
6. Focus on present realities and future ideals and possibilities and explore alternatives for achieving greater success.

Agree on the Changes to Be Made

7. Agree on the actions to be taken recognizing that it is better to do a few things well than many things poorly.
8. Evaluate the change from a systems perspective considering the implications of the changes and the alignment needed.

Develop a Change Strategy

9. Identify any forces working for or against the desired change.
10. Explore intervention alternatives.
11. Develop a change process based on a sound change model and set of change principles.
12. Develop a process for monitoring and managing the change process.

Clarify Roles and Follow-Through Responsibilities

13. Clarify the roles and follow-through responsibilities of all involved in the change process.
14. Commit to keeping the change process as clear and simple as possible

are with a small or large group, face-to-face or virtual, considerable planning is required to make them useful, positive, and productive experiences. Some issues that must be considered in preparing for the evaluation and prioritization of data and action planning are:

- Choose a skilled professional to facilitate the meeting.
- Send a carefully planned agenda to the participants ahead of time.
- Consider if the meeting needs training and possibly the establishment of ground rules.
- Consider the process used and any information and technology to evaluate and prioritize data and plan actions.
- Choose a meeting room that fits your process and any technology needed.
- Be clear on the end goal of the meeting and what is to be accomplished.

The data used in action planning may be simplistic or sophisticated, and the process used to evaluate and prioritize data may range from easy-to-use and understand processes to complex processes. Whatever the methodology used, the approach should be tailored to the audience and purpose selected. Where appropriate, it is also important to clarify the focus of change efforts (whole organization, group, intergroup, individual, systems, processes, structures, culture, etc.) and to consider the level of desired change (fine-tuning, incremental, and transformational).

Agree on the Changes to Be Made. Sometimes the actions to be taken are reasonably obvious. At other times, it is helpful to agree on criteria for deciding which actions to take. It may be helpful to classify actions as "quick and easy" and "high-impact" actions or "short-term" and "long-term" actions. It is also helpful to choose one or more "early win" actions that will reinforce the commitment to change. Another consideration is to recognize that it is better to choose a *few* actions and do them well than to overwhelm people with *many* actions that are unlikely to be accomplished. In choosing actions, take a systems perspective that considers the broad implications of changes and the support needed to make the change successful. Finally, actions, which sometimes are listed as goals, need to be simple and clear and should include: the action, a brief action plan of how the action will be accomplished, timelines, and who will champion getting the action accomplished (this could also include a team of people to work with the champion).

Develop a Change Strategy. Developing a change strategy for implementing the desired change based on a change process is as important as the actual changes. Even the right changes implemented the wrong way will fail and may have far-reaching consequences for change efforts. This important part of the action planning process can increase the probability of success, not only of the action planning process but also of the entire OD process. This is the part of action planning where OD contributes; yet, it is also the part sometimes left out. For some changes, the strategy may be fairly simple and clear and for others it requires a more in-depth analysis of the potential interventions and approaches that can be used.

One way to develop a change strategy is to do a force-field analysis. This is a technique developed from the work of Kurt Lewin that analyzes the forces working for change and the forces working for maintaining the status quo or resisting change (Lewin 1951). In its simplest form, this involves listing the forces working for and against the desired change, and then planning ways to increase the forces for change and reducing the forces against change.

The next step is to explore intervention alternatives. This requires an understanding of the individual, group, and organization interventions that OD offers. Once the interventions are selected that will best accomplish the desired goals, it is helpful to use a change model and change principles to create a model or descriptive explanation of the change process, or both, that can be used throughout the change process. An example is shown in Figure 10.1.

Clarify Roles and Follow-Through Responsibilities. The final step in the action-planning process is to assure that roles are clarified and responsibilities are followed through. Exhibit 10.5 shows the typical roles that must be covered in change efforts.

Keep in mind that—depending on the scale of the change and the training and skills of available resources—one or more persons may play multiple roles and not all roles are needed for all changes. The roles required and the persons fulfilling the roles may change throughout a change effort.

Exhibit 10.5. Roles in Successfully Managing Change

Change Agent (OD Practitioner): A person who is a specialist in organization development and change.

Change Leader: A person in a leadership position who can significantly influence the success or failure of a change effort and provide the support and the leadership necessary for change to succeed.

Change Champion: A person at any level of an organization who champions needed changes and has at least a basic understanding of how to successfully plan and implement changes.

Change Team: A team that is responsible for planning, managing, monitoring, and championing a change effort.

Note: The same person may play multiple roles in some situations, several people may occupy a role, and while at least one change champion is always needed, change agents and change teams may be needed depending on the change.

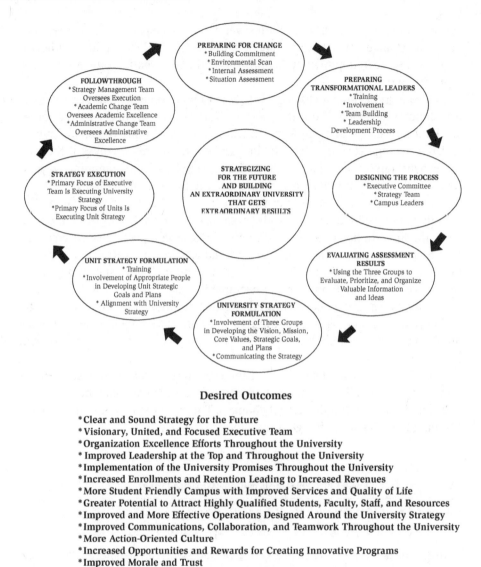

PREPARING FOR CHANGE
* Building Commitment
* Environmental Scan
* Internal Assessment
* Situation Assessment

FOLLOWTHROUGH
* Strategy Management Team
  Oversees Execution
* Academic Change Team
  Oversees Academic Excellence
* Administrative Change Team
  Oversees Administrative
  Excellence

PREPARING TRANSFORMATIONAL LEADERS
* Training
* Involvement
* Team Building
* Leadership Development Process

STRATEGY EXECUTION
* Primary Focus of Executive
  Team Is Executing University
  Strategy
* Primary Focus of Units Is
  Executing Unit Strategy

STRATEGIZING FOR THE FUTURE AND BUILDING AN EXTRAORDINARY UNIVERSITY THAT GETS EXTRAORDINARY RESULTS

DESIGNING THE PROCESS
* Executive Committee
* Strategy Team
* Campus Leaders

UNIT STRATEGY FORMULATION
* Training
* Involvement of Appropriate People
  in Developing Unit Strategic
  Goals and Plans
* Alignment with University
  Strategy

EVALUATING ASSESSMENT RESULTS
* Using the Three Groups to
  Evaluate, Prioritize, and Organize
  Valuable Information
  and Ideas

UNIVERSITY STRATEGY FORMULATION
* Involvement of Three Groups
  in Developing the Vision, Mission,
  Core Values, Strategic Goals,
  and Plans
* Communicating the Strategy

Desired Outcomes

* Clear and Sound Strategy for the Future
* Visionary, United, and Focused Executive Team
* Organization Excellence Efforts Throughout the University
* Improved Leadership at the Top and Throughout the University
* Implementation of the University Promises Throughout the University
* Increased Enrollments and Retention Leading to Increased Revenues
* More Student Friendly Campus with Improved Services and Quality of Life
* Greater Potential to Attract Highly Qualified Students, Faculty, Staff, and Resources
* Improved and More Effective Operations Designed Around the University Strategy
* Improved Communications, Collaboration, and Teamwork Throughout the University
* More Action-Oriented Culture
* Increased Opportunities and Rewards for Creating Innovative Programs
* Improved Morale and Trust

Figure 10.1. Change Process for a University's Transformation

IMPLEMENTATION

All previous phases of OD build toward the implementation phase where OD achieves results. Six steps are recommended for the implementation process: keep the big picture in mind; use a sound change plan and model to manage the change process; adapt the interventions to achieve the best results; keep people engaged; identify and manage resistance to change; and follow through and learn from the process (details are shown in Exhibit 10.6).

Exhibit 10.6. Implementation

Keep the Big Picture in Mind

1. Keep focused on the specific change and the end goal of improving the health, effectiveness, and self-renewing capabilities of the organization; approach changes from a systems perspective.

Use a Sound Change Plan and Model to Manage the Change Process

2. Use the action-planning change plan and change model to guide and manage the change process.
3. Build in feedback mechanisms so you will know what is working and not working and adjustments can be made.

Adapt the Action Plan and Interventions to Achieve the Best Results

4. Adapt the action plan and interventions to changing conditions.
5. Use strategic involvement to economize the time of the participants.

Keep People Engaged

6. Find ways to make the incentive to change greater than the incentive to stay the same.
7. Target and communicate early and continued wins.
8. Involve key leaders in keeping people focused, communicating progress, and providing encouragement.
9. Make sure that those involved in helping achieve the desired change are recognized and valued.

Identify and Manage Resistance to Change

10. Be aware of significant resistance to change and take positive steps to overcoming resistance.
11. Deal with continued resistance as quickly and constructively as possible.

Follow Through and Learn from the Process

12. Follow through until the desired goals of the change are achieved.
13. Assess what has been accomplished and what remains to be done.
14. Build in ways for the change to be sustained.
15. Learn from the process and share what has been learned.

When implementation is done well, it energizes people, results in needed changes, and produces confidence in the change process. However, it is also filled with many challenges as conditions may frequently change and guiding changes to successful completion requires considerable skill. The six implementation steps are discussed next.

Keep the Big Picture in Mind

Remembering the big picture in implementing changes from an OD perspective means keeping focused on the change goals *and* the end goal of OD and taking a systems approach to change. The end goal of OD has been defined differently by various experts in OD but usually includes increasing the health, effectiveness, and self-renewing capabilities of an organization. A systems approach considers the implications of changes on various parts of the organization and how organizational systems that could affect the change are aligned with the change.

Use the Action Plan and a Change Model to Manage the Change Process

This part of the implementation process includes using the previously developed action plan and a sound change model hopefully used in preparing the action plan to guide and manage the change process and adapt the plan to changing conditions. One often overlooked key to successfully implementing changes is building into the process feedback mechanisms so you will know what is working and what is not. It is common for changes to not be working and for those who initiated or are managing the changes to be unaware of how the changes that made such good sense to them are being experienced. Issues that could have been identified and addressed with good feedback mechanisms go undetected and can leave a path of unresolved issues, demoralization, and distrust of future change.

Adapt the Action Plan and Interventions to Achieve the Best Results

In a dynamic environment of constant change, even the best planned OD efforts must respond to changing situations. This is why it is so important to know of changing conditions and use feedback mechanisms to quickly detect what is working and not working in the change process. It is also important in adapting the action plan and interventions to changing conditions to strategically plan how to engage people without using too much time. Otherwise, the changes are not likely to be well received.

Keep People Engaged

Anyone who has made changes knows how challenging it is to keep people engaged in the change process. Leaders get busy with other tasks; key players often have too much going on to stay focused and carry out their responsibilities; and changes in leadership and circumstances can present obstacles to keeping changes alive.

Things can be done to keep people engaged. Use innovative thinking to make the incentive to change greater than the incentive to stay the same. Unless there is a compelling vision for the change and a change plan that provides opportunities for people to influence and possibly benefit from the change, changes are likely to be viewed as one more badly planned effort. Another way to keep people engaged is to seek early and visible wins that confirm the value of the change is producing results. It can also be helpful to involve leaders in the change process and in communicating progress. Finally, keep those involved focused on the purpose and goals of the changes, engage them where appropriate while protecting their time required for involvement, and recognize and value their efforts.

Identify and Manage Resistance to Change

There are many reasons people resist change. Some prefer the status quo to having to adapt to something new. Some resist for the sake of resisting. Some may resist for political, ideological, or self-serving reasons. However, some, if not most, resist for perfectly logical reasons … most changes are unsuccessful, the reasons for change are not clarified, the leaders are not vested in making the change succeed, and so forth. Exhibit 10.7 shows several reasons people resist change and how to overcome resistance to change.

The lesson is that people will support well-planned change and resist poorly planned change. Another lesson is that, while positive efforts should be made to win over resisters, if those efforts are unsuccessful and resisters are undermining the change process, at some point they need to be confronted and face consequences for their resistance. Failing to confront unwarranted resistance will cause involved leaders to lose credibility and could derail the change.

Follow Through and Learn from the Process

It takes considerable discipline and perseverance to follow through on changes to assure that the desired goals are achieved. However, this is not the end of the implementation. Plans also must be made to evaluate what has been accomplished and what remains to be done. In addition, plan ways to sustain the changes accomplished. A wrap-up step rarely pursued is to take the time to

Exhibit 10.7. Why People Resist Change and Overcoming Resistance to Change

Why People Resist Change	Overcoming Resistance to Change
• Lack of vision and purpose regarding the change	• Communicate compelling reasons for change
• Organizational memory about past change efforts	• Demonstrate visible and convincing leadership involvement and support
• Leaders not effectively leading or supporting the change	• Appoint a capable and respected champion
• Lack of involvement in the change process	• Involve key stakeholders and contributors
• Lack of incentive to change	• Make the incentive for change greater than the incentive to stay the same
• Fear of unknown	
• Personal threat or possible loss	
• Work overload	• Educate, train, and prepare people for change
• Change overload	• Communicate regarding the vision and progress
• Ideological differences or concerns	
• Political or self-serving reasons	• Listen to and address concerns and obstacles
• Lack of resources or institutional support	• Use assessments and data to motivate change
• Lack of skills to make the needed change	• Target early wins and use pilot projects to gain confidence
• Lack of information	• Be sensitive to time and action requirements
• Poor timing	• Take a positive approach to dealing with issues and resistance but know when to bite the bullet

learn from the process and document what has been learned so others can benefit from the experience.

SUMMARY

The launch phase of OD is the heart of OD. Skillfully assessing what is going on and what needs to be done, planning actions that can cause significant changes and improvements, and implementing changes in a way that has a high probability of success will make or break the OD process and can be critical to success. The skills required in the launch phase of OD are essential for OD practitioners. They are also invaluable to organizations facing nonstop change and experiencing a high failure rate at change, which puts them at a competitive disadvantage, demoralizes employees, and causes leaders to lose credibility. In dynamic times, the launch phase of OD provides skills that every organization should become proficient at.

Discussion Questions

1. Why is the launch phase of assessing, action planning, and implementation so important in the OD process?

2. What are some of the philosophical issues that should be considered between the change agent and the client before engaging in the launch phase of OD, and why are these issues important to the change process?

3. What are examples of how significant changes and decisions have been made by top level leaders without first assessing reality and listening to those closest to the issues involved?

4. What are important advantages and disadvantages of using various assessment methods?

5. What would you put on your checklist of criteria to remember in making action planning and implementation successful?

6. What do you believe are important pitfalls to avoid in the launch phase of OD?

Resources

A sample action plan for organization development: www.haltonccg.nhs.uk/Library/ public_information/Halton%20CCG%20OD%20Plan%202012%2015%20final?.pdf

A toolkit for action planning for change: http://vawnet.org/DELTAPREPToolkit/docs/ ActionPlanningWorkbook.pdf

A list of steps to take in developing an action plan to change organizational culture: www .nonprofitinclusiveness.org/developing-action-plan-organizational-culture

References

Anderson, D. L. 2012. *Organization Development: The Process of Leading Organizational Change.* Thousand Oaks, CA: Sage.

Burke, W. 2008. *Organization Change.* Los Angeles: Sage.

Cawsey, T., and G. Deszca. 2012. *Organizational Change: An Action-Oriented Toolkit.* Thousand Oaks, CA: Sage.

Church, A. H., and J. Waclawski. 2007. *Designing and Using Organizational Surveys.* San Francisco: Jossey-Bass.

Cooperrider, D. L., D. Whitney, and J. Stavros. 2008. *Appreciative Inquiry Handbook*. Brunswick, OH: Crown Custom Publishing and San Francisco: Berrett-Koehler.

Cummings, T. G., and C. G. Worley. 2014. *Organization Development and Change*. Cincinnati, OH: South-Western College.

Harrison, M. I. 2005. *Diagnosing Organizations: Methods, Models, and Processes*. Thousand Oaks, California: Sage.

Kaughman, R., and I. Guerra-Lopez. 2013. *Needs Assessment for Organizational Success*. Thousand Oaks, California: Sage.

Kotter, J. 1976. *Organization Dynamics and Intervention*. Reading, MA: Addison-Wesley.

Lewin, K. 1951. *Field Theory in Social Science*. New York: Harper & Row.

Weisbord, M. R. 1978. *Organization Diagnosis: A Workbook of Theory and Practice*. Reading, MA: Addison-Wesley.

CHAPTER ELEVEN

Evaluating Organizational Transformation

A Situational Approach

Steve H. Cady and Sheryl A. Milz

H ow does one evaluate organizational change, particularly when the change is transformative in nature? Within the field of organization development (OD), change initiatives are considered intentional interventions, which may be proactive or reactive, and can come in a variety of forms: training sessions, social programs, policy creation, projects or initiatives, strategic planning, organizational redesign or restructuring, cost-cutting programs, new product development, succession planning, implementing or upgrading technology, and more. When considering what's at stake with undertaking a change initiative, a question you will often hear from leaders, participants, and observers is, "Was the initiative worth the resources, the time, and money expended?" Another question often raised is, "Did it work and how do you know?" (Cady, Auger, and Foxon 2010).

In this chapter, we provide you with a way to navigate the myriad evaluation tools and choose the best combination for assessing the effectiveness of OD interventions from small-scale incremental change to large-scale transformation. The reason we address the full spectrum from small to large is that all change initiatives are comprised of a series of interventions woven together into a comprehensive whole. The chapter begins with a review of organizational change. Then, the paradox of competing demands is discussed. Finally, we provide a decision model to guide you in choosing an evaluation strategy for each situation.

DEFINING AND DIFFERENTIATING CHANGE

Something small or big happens, a disturbance if you will. This is the essence of change. On a personal level, it can be a health crisis. On an organizational level, it can be a merger. On a societal level, it can be a natural disaster. And, it is sometimes viewed as positive or negative, pending the "eye of the beholder," from the birth of a child to a new product line to a vote for independence. Regardless, disturbances, or changes, evoke and even provoke a response (Axelrod, Cady, and Holman 2010).

Whole System Collaborative Change

Whole system or large-scale organizational change has been defined as "A lasting change in the character of an organization that significantly alters its performance" (Mohrman et al. 1989, 2). Over the past 50 years, the pioneers of whole system approaches to change have led the way in inventing methods for engaging the people of the system in creating their future (e.g., Laszlo 2012). There are many practices now in use and more are emerging all the time. Some widely used methods include Appreciative Inquiry, Conference Model, Future Search, Open Space Technology, Whole-Scale Change, and World Café. These methods allow for groups to determine common ground and dispel assumptions so that the individuals participating actually generate better solutions together, taking ownership for resulting solutions (Holman, Devane, and Cady 2007). Large-group approaches provide dialogue-based activities that enable efficient facilitation of 50 to 5,000-plus people at one point in time, or over time with more asynchronous techniques. However, sustaining change requires continued processes, not just one event (Goldstein and Behm 2004).

Mohrman et al. (1989) summarize this as follows: "As the size of the organization grows, as the change becomes more pervasive, and as the depth of change increases, the risk, difficulty, complexity, unpredictability, and intensity of the change also become greater" (27). Manning and Binzagr (1996) noted that for large-scale change interventions, the intervention needs to be at the whole system level and cannot just be focused on system dynamics or ripple effects. Additionally, individuals must voluntarily take ownership for large changes to occur (Manning and Binzagr 1996). Covin and Kilmann (1988) demonstrated that the success of large-scale programs was positively correlated to the percentage of employees participating ($p < 0.01$). In other words, the higher the participation in the program, the more likely the program succeeded. Whole System Collaborative Change (WSCC) enables organizations to more effectively utilize people's time and effort to solve problems. These methods help provide:

- The forum for personnel to work together so that they arrive at a common understanding of an issue, are able to take ownership, and are able to commit to changes that will make a difference in the organization.
- The configuration allowing large amounts of information to be communicated in preparation for change.
- An efficient manner to harness employees desire to participate in the process and to create quality outcomes.
- The location for persons of all backgrounds and cultures to work together and participate in the changes and have their voices heard and understood.
- The prospect for people to state what is important to them, and to work together to understand these important issues so that actions can be taken for the good of the organization (Axelrod et al. 2010).

WSCC can also be described by a formula that explains what is necessary to overcome resistance within organizations. The formula states that $D \times V \times F \times S > R$, where D represents the desire for change, V represents the vision for change, F represents first steps toward change, S represents the supporting mechanisms that allow the change to occur, and R represents resistance to change. Therefore, if the desire, vision, first steps, and supporting mechanisms exceed the resistance to change, then change can occur. If any of these are zero, they cancel out the formula and resistance stops the change (Cady, Hine, Meenach, and Spalding 2011; Cady, Jacobs, Koller, and Spalding 2014).

Transformational versus Incremental Change

Transformation is defined as "a change that alters an entire organization, including strategy, structure, core processes, power distribution, controls systems, culture, and people's work" (Cady and Hardalupas 1999, 90). Collaboration is defined as "exchanging information, alteration activities, sharing resources, and enhancing the capacity of another for mutual benefit and to achieve a common purpose" (Himmelman 2002, 4). Combining these two concepts, we define collaborative transformation as occurring when information and resources are shared in order to alter an entire system (e.g., organization(s), community, industry, or bigger) for mutual benefit.

One view of transformation is that it requires two fundamental changes for it to be considered transformative. Using a biological perspective, the two key changes of transformation are the *mode* of production or delivery and the *resources* as a source of energy. While both the mode and resources can change dramatically, the core values and competencies of the system remain the same. Changes to both the mode and resources will result in a transformation. Incremental change occurs when only one of the aspects changes. Both transformational change and incremental change can be a punctuated or immediate change brought on by some event or the change can occur over time.

On the other hand, incremental change is the more traditional approach. Top management decides to make a change and then passes the expected changes down to middle management, who in turn pass the change down to the employees (Bunker and Alban 1997). Additionally, incremental change can be viewed, as stated above, to occur when just one of the key aspects change. In other words, either the mode changes or the resources change, but not both, during incremental change. Furthermore, incremental change occurs over time even when organizations are stable (van der Heijden 2010) or incremental change can occur as the result of some disturbance.

THE CHALLENGE OF EVALUATION

The question, "Did it work?" deals with the question of cause and effect. Interventions are developed, and then money and time are allocated for implementation. Sometimes, the impact of the intervention is evaluated. As organizations evolve, dramatic events and trends sweep the world, new technologies emerge, profit margins shrink, market demographics change, competition ebbs and flows ... leaders are exerting more and more pressure to see the value added by interventions (Cady et al. 2010).

Studying the effects of changes is highly dependent on the accuracy of measurements, but measuring change is difficult (Butler, Scott, and Edwards 2003; Terborg, Howard, and Maxwell 1980). However, Brennan, Sampson, and Deverill (2005) conclude that routine data are a necessary part of evaluating initiatives. Evaluation needs to be done in order to determine whether the change has been effective and whether the change should be retained (Kirkpatrick 1998). For example, Way and McKeeby (2012) reported the results for a research hospital from a two-day leadership retreat with 30-, 60-, and 120-day follow-ups. At 120 days, a performance setback was identified, while overall communication, teamwork, and morale had increased to an acceptable level that was not apparent prior to the leadership retreat. Should they hold another retreat in the future, as they set goals and identify priorities for the next year? With the evaluation report provided, they have the data necessary to make a more informed decision.

PARADOX OF COMPETING DEMANDS

There seems to be an underlying assumption, that in an ideal world, it is best to perform rigorous high-quality evaluations of all interventions. Therefore, it is necessary to balance the need of proving an intervention was successful or the need for improving the intervention with the cost of evaluating the intervention in terms of time and money.

Prove and Improve

When considering the why or purpose of an evaluation, it boils down to two aims. The first aim is to prove that the intervention worked. Proving is important to those who are responsible for the intervention's impact. In some cases, it is about accountability for results and in others it's about making the business case. The second aim is to evaluate an intervention in order to improve it for the future. A future focus is based on a need to understand how interventions work, identify the relative importance of a technique or method, advance theories, and create more robust approaches to change (Cady et al. 2010).

Time and Money

Conducting evaluations can be costly for all stakeholders involved in terms of both time and money. In terms of time, leaders will need to pull people away from other work in order to fill out evaluations, be interviewed, and provide data. Money may be necessary when outcomes are difficult to measure. Therefore, if either the time or the money or both are too high, it may lead the client and the consultant to decide against conducting any evaluation (Cady et al. 2010).

Paradox of Competing Demands

The paradox comes from wanting to prove the intervention worked and will improve for the future but not wanting to spend lots of time and money. As you focus on proving and improving an intervention, it will cost more in terms of time and money (see Figure 11.1). If you cannot do it all, then how do you make the tough choices?

On one hand, there is a costly intervention that has important implications for the organization or community. If there are long-term plans for the intervention, the intended impact is vital to the future. Further, continued funding will depend on demonstrating results in some objective fashion. On the other hand, evaluation will take time away from implementing the intervention. There may be no money in the budget allocated to the evaluation. Often, evaluation can be an afterthought. A leader might say, "Did that program work? ... Can you

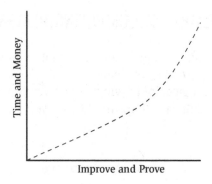

Figure 11.1. The Paradox of Competing Demands in Evaluation

confirm that it was worth our time and money? ... Are we better off? ... What next? ... We are not done, right? ... Oh, by the way, can you provide an update focused on these questions at our meeting next week?" Some believe that funds would be better spent on additional interventions. Some might even argue that evaluation is not necessary and it does not add value to the intervention. It is just a bureaucratic mechanism for show. The perception is that the outcomes of the process are so obvious it is not necessary to conduct an evaluation (Cady et al. 2010).

LEVELS OF EVALUATION

There are two particularly user-friendly models for evaluation. They are Kirkpatrick's (1998) Four Levels of Evaluation and Phillips's ROI (1996). While originally intended for the field of training, they have been applied to a variety of change initiatives (Russ-Eft, Bober, de la Taja, Foxon, and Koszalka 2008). The five levels can be thought to answer the following questions.

Level 1: Reaction—How satisfied are the participants?

Level 2: Learning—What do the participants know?

Level 3: Behavior—What are the participants doing?

Level 4: Results—What outcomes have been achieved?

Level 5: Return—What is the return on investment (ROI)?

While the higher levels provide more improving and proving data, they also cost more in terms of time and money. Some may argue that it is unrealistic to expect practitioners to conduct comprehensive evaluations in every situation.

They would argue that one should settle for evidence rather than seed proof (Kirkpatrick 1977). In this case, the evaluation will need to be less rigorous and less formal. While in other cases, it will be more formal and more rigorous.

The scope of Levels 1 and 2 includes participants in the moment. An example would be satisfaction surveys and quick multiple-choice testing done in the classroom during a training program. The scope focuses on the specific training program in isolation from the application context. Level 3 brings the evaluation into the organizational setting, by evaluating whether the initiative when implemented leads to actual change beyond reaction and learning. However, it doesn't indicate if there are benefits to organizational processes and productivity. Levels 4 and 5 provide that scope of data because they move from evaluating the specifics of an intervention to examining the intervention's impact on the whole organization (Kirkpatrick 1998). Level 5 data require the evaluation of monetary data and forces the intervention to align with the organization's strategic plan (Phillips, Phillips, and Zuniga 2013). Kirkpatrick (1998) suggests that evaluation should begin with Level 1, even if the goal is to evaluate at Level 3 or 4. By starting at the lower levels, results are obtained so that if no behavior change has occurred (Level 3), more information is available that may help explain why the behavior has not changed.

The challenge to be resolved is for evaluation to be fully utilized as a practical tool in the organizational toolkit. Consider utilization trends. Practitioners agree that Level 4 or 5 are the most desirable, yet they appear to be the least done. Twenty years ago, Foxon (1989) found that 30 percent of training practitioners consider evaluation to be one of "the most vexing problems" of the job. She found that more than 75 percent of organizations conducted only Level 1 evaluations. More recent data suggest little has changed. Rossett (2007) reports that Level 1 to 4 evaluations are being conducted 94 percent, 34 percent, 13 percent, and 3 percent of the time, respectively.

Qualitative and Quantitative Evaluations

Evaluation can be done both qualitatively and quantitatively for all five levels of evaluation. At times, evaluation can be less rigorous and formal and therefore qualitative data may be acceptable. Other times, evaluation needs to be more rigorous and formal requiring quantitative data. However, qualitative evaluation can be more formal and rigorous and quantitative evaluation can be less formal and rigorous. Qualitative evaluation includes collecting observations, feelings, and impressions of the participants, which is often analyzed using a thematic technique (Vaterlaus and Higginbotham 2011). Quantitative evaluation encompasses collecting measurable data on the effects of the training and can be analyzed using statistical software.

Case Example: International Organization

Phillips et al. (2013) provided an example of utilizing all five levels of evaluation at an international organization. High turnover rates and low employee satisfaction were a concern of the executive team for a U.S.-based company that operates in 12 countries with 21,000 employees. Diagnostics on the organization determined three key issues: (1) employees needed to have a clearer understanding of career paths; (2) to grow the business, more leaders were needed to take positions higher up in the company; and (3) the internal fill rate for leadership was 10 percent, and it would be beneficial to the company to groom more internal talent for higher positions. The OD team working with the company had managers throughout the company identify high-potential leaders. These potential leaders participated in a 360-degree feedback process based on established leadership competencies.

Evaluation was performed at all five levels. At Level 1, the OD team had participants complete a questionnaire immediately after the 360-degree feedback asking about satisfaction with the process and planned actions. The Level 2 evaluation was also completed immediately after the 360-degree feedback. The facilitator had participants complete a questionnaire regarding their learning on topics such as gaining business acumen, communicating effectively, and personal strengths and weaknesses. The Level 3 evaluation was not done until six months after the 360-degree feedback. The facilitator and store training coordinator completed a checklist of demonstrated competencies and a second 360-degree feedback was performed for each participant to determine what had changed over the six-month period. The Level 4 evaluation was also completed six months after the initial 360-degree feedback. The store training coordinator accessed company databases to determine if costs had been reduced, if the voluntary turnover rate had been reduced, if promotions had increased, and if employee satisfaction had increased. The Level 5 evaluation was a calculation of the ROI. The company's aim was for a 25 percent ROI (Phillips et al. 2013).

CHOOSING AN EVALUATION STRATEGY

Evaluation strategies can be visualized as a 3×5 matrix with the columns focusing on the five levels of evaluations and the three rows focusing on the rigor of the strategy. This matrix is shown in Figure 11.2. The result is 10 evaluation strategies, with five being a blend of low to high rigor.

The higher the rigor, the more formal and planned the evaluation. As for levels, the more whole the focus, the more the evaluation moves beyond examining the participants' perceptions of their experience to the intervention's impact on the entire system. In other words, evaluation at the lower levels focuses on participants, whereas evaluation at the higher levels focuses on the system

--- **Levels of Evaluation** ---

		Level 1 Reaction	Level 2 Learning	Level 3 Behavior	Level 4 Results	Level 5 ROI
	High	*Strategy 2* Validated Normative Survey	*Strategy 4* Piloted Pre/Post-Test Knowledge	*Strategy 6* Success Case Evaluation	*Strategy 8* Retention, Production, & Quality	*Strategy 10* Benefit-Cost Ratio Calculation
Degree of Rigor	Med	Blend	Blend	Blend	Blend	Blend
	Low	*Strategy 1* Live Verbal Poll or Flip Chart Survey	*Strategy 3* Oral Quizzes or Dialogue in Large-Groups	*Strategy 5* Participation Rates & Volunteering	*Strategy 7* Customer & Employee Intentions	*Strategy 9* Quick Group SWAG Calculation

Figure 11.2. Fifteen Situational Evaluation Strategies

(i.e., organization or community). Figure 11.2 provides examples for each of the 10 evaluation strategies based on levels of evaluation and rigor. Evaluations needing medium rigor, the middle five strategies, would require a blending of the two strategies. Listed below are more specific examples of ways to accomplish the 10 strategies.

- *Strategy 1*. Ask participants to provide a one-word or one-sentence "check out" on what was their greatest takeaway or learning from today's event. Ask participants for a "five finger evaluation" to rate each aspect of the intervention on a scale of 1 to 5.

- *Strategy 2*. Ask participants to complete a survey that has been validated; the results could be compared to responses from other events, times, or organizations.

- *Strategy 3*. Administer oral quizzes during the intervention to determine if the participants have learned the material presented. Use the large-group dialogue based techniques (e.g., World Café, Appreciative Inquiry, Open Space, Whole Scale Change, etc.) to engage the participants.

- *Strategy 4*. Ask participants to complete pre- and post-intervention tests to determine the knowledge they have gained during the intervention.

- *Strategy 5*. Determine the number of participants engaged in the process, volunteering for projects, offering ideas, and so forth, and track over time.

- *Strategy 6*. Perform a Success Case Evaluation in which both high performers and low performers are interviewed to determine the effects of the intervention (The Learning Sanctuary 2007).

- *Strategy 7*. Conduct a survey of customer and employee intentions to determine if employee morale has improved and whether customer satisfaction or recommendations have improved.

- *Strategy 8*. Verify actual changes in objective measures such as the degree to which production, retention, and quality changed.

- *Strategy 9*. Use group opinion or consensus for a quick SWAG. (scientific wild ass guess) to estimate the ROI (return on investment).

- *Strategy 10*. Calculate a benefit-cost ratio (BCR) on the intervention (Phillips and Phillips 2009).

The Evaluation Selection Process

Which strategy is best for your situation? Figure 11.3 presents a decision model that will guide you in picking the best strategy. Walk step by step through these questions; your answers will direct you to the appropriate evaluation for a situation. The decision model is organized into two sets or series of questions based on the competing demands: "Prove and Improve" and "Time and Money."

Start with the first series of questions that focus on the intention to prove and improve the intervention (Figure 11.3). This series of questions is based on your intention and it will help you determine the level of evaluation. Begin with determining the need or desire to prove whether or not the intervention had the intended impact. Next, answer the question, "Do you need to improve the intervention for later application or use (i.e., continuous improvement)?" It may be that the intention is to improve a change initiative that is in process over a period of time. If you need to prove and improve the intervention, then you are looking at a comprehensive evaluation utilizing all the levels of evaluation. If you don't need to prove or improve the intervention, then you don't need to conduct an evaluation at all.

The second series of questions addresses the constraints of time and money (Figure 11.4). This series of questions focuses on balancing constraints. These questions help you to determine the level of rigor to apply for any of the levels

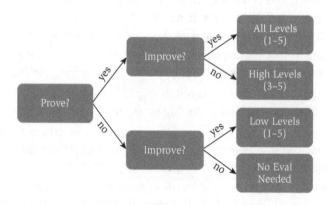

Figure 11.3. Question Series #1—Choosing an Evaluation Strategy

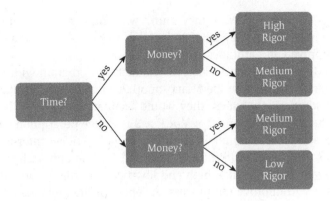

Figure 11.4. Question Series #2—Choosing an Evaluation Strategy

identified in the first question series. First, how much time do you have—a lot or a little? Then, consider how much money or resources you wish to use or have available to conduct the evaluation. If there is plenty of time and money, then it's recommended that you conduct a rigorous analysis. If you have little time and money, then choose a less rigorous approach.

CASE EXAMPLE: A TECHNOLOGY FIRM

In South Africa, an information technology service center's most important task was to keep their main customer's computers up and running. If an incident occurred that interrupted the computers, the number of incident-free days was reset to zero. The average number of incident-free days was 8.94, with a low of zero and a high of 24 days. This number of days between resets was low, so low that the contract was in jeopardy. In response, an intervention was launched, titled "80 Days Around the World." Management put up large banners and held a braai (i.e., a cookout) announcing a mandated goal of 80 incident-free days (Oelofse and Cady 2012).

Let's walk through the decision model and analyze what happened next. The first series of questions focus on "prove and improve." Do they need to prove that it worked? Yes. Do they need to improve the process? Yes. With that, the model suggests that all levels of evaluation are needed. The next series of questions in the decision model focus on "time and money." Do they have time? Not much—time is of the essence. They are on the verge of losing their contract. Do they have money? Yes. They are willing to spend money on banners, T-shirts, and more. However, they did not have a lot of resources to expend, and their budget was very lean. As a result, the consulting team working on the project tracked the incident-free days (*Strategy 8*) and also assessed employee morale in meetings (*Strategy 1*). What they found was employees did not understand nor see the need for such a goal of 80 incident-free days, and five months later, nothing improved and attitudes worsened.

Perplexed, management decided to relaunch the program with bigger banners, fancier T-shirts, more fliers, and another braai. The consultants offered a different solution, one where they would facilitate dialogue with employees based on the change formula $D \times V \times F \times S > R$ (see description earlier). The dialogue-based process would enable them to gather richer information at the lower levels of evaluation (*Strategies 1, 3,* and *5*). The approaches allow for a real-time evaluation, blending high and low rigor in order to provide information necessary to improve the process. A repeat of the previous results, using the same interventions, would be disastrous. There is an old saying, "The definition of 'crazy' is doing the same thing over and over, and expecting different results." They needed a different approach to solving this problem.

Reluctantly, upper management agreed to a two-hour session with all employees. Of the WSCC methods available, World Café was chosen as the medium in which the employees formed into groups to discuss the questions centered on the formula. Toward the end of the two-hour session, the manager was so impressed with the dialogue and great ideas being offered that he formed a cross-sectional team of volunteers (*Strategy 5*) to prioritize and coordinate the implementation. The organization saw immediate results. Utilizing *Strategy 1*

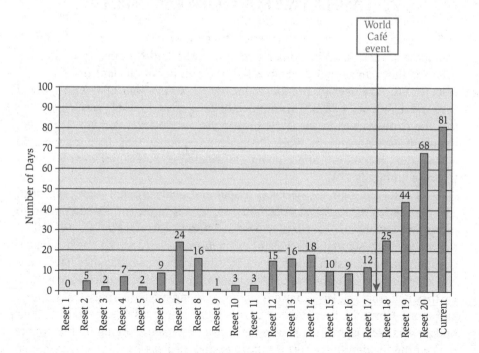

Figure 11.5. Trend of Incident-Free Days

and 2 evaluation, they showed that attitudes improved, and utilizing *Strategy 8*, they proved the positive impact of the intervention. Performance exceeded the expectations beyond the 81-day mark in the study to more than 120 incident-free days and counting, as shown in Figure 11.5. (Data were based on a presentation at the University of Johannesburg in South Africa on July 15, 2013, by E. Oelofse and Steve Cady.)

SUMMARY

Evaluation can be thought of as a research project. The evaluator is trying to disprove the hypothesis that no change had occurred from the intervention. Therefore, evaluation should be approached in the same manner as a research project. However, the research topic has already been chosen. The evaluation strategy chosen provides a starting point. An Internet search is then useful to determine if the type of evaluation chosen has been done before. It is generally easier to start with a survey or other instrument that has already been created and validated. Make sure you are using trustworthy sources such as government (.gov) and education (.edu) websites. Remember that anyone can post anything to the Internet (Antioch University). Additionally, it is helpful to focus your evaluation narrowly (Indiana University). The more comprehensive the evaluation, the more difficult it will be to perform. The focus of the evaluation can be on one of the objectives of the intervention.

This chapter has provided a foundation to evaluate the effectiveness of whole system collaborative change. Whole system collaborative change and organizational transformation were reviewed. The challenge of evaluation was presented, including a brief history of evaluation and a discussion of the paradox of competing demands. The five levels of evaluation were discussed along with guidance for choosing an evaluation strategy. The Phillips Case Example demonstrates the use of all levels, in a rigorous fashion. However, that is not always possible, as discussed with the competing demands. Taking a situational approach will enable you to choose a more realistic evaluation strategy. The World Café example shows how powerful a situational evaluation can be when blended with dialogue-based process. The belief in the wisdom of the people in the system is a fundamental principle of collaborative processes. Finding the right balance, the right blend, within the realities of the competing demands, is what differentiates masterful OD professionals from the good ones.

Discussion Questions

1. Describe a situation or scenario where you have had to compromise proving or improving, because of time and money limitations? How did you handle that situation, what did you learn, and what would you do differently next time?

2. What are the benefits to finding effective ways to balance these competing demands? What are some of the risks?

3. As you look at the 10 evaluation strategies, can you come up with more examples or options that you could utilize? Consider describing low- versus high-rigor strategies for one of the levels. Then describe a blended approach drawing from both.

4. In a small group, have one person bring an evaluation challenge. Walk through the two question series to identify a strategy, and then discuss the implementation of that strategy.

Resources

The ROI Institute's website: www.roiinstitute.net/applications

Training and Evaluation Methods by Kirkpatrick Partners website: www .kirkpatrickpartners.com/Resources/tabid/56/Default.aspx

NEXUS for Whole System Collaboration and Change website: www.nexus4change.org

References

Antioch University New England. "Research Tips." Retrieved from www.antiochne.edu/ library/researchassist.

Axelrod, E., S. H. Cady, and P. Holman. 2010. "Whole System Change: What It Is and Why It Matters." In *Practicing Organization Development: A Guide for Leading Change*, 3rd ed., edited by W. Rothwell, J. M. Stavros, and R. L. Sullivan, 363–376. San Francisco: Jossey-Bass.

Brennan, A., F. Sampson, and M. Deverill. 2005. "Can We Use Routine Data to Evaluate Organizational Change? Lessons from the Evaluation of Business Process Re-Engineering in a UK Teaching Hospital." *Health Services Management Research* 18: 265–276.

Butler, J., F. Scott, and J. Edwards. 2003. "Evaluating Organizational Change: The Role of Ontology and Epistemology." *Journal of Critical Postmodern Organizational Science* 2 (2): 55–67.

Bunker, B. B., and B. T. Alban. 1997. *Large Group Interventions: Engaging the Whole System for Rapid Change*. San Francisco: Jossey-Bass.

Cady, S., J. Auger, and M. Foxon 2010. "Situation Evaluation." In *Practicing Organization Development: A Guide for Leading Change*, 3rd ed., edited by W. Rothwell, J. M. Stavros, and R. L. Sullivan, 269–286. San Francisco: Jossey-Bass.

Cady, S. H., and L. Hardalupas. 1999. "A Lexicon for Organizational Change: Examining the Use of Language in Popular, Practitioner, and Scholar Periodicals." *The Journal of Applied Business Research* 15 (4): 81–94.

Cady, S., J. Hine, J. Meenach, and J. Spalding. 2011. "Collaborative Leadership: Using Large Group Meetings to Cause Rapid Change and Breakthrough Performance." In *Learning from Real World Cases: Lessons in Leadership*, edited by D. D. Warrick and J. Mueller, 153–163. Oxford, UK: RossiSmith Academic Publications.

Cady, S. H., R. Jacobs, R. Koller, and J. Spalding. 2014. "The Change Formula: Myth, Legend, or Lore?" *OD Practitioner* 46 (3): 32–39.

Covin, T. J., and R. H. Kilmann. 1988. "Critical Issues in Large-Scale Change." *Journal of Organizational Change Management* 1 (2): 59–72.

Foxon, M. 1989. "A Process Approach to the Transfer of Training." *Australian Journal of Educational Technology* 5 (2): 89–104.

Goldstein, R., and G. Behm. 2004. "Taking the Next Step: Reaching Higher Levels of Organizational Performance." *Organization Development Journal* 22 (1): 97–101.

Himmelman, J. T. 2002. *Collaboration for Change*. Minneapolis, MN: Himmelman Consulting.

Holman, P., T. Devane, and S. Cady. 2007. *The Change Handbook: The Definitive Source on Today's Best Methods for Engaging Whole Systems*. San Francisco: Berrett-Koehler.

Indiana University. "Doing Research." Retrieved from www.cs.indiana.edu/how.2b/how.2b.research.html.

Kirkpatrick, D. 1977. "Evaluating Training Programs: Evidence vs. Proof." *Training and Development Journal* 31 (11): 9–12.

Kirkpatrick, D. 1998. *Evaluating Training Programs: The Four Levels*. San Francisco: Berrett-Koehler.

Laszlo, K. C. 2012. "From Systems Thinking to Systems Being: The Embodiment of Evolutionary Leadership." *Journal of Organizational Transformation & Social Change* 9 (2): 95–108.

Manning, M. R., and G. F. Binzagr. 1996. "Methods, Values, and Assumptions Underlying Large Group Interventions Intended to Change Whole Systems." *The International Journal of Organizational Analysis* 4 (3): 268–284.

Mohrman, Jr., A. M., S. A. Mohrman, G. E. Ledford, Jr., T. G. Cummings, and E. E. Lawler III. 1989. *Large-Scale Organizational Change*. San Francisco: Jossey-Bass.

Oelofse, E., and S. H. Cady. 2012. "The World Cafe in South Africa: A Case Study on Improving Performance and Commitment." *Organization Development Journal* 30 (1): 79–89.

Oelofse, E., and S. H. Cady. 2013. "Whole System Collaborative Change." Mandela Day Talk, July 15. University of Johannesburg, Johannesburg, South Africa.

Phillips, J. 1996. *Measuring ROI: The Fifth Level of Evaluation*. Alexandria, VA: American Society for Training and Development.

Phillips, J. J., and P. P. Phillips. 2009. *The Bottom Line on ROI—A One-Day Workshop Describing How to Calculate the ROI in Government Training Programs*. Birmingham, AL: ROI Institute.

Phillips, P. P., J. J. Phillips, and L. Zuniga. 2013. *Measuring the Success of Organization Development*. Alexandria, VA: ASTD Press.

Rossett, A. 2007. "Leveling the Levels." *Training and Development* (February): 49–53.

Russ-Eft, D., M. Bober, I. de la Taja, M. Foxon, and T. Koszalka. 2008. *Evaluator Competencies: Standards for the Practice of Evaluation in Organizations*. San Francisco: Jossey-Bass.

Terborg, J. R., G. S. Howard, and S. E. Maxwell. 1980. "Evaluating Planned Organizational Change: A Method for Assessing Alpha, Beta, and Gamma Change." *Academy of Management Review* 5 (1): 109–121.

The Learning Sanctuary. 2007. *Success Case Evaluation*. amlconsultancy.com/wp-content/uploads/2007/05/success-case-brochure.pdf.

van der Heijden, J. 2010. "A Short History of Studying Incremental Institutional Change: Does Explaining Institutional Change Provide any New Explanations?" *Regulation & Governance* 4: 230–243.

Vaterlaus, J. M., and B. J. Higginbotham. 2011. "Qualitative Program Evaluation Methods." *The Forum for Family and Consumer Issues* 16 (1). http://ncsu.edu/ffci/publications/2011/v16-n1-2011-spring/vaterlaus-higginbotham.php.

Way, C., and J. McKeeby. 2012. "Systems Thinking as a Team-Building Approach." *Reflections* 11 (4): 44–49.

CHAPTER TWELVE

Measurement to Determine the Return on Change Management

Tim Creasey and D. Scott Ross

Organization development (OD) and change management (CM) make significant contributions to the achievement of change and organizational outcomes. Demonstrating the value of CM to organizations and leaders is an ongoing challenge. Effective CM is correlated with project success; however, executives and project leaders regularly press CM practitioners to measure their impact and show their value (Creasey and Taylor 2014). This chapter provides a concept-driven, research-based model for measuring CM and showing the contribution that effective CM makes to delivering change results.

MULTI-LAYERED, HOLISTIC MEASUREMENT

The Prosci® Change Measurement Framework™ is based on years of benchmarking research conducted by Prosci. In Prosci's 2013 research effort, study participants answered several new questions on CM measurement (Creasey and Taylor 2014). Analysis of responses produced the Prosci Change Measurement Framework™ comprising three levels: Organizational Performance, Individual Performance, and Change Management Performance, and three timeframes for measurement—early, mid-term, and late. The framework balances activity and outcomes measures to create a holistic assessment of CM's impact.

To provide a common platform for the measurement discussion, CM will be defined as "the application of processes and tools to manage the people side of change from a current state to a new future state so that the desired results of the change are achieved" (Hiatt and Creasey 2012, 9). Prosci's CM work focuses on driving adoption (individuals are performing in the new way) and usage (being proficient and completely capable). CM enables and catalyzes the individual transitions that deliver the portion of the outcomes that are dependent on adoption and usage.

HISTORY OF MEASUREMENT

OD and CM are challenged to measure the value of their contributions, but agreed upon standards are lacking. Some practitioners have devoted significant time and effort to responding to these challenges.

As Steven Cady, Julie Auger, and Marguerite Foxon note, the roots of measurement and evaluation efforts appear in education and social programs, in OD, and in training and development (Cady, Auger, and Foxon 2010). OD has a rich history of evaluating the impact of interventions, from the early days of Frederick Taylor and Kurt Lewin (Lewin 1946; Taylor 1911). In training and development, Donald Kirkpatrick and Patricia and Jack Phillips provide frameworks to gauge the impact of training and OD, evaluating reactions, learning, behavior, results, and return (monetized results) (Kirkpatrick 1998; Phillips 2010; Phillips and Phillips 2012; Phillips, Phillips, and Zuniga 2013). Other disciplines, such as communications and marketing, seeking to change individual or group attitudes, beliefs, or action, also seek tools to measure and evaluate effectiveness (Corder 2010; Farris, Bendle, Pfeifer, and Reibstein 2010).

These efforts struggle with two challenges: monetizing the value of the outcomes produced and determining the causal connection between their efforts and the outcomes. These challenges exist to varying degrees in all change, but the private sector can be especially demanding. To determine an ROI, the costs and benefits must be on the same scale for comparison. Monetary costs are relatively easy to determine. The question is what monetary value can be directly attributed to the OD or CM activity. This is compounded by the challenge of answering the conditional counterfactual question, "What would the outcome have been if the activity had not occurred?"

The approach described next addresses both, not with a silver bullet scale for the monetization or epistemological issues, but by changing the conversation. The following approach relies on a socially constructed prior agreement on the outcomes that CM will be accountable and responsible for delivering and their value. With that agreement, a scorecard can be constructed and CM can be held accountable for its role in and contribution to the outcome.

CHANGE MEASUREMENT FRAMEWORK

Prosci's 2013 benchmarking study involved 822 change practitioners from around the world, with 34 percent of respondents from the United States, 25 percent from Australia and New Zealand, 15 percent from Canada, 14 percent from Europe, and 12 percent from other regions. As in the previous seven studies, participants shared experiences regarding a variety of change management topics. In the 2013 study, practitioners were asked how they measured and reported on their effectiveness, measured whether changes were occurring at the individual level, demonstrated the value added from applying CM, and measured the overall impact of applying CM. Each question provided insight into the challenges of and potential considerations for CM measurement. A meta-analysis of the responses yielded patterns that created a picture that holistically measured change management's impact. Prosci's Change Measurement Framework (Figure 12.1) emerged from this analysis, comprised of three levels of measurement in each of three timeframes across the lifecycle of the change.

Three Levels of Measurement

Practitioner responses yielded three foundational questions for measurement. How much value did the organization realize from the initiative? How effectively did individuals bring the changes to life in their behaviors? How well did practitioners "do" CM? The first two—organizational results and individual transitions—measure the outcomes in the change, while the final level measures implementation of change management activities. This provides a multilayered view of CM measurement.

	Early	Mid	Late
Organizational Performance	Organization Readiness and Change Requisites	Progress to Plan	Results and Outcomes
Individual Performance	Individual Readiness	Engagement, Participation, and Adoption	Usage and Performance
Change Management Performance	Preparing: Strategy and Plans	Managing: Implementation Activities	Reinforcing: Sustaining Activities

Figure 12.1. Prosci® Change Measurement Framework™

Source: From T. Creasey, "Cracking the Measurement Code: Create Your Research-Based Change Measurement Scorecard." Paper presented at the ACMP Pacific Northwest Symposium, Redmond, WA, 2014. Reprinted with permission.

The three levels interact to create an integrated measurement system. The definition and measurement of initiative performance addresses why the change was undertaken and how the organization improved (or expected to improve). Some portion of expected benefits depends on individuals changing their behavior. Consider a new knowledge and content management system. Some of the project benefits may not depend on employee adoption and usage, say reduced data holding costs in the new system. However, benefits such as faster decision making and increased information flow depend on employee adoption and usage. In today's economy, the most important and strategic changes tend to have a greater dependence on individual adoption and usage. The benefits that depend on individual adoption and usage are the benefits that change management drives as outlined in Prosci's approach to Change Management Return on Investment (CMROI; Creasey, 2013, 2014a; Ross, 2013).

CM activities are the steps a team or change practitioner can take to facilitate needed individual transitions. Prosci's research identifies specific activities that drive adoption and usage, leading to success. These include active and visible sponsorship; effective communications; manager engagement; and employee participation. When CM activities are customized and scaled, and focused on helping individuals embrace a specific behavioral aspect of their job, the individual transitions that occur drive organizational outcomes. Linking CM activities to individual adoption and usage, and adoption and usage to organizational outcomes, creates an integrated framework for measurement.

Organizational Performance. The first level of measurement emerging from the analysis focuses on overall results and outcomes of the change, project, or initiative. This dimension asks whether the effort has delivered the expected benefits and improvement in performance. Were benefits realized (costs reduced, revenue increased, efficiencies improved, error lessened, risks mitigated, culture enhanced)? Was performance improved as expected? Was the targeted return on investment (ROI) achieved? Each effort has, or should have, specific results and outcomes it is attempting to deliver. Measurement begins with evaluating objective definitions and change requisites. During the implementation of the change, progress to plan is tracked, including milestone, budget, and deliverable adherence. Evaluating organizational performance resulting from the initiative provides the first level of outcome measurement.

Individual Performance. Achievement of the organizational outcomes requires individuals to behave differently. Change ultimately takes place one individual at a time. Whether a transformation, a program, or a project, some individuals in the organization will experience changes in the way they work, including changes in processes, systems, tools, job roles, critical behaviors, mindset/attitude/beliefs, reporting structure, performance measures, compensation, or location. Measuring individual transitions begins with ensuring awareness, understanding, and commitment or buy-in. When those occur among sufficient numbers of individuals, then participation, engagement, and adoption are measured to determine if and how many individuals are behaving in the new way. Beyond simple adoption, measurement efforts shift to usage, quality of compliance, and proficiency. Both adoption and the proficiency of usage determine the extent to which results are achieved and organizational outcomes are realized.

Change Management Performance. Research and experience show there are repeatable actions that can be taken within an initiative to support individual transitions. Over the past decade, the discipline of CM has evolved and matured with formalization of the processes and tools aimed at catalyzing individual adoption and usage. Formalization does not mean mechanization, but rather laying out a structured process and sequence of activities that, when customized for the situation at hand and adaptively applied, increase the likelihood of individuals successfully adopting the change. Prosci's research focused on scaling and customizing the approach used for the circumstances based on change history, culture, and underlying systems.

Research also shows that a structured approach applied by dedicated resources increases the overall effectiveness of change management and the likelihood of meeting of objectives. During the change effort itself, measures focus on the completion of CM activities and their impact. Late in the effort, measurement focuses on sustainment activities and outcomes. Evaluating CM performance requires answering both an "activity" question and an "outcome" question: Are best practice activities occurring? Are they having the desired impact on individual transitions?

Three Time Frames of Measurement

Each of the three levels—organizational performance, individual performance, and change management performance—is measured across the duration of the change, in each of three time frames—early, mid-term (during), and late in the change life cycle. However, in analyzing the results of the benchmarking data, what is measured differs in each of the three time frames. In the early stage, the focus is on readiness. In the mid-term, the focus shifts to progress. And late in the change, measurement focuses on outcomes and results.

CHANGE MEASUREMENT SCORECARD

The Prosci Change Measurement Framework presents three levels of measurement over three time frames. To create a Prosci® Change Measurement Scorecard™, the practitioner must identify specific measures for each of the nine cells (3 × 3) of the scorecard (see Figure 12.1).

The creation of a scorecard based on the framework should not be done by a single person working alone. Creating the scorecard as a collaborative team—including initiative leaders, sponsors, team members, subject matter experts, organization representatives, OD consultants, communication specialists, and training specialists—is an important step in creating a common vision of change success. The process of co-creating the scorecard drives agreement and clarity on organizational benefits, project objectives, and the change management effort required for success, establishing expectations and a shared platform. The goal of a scorecard creation conversation is to set a path for what will be measured and how success will be defined during and at the end of the initiative. Below are five steps for an effective co-creation effort.

Step 1: What Is the Initiative Trying to Achieve? The first step focuses on identifying the organizational benefits and objectives of the initiative or change. The team will function more effectively if it has a clear and shared vision of outcomes and what success looks like. Often, the initiative or project objectives are clear, but their connection back to organizational benefits and alignment with strategy is fuzzy at best. By incorporating these into the Change Measurement Scorecard, change practitioners are taking responsibility, even without sole influence or ultimate accountability, for delivering the expected benefits to the organization.

Step 2: Identify Affected Groups. The second step is identifying affected groups and individuals—the groups and individuals that will have aspects of their job changed because of the initiative. Many organizational initiatives, programs, projects, and even transformations move forward without ever defining the change at the individual, granular level. The team's inventory of affected groups is an important input into customized and scaled CM strategies, plans, and activities.

Step 3: Define "To Adopt and to Use" for Each Group. After identifying the affected groups, the team works to collaboratively define what "to adopt and to use" means for each group. Meaningful individual performance measurements depend on this crucial step: If we do not know how individuals and their behaviors will be affected, then we do not understand what to measure. Adoption and usage at the individual level can be defined by reviewing the aspects of an individual's current role that an initiative can affect: processes, systems, tools, job roles, critical behaviors, mindset/attitude/beliefs, reporting structure, performance reviews, compensation, or location. With the definitions from the team, the change practitioner can create measures and metrics to track progress.

Step 4: Evaluate Strategy and Plans to Drive Adoption and Usage. With a clear picture of expected change results and affected groups, the CM team reviews and plans how to drive and facilitate adoption and usage. The team should review the structured CM approach being used and the resources allocated for CM.

Step 5: Set Plan for Measuring. The outputs of the collaborative session may need to be translated into measures and metrics. The final step is to set a date for reviewing the initial draft and success targets created by the change practitioner and to establish a schedule for measurement throughout the initiative's life cycle.

A CASE APPLICATION OF CHANGE MEASUREMENT SCORECARD

A $20 billion financial services organization used the Prosci® Change Measurement Scorecard™ to plan, track, and evaluate the implementation of a customer relationship management (CRM) application designed to increase revenue, win rate, and opportunity size. A simplified version of their scorecard is shown in Figure 12.2.

Creation of the scorecard presented both challenges and opportunities. To create the scorecard, the team had to further clarify the organizational outcomes expected from the initiative. The team could recite the mantra for project objectives but was challenged when translating those objectives into the organizational benefits to be realized. While defining organizational outcomes was a difficult exercise, and one frequently skipped in many organizations, the

	Early	Mid	Late
Organizational Performance	Adoption of a nimble tool; Mobile solution; Increased speed to market	Software delivery methodology milestones met	Increase in revenue X%; Increase opportunity size Y% Improve win rates Z%
Individual Performance	Readiness assessments; Participation of change agent network	Awareness surveys; Knowledge checks; Logins to system	Behavior change; User productivity increases
Change Management Performance	Change management staffing; Key stakeholder alignment	Communication tracking; Manager involvement; Training delivery tracking	Follow-up assessments; Implementation reviews; Change outcome reviews

Figure 12.2. Prosci® Change Measurement Scorecard™

Source: From T. Creasey, "Cracking the Measurement Code: Create Your Research-Based Change Measurement Scorecard." Paper presented at the ACMP Pacific Northwest Symposium, Redmond, WA, 2014. Reprinted with permission.

team found great value in the exercise. Using the Prosci Change Measurement Framework enabled them to build a defined model that highlighted the connection between the change being introduced, the impact on individual behavior, and the specific, measureable outcomes desired. The integrated and multilayered view of change success enabled them to "connect the dots" in a novel way. The team developed measures and metrics for all the time frames with more than 25 metrics identified to assess individual performance. In addition, the scorecard integrated several existing tools being used to manage the change, producing a single big-picture view. In addition, the process of creating the scorecard increased the understanding of and commitment to CM, with one executive noting, "Now, I get it. I understand what change management is doing."

SUMMARY

The Prosci Change Measurement Framework provides an integrated measurement approach that links CM activities to individual performance focusing on adoption and usage, and connects individual adoption and usage to overall change outcomes and organizational results. A co-created scorecard that establishes metrics based on the Change Measurement Framework provides agreed upon targets directly tied to the delivery of organizational results. The CM team can use these to track and measure both activities and outcomes. The framework and scorecard's holistic and integrated view of measurement enables practitioners to build support for change management with leadership and ensure a unified, clear, and shared set of criteria for defining success and measuring impact. Experience with the Change Measurement Framework and Scorecard will help refine the approach and identify best practices for use.

Discussion Questions

1. What benefits result from a co-created, shared definition of change success?

2. How does the Change Measurement Framework build on earlier efforts to measure the impact of OD and CM activities?

3. For the CRM example described above, identify measures relevant to the individual adoption and usage outcomes.

4. Discuss the difficulties you would expect to experience when implementing the Prosci Change Measurement Framework.

Resources

Change Measurement: Cracking the Code: www.linkedin.com/pulse/article/
 20140916184352-33879-change-measurement-cracking-the-code

Cracking the Measurement Code: Create Your Research-Based Change Measurement Scorecard

Paper and presentation from ACMP Pacific Northwest Symposium, Redmond, WA: www .slideshare.net/TimCreasey/prosci-change-connect-2014-breakout-cracking

How to Calculate CMROI. [Webinar replay]: https://portal.prosci.com/resources/view/ 26

CMROI Calculator by Prosci: http://portal.prosci.com/

References

Cady, S., J. Auger, and M. Foxon. 2010. "Situational Evaluation." In *Practicing Organization Development*, 3rd ed., edited by W. Rothwell, J. Stavros, R. Sullivan, and A. Sullivan, 269–286. San Francisco: John Wiley & Sons.

Corder, L. 2010. *Marketing ROI: Measuring & Maximizing Campaign Results*. North Seattle, WA: CreateSpace Independent Publishing Platform.

Creasey, T. 2013. "ROI of Change Management: Connecting to Project Benefits." www .change-management.com/tutorial-roi-of-cm-mod3.htm.

Creasey, T. 2014a. "Adoption and Usage: The ROI of Change Management." Paper presented at the Conference Board 2014 Change Management Conference, New York.

Creasey, T. 2014b. "Cracking the Measurement Code: Create Your Research-Based Change Measurement Scorecard." Paper presented at the ACMP Pacific Northwest Symposium, Redmond, WA. www.slideshare.net/TimCreasey/prosci-change-connect-2014-breakout-cracking.

Creasey, T., and T. Taylor. 2014. *Best Practices in Change Management*. 2014 ed. Loveland, CO: Prosci.

Farris, P., N. Bendle, P. Pfeifer, and D. Reibstein. 2010. *Marketing Metrics: The Definitive Guide to Measuring Marketing Performance*. 2nd ed. Upper Saddle River, NJ: Pearson Education.

Hiatt, J., and T. Creasey. 2012. *Change Management: The People Side of Change*. 2nd ed. Loveland, CO: Prosci.

Kirkpatrick, D. 1998. *Evaluating Training Programs: The Four Levels*. San Francisco: Berrett-Koehler.

Lewin, K. 1946. "Action Research and Minority Problems." *Journal of Social Issues* 2: 34–46.

Phillips, P., ed. 2010. *ASTD Handbook of Measuring and Evaluating Training*. Alexandria, VA: ASTD Press.

Phillips, P., and J. Phillips. 2012. *Measuring ROI in Learning & Development*. Alexandria, VA: ASTD Press.

Phillips, P., J. Phillips, and L. Zuniga. 2013. *Measuring the Success of Organization Development*. Alexandria, VA: ASTD Press.

Ross, D. S. 2013. "Let's Talk Numbers: The Value of Change Management." Paper at the Association of Change Management Professionals (ACMP) Europe Conference, London.

Taylor, F. 1911. *The Principles of Scientific Management*. New York: W. W. Norton.

CHAPTER THIRTEEN

Closure

Mobilizing Energy to Sustain an Agile Organization

Ann M. Van Eron and W. Warner Burke

The last phase in the organization development (OD) consulting process is closure. This final phase is important for reaping and sustaining the benefits of an OD intervention. It needs to be conducted in a careful, planned manner. Few consultants or researchers choose to write or speak about this phase of the OD process (Anderson 2015; Block 2011). Given the rapid pace and complexity of change today, when leaders and organizations are faced with multiple challenges and the need to be innovative and responsive to demanding external pressures, the benefit of attending to closure is magnified.

Closure can be a valuable way to mobilize energy for agility and sustainability. Inadequate closure can limit the impact and learning of a successful OD intervention. More than simply separating from the OD process, there are benefits in a thoughtful and present attention to closure throughout an OD intervention. By stopping and reflecting, meaning can be made that will support future initiatives and enhance organization agility and growth.

We begin this chapter with a case example where closure was not successful and some related reasons for endings of OD projects. Then, we highlight the need to mobilize energy through closure. We suggest the value of attending to closing throughout the OD intervention to increase learning, agility, and sustainability. We also provide questions for a meaningful closure process. We share insights on determining next steps. As a summary, we provide an example of a successful closure process and offer discussion questions.

CASE EXAMPLE

While not atypical, the following synopsis of an actual OD effort provides an illustration of an OD practitioner managing the final phase rather poorly. The OD practitioner had worked with his client for about nine months conducting the usual steps. Data had been collected via interviews from a majority of management and key staff personnel. The data were reported back to the CEO and his direct reports, followed by a similar summary of the interview results to the larger system.

The OD practitioner's diagnosis was that most of the data collected were symptoms and that the major underlying cause was the existence of two "camps" within top management who vehemently disagreed with one another as to how the company should be managed and what business strategy was best regarding the future. The OD practitioner held an open discussion concerning the two-camp issue with the CEO alone and then with the entire top group of executives. The group verified that the OD practitioner's diagnosis was correct and that action should be taken to do something about this serious conflict. The CEO was very supportive of participation, that is, he wanted consensus within his top team. As a result, he was immobilized by the seemingly intractable differences of opinion, particularly regarding strategy. The OD practitioner provided coaching with suggestions for action steps. Changes within the top group needed to be made, but no action was taken. Time went by, with the CEO continuing to be in a "frozen" state.

The CEO did eventually modify the organizational structure somewhat and dismissed a key executive, but the OD practitioner believed that these changes were largely cosmetic and would not lead to the fundamental changes that were needed for significant improvement in organizational performance.

The OD practitioner had other clients at the time who were more demanding, and therefore, he allowed this client to drift away rather than pursuing potential options for change and working on his relationship with the CEO. Closure in this case occurred, not due to a planned process, but rather as a function of time passing and inadequate motivation on either the OD practitioner's or the client's part to try harder or to agree in a deliberate way to discontinue the relationship.

While real and not necessarily unusual, we are not recommending this case as an exemplary one for the closure phase. The fact that a careful closure phase is not common is no reason to overlook the importance of this final phase in OD practice. Closure is not easy, and, in any case, we should be clear that separations occur more often as a consequence of, say:

- A change in leadership due to retirement, a new and perhaps sudden assignment, or leaving the organization. For example, one of us had been a consultant to a large, global corporation for over three years and had worked closely with the CEO and head of HR. Both of these gentlemen retired at about the same time. The succeeding CEO, who had been with the corporation for a number of years, made it clear to the consultant that he would no longer be needed. In the eyes of the new CEO, the consultant had been "too close" to the retired CEO and the HR executive, and he needed to establish his own direction and bring in a new consultant who would not be seen as "linked to the old regime." Although not planned by the consultant, separation occurred nevertheless.

- Acquisition or merger where new leadership takes over and perhaps changes many of the old ways of doing things, including changing consultants. Often change initiatives are stalled or stopped with a merger. New leaders often bring their own OD practitioners based on their comfort and desire to signal a new way of working.

- Sudden change in organizational priorities due to an unforeseen crisis, for example, GM's massive recall of cars, changes in insurance and health care legislation, an economic downturn and downsizing, or perhaps some sudden change in technology that drastically affects the business. One of our clients stopped major change initiatives to focus attention on a hostile takeover. Sometimes change initiatives are stopped with little fanfare and often little attention to lessons learned when other pressures take precedence. One of our clients agreed to have quarterly dialogue sessions with the extended leadership team after other work. However, each quarter they were faced with more urgent demands, and they continued to postpone the follow-up intervention. While the OD practitioner highlighted the value of the intervention, there was no energy and closure occurred without reflection.

These examples represent frequent unplanned separations; therefore, these are rarely under the control of the OD practitioner. We will now address the closure phase in a more consciously planned manner.

THE PLANNED CLOSURE PROCESS

Done properly, the closure phase will be linked back to the contracting phase. What did the initial contract (probably revised a number of times along the way) call for? For the external OD practitioner, the contract covers the work to be done, of course, and is usually accompanied by specifications regarding time and money. This process may be less defined for internal consultants, since they are often considered to be "on call" much of the time. Yet, internal OD practitioners can conduct their practice in much the same way as externals, that is, moving through the phases from entry and contracting to closure. It's just that separation for internals is more like a clearly demarcated ending of a project but not ending a relationship with the client. Given that internal consultants are likely to be working on other OD projects, it is useful to take the time for closure in order to free up energy and the client to work on new projects. It is valuable to complete or close any unfinished business and reflect on learning that can be applied in the next initiatives.

In any case, closure is planned as a function of the content in the contracting phase. Good contracting on the part of the OD practitioner consists of agreements of who does what and when, and the specification of "deliverables"—the work to be performed—and how long everything is expected to take. Once these deliverables are achieved, then ending the project is in order. Separation can be difficult. Often clients and OD practitioners are more focused on the next initiative and may not take the time to benefit from the closure process.

MOBILIZING ENERGY

The Cycle of Experience, applied to organizations, by the Gestalt Institute of Cleveland, identifies closure and withdrawal to be a critical phase of the OD process (Stevenson 2013). The Gestalt process is unique since it highlights closure as an important phase. The Cycle of Experience is based on the view that we become aware and focus on a "figure" or issue. Then, energy is mobilized to take action, it naturally recedes, and we reduce our focus, withdraw our attention, and then turn our attention to another "figure." Gestalt practitioners focus on noting when attention to an issue is being withdrawn. It is always useful to notice what has occurred, what is finished, and what remains unfinished. The act of noting the shift frees energy for a new awareness.

Closing—identifying what has been achieved and what remains undone—supports learning and integration. Moving toward closure and separation does not imply that the work has been unsatisfactory, but that it is time to move on. By closing the engagement, there is space for new awareness and mobilizing energy for new beginnings. Closing must happen with the client and the OD practitioner. Each should pause and reflect on what went well, what is unfinished, and what was learned.

Effective closure mobilizes energy for new initiatives and next steps. Given the fast pace of change, it is easy to quickly shift focus and fail to effectively close. For example, when something is unfinished, such as the need to write a paper, pay taxes, or complete something, our energy is tied up with what we need to do. When we complete the task, we often have a sense of relief and a release of tension. We can redirect our attention and energy to the next project.

The Zeigarnik Effect is the psychological process of remembering an incomplete task that takes our mental and psychological energy. It was discovered and studied when Zeigarnik and her mentor Kurt Lewin noticed that waiters in Vienna could easily recall complex orders but immediately forgot or let go of them after a person paid for their meal. Without adequate closing, incomplete OD initiatives and other projects take mental space that could more easily be used for another creative endeavor. Incomplete projects drain our mental energy.

REFLECTING SUPPORTS AGILITY

We serve our clients and ourselves by making it a habit to regularly incorporate reflection related to closing in order to mobilize energy for moving forward. Research on how reflection aids performance, reported by Di Stefano, Gino, Pisano, and Staats (2014) in the *Harvard Business Review*, supports that a critical component of learning is reflection, which is the intentional effort to synthesize and articulate key lessons from experience. This study used both laboratory experiments and a field experiment in a large business to support that focusing augments learning or reflecting on what one has been doing. A significant performance differential was found when reflection was emphasized. Greater perceived self-efficacy was also an outcome of reflection. Our experience with closure reflection concurs that leaders experience a greater sense of self-confidence and self-efficacy through the process of considering what they have collectively learned from an intervention. Leaders are more likely to recall lessons learned from OD initiatives and incorporate useful behaviors in future initiatives after engaging in conscious reflection as they close a meeting or an intervention.

Given the rapid pace of change that most organizations are experiencing, we find that leaders are likely to be more agile—that is, more nimble, flexible, and able to move quickly when they have incorporated reflection and conscious closure into their interventions. Agility and sustainability requires being able to assess what has been achieved, what is unfinished, and what can be learned from what went well and what did not. This learning supports leaders as they approach their next change efforts. It seems that there is little space between such efforts these days. Leaders are continually embarking on new initiatives and benefit when they can incorporate their learning from experience and reflection on closing. This agility is more needed now in our fast-paced and complex organizations than ever. Research and our experience confirm the words of the American philosopher, psychologist, and educational reformer John Dewey, "We do not learn from experience ... we learn from reflecting on our experience."

When we do not take the time for closure, energy is tied up in the process, and we do not feel completely finished and ready to move on. For example, there was a premature closing to an initiative to bring together various parts of an organization where leaders were creating similar programs, thus duplicating efforts. It was a successful initiative to come to agreement on working together, presenting a cohesive message, and reducing costs dramatically. A new leader was assigned to the business and the OD initiative using the OD practitioner was abruptly ended. Meetings with the OD practitioner were stopped without an effective closure process. The incomplete process took psychological energy of the client team and the OD practitioner. It was not until later that they were able to formally close. After the dialogue, both felt satisfied and ready to move on. The client had the same dialogue with the leaders of the organization and all were better prepared to move forward.

We have closing ceremonies when we graduate from school, when we get married, or when we experience significant changes in our lives, such as birth or the death of a loved one. The opportunity to stop and reflect supports us in closing one experience and having the energy for moving to the next experience. When we fail to have such a ritual, it can take longer to mobilize our energy to go to the next phase or new beginning (Curtis 2013).

In her book *Honorable Closure*, Linda Curtis (2013) draws on the work of cultural anthropologist Angeles Arrien to emphasize the value of conscious reflection to effectively close experiences. Traditional cultures often have transition rituals to acknowledge the impact and lessons of an experience. Curtis emphasizes the importance of effectively navigating exits, endings, and good-byes. She highlights the value of the skill of honorably closing. Closings, even those we initiate and choose, always involve emotion. When we close with a sense of integrity—that is, honoring our emotions and speaking our truths—all involved seem to be better off. Closure is a process, and OD practitioners need to support their clients in reflecting and expressing emotions and learning to support effective transition and positive change. Curtis suggests that since endings are inevitable, why not become skillful at them? When we pause to reflect on what we have learned as we close, we become more open to possibilities.

ATTEND TO CLOSING THROUGHOUT AN ORGANIZATION DEVELOPMENT INTERVENTION

Most organizations are embarking on multiple change efforts and seem to be continually introducing new initiatives. It is not always easy to see clear endings. We have experienced the benefits of attending to closing in order to mobilize energy and agility throughout an OD intervention for those in the system to move forward without necessarily having an OD practitioner there. For example, we noticed, after facilitating an important leadership team intervention with two merging organizations, that when we met again after several weeks, team members did not incorporate what we thought was a significant breakthrough. Upon reflection, we realized an outside speaker had joined the meeting, and we did not effectively close that intervention and take the time to reflect on how to incorporate the insights. We have noticed similar experiences in executive coaching sessions, where a leader may not recall or act on an important insight.

Often leaders are running from one meeting to the next with little opportunity for integration and reflection. When leaders learn to make reflecting, learning, and identifying intentions for future initiatives a part of the OD process, they more effectively close and incorporate the learning in the next endeavor. This supports them in being more agile and they can quickly adapt. This is particularly true when a leadership team builds the habit of effective closure. We have seen members of leadership teams, keeping the team focused and benefiting from past learning. For example, one leadership team recalled that they had made a quick decision to move ahead on implementing a significant change in the organization's performance review process. In their haste to demonstrate a change in culture to stronger accountability, they failed to get full support from the business leaders and the rest of the human resource community. In their haste to change the culture, they had not prepared the organization and rather than positive change, the quick move cost the leaders much goodwill. The closure process enabled the team to see they had not engaged in careful enough reflection and did not involve key stakeholders. Later, when they were about to quickly approve another significant cultural change, the leadership team was able to recall their previous closure conversation and take steps to ensure stakeholder buy-in and to more widely share the key goals of the initiative. Without the previous effective closure conversation, this leadership team would have likely made similar mistakes. In fact, we often hear members of organizations question how leadership teams can continue to make some of the "same mistakes." Without clear reflection and agreement on learning and closure, it is not surprising that leaders continue with habitual responses.

It is important to create an environment where leaders can share their emotions and thoughts about a change initiative. When leaders can openly share their disappointment, frustration, excitement, and other emotions and receive empathy, there is more energy for taking on the next initiative. After all, organization change is not easy. While significant changes are being made there are pressures on many fronts while keeping the organization functioning. OD practitioners can support open dialogue where leaders can safely share their experience of the unchartered change process during closure.

Continual reflection, learning, knowledge sharing, knowledge creation—effective closure—supports agility and ultimately sustainability. Those organizations that routinely reflect and effectively close initiatives are more likely to see where changes are needed and be more nimble in making future changes. By making closure a regular part of the change process, participants are in a continual process of learning and taking actions based on learning throughout the change effort. From our many years of experience, we are convinced that teams and organizations that take the time for effective closure are more resilient and often more effective.

By building in reflection and attention to closing throughout an OD intervention, closing becomes a normal part of the process. We find this enhances the agility that is needed these days. Leaders and others learn to value closing as a part of all interventions. Many of our clients have adapted the process of attending to closing and report positive outcomes. We allow time for closing in each meeting as a normal part of the OD process. Clients learn to incorporate the closing reflection questions into their processes. In this way, they learn to appreciate and understand the benefits of interventions.

By highlighting the value of closing in each team meeting or component of an OD intervention, clients get in the habit of pausing for reflection on what they have learned and what is finished and what is not finished. With the habit of allowing time at the end of meetings for closings, clients learn to value and attend to closure. Just as openings are important, closures contribute to the success of OD interventions. By attending to closure throughout an OD intervention, clients are more nimble in making adjustments and learning throughout the process. This agility supports the long-term success and sustainability and viability of the organization

GUIDELINES FOR THE CLOSING PROCESS

A simple process for closure is having the client and OD practitioner reflect and answer a few questions. It is useful to take a positive perspective and begin with an overarching question.

- What are you leaving with from this experience? What meaning are you making?
- What has worked well?
- What is unfinished?
- Is there anything else that needs to be said for closure?

While our clients have become used to questions to help bring closure, we have found it useful to share these questions in advance and then meet with our clients in a conducive environment where we can take the time to reflect and talk about the questions as a contract comes to a formal end. An open conversation where the client and the OD practitioner share their thoughts, emotions, and reflections related to closing is impactful. One of our clients shared specifically how she had grown as a leader and benefited from our support. She acknowledged what her leadership team achieved—how they created a compelling vision and made progress in changing the organization's culture. She also identified the areas that still needed attention. We appreciated the leader's courage. Years later, both the OD practitioners and the client consider the intervention to have influenced who we are and our future endeavors. We doubt the experience would have contributed to our development without the purposeful reflection on closing. Other successful OD projects where we were not able to have such closure did not provide some of the same learning benefits.

HEALTHY CLOSURE

It is important for OD practitioners to transfer their skills to clients and to identify resources in client organizations to carry on change efforts. When independence is fostered, closure comes more easily for all involved. At the same time, practitioners must avoid becoming dependent on their clients as a means to meet their needs for work, money, or affiliation, because these needs can lead to unnecessary change efforts and wasted resources. OD practitioners should respond to actual needs in client organizations rather than to their own needs. Given the growing need for internal OD practitioners with numerous change initiatives, it is useful to have clear closure of projects. In this way, clear lines of responsibility are established and confusion avoided.

Ideally, the OD practitioner and client mutually agree that it is time to close the engagement. Otherwise, there are challenges when only one party sees the need to close. The client and the consultant can experience a sense of loss that may result in depression and dependence as a positive working relationship comes to a close (Block 2011). In some societies, endings often initiate anxiety, discomfort, sadness, or depression. Therefore, some people may avoid terminating relationships. They may postpone completing projects by beginning new projects or by procrastinating in completing assignments.

The client and the OD practitioner may have shared important experiences and are likely to have developed a mutual interdependence. It is important that the OD practitioner initiate a discussion to address and deal with the emotions associated with disengagement. Otherwise, these feelings may linger and lead to an unproductive extension of the OD process.

In a healthy but terminating OD relationship, the client may miss the confidential, candid, and stimulating discussions he or she had with the OD practitioner. Both the client and the OD practitioner can experience the loss of friendship. The OD practitioner may also sense a loss of challenge. The process of jointly determining the appropriate time to terminate the relationship allows the client and the OD practitioner an opportunity to share their feelings and perspectives. An open discussion about the discomfort in separation is important and healthy. The OD practitioner and the client will find it valuable to understand the stages and the behavioral outcomes of the mourning process for long-term relationships (Bridges 2010).

DETERMINING NEXT STEPS

After the client and the OD practitioner have reviewed the initial agreement or contract and determined the results of the change effort, they can then identify any remaining tasks and determine whether to continue the services of the OD practitioner. The client and the OD practitioner should develop an outline of next steps and decide who will be involved in these. If the goals of the change effort were not realized, the OD practitioner and the client will have to redefine the challenge or desired state and/or generate new intervention options. Even if the goals of the effort were realized, there still may be additional or related work for the OD practitioner. In this case, the process moves to one of exploring needs and contracting anew. Alternately, the OD practitioner and client may decide that additional work is not required at this time.

Often a friendship develops with a client and the OD Practitioner chooses to stay in touch. One way to stay in touch with clients is to contract for a different relationship as the OD practitioner departs. We have coached clients after the completion of change initiatives on a regular basis or for quarterly check-ins to assess progress or facilitate annual summit events. Even when a formal arrangement is not made, it is useful to touch base with clients to renew friendships and engage in dialogue regarding new initiatives and developments.

When a successful closure is made, it is not uncommon for clients to call even years later for another engagement. After we assisted a client with a large cultural change effort, she called for assistance with an even more complex cultural change process when she moved to a different organization five years later. Because time had been spent to evaluate and successfully separate, the client had positive feelings about the work, and we were able to start a new process in an efficient manner. We were able to recall our learnings from the first project and build the structures and support needed to be successful. In addition, we had a basis of trust and a positive style of working together.

A consulting project with a different organization was successful, but the client became very busy and time was not taken to effectively separate. A few years later, the client was grateful when the OD practitioner stopped to visit, and they were able to adequately close when he had more time and energy. It is likely he did not call for additional projects because he felt awkward about the ending. It's often not too late to close. Some ways to stay in touch and maintain a relationship include sending blog articles and emails, visiting the client when nearby, encouraging the client to call anytime, helping clients find resources, suggesting articles and books, providing recommendations for opportunities that may be of interest, such as conferences, and calling to ask to use the client's name as a reference for other projects (Biech 2013; Weiss 2011).

SUMMARY

We'll conclude with a case of closure to an OD project to change a global organization's culture. A major reorganization caused a rift between senior staff and top management and the tension extended throughout the system. The goal of the OD initiative was to help the organization to become unstuck, create open-minded conversations, and develop a plan for changing the climate. We conducted interviews and focus groups across the organization, coached senior leaders, and facilitated dialogue between management and staff. We worked with a sounding board of well-respected staff and forged a plan to change the culture to be more open and collaborative.

Through many dialogue sessions, the senior leadership team and the directors and staff representatives developed a plan to change the polarized environment to be more collaborative. After there was agreement on the plan and communication throughout the organization, we established a process for senior leaders to communicate to staff what actions were being taken in specific areas. In this way, the desired change and progress on recommendations was transparent. Each month, progress was reported to staff. We provided coaching to leaders and supported accountability.

As we came to the end of our contract and the organization was more stabilized, we reduced our involvement and the internal change office monitored and reported on progress. We agreed to facilitate quarterly conversations on progress. After a year, we formally closed the engagement. The sounding board members and senior management had a lunch focused on closure. Each person shared their personal learning from the experience and what was still unfinished. A document of lessons learned was prepared and shared with the whole organization. The CEO at an annual leadership summit recognized the OD practitioner and the sounding board. While a difficult moment for this organization, all agreed that the organization became stronger for the experience. One outcome was regular team-building meetings with the directors of the organization. This cross functional leadership group met for a number of sessions with the OD practitioner and then this group moved to be self-managing with a similar closure process. Each shared what they were leaving with from the experience, what was still unfinished, and next steps were identified.

A learning experience for the OD practitioner was seeing how difficult organization experiences with opportunities for dialogue, reflection, and conscious closure throughout the intervention could be used to strengthen and sustain the system. Years later, most agreed that the intervention made the organization more agile and shored them up for significant changes in the marketplace. The conscious process of closure, and in this case documenting the lessons learned for the rest of the organization, enabled us to all feel stronger for the experience. In this case, the organization shared the lessons with other companies too. They also recommended the OD practitioner to other organizations for similar projects. We were glad to understand the value of closure and to extend the understanding to this system. When it was time for formal closure, the leaders had already had many opportunities to see the benefits of closure in other settings and they recognized the value of reflecting, sharing their emotional reactions, and learning and consciously closing.

Taking the time for reflection about fulfillment of the contract and the process, recognizing the emotional component of closure, agreeing on next steps, saying good-bye, and following up enable the client and the OD practitioner to benefit from this last phase of the OD process.

Discussion Questions

1. What have been your experiences with closing OD engagements?
2. What is a healthy mindset to have around closure?
3. How can you incorporate the closing questions to mobilize energy throughout the OD process?

Resources

Project Management Essentials: Closing (Skillpath Seminars): www.youtube.com/watch?v = MWu8B8rcS2g

What Is Honorable Closure? (Linda Curtis): www.youtube.com/watch?v = mGkcGBAHjyI

Closing the Consulting Assignment Video Tutorial (Derek Hendrikz): www.youtube.com/watch?v = rqCjvsVQ0K8

References

Anderson, D. L. 2015. *Organization Development: The Process of Leading Organization Change.* 3rd ed. Thousand Oaks, CA: Sage.

Biech, E. 2013. *The 2013 Pfeifer Annual: Consulting.* San Francisco: John Wiley & Sons.

Block, P. 2011. *Flawless Consulting: A Guide to Getting Your Expertise Used.* 3rd ed. San Francisco: Pfeiffer.

Bridges, W. 2010. *Managing Transitions: Making the Most of Change*. 3rd ed. Boston: Nicholas Brealey.

Curtis, L. A. 2013. "Honorable Closure: The 4-Step Process to Skillful Endings." www .HonorableClosure.com.

Di Stefano, G., F. Gino, G. Pisano, and B. Staats. 2014. "Learning by Thinking: How Reflection Aids Performance." Working Paper 14-093. Harvard Business School.

Stevenson, H. 2013. Herb Stevenson website. "Chapter Two: Gestalt Cycle of Experience." www.herbstevenson.com/chapters/gestalt-cycle-of-experience-chapter-2.php.

Weiss, A. 2011. *The Consulting Bible: Everything You Need to Know to Create and Expand a Seven-Figure Consulting Practice*. Hoboken, NJ: John Wiley & Sons.

CHAPTER FOURTEEN

Taking Culture Seriously in Organization Development

Edgar Schein

WHAT IS CULTURE AND HOW DOES IT WORK?

The simplest way of thinking about culture is to liken it to personality and character in the individual. As we grow up, we learn certain ways of behaving and have certain beliefs and values that enable us to adapt to the external realities that face us and give us some sense of identity and integration. As groups and organizations grow, they undergo the same kind of learning process. The initial beliefs and values of the group's founders and leaders gradually become shared and taken for granted if (1) the group is successful in fulfilling its mission or primary task and (2) if it learns how to manage itself internally. The group's culture consists of its accumulated learning, and if the group builds up a history, the beliefs, values, and norms by which it has operated gradually become taken for granted and can be thought of as shared assumptions that become tacit and nonnegotiable.

However, as organizations grow and age, they also develop subunits in which the learning process described above occurs as well, since they have different tasks and issues of internal integration. Therefore, an organization will eventually develop both an overarching culture and subcultures that will vary in strength and degree of congruence with the total organization culture.

The strength of a given culture or subculture depends on several factors:

- The strength of the convictions of the original founders and subsequent leaders.

- The degree of stability of the membership and leadership over a period of time.

- The number and intensity of learning crises that the group has survived.

The stability of the leadership and membership is the most critical in that high turnover, especially of leaders, would keep the organization from developing a shared set of assumptions in the first place. Beliefs and values would continue to be contested between various subgroups, which would prevent the kind of consensus that would, over time, lead to shared tacit assumptions. How well the organization succeeded would then depend on the degree of interdependence of the tasks of the subgroups. As coordination needs increase, subcultural alignment becomes more critical.

The *content* of a given culture is generally the result of the *occupational* culture of the founders and leaders of the group or organization. Since the mission or primary task of an organization is to create products or services that society wants and needs, successful organizations usually reflect some congruence between the core technology involved in the creation of the products and services and the occupational skills of the founders and leaders. Thus, a computer company tends to have been founded by electrical engineers, a chemical company tends to have been founded by chemists and chemical engineers, and a bank or financial institution tends to have been founded by people trained in the management of money. There will be many exceptions, of course, such as IBM, which was founded by a salesman, but ultimately there will be congruence between the core technology and the core occupations of the founders and leaders.

An *occupational* culture can be thought of as the shared beliefs, values, and norms of an occupational community, based on their formal training and practical experience in pursuing the occupation, leading to shared tacit assumptions that govern the occupation. In the traditional professions, such as medicine or law, these beliefs, values, and norms are codified and formalized, including codes of ethics designed to protect the vulnerable client from professional exploitation. Underneath these codes are the tacit assumptions such as "a doctor must do no harm," or "a scientist must not misrepresent data." As organization development (OD) has evolved, the field has sought to professionalize themselves by developing formal educational and training programs for future OD practitioners and codes of practice and ethics designed to reassure clients and set standards. These codes are sometimes expressed legally and enforced through licensing procedures. OD has not reached that status, though some of its subsets of practitioners are licensed counselors, social workers, or coaches.

The process by which this happens is the same as in the growth of other group cultures. OD founders and leaders, such as Kurt Lewin, Lee Bradford, Rensis Likert, Ron and Gordon Lippitt, Eric Trist, A. K. Rice, Tommy Wilson, Harold Bridger, Elliot Jaques, Doug McGregor, Chris Argyris, Richard Beckhard, Herb Shepard, Warren Bennis, Bob Blake, and Bob Tannenbaum—to name a few of the first generation of forerunners—have shared certain beliefs, values, assumptions, and practices that they have taught to successive generations.

However, as this long list of OD leaders indicates, the process of forming consensus around occupational norms takes longer and is more complex because the client systems respond differently to different practices that come from the same occupational community. And in this way, an occupation spawns subgroups and subcultures in the same way that a given organization does. For example, the Tavistock group, built around A. K. Rice and Wilfred Bion, developed very different theories and assumptions about how to work with groups and organizations than the Lewinian group that developed in Bethel, Maine, or the Human Potential group that evolved in California around Bob Tannenbaum and John and Joyce Weir.

Even the OD group working in Bethel eventually divided over the issue of whether to stay focused on leadership training and community building or to become more individually oriented. Within 10 years, this group had divided into at least two factions—those wanting to continue to work with organizations and managers and those who saw in sensitivity training the potential for "therapy for normal individuals" and who allied themselves with the human potential movement.

The field of OD today is, therefore, considered to be more of a confederation of subcultures trying to become a single occupational community rather than a profession in the more traditional sense. It is missing a core content that would be embodied in a formal training program and licensing process, and there is little consensus on what is an appropriate or inappropriate form for working with client systems. The same statement applies to the larger field of consultation, especially management consultation, where it is obvious that consulting companies and individual consultants are quite diverse in what they advocate is the "correct" way to deal with clients and what they think the goals of consultation should be.

Within this confederation there has grown up in the last 10 years a kind of further distinction that may or may not ultimately lead to two different OD cultures—what Gervase Bushe and Robert Marshak (2014) have identified as "*Dialogic* OD" as contrasted with "*Diagnostic* OD." In some of my previous critiques of OD, as in the third edition of this handbook, I made several points which, I now realize, apply primarily to diagnostic OD and reflect some growing subcultural occupational differences within the broader OD confederation.

DIALOGIC AND DIAGNOSTIC ORGANIZATION DEVELOPMENT

The basic distinctions between these two types of OD (dialogic and diagnostic) will be discussed by Bushe and Marshak (in Section 5 of this handbook) so I will not repeat here their analysis but rather discuss what I see to be the differences in the evolving cultures of these two sets of practices and how this impacts work with organizational cultures.

At the most fundamental level, many OD practitioners start with the tacit assumption that organizations can be improved, and there is an ideal model of what that improvement should entail. From McGregor's Theory Y to Maslow's and Argyris's concepts of self-actualization, OD has held up a set of humanistic values that are constantly expressed as making work a more fulfilling activity that engages the whole person not just "his hands." Some practitioners make these values quite explicit, but others are conflicted about them when they encounter complex organizational situations that seem to require an even higher-level pragmatic value of improving what the organization is trying to do, even if that involves some personally unpleasant activities.

I encountered this issue early in my career when I realized that the T-group was a laboratory in which neither the participants nor the staff knew exactly what would be learned and, therefore, touted as our ultimate goal a "spirit of inquiry" and "learning how to learn." However, when we analyzed group behavior, it was clear that we disapproved of groups "shutting down" a member, interrupting members, or, in other way violating some of the norms of civility. A model of good group behavior clearly emerged and was valued.

My learning occurred when in my working with the Operations Committee of Digital Equipment Corporation (DEC) in the mid 1960s, when I discovered a group that violated just about every concept of good group behavior I had brought with me from my training in Bethel (Schein 2003). I focused on pointing out as best I could the dysfunctional behavior of constantly interrupting each other, emotional arguments, shouting, putting others down, and so on. I got nowhere with this approach; therefore, I gave up, sat back, and began to wonder why a very smart group of successful electrical engineers were so rude. That is when I first encountered organizational and occupational culture.

DEC was a young, very successful company that had adopted many of the academic norms that one should not trust an idea unless it can stand up to any amount of criticism. This group was, after all, fighting for its economic survival and growth. Its members were not only smart but very passionate about their ideas and had low impulse control. I did realize that if ideas were important that their constant interruption was keeping ideas from being fully heard. So at one meeting I went to the flipchart and when Person A started into an idea, I started to write it down. Needless to say, the idea was interrupted immediately, but at this moment, I did something different. I turned to Person A, locked in on his eyes and said: "I did not get all of that ... what was the rest of your idea?"

To my relief and amazement the group shut up while Person A finished his thought, and I was able to write it all down. When another idea came up, writing it down again controlled the group, and we discovered that having the full ideas in front of us made it easier to discuss them and decide how to proceed. What had happened from a cultural point of view is that I had finally figured out a key element of the DEC culture—it was about processing ideas, not about being nice to each other. I had finally helped them by helping them process ideas, not telling them how to behave. I had abandoned my ideal model of what a group should be and what human discourse should be and begun to help them with their need to make better choices among idea alternatives.

To me this was the moment where I think I conceptualized what I later called "process consultation," (Schein 1969, 1999) reflecting the reality that I was now helping them with their process in the context of their culture and that humanistic values or ideal models of group or organizational behavior became irrelevant. This did not mean that I gave up my humanistic values, but it did imply that I had to resolve in my mind whether this group's need to solve problems and make decisions was more important than being nice to each other. In fact, when their leader would from time to time rudely and angrily criticize one of his subordinates in public, we would all cringe and wish that this did not occur. But none of us knew how to change that behavior until we sat down and figured out that his rants were likely to occur when he was anxious about something; therefore, the solution was to reassure him when we first saw symptoms of growing anxiety.

My point is that in the 25 years of working at DEC, *helping* was defined in many different ways that often had little to do with ideal models or humanistic values. If it made me too uncomfortable, I would get out. If I stayed, I would work with them on their issues. My conceptualization of this as "process consultation" is, as I now understand it, one of the key assumptions of "dialogic OD"—that the consultant must facilitate the organization's efforts to improve its functioning but that the consultant does not know at the outset what the nature of that improvement will be. In pure dialogic OD, this conclusion would be reinforced by the adoption of a more general model of human society as being perpetually socially constructed and reconstructed and, therefore, by definition no one would know "the answer" for a given problem.

It is, of course, not necessary to take the extreme either/or position on whether problems are ever solvable or not, and whether culture itself is always socially constructed. As OD practitioners, we can work with the distinction made by Heifetz between problems that cause immediate crises but have solutions, which he calls "technical problems," and problems that are perpetually bubbling up but have no immediate solution because they exist in a dynamic perpetually changing, socially constructed context, which he says require "adaptive" processes (Heifetz 2009). The broad argument might then be made that diagnostic OD is all about solving technical problems and dialogic OD is all about helping clients to adapt to their complex, ever-changing environment. The practitioner must, therefore, be diagnostically agile in determining what kind of problem or issue the client is facing. That leads to the question of how diagnosis and intervention are connected.

DIAGNOSIS AND INTERVENTION

Much of the OD and traditional consulting literature takes it for granted that, before one makes an intervention, one should make some kind of diagnosis of what is going on. That diagnosis is typically based on several factors: (1) the OD practitioner's insights based on prior education and experience, operating in the form of mental models and organizational stereotypes that structure expectations, predispositions, and communication filters; (2) the OD practitioner's personal style and preferences operating as predispositions to perceive the new situation in a way that is comfortable for that person; (3) supplemented by the here-and-now "online" interpretation of the spontaneous reactions of the client to whatever the consultant does; and (4) the consultant's reactions to what the client says and does, leading to formal or informal activities by the consultant in the form of questions, surveys, or observation periods designed to elicit data (most models talk about a "stage" of data gathering) that are then interpreted by the consultant as a basis for deciding how to intervene.

It is my belief that the first and second factors, the OD practitioner's theoretical biases and personal style, are inevitable and ever-present sources of whatever diagnostic insights the practitioner possesses. I also believe that the third factor, the immediate "online" interpretation of here-and-now events as the consultant and client interact, *is the only valid basis for diagnostic insights*. And, by implication, it is my belief that the fourth factor, the active diagnostic activities that practitioners engage in for "gathering data" are, in fact, *interventions* in disguise that, if not treated as interventions, change the system in unknown ways and, thereby, invalidate whatever is found by the interviews, surveys, or observations in the first place. In other words, formal diagnostic processes launched by the OD practitioner through surveys, assessment processes, tests, or interviews may be neither scientifically valid nor good practice when we are dealing with human systems that have cultures and are perpetually evolving.

In stating this so bluntly, I am de facto allying myself with *dialogic* OD. In contrast, the model of OD as a set of stages beginning with contracting, then doing data gathering and then intervening is in fact the model of *diagnostic* OD in which the cultural assumption exists that there will be an answer that can lead to expert solutions. The diagnostic model would, as in "action research," argue for involving the client, but it would also be understood tacitly that the OD practitioner's knowledge and experience would influence how the client thinks and what solution might be developed.

When we engage in any kind of interaction with another person or group, whether in the role of a consultant, friend, casual acquaintance, or stranger, we are in a process of dynamic, mutual influence that simultaneously reveals data to be interpreted and learned from and changes the situation as a result of the interaction. Even if we take a completely passive listener's role, like the psychoanalyst sitting in a chair behind the patient on the couch, our silence is still an intervention that influences the patient's thoughts, feelings, and behaviors. When therapists talk of transference and countertransference, they are talking of the reactions both in the patient and in the therapist, through their ongoing interaction.

For some reason, in the OD field, many practitioners have deluded themselves that they can engage in data gathering *prior to intervention* and have, thereby, created a monumental fantasy completely out of line with reality—that data gathering *precedes* intervention rather than being one and the same process *simultaneously*. When I first wrote about process consultation and then helping (Schein 2009), I always found it necessary to distinguish these three fundamentally different helping roles: (1) the *expert* who provides information that the client needs; (2) the *doctor* who makes a diagnosis and then prescribes a remedy; and (3) the *process consultant* who stays in the dialogic role of helping the client to solve a problem or achieve whatever it is that the client aspires to.

However, I found myself arguing a very central principle that the human process with the client must always start in the process consultant role and must start with *humble inquiry* (Schein 2013). The reason for this conclusion is that the helper cannot know what kind of help is needed and what role to be in without first establishing a relationship that elicits a feeling of security in the client and motivates the client to reveal what is really bothering him or her. That may be just one question or hours of relationship building but the helper is intervening all this time to create a trusting relationship as a prerequisite to further helping. Until I know what the problem or aspiration is, this is by definition a *dialogic process* because I don't know the outcome and the client may not know either until we have interacted for some time.

If it turns out that the problem is a technical one that the client and I believe has a solution, then I must use my agility to drop into the right role to be helpful. Again two examples from DEC make this clear. The operations committee meetings never got through their agenda. I asked a question to which I did not know the answer, hence by definition, this was "humble inquiry": "Where does this agenda come from?" Surprisingly the group members did not know—it was

just there when they got to the meeting. The boss said that his assistant prepared it, but he did not know how she did that so they called her in, and she
explained that she took items by phone in the order in which they were called
in. This news raised a lot of knowing eyebrows. They decided to keep her doing
that but also decided at every meeting they would first rearrange the items by
importance before they started to discuss them. I considered this good process
consultation that would fit into the dialogic framework since none of us knew
the outcome.

But the group still never got through their agenda because they put off some
of the more complex strategy items to the end and never got to them. These were
Friday afternoon meetings and I "knew from experience" that they needed a
different kind of meeting to deal with these items, so I asked a pointed question
which, in retrospect, fit better into the model of diagnostic OD and shifted into
a "doctor" role: "Should you have a different kind of meeting to discuss the
policy issues?"

The group immediately responded "yes" and proposed that they alternate
Fridays for "fire fighting" and "policy" items. At this point, I felt completely
in the doctor role in "knowing" that Friday afternoons was not a good time for
heavy policy questions. I said, still in questioning mode but with a confrontative
intention, "Shouldn't the policy issues be discussed away from the office where
you have more time?" I knew of many successful "retreats" that companies were
using for such purposes. Evidently, I struck the right key because the president
immediately volunteered his cabin in Maine for a weekend overnight. Others in
the group also had houses in New Hampshire and Maine so the group decided
on the spot to start quarterly two-day meetings to tackle the big questions,
called them "Woods Meetings," and launched what became a 25-year quarterly
tradition. The engineering group decided a few years later to also have such
retreats and called them "Jungle Meetings." If I had the time, I was to join such
meetings and to be, from their point of view, the "helper," which turned out
to include the "doctor" role of helping the internal designers of these weekend
meetings formulate an agenda that would enable them to move forward. The
insider OD people knew what problems really needed to be addressed, and
it was my job to help them design a meeting that would work on the issues
constructively.

THE U.S. CULTURE OF DOING
AND MEASURING

In summarizing the previous section, I was simultaneously both diagnosing
and intervening throughout this process, even when I was in the doctor role.
That conclusion leads to the interesting question of why the diagnostic OD

practitioners and theorists keep seeing the process as a series of stages of contracting, diagnosing, intervening, and then terminating (e.g., Gallant and Rios
2014). The answer to that question might be cultural, in this case the U.S. culture with its pragmatic obsession with doing things, accomplishment, efficiency,
timeliness, and individual achievement. With those concerns comes the need
to measure and assess accomplishment, and with that need comes the need
to break what is an integral systemic process into definable and measurable
components.

The OD function is, after all, being performed primarily in Western, cap-
italist countries so one would expect that the larger culture of Do, Tell, and
Measure individual accountability would override the values of Ask, Listen,
Relate, Collaborate (Schein 2009, 2013). I am well aware that my book *Humble Inquiry* is, in a sense, countercultural in asking even bosses to accept their
dependency on subordinates and to build personal relationships with subordinates if they are in complex interdependent tasks. There are two different
cultural issues involved in thinking about this. The first issue is that tasks to
be performed are increasingly complex, interdependent, and adaptive (often
uncertain outcomes). In many such tasks as in a surgical team, there is a clear
hierarchy and power differential, but the higher-status person is nevertheless
at various times dependent upon the collaboration and open communication of
the subordinates, especially if a mistake is about to be made.

The second issue, a more complex cultural one, is that many cultures do
put more of a value on relating, on groups, on loyalty, and on dependency,
but not necessarily downward across rank and status barriers. A boss in such
cultures may be even more resistant to accepting his or her dependency on
subordinates even if the task clearly requires it. The dilemma for the OD practitioner then is how to design a diagnostic or intervention process that values
humble inquiry for purposes of relationship building but not across status or
hierarchical barriers, and especially not downward.

Of course, the astute reader will note that in making this point I have lapsed
back into my expert/doctor model in assuming that in a relational culture the
same kind of boss behavior is needed to open communication channels. One
year at MIT, we had a German middle-level executive who was very formal
and was often teased by his American peers about this. He finally retaliated
one day by saying: "Look guys, when I go into my boss's office I bow, I click
my heels, I shake his hand, but then I tell him the truth." Another example
along the lines of how open one can and should be occurred in a competition
simulation game among executives. The game involved some negotiation in
which an American Jesuit priest lied to gain advantage for his team which won.
Several Catholic managers from a South American country were so outraged
that a priest would lie, game or not, that it destroyed the relationships between
some of the group permanently and led to abandoning the game. The big lesson

for me is not to try to do OD in another culture without an insider to work with you and advise you how diagnostic or dialogic to be. Yet another example that illustrates cultural complexity was the heartfelt complaint of a woman from India that in her company in the United States, they were much "too open" talking about things that she felt uncomfortable about, yet expected her to be equally open.

WHAT IS ORGANIZATION DEVELOPMENT'S MODEL OF ORGANIZATIONAL FUNCTIONING?

How we end up doing our OD work will inevitably reflect our own mental models of what an organization is and what constitutes improvement in how it functions. My mental model has evolved from focusing on total *corporate* culture—the things that everyone in the organization agrees on—to worrying more about *occupational* cultures and three kinds of *generic subcultures* that seem to arise in all organizations and reflect the very nature of organizing.

1. *An operator culture, the line organization that delivers the basic products and services.* This would be production and sales in businesses, nursing and primary care in hospitals, the infantry in the army, and so on. These units are always built around people and teamwork and are embedded in the organization. The operators come to believe that they are the key to performance because they have to innovate and cope whenever there are surprises or events not anticipated by the formally engineered processes.

2. *An engineering or design culture, the research and development function, and/or the design engineering function.* This group is not necessarily identified with the organization but is embedded in the larger occupational community that constitutes their profession. It is their job to design better products and processes, which often means engineering the people out of the system through automation, because it is people who, in their view, make mistakes and foul things up. These are the design engineers in business, the experimental surgeons in the hospital, and the weapons designers in the military. Their solutions are often expensive, which reveals the third critical culture.

3. *The executive culture, the CEO, whose primary job is to keep the organization afloat financially.* The CEO culture is also a cosmopolitan culture that exists partially outside the organization in that the CEO is most responsive to the capital markets, to the investors, to Wall Street and the analysts, to the board of directors, and, paradoxically, to the CEO's peers. CEOs believe their jobs to be unique.

For any organization to function well, these three subcultures must be aligned and collaborate, and should not compete for resources. The Dialogic OD practitioner will realize that in order to become aligned the organization must be able to: (1) sense and detect changes in the environment; (2) get the information to those subsystems that can act on it, the executive and operating subsystems; (3) be able to transform its production processes; (4) develop the capacity to export its new productions; and (5) close the cycle by observing accurately whether its new products, processes, and services are achieving the desired effect, which is again an environmental sensing process.

The OD practitioner can be helpful around any of these five processes and, most importantly, make the organization aware of its general subcultures, its cultural biases based on the occupations of its members, and its need to worry about the alignment of these subcultural biases.

SUMMARY

To take culture seriously, we must start with understanding our own occupational culture in which we are embedded and that we take for granted. Having understood that, we can then examine the cultures and subcultures of our client systems and decide whether or not there is enough value congruence to proceed with the project. If we pass that test in our own minds, we can proceed to help the client by intervening in a helpful, constructive way to build a relationship with each part of the client system that will reveal cultural strengths and weaknesses on the path to helping the clients with whatever problems they want help with.

This process must start by intervening in a *Dialogic OD* manner using humble inquiry to build a relationship with the client that enables us to determine how best to help. We can then decide whether to continue in a dialogic manner or shift to being an expert or doctor in the more *Diagnostic OD* process. That, in turn, will be determined by our joint assessment with the client of whether we are dealing with a technical or adaptive type of problem.

Discussion Questions

1. As an OD practitioner, if a client asks you what your values are, what would be your answer? Does it matter?

2. Do you identify yourself more with Diagnostic OD or Dialogic OD? Why?

3. Think about a current or recent client and identify in that organization the operator, engineering/design, and executive cultures.

4. As you think about that client, what are the major occupations of the key managers and employees, what technologies drive the organization, and what occupational cultures are involved?

Resource

Culture University: Culture Fundamentals: 9 Important Insights from Edgar Schein (includes a video clip): www.cultureuniversity.com/culture-fundamentals-9-important-insights-from-edgar-schein/

References

Bushe, G. R., and R. J. Marshak. 2014. "Dialogic Organization Development." In *The NTL Handbook or Organization Development and Change*, 2nd ed., edited by B. B. Jones and M. Brazzel, 193–211. Hoboken, NJ: John Wiley & Sons.

Gallant, S. M., and D. Rios. 2014. "The Organization Development (OD) Consulting Process." In *The NTL Handbook or Organization Development and Change*, 2nd ed., edited by B. B. Jones and M. Brazzel, 153–174. Hoboken, NJ: Wiley.

Heifetz, R. 2009. *The Practice of Adaptive Leadership*. Boston: Harvard University Press.

Schein, E. H. 1969. *Process Consultation*. Reading, MA: Addison-Wesley.

Schein, E. H. 1999. *Process Consultation Revisited*. Englewood Cliffs, NJ: Prentice-Hall.

Schein, E. H. 2003. *DEC Is Dead: Long Live DEC*. San Francisco: Berrett-Koehler.

Schein, E. H. 2009. *The Corporate Culture Survival Guide*. 2nd ed. San Francisco: Jossey-Bass.

Schein, E. H. 2013. *Humble Inquiry*. San Francisco: Berrett-Koehler.

PART THREE

LEVELS AND TYPES
OF CHANGE

CHAPTER FIFTEEN

Individual Development in Organization Development

Making Change Stick

Marshall Goldsmith

S uccessful leaders can achieve positive, long-term, measurable change in behavior for themselves, their people, and their teams. While behavioral coaching is only one branch in the coaching field, it is the most widely used type of coaching for individual development. There is nothing more important in organization development (OD) than positive role modeling from the leaders of the company. When leaders' behaviors vary from the desired behavior in the OD intervention, the intervention will not work. When leaders' behaviors are aligned with the needed behavior for the OD intervention, the odds on successful implementation are much greater.

Does behavioral coaching work? Can people *really* change their behavior? The answer is definitely yes. At the top of major organizations, even a small positive change in behavior can have a big impact. From an organizational perspective, that the executive is trying to change leadership behavior (and is being a role model for personal development) may be even more important than what the executive is trying to change. One key message I have given every CEO I coach is, "To help others develop—start with yourself."

When the steps in the coaching process described in this chapter are followed, leaders can achieve positive behavioral change—not as judged by themselves, but as judged by preselected, key stakeholders. While this process can be very meaningful and valuable for top executives, it can be just as useful for high-potential future leaders. Increasing effectiveness in leading people can have an even greater impact if it is a 20-year process, instead of a one-year program. This process has been used around the world with great success—by both external and internal coaches. Taking a similar process and using it with teams, as described in the second half of the chapter, furthers positive change throughout the organization.

COACHING STEPS FOR BEHAVIOR CHANGE PROCESS

The following steps describe the basics of the coaching for behavioral change process. If these basic steps are followed, leaders almost always achieve positive change!

1. *Involve the leaders being coached in determining the desired behavior in their leadership roles.* Leaders cannot be expected to change behavior if they have no clear understanding of what desired behavior looks like. The people I coach (in agreement with their managers, if they are not the CEO) work with me to determine desired leadership behavior.

2. *Involve the leaders being coached in determining key stakeholders.* Not only must clients be clear on desired behaviors, they need to be clear (again in agreement with their managers, if they are not the CEO) on key stakeholders. There are two major reasons people deny the validity of feedback—wrong items or wrong raters. Having clients and their managers agree on the desired behaviors and key stakeholders in advance helps ensure their "buy-in" to the process.

3. *Collect feedback.* Interview all key stakeholders to get confidential feedback for our clients. The people who I am coaching are either CEOs or potential CEOs, and the company is making a real investment in their development. This more involved level of feedback is justified. However, at lower levels in the organization (that are more price sensitive), traditional 360° feedback can work well. In either case, feedback is critical. It is impossible to get evaluated on changed behavior if there is not agreement on what behavior must be changed!

4. *Agree on key behaviors for change.* As I have become more experienced, my approach has become simpler and more focused. Select only one to three key areas for behavioral change with each client. This helps ensure maximum attention to the most important behavior. My clients and their managers (unless my client is the CEO) agree upon the desired behavior for change.

5. *Have the coaching clients respond to key stakeholders.* The person being reviewed should talk with each key stakeholder and collect additional "feed*forward*" suggestions on how to improve on the key areas targeted

for improvement. In responding, the person being coached should keep the conversation positive, simple, and focused. When mistakes have been made in the past, it is a good idea to apologize and ask for help in changing. Suggest that those you are coaching *listen* to stakeholder suggestions and not *judge* the suggestions.

6. *Review what has been learned with clients and help them develop an action plan.* My clients must agree to the basic steps in this process. Outside of the basic steps, all of the other ideas are *suggestions*. Ask them to listen to your ideas as they are listening to the ideas from their key stakeholders. Then, ask them to come back with a plan of what *they* want to do. After reviewing their plans, encourage them to live up to their own commitments. I am much more of a facilitator than a judge. The coach's job is to help great, highly motivated executives get better at what *they* believe is most important—not to tell them what to change.

7. *Develop an ongoing follow-up process.* Ongoing follow-up should be very efficient and focused. Questions such as, "Based upon my behavior last month, what ideas do you have for me next month?" can keep a focus on the future. Within six months, conduct a two-to-six-item mini-survey with key stakeholders. They should be asked whether the person has become more or less effective in the areas targeted for improvement.

8. *Review results and start again.* If the person being coached has taken the process seriously, stakeholders almost invariably report improvement. Then, build on that success by repeating the process for the next 12 to 18 months. This follow-up will assure continued progress on initial goals and uncover additional areas for improvement. Stakeholders almost always appreciate follow-up. No one minds filling out a focused, two-to-six-item questionnaire if they see positive results. The person being coached will benefit from ongoing, targeted steps to improve performance.

9. *End the formal coaching process when results have been achieved.* The goal is not to create a dependency relationship between coach and client. While I almost always keep in touch with my coaching "graduates" for the rest of their lives, we have no ongoing business relationship.

CASE STUDY

This case study shows how an executive can expand a simple coaching assignment to benefit his or her team and the entire company. Joe Smith is the president and chief executive officer of Clarkson Products. Clarkson Products is a key division of Clarkson Enterprises and employs over 40,000 people. Clarkson Enterprises is a Fortune 100 company that employs over 100,000 people and is a leader in its industry.

I worked with Joe as an executive coach for over a year. Although I am not sure how much Joe learned from me during this period, I learned a lot from him and his team! Hopefully, the great work done by Joe and his team gives you a few ideas you can use, either as a coach or as a person being coached.

This real life case study shows how an executive can expand a simple coaching assignment to benefit his team and the entire company. This case study also reinforces my observation that the most important factor in executive coaching is not the coach. It is the executive being coached and his or her coworkers.

Getting Started

The project began when I met with Bruce Jones, the CEO of Clarkson, and Mary Washington, the executive vice-president of human resources. Bruce was a "fan" of Joe's. He let me know that Joe was a fantastic leader who had produced consistent results. He felt that Clarkson would benefit if Joe played a greater role in reaching out across the company and building relationships with his colleagues in other divisions. Mary agreed that Joe was a key resource for the company and that the entire company could benefit from his increased involvement. Clarkson, like many of my clients, is trying to increase synergy across divisions and build more teamwork across the company.

When I first met Joe, I was impressed with his enthusiasm and love for his job. He was in a place where he wanted to be. Joe was very proud of what Clarkson Products produced and proud of the people who worked with him. I have worked with over 150 major CEOs. I have met a lot of committed leaders. Joe is one of the most committed leaders I have ever met.

Joe liked the design of our coaching process. He developed a list of key stakeholders and called Bruce to validate his list. He worked with me.

Collecting Information

One-on-one confidential interviews were conducted with each of Joe's preselected stakeholders. Both colleagues and direct reports agreed that Joe was brilliant, dedicated, hardworking, high in integrity, great at achieving results, well organized, and an amazing leader of people.

Joe's peers felt that the company could benefit if he did a better job of reaching out and forming partnerships with them. Some believed that Joe and his team were so focused on achieving results for the products division, they had not placed enough emphasis on building synergy and teamwork across the entire Clarkson business.

Joe's direct reports agreed that Joe, his team, and the company would benefit if the products team did a better job of reaching out across the company. They also wanted Joe to focus on making sure that everyone felt included.

Some mentioned that Joe was so focused on achieving his mission he could (unintentionally) leave out people or ideas not on his "radar screen."

All of the interview data was collected by topic, so that no individual could be identified. After reviewing the summary report of the interviews with Joe, he agreed that he wanted to work on "reaching out across the company and building partnerships with colleagues" as a goal. He also expanded the goal to include his entire team. Joe also worked on "ensuring involvement and inclusion" with his direct reports. Joe checked in with Bruce and both agreed these were worthwhile goals.

Involving Team Members

Our research on behavior change is clear. If leaders get feedback, follow up, and involve their coworkers in the change process, they get better. If they do not follow up and involve their coworkers, they usually are not seen as improving.

As part of the coaching process, Joe had one-on-one discussions with each of his colleagues and direct reports about what he had learned in his initial feedback. He thanked them for their input, expressed gratitude for their involvement and positive comments, openly discussed what he wanted to change and asked them for their ideas on how he could do a great job.

After the initial discussions with his direct reports, Joe made a minor modification in one of his goals. He decided that his direct reports wanted him to do a great job of "inclusion and validation." The products division was going through very turbulent times. Several of Joe's team members wanted to make sure that he was "checking in" with them and validating that they were headed in the right direction during these changing times.

While I always recommend that my coaching clients follow up with their key stakeholders to get ongoing ideas for improvement, Joe came up with a much better idea. He got his entire team involved! Not only did Joe pick key colleagues to connect with regularly, so did everyone on this team. This expanded the benefit "reaching out" far beyond anything that Joe could do by himself. Joe's team established a matrix with ongoing process checks to ensure that everyone was "sticking with the plan." All members of Joe's team talked about whom they were contacting and what they were learning regularly. They shared information with each other to help improve cross-functional teamwork, synergy, and cooperation.

In ensuring inclusion and validation with direct reports, Joe developed an amazing discipline. He would consistently ask, "Are there anymore ideas that we need to include?" and "Are there any more people that we need to include?" at the end of each major topic change or meeting. This gave everyone a chance to reflect and made sure that everyone made a contribution.

Often in the meetings of high-level executive teams (like Joe's), there is an "outer ring" of people who may attend meetings. These are people who may report to team members and may provide information on key topics to be discussed. Not only did Joe make sure that his team members were included, he also ensured that everyone in the room was invited to participate.

During the year, I had follow-up discussions with Joe's direct reports. Not only did Joe pick an area for personal improvement, each one of his direct reports did. This way the process of change not only benefited Joe; it benefited everyone.

Two of his direct reports showed great maturity by telling Joe, "When we started on this process, I was critical of you for not being inclusive. In the last few months, you have been doing everything that you can do to include people. You have asked me for my input regularly. I have to admit something. You were not the problem. Sometimes I just was not assertive enough to say what I was thinking. It was easier for me to blame you than to take responsibility myself."

A Year Later

At the end of the coaching assignment, I interviewed each of Joe's 15 direct reports and his 10 colleagues from across the company. They were asked to rate his increased effectiveness on each item on a "−5" to "+5" scale (with "0" indicating "no change"). His improvement scores were outstanding. Forty percent of all numerical responses were a "+5" and over 85 percent were a "+3" or above. No individual had a negative score on any item. I have seen hundreds of reports like this. These scores were exceptionally positive.

In "reaching out across the company and building partnerships," both his direct reports and colleagues were satisfied with his progress. They commented on his ongoing dedication to being a great team player. They noticed how he had "gone out of his way" in meetings, phone calls, and emails to be a good partner.

In "ensuring that his team does a great job of reaching out and building partnerships," his scores were equally positive. Both groups commented on the ongoing process he put in place with his team. Some of his direct reports commented that their colleagues across the company had also become better team players. (It is much easier to be helpful and supportive to someone else if they are trying to be helpful and supportive to you!)

In "ensuring validation and inclusion," his direct report scores were not just positive, they were amazing! His 15 direct reports had over 100 positive comments and nothing negative to say. They almost all talked about the value of his asking for input on an ongoing basis and including everyone who was involved in the decision.

Like many companies, Clarkson's business was dramatically affected by September 11 and its aftermath. This was a hard year for Joe, his team, and his company. Many of his team members noted how easy it would have been for Joe to "lose it" and not contact others during this tough time. He had every "excuse" not to put in the time. They were amazed at his ability to involve, inspire, and motivate people when times were so tough. Some of the written comments were more than positive, they were moving.

Learning Points for Coaching

As we discussed earlier, individual leader change is critical for the successful implementation of organizational change. My friend and former coaching client, Alan Mulally, did a spectacular job of creating change as the CEO of Ford (he was ranked in 2014 as the third Greatest Leader in the World—behind only the Pope and Angela Merkel). He began by helping his executive team agree on desired leadership behaviors and then coached his team members to ensure they would be great role models for the desired change at Ford. From his team, this process spread throughout the organization. Most OD interventions require changed leadership behavior and improved team coordination—the best place to start is at the top!

Point 1: The key variable in determining the success of coaching is not the coach; it is the person being coached and his or her coworkers. Joe had greater challenges and problems than almost any of the people I have coached. In spite of this, he achieved outstanding results in building relationships with his colleagues and being inclusive with his team. He did not get better because I did anything special. I have put in much more time with people who have achieved much less. He reinforced an important lesson for me (as a coach)—I only work with people who care!

As a person being coached, never put the responsibility for your change on the coach. It is your life. Like a personal trainer, the coach can help you get in shape. You have to do the work. Not only was Joe a model of ongoing dedication and commitment, so was his team. Every team member had a positive, "can do" attitude toward improving teamwork across Clarkson. Joe's positive results were not just a reflection of his efforts, they reflected his team's efforts.

Point 2: True long-term change requires discipline over time and process management. One of the great false assumptions in leadership development is, "If they understand, they will do." If this were true, everyone who understood the importance of going on a healthy diet and exercising would be in shape. Every executive I meet is smart. In terms of behavior, they all understand what they should do. Joe did it! Joe established an ongoing process and discipline and "stuck with it." He managed a process. He made sure the follow-up discussions were scheduled. He had the discipline to ask, "Are there any people or ideas that we need to include?" over and over again. Joe worked with Carrie, a great executive assistant, who helped keep him and his team on track.

Point 3: By involving team members and key stakeholders, the value of the coaching process can be increased exponentially. Joe and everyone around Joe got better! Joe's entire team was involved. Everyone in his team reached out across the company to build partnerships and increase synergy. Everyone on

Joe's team picked personal areas for improvement and focused on getting better. Many of the members of Joe's team implemented the same process with their own teams. Sometimes, people across the company reached out to Joe's team in a much more collaborative way.

Joe was given a simple challenge to change his own behavior. Through his effort at personal improvement, Joe ended up benefiting hundreds of people across Clarkson. This can be done with teams, as you'll discover in the next section.

COACHING TEAMS FOR BEHAVIOR CHANGE

Recently, I coached a team in a group session. The team members rated the team a 6.1 (out of 10) to work together. Each team member was asked to reflect on a challenge he or she is having and share it with me and the group. There were about ten people, and six focused on changing what they could not change. It was an epidemic! The team prioritized this behavior as the one to focus on in their team change efforts. Over the next six months, the group participated in the Team Building without Time Wasting process, and it is now a highly functional team, with members rating the team an 8.6!

Following are the steps the team took to change this endemic challenge of focusing on what they could not change. All of the steps are critical, and Step 7 is the one that will take your team to the next level—it is follow-up—and it will ensure that the change sticks!

1. Ask all members of the team to confidentially record their individual answers to two questions: (1) On a 1 to 10 scale (with 10 being ideal), how well *are* we doing in terms of working together as a team? and (2) On a 1 to 10 scale, how well *do we need to be* doing in terms of working together as a team?

2. Have a team member calculate the results. Discuss the results with the team. If the team members believe that the gap between current effectiveness and needed effectiveness indicates the need for team building, proceed to the next step.

3. Ask the team members, "If *every* team member could change two key behaviors that would help us close the gap between *where we are* and *where we want to be,* which two behaviors should we all try to change?" Have each team member record his or her selected behaviors on flip charts.

4. Help team members prioritize all the behaviors on the charts (many will be the same or similar) and (using consensus) determine the most important behavior to change (for all team members).

5. Have each team member hold a one-on-one dialogue with all other team members. During the dialogues, each member will request that his or her colleague suggest two areas for personal behavioral change (other than the one already agreed on above) that will help the team close the gap between *where we are* and *where we want to be*.

6. Let each team member review his or her list of suggested behavioral changes and choose the one that seems to be the most important. Have all team members then announce their one key behavior for personal change to the team.

7. Encourage all team members to ask for brief (five-minute), monthly three-question "suggestions for the future" from all other team members to help increase their effectiveness in demonstrating (1) the one key behavior common to all team members, (2) the one key personal behavior generated from team member input, and (3) overall effective behavior as a team member.

8. Conduct a follow-up mini-survey in approximately six months. From the mini-survey, each team member will receive confidential feedback from all other team members on his or her perceived change in effectiveness. This survey will include the one common behavioral item, the one personal behavioral item, and the overall team member item. A final question can gauge the level of follow-up—so team members can see the connection between their level of follow-up and their increased effectiveness.

This team-building process works because it is highly focused, includes disciplined feedback and follow-up, does not waste time, and causes participants to focus on self-improvement. There is more to read on creating teams, especially innovative teams, in Chapter Sixteen.

SUMMARY

Let me close this chapter with a challenge to you: Try this process. The "downside" is low; and the "upside" can be high. As effective leadership and teamwork become more important, the time that the leader, organization, and team members invest in this process can produce a great return for the leader and the team and an even greater return for the organization!

Discussion Questions

1. Has your organization used behavioral coaching in its improvement attempts? Was the effort successful? Why? Why not?

2. As a member of an organization, at whatever level, consider this statement: "To help others develop, you must start with yourself." What does this mean for you, your team, or organization?

3. Think about team(s) you have led or been a part of. How might the Team Building without Time Wasting process have been implemented?

4. Have you ever been part of a "dysfunctional" team? How did that work out? How about a functional team? What did you find was the biggest difference being dysfunctional or functional made to you, to your team, to the organization?

Resources

Coaching for Behavioral Change: Steps in the Coaching Process: http://youtu.be/Hwn_W-X2Rds

Team Building without Time Wasting: www.youtube.com/watch?v = hq2CnccWdPs

Feed*Forward*: www.youtube.com/watch?v = BlVZiZob37I

CHAPTER SIXTEEN

Leading Innovative Teams

Jeffrey H. Dyer and W. Gibb Dyer

*When you create something that people didn't think could be
created, it's never one person. It's always a group.*
—A. G. Lafley, former Chairman and CEO, Procter & Gamble

In our previous chapter in *Practicing Organization Development* on team
building, we outlined the "4Cs" that determine the performance of teams.
These are: Context, Composition, Competencies, and Change (Dyer, Dyer,
and Dyer 2013). "Context" refers to the organizational factors—leadership, culture, structure, systems, and processes—that either support or undermine teamwork. "Composition" refers to the skills, experience, and motivation of team
members and team size. "Competencies" concerns the ability of the team to
make decisions, solve problems, deal with conflict, and so forth, while "change"
is a team's "meta-competency," and concerns the team's ability to monitor
its performance and make changes—usually in the form of team building—to
improve the team's performance.

In this chapter, we focus on the team competency of "innovation." A key
question for team leaders and those that work with them is: "Do you have
what it takes to create an innovative team?" Most managers spend little time
thinking about this question because they are too busy focusing on execution:
delivering results through the current strategy, business model, and processes.
In the short run, this may work, but in the long run, it will not differentiate
one's organization. An organization's most valued leaders are those who create

With the permission of John Wiley & Sons, this chapter is adapted from: Dyer, W. G.,
Jr., J. H. Dyer, and W. G. Dyer, *Team Building: Proven Strategies for Improving Team
Performance* (San Francisco: Jossey-Bass, 2013), 183–203.

and lead innovative teams—teams that generate and implement valuable new products, processes, and strategy ideas. The ability of the OD practitioner to use team building to foster innovation in teams is very important as organizations attempt to adapt and survive in a global economy.

So what are the characteristics of leaders—and teams—that excel at innovating? Our research (Dyer, Gregersen, and Christensen 2011) suggests that innovative teams have:

1. A leader with strong innovation skills who leads by example (contributes directly to innovation) and instead of dominating others, creates a safe space for them to shine.

2. Team members who possess a complementary mix of innovation and execution skills, as well as complementary expertise in multiple functions and knowledge domains.

3. Team processes that explicitly encourage, support, and even require team members to engage in questioning, observing, networking, experimenting, and associational thinking as they hunt for creative solutions to problems.

When a team has all of the above, it has the capacity to become an innovation lighthouse for an organization. To realize this role, it requires a leader fully capable of leading an innovative team.

EXAMINING THE TEAM LEADER

As a first step to leading an innovative team, team leaders and/or the OD practitioner working with the team must take a look at those who report to the team leader, the team leader's peers, and the team leader's manager. They might ask the following questions of those individuals: "How would you describe the team leader? Would you describe the leader as innovative? How creative do you feel in the leader's presence?" Answering these questions requires a hard look at the team leader and asking another question: On what activities does the team leader typically spend time at work?

When team leaders are asked this question, we suggest that they divide their core tasks at work into two categories: discovery activities and execution activities. Discovery focuses on innovation and includes spending time actively engaged in questioning, observing, networking, and experimenting in search of new ideas to change or improve products, services, or processes. Execution is all about delivering results, analyzing, planning, executing, and implementing strategies.

Team leaders need to look at their calendars for a typical work week and ask: What percent of my time do I personally spend on discovery versus execution activities? Is innovation a priority for my team and me?

A long-term research project on business innovators by Jeff Dyer, Hal Gregersen, and Clayton Christensen (2011) suggests that particular skills separate business innovators like Jeff Bezos, the late Steve Jobs, and Marc Benioff of Salesforce.com from ordinary managers. They refer to these as the five skills of disruptive innovators, and describe them as follows:

1. Questioning allows innovators to challenge the status quo and consider new possibilities.
2. Observing helps innovators detect small details—in the activities of customers, suppliers, and other companies—that suggest new ways of doing things.
3. Networking permits innovators to gain radically different perspectives by talking to individuals with diverse backgrounds.
4. Experimenting prompts innovators to relentlessly try out new experiences, take things apart, and test new ideas through pilots and prototypes.
5. Associational thinking is a cognitive skill of finding connections between questions, problems, or ideas from unrelated fields that is triggered by new information brought in through questioning, observing, networking, and experimenting and is the catalyst for creative ideas.

The leader should ask: To what extent do I question the status quo, engage in observations of customers or companies for new insights, network far and wide with diverse people to spark new ideas and get different perspectives, and experiment by learning new skills, taking apart products or processes, or launching a pilot or creating a prototype? If the leaders find that they are not engaged in these behaviors very frequently, they probably are not triggering lots of new creative ideas in their team.

After assessing the leader's strengths and weaknesses on these discovery skills, the next step is to encourage the leader to find a specific, current innovation challenge or opportunity so that the leader can practice these skills with the team. This challenge might range from creating a new product or service, reducing employee turnover, or coming up with new processes that reduce costs by 5 percent in the business unit. With this innovation challenge clearly in mind, the leader with the team develops a plan to practice some of the discovery skills as the team searches for creative solutions.

We propose working on questioning skills first, since innovation often starts with a compelling question. The leader, perhaps with the team, should brainstorm (Question-Storm) at least 25 questions about the team's innovation challenge. A sample question might be: "What resources will we need to solve this innovative challenge?" This process of questioning will help the leader and the team identify the key issues to be addressed in the search for a creative solution. It will also help create a safe space for others on the team to ask questions. The team should identify the top three to five questions that need to be answered in order to come up with a creative solution to its challenge.

After identifying the key questions, the team should identify some activities that the team could do to answer the key questions or generate ideas that might be relevant to its innovation challenge. For example, the team could identify some individuals that the team or team leader should talk to about its innovation challenge to get their perspective. Finally, the team should consider pilot studies it could run, or prototypes it could build to answer some of those key questions. Try to identify some experiments that might answer "what if" questions about the team's innovation challenge. The team leader should involve the team as much as possible in observing, networking, or experimenting as it searches for a solution to its challenge.

The team should then repeat the process. Improving discovery skills requires building new habits. This takes time, practice, and self-discipline. The innovative leaders we studied were often very conscious that they set the example by modeling behavior for others. A. G. Lafley, former chairman and CEO of Procter & Gamble, recognized the need to be an in innovative leader. "Lafley always gets out in market places and wants consumer interactions," says Gil Cloyd, a member of his top management team and former chief technology officer. "He's genuinely curious about it. This becomes important because it's not just role modeling of something you'd like, but it's an infectious curiosity to discover how we can provide an ever more delightful experience for our consumers" (Dyer et al. 2011, 179). Lafley also showed that innovation is not an individual game, but in the end, a powerful team effort. "You remember the times when nobody knew what to do and you came through with something that people didn't think you could come through with or when you create something that people didn't think could be created," Lafley observed. "When this happens in our company, it's never one person. It's always a group. . . . Getting everybody in the same boat, rolling in the same direction, that is really what is fun. Especially when you win" (Dyer et al. 2011, 180). To encourage leader modeling of innovative behaviors, the OD practitioner may need to initially educate team leaders about the key concepts regarding innovation and help them practice innovative behaviors.

CREATE A SAFE SPACE FOR OTHERS TO INNOVATE

Having the team leader lead by example lays the foundation for what is arguably the most difficult part of leading innovative teams—creating a safe, encouraging space for others to innovate. Researchers call this creating "psychological safety," a condition in which team members are more willing to express opinions, acknowledge mistakes, and have confidence that they can engage in risky, learning-related behaviors without punishment (Edmondson 1999). Leaders of innovative teams possess a rare talent: They somehow establish a sense of psychological safety so that people feel empowered to produce insights with impact. "If you foster an environment where people's ideas can be heard," says AZUL and JetBlue founder David Neeleman, "things naturally come up" (Neeleman 2007).

How do leaders create a safe space for others to innovate? First, they inspire team members to show the courage to innovate by asking for game-changing ideas. Just ask! Asking people to be creative legitimizes the generation of original—even wild and crazy—ideas. We've seen this first-hand when watching graduate student teams come up with solutions to a business problem facing a company. In most cases, an easy way to cultivate more innovative solutions is to give the assignment and say, "Be creative in your solution. I'm looking for something innovative." We get far more innovative solutions when we ask than when we do not.

Second, creating a team culture that encourages questions can make a big difference in establishing psychological safety. At Southwest Airlines, Herb Kelleher was known for creating an innovation safe space by soliciting challenging questions from direct reports. "I just watch, I listen," he says. "And, I want them to ask me tough questions" (Kelleher 2003).

Third, encouraging and supporting team members to engage not only in questioning, but also in observing, networking, and experimenting activities helps establish psychological safety. This means not only giving team members time to engage in those activities, but applauding what they learn by doing so. Building psychological safety happens interaction by interaction, moment by moment, one-on-one as well as with the entire team. Leaders should ask themselves honestly whether they applaud and support others' innovative behaviors. Research shows that out of 60 new product ideas that are generated, only about one or two will eventually get to market. Hence, failure is a common experience of teams that are trying to innovate. Thus, the leader must continually encourage, challenge, and support those who try new ideas, even when they are not successful.

In our work with executives around the world, we often ask large groups, "Do you get as excited about others' ideas and achievements as you do about your own?" More often than not, about half the hands go up in the room. Then, we ask a tougher version of the question, "Do you get more excited about others' ideas and achievements than you do about your own?" Far fewer hands go up for this question. Yet enthusiasm for others' ideas remains a fundamental condition for our teams to feel "safe" in our presence.

BUILDING A TEAM WITH COMPLEMENTARY SKILLS AND EXPERTISE

Innovative teams work best when comprised of people with complementary skills in two areas. First, the team needs complementary innovation and execution skills to effectively generate novel ideas as well as implement them. Second, it helps immeasurably if team membership reflects a complementary set of functional skills—different types of expertise. Innovation design firm IDEO's substantial experience designing innovative teams recommends the importance of complementary expertise among members in understanding human factors (the *desirability* of an innovative idea), technical factors (the technical *feasibility* of an innovative idea), and business factors (the business *viability* and profitability of an innovative idea).

Complementary Innovation and Execution Skills

Effective leaders of innovative teams understand their personal strengths and weaknesses with regard to innovation and execution and strategically balance their weaknesses with other people's strengths. For example, during the highly successful 1990–2005 run at Dell Computer, Michael Dell engaged in a frequent tug of war between discovery and delivery with then president Kevin Rollins. "Kevin gave me a toy bulldozer driven by a little girl with a huge smile on her face," Dell recalled. "Sometimes, I'll get really excited about an idea and just start driving it. Kevin put the bulldozer on my desk, and it's a signal to me to say 'wait a second, I need to push it a little more and think through it for some others and kind of slow down on this great idea that I'm working on.' I gave Kevin a Curious George stuffed animal. The Curious George is for Kevin to ask questions, to be a little more inquisitive. We don't use them that much, but they're subtle little jokes between us" (Dell 2004).

The takeaway from this story is that teams that innovate successfully need the ability to generate novel ideas and the ability to execute on those ideas. Both skill sets are necessary. Smart leaders know this and consciously think about team composition—making sure the team is balanced enough in terms of discovery and delivery skills. Figure 16.1 shows discovery and delivery skills temporarily "in balance" on a team. Sometimes discovery skills should weigh more heavily on a team or throughout an organization (particularly during the founding stage of an organization or if the team is charged with product development or other business development tasks), while, at other times, delivery skills are relatively more important and those skills should be given greater weight (during the growth or mature stage of a business, or in functional areas related to operations and finance).

THE BALANCING ACT

Discovery-Driven	Delivery-Driven
• Associating	• Analyzing
• Questioning	• Planning
• Oberving	• Detail-Oriented Implementing
• Idea Networking	• Self-Disciplined
• Experimenting	

Figure 16.1. Balancing Innovation and Execution Skills

Complementary Human, Technical, and Business Expertise

Making sure that innovative teams possess complementary innovation and exe-cution skills matters, but we learned that making teams multidisciplinary—comprised of individuals with deep expertise in different disciplines—matters even more when it comes to innovation. To illustrate this idea, consider how IDEO, the hottest innovation design firm in the world (they've won twice as many Industrial Design Excellence Awards as any other firm) staffs innovation design teams.

In general, IDEO tries to create multidisciplinary teams comprised of indi-viduals who are "T" shaped in terms of expertise: deep in at least one area of expertise with shallow expertise in multiple knowledge domains. The deep area of expertise often falls in one of three domains that they call "human factors," "technical factors," or "business factors." First, they like to have a "human fac-tors" expert on a product or service design team, someone with a background in one of the behavioral sciences like cognitive psychology or anthropology. This person's role is to provide insight into the desirability of a new product (or service) from the user's perspective. The human factors person orchestrates in-depth observations of customers to understand customers' latent needs and wants and to acquire deep user empathy. For example, when designing a prod-uct or service for people in wheelchairs, the human factors person might make sure that folks on the team spend a day a week in a wheelchair, experiencing the world as someone confined to a wheelchair. By gaining insight and empathy into the user experience, the human factors person brings insight into the desir-ability of an innovative new design. This perspective is particularly important in early stages of designing a new product or service.

The "technical factors" person brings deep expertise in various technologies that the team might employ in the design of a new product or service. This person likely comes from an engineering or science background. This expertise is important for the team to understand what technologies are feasible for use in a particular new product or service design. Technical expertise is particularly critical after the user's needs have been clearly identified (the "job to be done") and the team is searching for and deciding which technologies might provide the optimal solution.

Finally, the "business factors" person brings the business expertise necessary to figure out whether an innovative new product or service design will prove viable in the market. This person likely has a business background, such as a master's degree in business administration (MBA) with expertise in operations, marketing, or finance. Naturally, this expertise becomes critical in the later stages of the innovation process when a team must figure out the optimal way to manufacture, distribute, promote, and price the product for profitability.

In summary, effective innovation teams at IDEO possess the necessary complementary expertise to figure out how to create a product or service that is desirable, feasible, and viable. This requires multifunctional expertise within the innovation team. Most organizations attack problems within functional silos—which means those on the team bring limited perspectives to the problem.

TEAM PROCESSES THAT ENCOURAGE INNOVATION

The final piece of the team innovation puzzle is having team processes that encourage—even require—team members to question, observe, network, and experiment in search of new ideas. Research on successful innovators shows that they engage in those four behaviors more than noninnovators (Dyer, Gregersen, and Christensen 2008). Not surprisingly, the same is true for innovative teams. Beyond diverse team composition, IDEO founder David Kelley attributes IDEO's success at innovating to its team processes. "We're experts on the process of how you design stuff," Kelley says. "We don't care if you give us a toothbrush, a tractor, a space shuttle, a chair; we want to figure out how to innovate by applying our process" (Nightline 1999).

So what team processes does IDEO rely on to innovate? Not surprisingly, IDEO teams start with a questioning process, move to observing and networking processes to gather data about their initial questions, and conclude with an experimenting process where innovative ideas emerge and evolve through rapid prototyping. These processes stood out in the now famous *Dateline* TV episode that shows an IDEO team redesigning a shopping cart. Today IDEO takes the same approach in their quest for more innovative products and services with a variety of clients. For example, these processes formed the core of IDEO's work with Zyliss, a maker of kitchen products, to completely redesign its kitchen gadget line from cheese graters to pizza cutters and mandolines (slicers).

Process 1: Questioning

The IDEO project team begins its quest for an innovative cheese grater (or pizza cutter, or mandoline) by asking a series of diverse questions to better understand the problems associated with using traditional cheese graters. "What are the problems with cheese graters? What don't people like about existing cheese graters? How important is safety? What other things do people want to grate with a cheese grater? Who are the 'extreme users' of cheese graters (highly skilled and highly unskilled users) and how do their needs differ?" As far as kitchen gadgets go, extreme users are cooks and chefs (those using kitchen gadgets for hours each day) as well as those who are first-time or rare users of kitchen gadgets, such as college students, children, or the elderly.

This initial process has been referred to by Dyer et al. (2011) in *The Innovator's DNA* as "Question Storming," a method to ensure that teams ask questions about a problem before jumping to offer solutions. At IDEO, they not only ask lots of questions, but they put them on small Post-it notes so they can easily rearrange and prioritize them. As Matt Adams, product design director at IDEO told us, "By having the right questions, it becomes clearer how you might go about answering those questions." Then, IDEO teams have a much better sense of "what to ask, how to ask it, and what kinds of people to ask" as they move to the next processes: observing and networking.

Process 2: Observing

This phase involves sending the IDEO design team out into the field where they observe and document the customer experience first-hand. "Our process is to go in and try to really understand the people that you are designing for," says Kelley. "We try and look for a latent customer need, a need that's not been seen before or expressed in some way." So the Zyliss team spent hours observing various product users, particularly extreme users, in Germany, France, and the United States trying to intuit what they're thinking and feeling. They took photos and videos of customers using kitchen gadgets to document what they noticed.

Through observations, the team captured many problems with using traditional kitchen gadgets. For example, they saw that traditional cheese graters easily clogged, were hard to clean, and often required considerable dexterity to be used safely. They noticed that the mandoline, a slicer well-beloved by advanced cooks, presented severe safety hazards due to extremely sharp blades that were often exposed.

During these observations, they look for ways to optimize ergonomics (ease of use), cleanability, and functionality. For example, to optimize ergonomics, they carefully observe hand and arm movements to make subtle adjustments in handle shape or tool angle for tremendous ergonomic benefit.

Process 3: Networking

As IDEO team members observe, they also talk to as many product users as they can about the kitchen gadgets they are using. In particular, they want to visit with users while they are operating a particular kitchen gadget because this is when users are most likely to offer ideas or insights about the things they like and hate about it. They especially like to talk to "experts" (e.g., chefs; stay-at-home cooks) because they are the most demanding and difficult-to-please users and often have great suggestions for product improvements.

Through these unscripted conversations, IDEO team members gain critical insights for designing novel kitchen gadgets. They're trying to gain deep empathy to the point that they can champion a particular user, such as a chef. They come to understand what she loves, what her challenges are, and what's important so they can share that person's story later with other team members. Peter Killman, a project leader at IDEO, says that during the observing and networking phase, IDEO teams "go out to the four corners of the earth and come back with the golden keys of innovation" (Nightline 1999). Those keys help unlock the doors to innovative ideas.

Process 4: Brainstorming Solutions and Associating: The Deep Dive

The next phase involves bringing all of the insights acquired through observation and interviews back to a brainstorming session that IDEO calls a "Deep Dive." During the Deep Dive brainstorming session, everyone openly shares all of the knowledge acquired during the data collection phase. It is basically a storytelling session with lots of details about individual lives where they capture insights, observations, quotes, and details and share photos, videos, and notes.

The team leader or OD practitioner facilitates the discussion, but there are no real titles or hierarchy at IDEO—status comes from coming up with the best ideas, and everyone gets an equal opportunity to talk. After the ideas are shared, the team starts to brainstorm design solutions to the problems they have witnessed. To actively support associational thinking during the brainstorming phase, IDEO maintains a "Tech Box" at every office (full of a fantastic range of odd, unrelated things from model rockets to slinkies). Many items are often spread in view of the team to stimulate creative thinking as they brainstorm innovative product designs.

Process 5: Prototyping (Experimenting)

The final phase is "rapid prototyping" where the designers build working models of the best kitchen gadget ideas that emerge from the brainstorming session. Kelley argues that prototyping is critical: "You know the expression 'a picture is worth a thousand words.' Well if a picture is worth a thousand words, then a prototype is worth about a million words. . . . Prototyping is really a way of getting the iterative nature of this design going through feedback from others. If you build a prototype, other people will help you" (Kelley, 2006). IDEO takes its kitchen gadget prototypes to a variety of different product users—from chefs to college students to children—for feedback. For example, the new cheese grater design has a large drum to grate cheese as it rolls and can grate more cheese (or chocolate or nuts) with less cranking. An optimized, clog-resistant tooth pattern provides maximum grating with minimal resistance for older users and people with small hands. The foldable and opposable hand crank makes for more efficient drawer storage, and for easier use by right- and left-handed users. These innovations get refined with each new prototype because they "build to think and think to build," as Matt Adams, IDEO consultant, put it (Adams 2010). Taking the prototype out for a test drive is the fastest way to get great feedback on new product ideas.

Finally, IDEO teams follow a set of guiding principles that give them the courage to innovate. Among these philosophies, which are posted in their work spaces, are: "Fail often to succeed sooner," "Encourage wild ideas," and "Build on the ideas of others." "You have to have some wild ideas," claims Kelley. "And, then you build on those wild ideas to build a really innovative idea" (Nightline 1999). As mentioned earlier, a critical step in leading an innovative team is to ask them to be creative. By asking for creative and wild ideas, you legitimize it. That way people don't have to worry about being shot down for a "wild" idea.

SUMMARY

Mahatma Gandhi once suggested that each of us "be the change you want to see in the world." Is the team leader seen as someone who contributes to innovation? Or, do team members see the leader mostly admonishing others to innovate? When it comes to innovation and creating highly innovative teams, doing what innovators do—as a leader—gains much greater traction than talking about it. Given the importance of leadership in team innovation, the role of the OD practitioner is to train team leaders and members in the innovation model we have discussed in this chapter and encourage the team to experiment with the various activities that encourage innovation. Organizations like IDEO have been successful at innovating as a result of implementing these techniques in their teams.

Without question, the most effective innovation leaders are good at questioning, observing, networking, and experimenting (Dyer et al. 2011). They lead by example and can mentor and coach others because they are capable innovators. But even if team leaders are not particularly skilled at innovating, they can still lead an innovative team if they understand how innovation happens at the individual and team level. The OD practitioner as a mentor and coach can help the team leader implement these practices, monitor the team's innovative behaviors, and help the team set benchmarks to track its performance in regards to innovation. Furthermore, the OD practitioner can encourage team leaders to select team members with complementary discovery and execution skills (as well as multidisciplinary expertise) to ensure that novel ideas can be generated and executed. And the OD practitioner can help to establish processes in the team that encourage and support team members in questioning, observing, networking, and experimenting. Finally, it requires establishing a culture that creates psychological safety on the team—where team members trust that they can throw out wild ideas, experiment, and take risks without retribution as we have described in the case of IDEO. While certain teams might have the skills and ability to create a culture that fosters innovation, we have found that a skilled OD practitioner can be an invaluable resource to any team and team leader who wants to implement the strategies for innovation that we have outlined in this chapter.

Discussion Questions

1. Why are some teams unable to be as innovative as they would like to be?
2. Which of the five innovation skills—questioning, observing, networking, experimenting, associative thinking—are most important? How can OD practitioners help teams develop each of these skills?
3. How can OD practitioners encourage team leaders to be more innovative in their approach to managing their teams? How might the practitioner help the team in general to be more innovative?

Resources

Dyer Team Building Assessment: www.josseybass.com/go/dyerteamassessments

Becoming a World Class Innovator: www.innovatorsdna.com

IDEO: Helping Organizations Innovate: www.ideo.com/

References

Adams, Matt. 2010. Author interview (October 18).

Dell, Michael. 2004. Author interview (June 25).

Dyer, W. G., Jr., J. H. Dyer, and W. G. Dyer. 2013. *Team Building: Proven Strategies for Improving Team Performance*. San Francisco: Jossey-Bass.

Dyer, J. H., H. Gregersen, and C. M. Christensen 2008. "Entrepreneur Behaviors, Opportunity Recognition, and the Origins of Innovative Ventures." *Strategic Entrepreneurship Journal* 2: 317–338.

Dyer, J. H., H. Gregersen, and C. M. Christensen. 2011. *The Innovators DNA: Mastering the Five Skills of Disruptive Innovators*. Boston, MA: Harvard University Press.

Edmondson, A. 1999. "Psychological Safety and Learning Behavior in Work Teams." *Administrative Science Quarterly* 44: 350–383.

Kelleher, Herb. 2003. Author interview (November 11).

Kelley, David. August 21, 2006. Stanford University podcast, http://iinnovate.blogspot .com/2006_08_01_archive.html.

Neeleman, David. 2007. Author interview (April 4).

Nightline. 1999. "The Deep Dive" (February 9).

CHAPTER SEVENTEEN

Transformation and Change in Large Systems

Thomas G. Cummings and Ann E. Feyerherm

Organization development (OD) interventions can help large systems change themselves to keep pace with the challenges of rapidly changing and highly competitive environments. Building an organization capable of change and agility or creating a network organization comprised of different organizations that join together to tackle complex problems are both examples. This chapter describes a coherent set of OD practices for large systems, which generally proceed from assessment and action planning to change implementation. It defines interventions in large systems, describes their characteristics, and presents examples of these change methods.

DEFINING TRANSFORMATION AND CHANGE IN LARGE SYSTEMS

OD interventions in large systems involve changes in organizational entities that are relatively large in size (e.g., members, budget, or sales), such as a large global firm or government agency, one of their major divisions, or an alliance they might enter with other organizations. These change programs include significant transformations in large systems' character and performance. The *character* of a large system includes the pattern of exchanges between the system and its environment as well as the design of the system's internal structures, processes, and procedures for producing products or services.

The *performance* of a large system concerns how effective and efficient those outcomes are produced, which can include measures such as productivity, return on investment, environmental impact, and employee satisfaction and retention. A large system's character directly affects its performance. Performance is likely to be high when exchanges between the system and its environment are effective and the system's internal-design features fit together and mutually reinforce strategic behavior (Mohrman et al. 1990).

Figure 17.1 illustrates the two basic features of a large system's character: system-environment relations and internal-design components. The figure relies heavily on open-systems theory, which views systems as embedded in a larger environment (Cummings and Worley 2015). The environment provides the system with inputs (such as raw materials) that are converted by transformation processes (such as manufacturing technologies) into outcomes (such as products and services). The environment also provides feedback on how well the system is performing. The system's transformation processes include several interrelated design components. A key concept in open-systems theory is congruency or alignment among these components (Ritson, Johansen, and Osborne 2012). They must fit and work together to attain the most effective results (Hanna 1988). Large-system interventions generally change most if not all of the design components to assure that they are aligned with each other to increase system performance (Macy, Bliese, and Norton 1994). These changes are transformational because they fundamentally alter the large system's character.

The open-systems model applies to different levels within a large system as well as the entire system. It is appropriate for large-system change because a

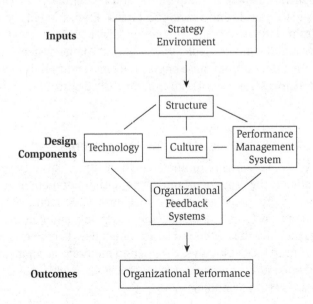

Figure 17.1. Model of a Large System

system's components must be viewed with the total system in mind. The system provides the overriding logic for organizing its components so they motivate and reinforce behavior in a particular strategic direction.

Large-system interventions seek to improve the two main features of a system's character: the system-environment relationship (how well the system interacts with its environment) and the fit among the internal-design components (how well the design components mutually reinforce strategic behavior). Large-system interventions directly influence the system's character which, in turn, affects its performance. The two features of a large-system's character are defined next, and then examples of large-system interventions are described.

System-Environment Relationship

The system-environment relationship is defined as the fit or congruence between the system's inputs and its design components. The key inputs include strategy and environment.

Strategy defines how a large system will use its resources to gain a competitive advantage in the environment (Hill and Jones 2004). It includes choices about which functions the system will perform, which products or services it will produce, and which markets and populations it will serve. Strategy defines the relevant environment within which the large system chooses to compete (Porter 1985).

The *environment* consists of those external elements and forces that affect a large system's ability to achieve its strategic objectives. The environment includes suppliers, customers, competitors, and regulators. It also includes cultural, political, technical, and economic forces. Environments range along a continuum from static to dynamic (Emery and Trist 1965). A dynamic environment changes rapidly and unpredictably. It requires large-system strategies and designs that are different from those appropriate in a static environment. System members need to assess their environment in order to plan a large-system intervention.

Internal-Design Components

In addition to the system-environment relationship, a large system's performance depends on the alignment among its design components. The following five design components are shown in Figure 17.1: technology, structure, feedback systems, performance-management systems, and culture.

Technology includes the methods a large system uses to convert raw materials into products or services. It involves production methods, equipment, and work flow. Lean manufacturing and total-quality processes, such as statistical process control, also are part of technology.

Structure is the way in which a large system divides tasks into departments or groups and coordinates them for overall task achievement. Alternative structures can be differentiated by function (such as engineering, manufacturing, and sales), by product and service (such as detergents, food, and paper), or by a combination of these (a matrix). Structures also can be based on business processes (such as product development, order fulfillment, and customer support).

Feedback systems are the methods a large system uses to gather, assess, and disseminate information relevant to its performance. Management information systems help a large system ensure that each of its subunit's activities are consistent with its objectives.

Performance-management systems focus on selecting, developing, and rewarding people. These systems help shape employees' behavior and activities within a large system. For example, rewards systems induce people to join, remain, and work toward specific objectives. They provide employees with incentives for achieving the system's goals.

Culture includes the basic assumptions, values, and norms shared by members of large systems (Schein 1985). It guides and coordinates members' decisions and behaviors by providing a shared understanding of what actions are needed for successful performance. Culture is central among the design components shown in Figure 17.1 because it is so pervasive and embedded in a large system's design. Thus, it can significantly impact the success or failure of large-system transformation and change (Cameron and Quinn 2011).

Research suggests that large systems achieve high performance when all five design components fit with one another and mutually reinforce behaviors needed to achieve the system's strategic objectives (Daft 2012; Galbraith 2008, 2014). For example, when a large system's strategy and environment demand innovation and change, its design elements should promote flexibility and experimentation, such as those found in high-involvement organizations (Ashton 2000).

While open-systems theory is useful for framing transformation and change in large systems, complexity theory also can provide insights into these interventions (Vessey and Ward 2013). Complex systems display characteristics of learning and adaptability, spontaneous self-organizing, and emergent phenomenon from interactions among system members. The inherent paradox or tension between freedom and control in complex systems can spur creativity and innovation. Based on complexity theory, large-system interventions seek to create greater connectivity among system members and significant external stakeholders. This results in large-system designs that encourage self-organizing, learning, and self-motivation (Brodbeck 2002; Hammer, Edwards, and Tapinos 2012).

Characteristics of Interventions in Large Systems

OD interventions in large systems have the following common features that distinguish them from other change methods. They are triggered by environmental jolts and internal disruptions that provoke revolutionary or transformational change. These changes incorporate new organizing paradigms that significantly alter how the organization is designed and managed. Large-system interventions are typically led and supported by senior executives. Considerable organization and personal learning is required to execute the changes. Consequently, multiple organization levels and large numbers of organization members are involved in planning and implementing them.

Environmental jolts and internal disruptions can be compelling reasons for large systems to change. Such interventions generally occur in direct response to at least three kinds of disturbance (Tushman, Newman, and Romanelli 1986):

1. Industry discontinuities such as dramatic changes in legal, political, economic, and technological conditions.

2. Changes in a product's life cycle that require different business strategies.

3. Internal system dynamics such as changes in size, strategy, or leadership.

These disruptions jolt a large system at a basic level, and if identified correctly during diagnosis, can provide the strong "felt need" necessary to embark on large-system change.

OD interventions in large systems involve changes that dramatically reshape the system. Such changes generally transform all of the system's design components. Although evolutionary changes that fine-tune a large system also can occur, the primary focus is revolutionary change (Zeid 2014). Most interventions in large systems attempt to restructure or redefine the system. The goal is to create commitment-based systems that are better suited to adapt to rapidly changing conditions than the old compliance-based systems. Commitment-based systems have the following mutually reinforcing elements:

- Lean and flexible structures
- Information and decision making diffused throughout the system
- Decentralized teams and subunits accountable for specific products, services, processes, or customers
- Participative management and teamwork
- Strong customer orientation
- Commitment to quality concepts and practices

A large system's senior executives must lead and take an active role in these interventions (Kotter and Cohen 2014; Winn 2013). Change leadership in large systems generally involves the following essential capabilities (Feyerherm and Parker 2011; Metcalf and Benn 2013):

1. *Understands complexity*. The complexity of large-system change is often accompanied by paradox and tension that leaders must psychologically, cognitively, and behaviorally address (Peters 2012). When paradox and tension are handled skillfully, innovation and learning can emerge.

2. *Engages groups of stakeholders*. Since transformation in large systems involves multiple stakeholders, leaders need to know how to engage with them to enable shared leadership and commitment to change (Mayfield 2014).

3. *Manages emotions*. Change in large systems is often unsettling, and leaders need to manage their own emotions and help others to do so as well (Foltin and Keller 2012).

The problem solving and innovation necessary to change large systems require considerable system and personal learning (Brown 2012; Mohrman and Cummings 1989; Senge et al. 1999; Shani and Docherty 2008). Learning helps to manage the uncertainty involved in transformational change by bringing new information to the system and providing a constructive element of control. Unlearning old ways is equally important as people's traditional values, worldviews, and behaviors are challenged and replaced with new ones. Because members spend considerable time and effort learning how to change themselves, large systems need to create norms and practices that support learning for the entire system.

OD interventions in large systems require considerable involvement and commitment from members throughout the system. Consequently, everyone or at least a cross section of the system needs to be involved in planning and implementing change (Haggroth 2013). Ideally, this includes getting all system members or their representatives in the same room at the same time. As members of the large system directly communicate and interact with each other, they can begin to understand the issues confronting the system and to devise better responses to them. Methods for bringing members of large systems together for change are called *large-group interventions* (Bunker and Alban 1996; Worley, Mohrman, and Nevitt 2011). These include techniques such as conference boards, future searches, open space technology, and Appreciative Inquiry; each having its own proponents and rhythm. The values and assumptions that underlie these large-group interventions include beliefs that people in the system have the capacity to self-organize, that perception becomes reality, and the system needs to be seen in its entirety. While pragmatically having all members of a large system in the room at the same time may be difficult if not impossible to accomplish, at least representatives of all relevant stakeholders should be included.

Examples of Selected Interventions in Large Systems

OD interventions in large systems generally fall into two categories: those that create changes in the system-environment relationship and those that reshape the internal-design components of a large system. Examples of both interventions are presented in the following sections.

Interventions in System-Environment Relationship. Two OD interventions that change system-environment relationships are dynamic strategy-making and network organizations.

Dynamic strategy-making. Fast-paced environments require rapid strategic responses. Yet, conventional approaches for planning and executing strategy are highly formal, detailed, and time consuming and often create obstacles to quick thinking and action. Dynamic strategy-making is a type of OD intervention aimed at overcoming the problems with traditional strategic planning. It provides large systems with the capability to strategize continuously and to execute quickly (Greiner and Cummings 2009). It enables them to engage effectively with rapidly changing environments.

Dynamic strategy-making treats the content (the what) and the process (the how) of strategy-making as inseparable, integrating them to create strategies that are relevant and implementable. Dynamic strategy-making forges a strong link between strategy and execution, addressing them together rather than separately. It builds strategy-making and implementation into the design of the system—its structure, systems, and culture—so strategic behaviors are constantly directed and reinforced.

Dynamic strategy-making involves large system members directly in creating strategic content—what the system intends to do to achieve specific outcomes in a particular market. Determining strategic content involves two broad activities. The first is *strategic assessment,* which involves collecting and analyzing data about the system and its environment to inform strategic choice. The system is diagnosed to identify core capabilities and resources; the environment is scanned to discover opportunities where the system can gain competitive advantage. Based on this assessment, the second activity involves drafting a *statement of strategic direction*. It includes the business model for how the system will gain competitive advantage and the strategic goals that will direct and motivate members' behavior. The statement also contains guidelines for structuring the system's activities, and an action plan for implementing strategic initiatives.

Dynamic strategy-making also addresses strategic process—those activities used to create, execute, and update strategic content. Choices about process can powerfully affect whether strategic content is relevant, timely, and accepted throughout the large system. Strategic process identifies the key stakeholders who should be involved in strategy-making and organizes their interaction and decision making. It includes two key issues. The first has to do with *strategic leadership and change,* which are essential for guiding strategy-making and making sure the strategy is enacted effectively throughout the system. Strategic leaders show behaviorally how to create the strategy and make it happen. They hold themselves and others accountable for changing the system to enact the strategy and to keep it up to date.

The second issue involves *guided involvement,* which helps members rapidly assess the system and its environment, share their knowledge and experience, and choose the right strategic direction. Guided involvement is generally carried out by OD practitioners with skills and experience in both the content and process of strategy-making. They help large systems involve key stakeholders in strategy-making, facilitate their interactions and choices, and encourage wider understanding and commitment to the strategic content throughout the system. In Chapter Eighteen, you will be introduced to the SOAR framework and approach, which is one way to build and execute dynamic strategy.

Network organizations. An OD practitioner can use network concepts to help large systems join in partnerships with other large systems to solve problems and perform tasks that are too complex and multisided for single systems to handle alone (Boje and Hillon 2008; Chisholm 2008; Cummings 1984; Gray 1989). Typically called *network organizations,* these multi-organization partnerships are used increasingly to respond to the complexities of today's dynamic environments (Steele and Feyerherm 2014). Examples include joint ventures, research and development consortia, public-private partnerships, and customer-supplier networks. Four basic types of networks have been identified: an internal market network, a vertical market network, an inter-market network, and an opportunity network (Chisholm 2008; Halal 1994). The opportunity network tends to be the most loosely coupled, nonhierarchical, and under-organized. Consequently, it requires large-system interventions that help members recognize the need for such partnerships and develop mechanisms for organizing their joint efforts.

OD interventions to create and develop network organizations generally follow four stages that are characteristic of planned change in under-organized settings: identification, convention, organization, and evaluation.

In the *identification* stage, an OD practitioner helps organization members identify potential network members. The organization or person that is motivated to form a networked organization generally takes the lead, which is key in the early stages. The main activities include determining criteria for membership and identifying organizations that meet them. Often a network of leaders from different organizations emerges, which mimics the characteristics of the network.

In the *convention* stage, OD practitioners bring potential members together to assess the feasibility of forming a network organization. At this point, the potential members evaluate the costs and benefits of forming, and determine an appropriate task definition. Key activities in this stage include reconciling members' self-interests with those of the network and working through differences.

In the *organization* stage, the network takes shape. Members organize themselves for task performance by creating key roles and structures. Legal obligations and member rights are determined at this point.

In the *evaluation* stage, the OD practitioner gives network members feedback about their performance so they can start identifying and resolving problems. The members assess how the network is working and how it can be improved.

INTERVENTIONS IN INTERNAL-DESIGN COMPONENTS

This section describes two interventions that reshape the internal-design components of a large system so they fit better with the system's strategy and with one another. These interventions are culture change and built-to-change organizations. They transform most of the large system design components.

Culture Change

While there is some debate on the possibility of changing a system's culture, most would agree that culture plays a central role in system functioning and performance (Schein 2011). Culture is the unique pattern of assumptions, values, and norms that guide system members in how to solve problems, perform tasks, and interact with each other and with key elements of the environment such as suppliers, customers, and government regulators. Culture is the outcome of social learning and emerges from past decisions and behaviors that have proved successful for system performance and become part of the system's values and norms. Because culture is deep-seated and taken for granted, it is difficult to change. Thus, it can be a liability when a system's environment is rapidly changing and past practices and behaviors are no longer effective (Schein 2010). It is not surprising, then, that culture change is a compelling intervention in today's fast-paced world.

Changing the culture of a large system commonly starts with an assessment of the existing culture to determine how well it fits with the system's strategy and environment. This can be accomplished with culture surveys, such as Cameron and Quinn's (2011) survey based on typical archetypes of system culture. Similarities and differences in survey responses might reveal the strength of a culture or the existence of subcultures within the system. Another approach relies on interviews and focus groups (Schein 2010), which seek to tap into members' strongly held assumptions and values.

Culture change also requires a widely shared vision of the system's strategic direction and what values and norms are needed to support it. This provides a clear path for members to follow as changing a culture can feel like the ground is shifting below. Top management is responsible for leading culture change and consequently must be committed to the change and visibly enact the values and norms that are espoused for the new culture. Chatman (2014) provides a cogent example of culture change at Genetech, outlining the kind of leadership that is needed for implementation success. Also, since culture is intertwined with the other components of system design, such as reward systems, human resource practices, structure, and information processes, these components may need to be changed to align with the new cultural values and norms. Such fit with the other design components is essential for a new culture to "take hold." Finally, since culture is embedded in members' thoughts and feelings, one of the most effective ways to change culture is to identify and recruit people who fit the new culture or can easily be socialized into it. Training and developing existing members also can help culture change, though changing entrenched thoughts and habits can be difficult.

Building Systems for Change and Agility

Several OD interventions are aimed at creating large systems that are capable of constant change and agile performance (Lawler and Worley 2006; Worley, Williams, and Lawler 2014). Their design components and managerial practices all work together to encourage and reinforce change and agility. These large system designs contrast with traditional designs that support stability and reliability, a recipe for failure in a fast-paced world. Large systems that are built for change and agility can compete in rapidly changing environments in which constant change is essential for success. They also can achieve sustainably managed performance (Lawler and Worley 2011).

Large systems that are built for change and agility include the following design features: talent management practices that select quick learners and provide them with constant training and development; reward systems tied to change goals and continuous learning; flat, lean structures that promote flexibility and innovation; transparent information systems that move information rapidly to where it is needed; and shared leadership that disperses power and control throughout the organization. Developing these features can be a daunting task, especially for large systems that have been designed for stability. The following interventions can help them gain change and agility capabilities (Lawler and Worley 2006):

- *Create a Change-Friendly Identity*. This addresses the core values, norms, and beliefs shared by system members, who can either hinder or support change. Existing values and norms are surfaced, assessed for their relevance to change and agility, and appropriate adjustments are made. Attention is directed at creating values and norms that help members see change and agility as necessary and natural.

- *Pursue Proximity*. This helps the system get closer to current and possible future environments by focusing outward to gain a clearer picture of environmental demands and opportunities. Scenarios of possible and desired future environments are developed, and a strategy for moving the system and its environment in the favored direction is developed.

- *Build an Orchestration Capability*. This helps the system build its own change and agility capability. It develops members' change management skills, creates a design and change function into the system, and helps members learn how to apply their change capability by engaging in system changes and agile performances and reflecting on that experience.

- *Establish Strategic Adjustment as a Normal Condition*. This helps large systems constantly work at changing and coordinating all of their design components to fit changing conditions. It includes empowering members to make relevant decisions, giving them the necessary skills and knowledge, sharing information widely, and measuring and rewarding the right things.

- *Seek Virtuous Spirals*. This helps large systems constantly develop their change capabilities to create even better system designs and competitive strategies. This results in a series of competitive advantages as large systems improve their capabilities and designs to take advantage of emerging prospects.

SUMMARY

Today's organizations are facing unprecedented levels of complexity and uncertainty that require continuous change in how they are designed and managed. Transformation in large systems can affect all aspects and components of the system. It is led by senior executives and can involve all levels of the organization and many members in planning and implementing the changes. An important consideration for OD practitioners is to diagnose what intervention is most appropriate for a particular large system. Some large-system interventions relate the organization to its environment (such as dynamic strategy-making and organization networks) while others are directed at internal design components (such as culture change and building systems for change and agility). Changing a significant aspect or component of a large system will have implications for the entire system; thus it is essential to plan how a large-system intervention may cascade throughout the system.

Discussion Questions

1. In what ways does transformation and change in large systems differ from change in small systems such as leader-subordinate dyads or work teams?

2. What special knowledge and skills are needed to practice OD in large systems?

3. OD has traditionally been applied within a particular system. Large system change may require interventions that go beyond the system's boundaries to influence parts of the environment. What are the challenges of moving beyond the system?

4. It has often been said that large systems cannot rely on outside experts to transform and change them but must build their own change capability within the system. What does this mean for large systems? What does it mean for OD practitioners?

Resources

The Center for Effective Organizations at the Marshall School of Business, University of Southern California: http://ceo.usc.edu/

The Change Leaders Network: http://changeleadersnetwork.com/

Strategy & Business: The Agility Factor: www.strategy-business.com/article/00188? pg = all

References

Ashton, C. 2000. "KI Pembroke Succeeds Through Teamwork, Empowerment and Rewards." *Human Resource Management International Digest* (November/December): 21–23.

Boje, D., and M. Hillon. 2008. "Transorganizational Development." In *Handbook of Organization Development*, edited by T. G. Cummings, 651–664. Los Angeles: Sage.

Brodbeck, P. W. 2002. "Complexity Theory and Organization Procedure Design." *Business Process Management Journal*, 377–402.

Brown, B. C. 2012. "Leading Complex Change with Post-Conventional Consciousness." *Journal of Organizational Change Management* 25 (4): 560–575.

Bunker, B., and B. Alban. 1996. *Large Group Interventions: Engaging the Whole System for Rapid Change*. San Francisco: Jossey-Bass.

Cameron, K., and R. Quinn. 2011. *Diagnosing and Changing Organizational Culture*. 2nd ed. San Francisco: Jossey-Bass.

Chatman, J. 2014. "Culture Change at Genentech: Accelerating Strategic and Financial Accomplishments." *California Management Review* 56 (2): 113–129.

Chisholm, R. 2008. "Developing Interorganizational Networks." In *Handbook of Organization Development*, edited by T. G. Cummings, 629–650. Los Angeles: Sage.

Cummings, T. 1984. "Transorganizational Development." In *Research in Organizational Behavior*, vol. 6, edited by B. Staw and L. Cummings, 367–422. Greenwich, CT: JAI.

Cummings, T., and C. Worley. 2015. *Organization Development and Change*. 10th ed. Cincinnati OH: South-Western.

Daft, R. 2012. *Organization Theory and Design*. 11th ed. Mason OH: South-Western Cengage Learning.

Emery, F., and E. Trist. 1965. "The Causal Texture of Organizational Environments." *Human Relations* 18 (1): 21–32.

Feyerherm, A. E., and S. B. Parker. 2011. "Emergent Collaboration and Leadership for Sustainable Effectiveness: The Metropolitan Housing Authority." In *Organizing for Sustainable Effectiveness*, vol. 1., edited by S. A. Mohrman and A. B. Shani, 127–153. Bingley, UK: Emerald.

Foltin, A., and R. Keller. 2012. "Leading Change with Emotional Intelligence." *Nursing Management* 43 (11): 20–25.

Galbraith, J. 2008. "Organization Design." In *Handbook of Organization Development*, edited by T. G. Cummings, 325–352. Los Angeles: Sage.

Galbraith, J. 2014. *Designing Organizations: Strategy, Structure, and Process at the Business Unit and Enterprise Levels*. 3rd ed. San Francisco: Jossey-Bass.

Gray, B. 1989. *Collaborating: Finding Common Ground for Multiparty Problems*. San Francisco: Jossey-Bass.

Greiner, L., and T. Cummings. 2009. *Dynamic Strategy-Making*. San Francisco: Jossey-Bass.

Haggroth, S. 2013. "Leading Change by Including Stakeholders." *Public Administration Review* 73 (4): 550.

Halal, W. 1994. "From Hierarchy to Enterprise: Internal Markets Are the New Foundation of Management." *Academy of Management Executive* 8 (4): 69–83.

Hammer, R. J., J. S. Edwards, and E. Tapinos. 2012. "Examining the Strategy Development Process Through the Lens of Complex Adaptive Systems Theory." *Journal of the Operational Research Society* 63: 909–919.

Hanna, D. 1988. *Designing Organizations for High Performance*. Reading, MA: Addison-Wesley.

Hill, C., and G. Jones. 2004. *Strategic Management: An Integrated Approach*. 6th ed. Boston: Houghton Mifflin.

Kotter, J., and D. Cohen. 2014. *Change Leadership: The Kotter Collection*. Boston, MA: Harvard Business School Press.

Lawler, E. E., and C. Worley. 2006. *Built to Change: How to Achieve Sustained Organizational Effectiveness*. Hoboken, NJ: John Wiley & Sons.

Lawler, E. E., and C. G. Worley. 2011. *Management Reset: Organizing for Sustainable Effectiveness*. San Francisco: Jossey-Bass.

Macy, B., P. Bliese, and J. Norton. 1994. "Organizational Change and Work Innovation: A Meta-Analysis of 131 North American Field Experiments—1951–1990." In *Research in Organizational Change and Development*, vol. 7, edited by R. Woodman and W. Pasmore, 235–314. Greenwich CN: JAI Press.

Mayfield, P. 2014. "Engaging with Stakeholders Is Critical When Leading Change." *Industrial and Commercial Training* 46 (2): 68–72.

Metcalf, L., and S. Benn. 2013. "Leadership for Sustainability: An Evolution of Leadership Ability." *Journal of Business Ethics* 112: 369–384.

Mohrman, S., and T. Cummings. 1989. *Self-Designing Organizations: Learning How to Create High Performance*. Reading, MA: Addison-Wesley.

Mohrman, A., S. Mohrman, G. Ledford, T. Cummings, E. E. Lawler, and Associates. 1990. *Large Scale Organizational Change*. San Francisco: Jossey-Bass.

Peters, L. 2012. "The Rhythm of Leading Change: Living with Paradox." *Journal of Management Inquiry* 21 (4): 405–411.

Porter, M. 1985. *Competitive Advantage*. New York: Free Press.

Ritson, G., E. Johansen, and A. Osborne. 2012. "Successful Programs Wanted: Exploring the Impact of Alignment." *Project Management Journal* 43 (1): 21–36.

Schein, E. 1985. *Organizational Culture and Leadership*. 1st ed. San Francisco: Jossey-Bass.

Schein, E. 2010. *Organizational Culture and Leadership*. 4th ed. San Francisco: Jossey-Bass.

Schein, E. 2011. *Corporate Culture: What It Is and How to Change It*. New York: Nabu Press.

Senge, P., A. Kleiner, C. Roberts, R. Ross, G. Roth, and B. Smith. 1999. *The Dance of Change: The Challenges of Sustaining Momentum in Learning Organizations*. New York: Doubleday.

Shani, A. B., and P. Docherty. 2008. "Learning by Design: Key Mechanisms in Organization Development." In *Handbook of Organization Development*, edited by T. G. Cummings, 499–518. Los Angeles: Sage.

Steele, B., and A. Feyerherm. 2014. "Loblaw Sustainable Seafood: Transforming the Seafood Supply Chain Through Network Development and Collaboration." In *Building Networks and Partnerships: Organizing for Sustainable Effectiveness*, vol. 3, edited by C. G. Worley and P. H. Mirvis, 101–132. Bingley, UK: Emerald Group.

Tushman, M., W. Newman, and E. Romanelli. 1986. "Managing the Unsteady Pace of Organizational Revolution." *California Management Review* (Fall): 29–44.

Vessey, I., and K. Ward. 2013. "The Dynamics of Sustainable IS Alignment: The Case for IS Adaptivity." *Journal of the Association for Information Systems* 14 (6): 283–311.

Winn, B. 2013. "Leading Big Change and Employer Re-Branding: Is This Still a Great Place to Work?" *People and Strategy* 36 (2): 20–22.

Worley, C., S. Mohrman, and J. Nevitt. 2011. "Large Group Interventions: An Empirical Field Study of Their Composition, Process, and Outcomes." *Journal of Applied Behavioral Science* 47 (4): 404–431.

Worley, C. G., T. D. Williams, and E. E. Lawler. 2014. *The Agility Factor: Building Adaptable Organizations for Superior Performance*. San Francisco: Jossey-Bass.

Zeid, A. 2014. *Business Transformation: A Roadmap for Maximizing Organizational Insights*. Hoboken, NJ: John Wiley & Sons.

CHAPTER EIGHTEEN

SOAR

Building Strategic Capacity

Jacqueline M. Stavros and Patricia Malone

S trategy should be more fluid, generative, and dynamic to make a positive impact. This suggests a perspective of strategy that requires organizations to build strategic capacity. Strategic capacity is "the ability of an organization to obtain its vision, mission, and goals, ultimately leading to its sustainability. In short, strategic capacity is a deeply embedded ability that enables an organization to bridge the gap between its current performance and its potential" (Malone 2010, 8). Malone researched strategic capacity and the impact of the SOAR framework on building strategic capacity.

SOAR is "a profoundly positive approach that allows an organization to construct its future through collaboration, shared understanding, and a commitment to action" (Stavros and Hinrichs 2009, 3). The SOAR acronym stands for strengths, opportunities, aspirations, and results. SOAR is best understood as a strengths-based framework with a participatory approach to strategic thinking, planning, and leading "that allows an organization's stakeholders to co-construct and execute its future through collaboration, shared understanding, and a commitment to action" (3). SOAR is a generative framework that supports and accelerates building strategic capacity, ultimately transforming individuals and organizations (Malone 2010; Stavros 2013).

This chapter starts with a brief historical perspective of strategy and highlights the connection between organization development (OD) and strategy. Next, we present what SOAR is, examples of SOAR applications, and how to apply SOAR. Then, we share an illustration of SOAR at a global consumer products organization that resulted in a positive transformation with impactful results. SOAR has been used by hundreds of small and large organizations throughout the world to support strategy generation, strategic planning, and implementation.

STRATEGY—A HISTORICAL PERSPECTIVE

Over time, strategy research evolved from studying strategic planning and implementation processes to the configurations and strategic positioning of organizations. By thinking about organizations as configurations, strategy researchers began to explore the structuring of mutually supporting and interrelated practices in an organization that enable it to achieve internal harmony and adapt to the external environment (Miller and Mintzberg 1984). As the configuration perspective of strategic management matured, other strategy researchers began to focus more on the content of strategy and how organizations use strategy for positioning within an industry. Michael Porter's classic 1980 book, *Competitive Strategy*, became the focal point for this positioning perspective by looking at how industry forces shape an organization's strategy. From this viewpoint, the market structure and the desire to find a niche within an industry dictates the positioning of strategy and structure, and this determines an organization's performance (Hofer and Schendel 1978).

Embedded in these various schools of strategy research is the idea that strategy is a rational, leadership-driven process that should be comprehensive and analytical, involving tasks such as market research, competitor analysis, and the alignment of internal resources with an organization's external environment. Moreover, these classical perspectives of strategy created an artificial dichotomy that segments strategy formulation from strategy implementation by separating the planners from the doers (Barrett, Cooperrider, and Fry 2005). Yet, researchers acknowledge that, in practice, strategy formulation and implementation are an intertwined dynamic process that involves the entire organization (Hart 1992). Furthermore, the involvement of organizational members beyond the leadership ranks is critical to the success of the strategy because these are the people responsible for co-creating and executing the strategy (Hauden 2008; Stavros and Wooten 2012).

LINKING STRATEGY AND ORGANIZATION DEVELOPMENT

As the strategy field evolved, OD researchers became interested in integrating the two fields. OD emerged from research on group dynamics, behavioral sciences, and experiential learning by the National Training Lab (Cummings and Worley 2005). Research on OD emphasizes system change in the character and performance of an organization (Cummings and Feyerherm 2010). The character of an organization reflects the pattern of exchanges between the organization and its environment through the design of internal practices and structures that produce the organization's desired service or product. An organization's character directly influences its performance and is measured by outcomes, such as productivity, return on investment, customer satisfaction, and employee engagement.

OD scholars contend that the blend of their research and practices offers the field of strategic management a lens for exploring processes associated with formulating, planning, and implementing strategy from a whole system perspective. Integrating this perspective provides a dynamic view of strategy-making by emphasizing both the content and process of strategy-making that enables an organization to engage its relevant stakeholders in rapidly changing environments (Greiner and Cummings 2009; Stavros and Hinrichs 2009). From this blended lens, strategy-making processes can be designed so that strategic behaviors are institutionalized throughout the organization by members assessing the environment, sharing knowledge, identifying strengths and opportunities, and choosing the right direction. This is a by-product of a learning organization that values the process of strategy-making by listening to different voices, engaging in reflection, and creating systems to synergistically combine personal and team mastery for collective strategic action (Barrett et al. 2005).

The foundations of historical perspectives of strategy and OD open the doors to explore strategy from a positive perspective and provide us with an alternative way of thinking about framing strategy and strategic conversations by using SOAR. A SOAR-based perspective takes into account emergent and planned strategies that capitalize on the full human potential within an organization by engaging the hearts, hands, and minds of its members (Malone 2010).

SOAR

What Is SOAR?

The Appreciative Inquiry (AI) paradigm led to shifting to a new framework to support strategic analysis, formulation, and planning, leveraging the "S" and "O" from SWOT into SOAR. The traditional SWOT approach begins with a scan of internal strengths and weaknesses and an external scan of opportunities and threats. From the recent advances in OD theory, we realized that any consideration of strengths implicitly considers weaknesses and, similarly, opportunities are developed in consideration of threats. There is also an intentional shift in language from problems to possibilities that is subtle yet powerful when engaging in strategic conversations. Rather than focusing attention on weaknesses and threats directly, organizations can reframe their perspective to optimize their path toward their highest possible achievements. SOAR does not ignore an organization's challenges; it reframes them into possibilities, thus creating a strengths-based *opportunity approach* to the strategic plan.

SOAR places the focus on finding a strategic fit between positive aspects of internal environment (strengths) and external environment (opportunities) that invites a dialogue to continue into aspirations and results. Thus, SOAR was created to help organizations generate innovations and design strategy around strengths (S) and opportunities (O). The "A" in SOAR inspires teams to explore their values, vision, and mission statements, and sets of strategic goals and objectives through discovering their *aspirations* for their most desirable future and what is valued from the organization's stakeholders. The "R" element in SOAR connects strategy formulation and implementation through a focus on measurable and meaningful *results*.

The SOAR framework provides a flexible approach to strategic thinking, planning, and leading that invites the whole system (i.e., stakeholders beyond the senior management) into a strategic planning or strategy process by including relevant stakeholders with a stake in the success of the organization's future. These stakeholders can be internal (i.e., employees) or external (i.e., customers, suppliers, and communities). Utilizing a whole system perspective provides a more complete picture of how an organization best serves its customers and what its future can become by considering many different stakeholders' perspectives.

Who Is Using SOAR?

Since 1999, the application of SOAR has offered a wide-range of options to each organization that has adopted it to help them meet their strategic needs. Organizations' use of SOAR varies from strategy, strategic planning, coaching, leadership development, team-building, and other areas. The broad categories of organizations (Types of Organizations) and locations (Continents) where SOAR has been applied are listed in Table 18.1. This demonstrates robust nature, flexibility, and the global growth of applications that the SOAR framework has gained since 1999. Furthermore, organizations are adopting the SOAR framework to be used at different levels of strategy or strategic conversations including industry-wide, organization-wide, group, and individual.

Table 18.1. SOAR's Application in Types of Organizations and Global Growth

Types of Organizations	Continents
For-profit organizations, at every level	Africa
Non-profit organizations	Asia
Governments	Australia, New Zealand
Nongovernmental organizations (NGOs)	Europe
Education: primary, secondary, and higher education	North America, South America

SOAR helps organizations create dialogue about how best to build and deliver their unique value through creating a positive strategy that is now supported by hundreds of case studies on the benefits of employing the SOAR framework.

How to Use SOAR

SOAR features a disciplined 5-I approach that starts with *initiate* to helping an organization *inquire* into strengths, opportunities, aspirations, and results; *imagine* its best possible future; *innovate* strategies, strategic initiatives, plans, systems, designs, and structures; and *inspire* the strategic plan and strategies to create positive results. SOAR uses a whole system (stakeholder) approach to strategic thinking, planning, and leading (see Figure 18.1).

SOAR asks the questions:

Strengths: What can we build on? What makes us unique?

Opportunities: What are our stakeholders asking for? What are the top three to five opportunities on which we should focus our efforts?

Aspirations: What do we care deeply about? What are our most compelling aspirations?

Results: How do we know we are succeeding? What are meaningful, measurable results?

These SOAR-based questions and their collective responses can start the journey to understand the past and present strategic situation and imagine the best

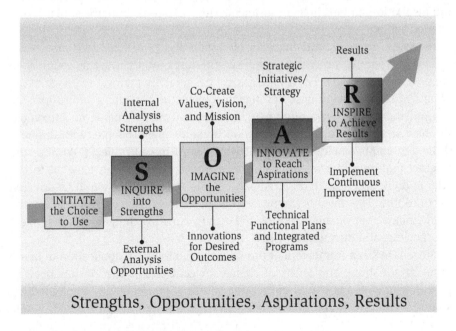

Figure 18.1. SOAR Framework and 5-I Approach

future for the organization's stakeholders. The questions are designed to create positive conversations about strategic direction and strategy. The key is to make sure stakeholders' voices are represented, and that there is space and time to inquire, imagine, innovate, and make decisions in the strategic planning process and its implementation. It has been our experience that a SOAR workshop can be designed with 10 to hundreds of participants, with sessions that range from a half day to three days. The differences in these ranges depend on what the organization wants to achieve as determined in the initiate phase.

A 5-I approach guides the SOAR process: Initiate, Inquire, Imagine, Innovate, and Implement, which can be used to guide the delivery of the questions highlighted above. Some organizations use the AI 4-D or 5-D cycle when applying the SOAR framework. The phases are briefly defined next.

Initiate. *How shall we work together?* The organization's leadership team or a core strategic planning team meets to determine how to use SOAR. They identify the relevant stakeholders to invite and discuss ways to engage stakeholders in and throughout the process.

Inquire. This is a strategic inquiry into values, mission, vision, internal strengths, and external environment to identify opportunities, and conversations of aspirations and results. This phase explores the "as is" state of the organization and "might be" of future states of the organization.

Imagine. A dialogue takes place that considers the combination of strengths and opportunities to create a shared vision that aligns with aspirations. Participants use the power of positive images of the future as a basis for envisioning actions and results. These images and supporting dialogue create the inspiration and excitement to fuel strategy, strategic initiatives, plans, and aligned action.

Innovate. Strategic initiatives are identified and prioritized that may result in new or changed processes, systems, structures, and culture as required to support the new goals. These changes are designed by taking advantage of the identified strengths and opportunities to achieve the aspiration and results.

Implement. Energy, commitment, and tactical plans emerge to implement the new strategic plan. Implementation involves many people, with different skills and competencies aligned and working on linked projects. Because the original inquiry and strategic dialogue connects each person to what to do, why to do it, and how to do it, all participants are more likely to be motivated to contribute. The rewards can be tangible in terms of a successful result in the marketplace or in financial returns and also in knowing the work served others in a positive and meaningful way.

Since SOAR is a framework, it provides the flexibility of application in many different situations and levels of change. A goal of this section has been to provide you with a new way of thinking, crafting, planning, and implementing strategy. We have found that creating strategy from a strengths-based, whole system perspective builds confidence and momentum to move people forward in an uncertain environment. The following story brings this concept to life.

SOAR: A POSITIVE TRANSFORMATION

Overview

This story is set within the operations finance function of a division of a large Midwestern global consumer products manufacturer with $4 billion in sales. This division is responsible for the manufacture of five different personal product categories across four different brands representing over $1 billion in sales and 2,000 employees in seven countries.

The operations finance team was experiencing a crisis in performance and leadership in delivering core financial services such as budgeting, forecasting, reporting, and strategic analytics to their operations team. A new finance director was brought in to provide strong leadership in driving an operations finance team transformation. Over a period of 18 months, the director applied positive organization approaches, including SOAR, Appreciative Inquiry (AI), lean management, and business process management techniques to build and develop a team of finance professionals who became strategic business partners and leaders across the greater consumer products organization.

The Personal Care Division Story

At first, the director concentrated on just getting up to speed on the annual budgeting process (ABP), which culminates in the setting of new standards. This process was very complex, involving many people across the division and taking several months to complete. In general, the ABP appeared to be a free-for-all with few defined responsibilities. Not only were roles unclear, but the team was experiencing a crisis in both leadership and performance. The director conducted a requirements gathering exercise that attempted to define the key issues for the personal care division (PCD) team. She interviewed a number of key operations leaders to determine what they thought the issues were and their vision of a high-performing finance team.

The feedback was not good regarding performance to date. Key operations leaders wanted (1) improved business partnering, (2) ability to meet deadlines, (3) greater speed and accuracy in standards and forecasting, (4) stronger analytics, (5) effective new product development (NPD) process, (6) greater consistency, (7) proactive reporting and analysis, (8) deeper understanding of cost drivers, (9) improved capital budgeting process, (10) greater visibility, (11) opportunities to improve, and finally, (12) a better understanding of the business and ability to make a meaningful contribution to its strategic competitiveness.

In summary, every finance process was broken, and the stakeholders were unhappy with the finance team's performance. In addition, the team lacked effective tools for insightful reporting and analysis. Given this situation, the finance team was unable to successfully serve as a strategic business partner to the operations team. As a result, the finance team was frustrated and demoralized.

Whole System Strategic Planning—Learning to SOAR

After the annual ABP was completed, the new director launched a week-long Hoshin (strategic) planning meeting where she included the entire team (i.e., engaging the whole system). A key event on the agenda was a quick SOAR using the 5-I approach. A quick SOAR is basically a half-day to full-day session allowing teams 60 minutes of dialogue for each of the four SOAR elements (Stavros and Hinrichs 2009). Some quick wins emerged from this session around the ABP process to build momentum and the finance vision and key strategic initiatives for the following year. Overall, a great deal of energy, alignment, and trust were created around what the team wanted to achieve together in the coming year.

SOAR was chosen to build strategic capacity and create whole system engagement in transforming the finance organization to achieve its ideal future in support of the organization and its stakeholders. As a result, the team discovered that SOAR:

- Builds trust
- Promotes relationships
- Provides a safe environment
- Empowers
- Develops efficacy
- Enables innovative thinking

- Creates alignment
- Evokes action and accountability
- Fosters engagement and energy
- Promotes learning
- Is versatile and simple to use
- Is flexible in working with other tools and frameworks

The SOAR journey unfolded through 5-I phases: Initiate, Inquire, Imagine, Innovate, and Implement.

Initiate. Interviews of key operational leaders (stakeholders) were completed to gain feedback regarding performance. This feedback was presented at the planning event as part of the planning process. SOAR was used with 12 colleagues representing the entire finance core team who traveled to the Hoshin meeting to participate in the one-and-a-half-day quick SOAR. An agenda outlining the planning process utilizing SOAR is in Exhibit 18.1.

Inquire. The 12 colleagues were divided into teams of two who interviewed each other using the AI and SOAR-based questions in Exhibit 18.2. Small groups

Exhibit 18.1. PCD Planning Process Agenda

SOAR Introduction and Interviews	(90 min)	
Strengths Conversation: What can we build on?	(90 min)	What are we most proud of as an organization? How does that reflect our greatest strength? What makes us unique? What can we be best at in our world? What is our proudest achievement in the last year or two? What do we do or provide that is world class for our customers, our industry, and other potential stakeholders?
Opportunities Conversation: What are our stakeholders asking for?	(90 min)	Stakeholder needs reviewed What are our potential opportunities/ innovations? What are the top three opportunities on which we should focus our efforts? Are there any challenges that can be reframed into opportunities? What new skills do we need to move forward?
Aspirations Conversation: What do we deeply care about?	(90 min)	When we explore our values and aspirations, what are we deeply passionate about? Reflecting on our strengths and opportunities conversations, who are we, who should we become, and where should we go in the future? What strategic initiatives would support our aspirations?
Results Conversation: How do we know we are succeeding?	(90 min)	Considering our strengths, opportunities, and aspirations, what meaningful measures would indicate that we are on track to achieving our goals? What are three to five indicators that would create a scorecard? What resources are needed to implement our most vital projects? What are the best rewards to support those who achieve our goals?

Adapted from J. Stavros and G. Hinrichs, *The Thin Book of SOAR: Building Strengths-Based Strategy* (Bend, OR: Thin Book Publishing, 2009), 16–17.

Exhibit 18.2. Discovering the Best of Our PCD Team (Interview Questions)

What Attracted You?	Think back to when you first got involved with PCD—what attracted you? What were your initial excitements and impressions?
High Point Experience	During your relationship with our team, I'm sure you've had some ups and downs, some peaks and valleys, some high points and low points. I'd like you to reflect for a moment on a high point experience, a time when you felt most alive, most engaged, most proud of your involvement with our team … tell the story. What happened? What made the experience exceptional?
Root Causes of Success	As you reflect on your high point, I'd like you to identify some of the "root causes" that contributed to making it a peak experience. First, what was it about you that made it a great experience? If we had a conversation with the people who know you best and asked them, "What are the three best leadership qualities they value in *you*, qualities or capabilities that you bring to our team and the building of its future—what would *they* say? Second, who were significant others and what was it about them that made it a high point? Third, what was it about the nature of your work … the things you most value … that made it a great experience? Finally, what was it about our team as a group (e.g., culture, values, relationships, leadership, systems, ways of working, etc.) that made it a high point for you?
Strategic Core Factor	Based on the last three questions, if you could boil it down to one thing, what would you say is the strategic core factor (a distinctive competency) that gives life, health, and vitality to our team—*our strengths*?
Exploring the Best Qualities and Hopes for the Future	Organizations work best when team spirit and enthusiasm are high and everyone is a valued member of a group where his or her ideas are heard. To be effective over time, organizations need cooperation within groups as well as between groups that cross department lines, jobs, and levels in the hierarchy. Teamwork requires trust, open channels of communication, appropriate business information, responsiveness to others' needs, good training, and interpersonal skills. Think of an example for

Exhibit 18.2. (*Continued*)

	the most effective team or group effort you have been part of at some point during your career or elsewhere. Tell the story of what happened. Who was involved? What made the teamwork effective? What were the important lessons?
Leadership in Finance	As you think today about the larger context and purpose of our team, there are many trends, events, and developments that will call on our group (like any high-purpose organization) to change, develop, and play an even more significant role in the future. In your view, what are the two or three most important *opportunities* affecting our finance group today (e.g., opportunities to better serve our customers in the finance realm)?
Images of the Future	Imagine five years have gone by, major changes have taken place, and our team has become everything you hoped it could be. You can truly say, without reservation, that this is the team of your dreams. What do you see? What does it look like? What's going on in finance? What's happening that's new and different? What is our team's culture and distinguishing characteristics? What is our reputation in the broader organization? In what ways are we leading in the field of finance? What do you see in terms of purpose, values, systems, people, ways of working, fiscal performance, others—*aspirations*?
How Do We Get from Here to There?	If you could develop or transform our team in any way, what three wishes, in order of priority, would you make to heighten our team's overall health and vitality? What *results* would define our success?

were formed combining two teams for debriefing. Each colleague presented what each partner had relayed during the interview process within the small group using the SOAR framework. Wonderful stories were shared around past successes, and a feeling of deep engagement and energy permeated the sessions. One colleague per team captured the emerging themes and ideas. At the end of the conversations, several key themes emerged: (1) standardized processes and reporting, (2) better tools and capacity building, (3) strong communication within our team and externally with our business partners, (4) restored trust and credibility, (5) a lean culture was created, and (6) partnership with operations.

Imagine. The small groups reconvened within the large group and shared stories and key themes. The large group continued the conversation to imagine the future through using the interviews as a core foundation for exploration. The large group identified key strengths, opportunities, aspirations, and results (see Exhibit 18.3) as part of this phase utilizing the SOAR framework questions.

The team's core values emerged from the dialogue based on the interview questions (Exhibit 18.2 and SOAR factors summarized in Exhibit 18.3) as (1) passion, (2) respect, (3) integrity, (4) trust, and (5) appreciation. The team developed a shared vision: "To become a highly credible finance team who is a trusted partner in making a difference for our company. Together we will grow, care, share credit, and become a smoothly functioning team that is able

Exhibit 18.3. SOAR: Strengths, Opportunities, Aspirations, and Results

	Strengths	**Opportunities**
Strategic Inquiry	People	Better tools
	Experience	Clear roles and responsibilities
	Tenacity and dependability	Standardized processes
	We deliver/make our deadlines	Communication
	Relationships—internal/external and with our customers	Proactive reporting
		Capacity building
	Flexibility—we seek new challenges	Cross-training and cross-teaming
	Hunger for learning	Lean culture
		Share best practices
		Restore trust and credibility
	Aspirations	**Results**
Appreciative Intent	Being winners	Close the books in three days
	Make a difference	Improve forecast accuracy by 90 percent
	Finance is the go-to person on all projects	100 percent of finance core value streams are streamlined and standardized using best practices
	High credibility	
	Trusted partner	
	We all care about each other	
	Everyone has grown and achieved personal career dreams	Standards delivered on time and with high accuracy
		Controllable variances = $0
	Smoothly functioning team	Communication plan and team established
	Good data and the right tools	
	Save the company millions!	Team 100 percent cross-trained
	Agile and fluid	SAP and EXCEL training delivered
	Premier team within PCD	

to achieve our collective dreams." This information was put on all the finance badge tags to remind the team of their values and vision every day.

Innovate. Based on the identification of strengths, opportunities, aspirations—image of the future, core values, and understanding the mission, the team identified the following strategic initiatives:

- Implement lean management techniques to streamline, standardize, innovate, and define the future state for all key finance processes
- Create a new division-wide strategic planning process using tools for business process management such as the inputs, guides, outputs, and enablers (IGOE) and stakeholder analysis
- Develop a business partner scorecard to promote better freight management
- Adopt lean leadership practices to enhance communication and coordination among the team
- Host Lunch & Learns and Power Hours to build the team's strategic capacity

The team also discussed necessary changes to structure, processes, systems, and resources to support the strategic initiatives. These strategic initiatives drove the action plans.

Implement. Moving from identification of strategic initiatives to implementation of the plan, the team showed high energy and commitment to their findings. Many team members joined together to work on projects to obtain positive results. Focusing on newly identified individual strengths, the finance team was reorganized around product value streams to promote better support of their operations business partners. This support by value stream was aligned with how operations were organized. The reorganization provided clear roles and responsibilities and customers for each finance colleague and key financial process. A change management plan was developed and implemented utilizing the ADKAR® framework along with a robust communication plan. ADKAR® is a change management tool used to diagnose and improve the people side of a change management initiative. Developed by Prosci, ADKAR stands for Awareness, Desire, Knowledge, Ability, and Reinforcement, which represent critical stages in an individual's adoption of change (Hiatt 2006).

A whole system, collaborative approach was utilized to implement the reorganization. Each team member met with individuals they were giving duties to and getting duties from. These meetings resulted in specific project plans to accomplish the new organization. As part of this effort, core processes and procedures were documented to promote team learning. Each individual was accountable to carry out the action plan accomplishing their transition. During implementation, each major initiative identified in the Innovate phase was assigned a lead person from the finance team. Then, individuals self-selected into projects supporting each initiative based upon interest and ownership of the topic under the new organization structure.

Lean project management templates were utilized (A3s) as a tool to manage each initiative. These A3 templates were living documents posted on an intranet site so that the entire team could access and review progress. In addition, monthly half-day Hoshin reviews were established for each team to report to the larger team progress on their projects in order to receive help and advice. Individual performance scorecards were created to measure actual results against individual key performance indicators. These scorecards were reviewed with the colleague by their manager each month to assess progress and provide coaching/help. These scorecards were utilized as part of the annual review process to establish overall scores for each colleague. This performance tool promoted high communication, coaching, and strategic focus.

Results

Through the project management structure and activities specified in the implementation phase, including monthly Hoshin reviews, daily stand-up meetings, and regular management reviews of individual performance scorecards, the strategic initiatives were accomplished within 12 months.

The team was successfully reorganized with no disruption in service levels. New tools were implemented and training provided to the finance team to build their capability. Standardized reports focusing on stakeholder requirements were created and refined. Every core finance process (value stream) was redesigned, streamlined, stabilized, and standardized. Because operations had been involved in many of the process redesign efforts, there was greater accountability on the part of the operations team for achieving the targeted financial results of the division. In addition, these processes became highly focused on stakeholder requirements, which were much more valuable to accomplishing the operations team objectives. Forecast accuracy improved dramatically, and the division met their budgeted targets. As a result of these efforts, the finance team improved in their ability to become a trusted strategic business partner.

A Finance Customer Scorecard was created and completed by every operations leader at the end of the fiscal year. The scorecard showed dramatic customer satisfaction improvement in the areas of providing basic financial services, reporting, and overall customer service levels to the organization. However, scores for analytical services showed low satisfaction. This instrument served as the starting point for another SOAR cycle that occurred at the annual Hoshin planning event in the new year.

The finance team experienced a positive transformation from demoralization and disrespect to highly functioning, positive financial leadership of the division. SOAR enabled the team to bridge the gap between its current performance and its potential, by building the team's capacity to identify and meet its strategic goals. Some of the results realized:

- A kaizen session (a Japanese philosophy for continuous improvement) was held for closing the books, which resulted in the ability to close the books in three days (this process was formerly taking seven days to accomplish).
- All major finance value streams were streamlined, standardized, measured, and managed.
- A new financial model and process was developed to bring greater visibility, accountability, and transparency to divisional strategic planning targets.
- A new process was designed for new product development costing, resulting in improved analytics and greater functional coordination.
- Best practices for financial modeling and EXCEL techniques were developed and shared among the team. This built the team's capacity and offered a vehicle for recognition.
- Cross training and standardized work (documented work processes) were completed for all major processes to enhance team scale and scope.
- The team created a peer recognition award: the *Yeoman Award* for great and noble service.

The results were celebrated each month at Hoshin reviews in order to build and leverage momentum. A communication committee was established to ensure high communication, collaboration, sharing of best practices, and fun celebrations among the team. The team eventually became recognized as the highest achieving finance team in the organization. The team built strategic capacity through this experience and subsequently was able to leverage this capacity in a second major transformation 18 months later as the entire finance team was reorganized into centers of excellence.

SUMMARY

SOAR engages the entire system (or representatives of key stakeholders) to build upon strengths, engage in possibility thinking, and expand participation in the development of goals and objectives for strategizing in developing and implementing strategic plans. SOAR creates positive energy that informs action. The SOAR framework is very versatile and can be utilized for many applications such as individual coaching, leadership development, brand management, problem-solving, continuous improvement, and conflict management. SOAR also fosters learning and engagement, allowing for a shared learning system in its different applications. SOAR functions as a sense-managing tool that enables individuals across the organization and multiorganizations to better understand the values, mission, vision, and strategies of the organization and relate them back to individual actions. Finally, SOAR can be utilized throughout an organization to foster trust and build relational generativity. Generativity refers to the ability to create something new and unique as the offspring from an initial condition. Ultimately, SOAR builds strategic capacity enabling individuals and organizations to achieve their latent potential.

In a *McKinsey Quarterly* survey of 1,200 global executives, it was found that organizations with the highest performance had a clear purpose, an understanding of *strengths,* shared *aspirations,* and leaders who know how to unleash ideas (*opportunities*) with a *results*-driven process (Isern and Pung 2007). As a result, those responsible for strategy formulation and execution are placing a new emphasis on positive strategy and the SOAR framework. SOAR is gaining attention and actively emerging as an effective and flexible strategic framework that releases an organization's energy, creativity, and engagement to build strategic capacity that achieves positive results. SOAR builds strategic capacity that creates an environment where strategy is fluid, generative, and dynamic.

Discussion Questions

1. How can SOAR be combined with other change management techniques to bring about transformation within your organization?

2. How can SOAR be utilized to build strategic capacity within the teams that you work with?

3. How can SOAR and lean management methodologies create culture change in back office processes?

4. How does SOAR support holistic transformation?

5. How can SOAR be used at your organization to release energy, creativity and engagement?

Resources

ADKAR: Awareness, Desire, Knowledge, Ability, and Reinforcement: www.change-management.com/

Lean Enterprise Institutes (includes Hoshin and project management): www.lean.org/

Kaizen Institute: www.kaizen.com

Project Management: www.pmi.org/default.aspx

SOAR website: www.soar-strategy.com/

SOAR Facebook: www.facebook.com/SOAR.Strategy

Business Process Management and Redesign—BP: Trends: www.bptrendsassociates.com/

References

Barrett, F. J., D. L. Cooperrider, and R. E. Fry. 2005. "Bringing Every Mind into the Game to Realize the Positive Revolution in Strategy: The Appreciative Inquiry Summit." In *Practicing Organization Development: A Guide for Consultants*, 2nd ed., edited by W. J. Rothwell, R. Sullivan, and G. McLean, 501–549. San Francisco: John Wiley & Sons.

Cummings, T. C., and A. Feyerherm. 2010. "Interventions in Large Systems." In *Practicing Organization Development: A Guide to Leading Change*, 3rd ed., edited by W. J. Rothwell, J. Stavros, and R. Sullivan, 345–362. San Francisco: John Wiley & Sons.

Cummings, T., and C. Worley. 2005. *Organization Development & Change*. 8th ed. Mason, Ohio: Thomson/South-Western.

Greiner, L., and T. Cummings. 2009. *Dynamic Strategy-Making: A Real-Time Approach for the 21st Century Leader*. San Francisco: Jossey-Bass.

Hart, S. 1992. "An Integrative Framework for Strategy Making Processes." *Academy of Management Review* 17 (2): 327–351.

Hauden, J. 2008. *The Art of Engagement: Bridging the Gap between People and Possibilities*. New York: McGraw-Hill.

Hiatt, J. 2006. *ADKAR: A Model of Change in Business, Government, and Our Community*. Loveland, CO: Prosci Learning Center.

Hofer, C. W., and D. Schendel. 1978. *Strategy Formulation: Analytical Concepts*. St. Paul, MN: West Publishing.

Isern, J., and C. Pung. 2007. "Driving Radical Change." *The McKinsey Quarterly* 4: 1–12.

Malone, P. 2010. *An Appreciative Exploration of Strategic Capacity and the Impact of the SOAR Framework in Building Strategy Capacity*. Unpublished dissertation, College of Management, Lawrence Technological University, Southfield, MI.

Miller, D., and H. Mintzberg. 1984. *Organizations: A Quantum View*. Englewood Cliffs, NJ: Prentice Hall.

Stavros, J. M. 2013. "The Generative Nature of SOAR: Applications, Results, and the New SOAR Profile." *AI Practitioner: International Journal of Appreciative Inquiry* 15 (3): 6–26.

Stavros, J. M., and G. Hinrichs. 2009. *Thin Book of SOAR: Building Strengths-based Strategy*. Bend, OR: Thin Book Publishers.

Stavros, J. M., and L. Wooten. 2012. "Positive Strategy: Creating and Sustaining Strengths-based Strategy That SOARs and Performs." In *The Oxford Handbook of Positive Organizational Scholarship*, edited by K. Cameron and G. Spreitzer, 825–842. New York: Oxford University Press.

PART FOUR

SPECIAL ISSUES IN ORGANIZATION DEVELOPMENT, TRANSFORMATION, AND CHANGE

CHAPTER NINETEEN

Sustainability and Transformational Work

What Should Business Do?

Nadya Zhexembayeva

In recent years, three big trends—declining resources, radical transparency, and increasing expectations—have redefined the way companies compete. The linear throw-away economy, in which products and services follow a one-way trajectory from extraction to use and disposal, can no longer be supported, as we are simply running out of things to unearth and places to landfill. Consumers, employees, and investors are beginning to demand socially and environmentally savvy products without compromise, while radical transparency is putting every company under a microscope.

Together, these challenges have been addressed by the global sustainability movement, which at its best calls for embedded sustainability—defined as "the incorporation of environmental, health and social value into the core business with no trade-off in price or quality—in other words, with no social or green premium" (Laszlo and Zhexembayeva 2011, 100). Yet, embedding sustainability into the core of business without compromises on price or quality requires a comprehensive business makeover. This transformation does not happen overnight, and it requires strategic and systemic change management efforts by everyone involved. Here, organization development (OD) professionals have a special role to play. So, what are the most crucial considerations for transformational work done in the field of sustainability? It boils down to three aspects:

1. The emergent nature of sustainability strategy
2. The need for rich harvest of low-hanging fruit
3. The call for new competence development

In this chapter, we will explore these considerations and discuss implications and insights for OD professionals thriving to assist businesses in building and executing their sustainability strategy.

CONSIDERATION 1: MOVE FROM A PREPLANNED TO AN EMERGENT PROCESS

Modern management has a thing for putting the world in boxes. Whether it is a dip in performance that drives our companies to embark on a grand change program, or pressure from legislators, consumers, or investors—whether it is inside-out or outside-in—it seems that all of us are expected to go through the same process. Step one: Identify the problem. Step two: Conduct a thorough root-cause analysis. Step three: Brainstorm and analyze possible solutions. Step four: Choose and develop a clear course of action. Step five: Implement. Managing strategic change for sustainability seems no different: We need clear, manageable steps—from plan to implementation—and no other way will do. Sounds easy, right?

I have yet to find a company where this perfect step-by-step plan ever worked. Yet, we insist on taking this route again and again—and every time I ask a group of managers to draw me a change-management plan, they produce the same five steps. Perhaps, that is exactly the reason why so many change efforts fail miserably. In 1996, in his blockbuster *Leading Change*, John P. Kotter revealed a shocking number: Only 30 percent of change efforts succeed (Kotter 1996). Considering that change management was a very new discipline at that time, we can give it the benefit of the doubt; it has to have gotten better since then, right? Unfortunately, the progress was not visible. In 2008, a McKinsey survey of 3,199 executives around the world found, just as Kotter had, that only one transformation in three attempted succeeds (Aiken and Keller 2009).

Sustainability is a complex, multi-activity, and multi-actor challenge; no simple recipes are possible. The task of embedding social and environmental value into the DNA of a business is iterative, repetitive, and chaotic. Embedded sustainability demands new thinking and unorthodox solutions that can spring from unlikely sources and in improbable ways. The challenge of strategic sustainability breaks the expected sequence of change management. Customarily, it is assumed that you first develop the strategy and then implement it. In fact, the line between strategy and execution has become so sharp that it is taken as a sign of great wisdom to hear business leaders such as Jamie Dimon, CEO of JPMorgan Chase, assert, "I'd rather have a first-rate execution and second-rate strategy any time than a brilliant idea and mediocre management" (Martin 2010, para. 1).

Yet, for most of us who lived through at least one successful strategic management and OD process, it is rather clear that the line, if it exists at all, is less of a Great Wall of China and more of a jagged set of dots guiding the ever-changing dance between strategy and execution. Roger Martin, a strategy theorist and practicing manager, offered this passionate illustration in a 2010 *Harvard Business Review* article:

> If a strategy produces poor results, how can we argue that it is brilliant? It certainly is an odd definition of brilliance. A strategy's purpose is to generate positive results, and the strategy in question doesn't do that, yet it was brilliant? In what other field do we proclaim something to be brilliant that has failed miserably on its only attempt? A "brilliant" Broadway play that closes after one week? A "brilliant" political campaign that results in the other candidate winning? If we think about it, we must accept that the only strategy that can legitimately be called brilliant is one whose results are exemplary. (Martin 2010, para. 5)

Indeed, early successes with innovating for a resource-deprived, demanding, and transparent world echoed Martin's strong questioning of the illusory line between strategy and execution. But even more so, they challenge the sequence of change itself. Every company I studied or worked with that dared to venture into the unknown terrain of sustainability had to do so in the nearly complete dark, each step suggesting the next, experimenting heavily, taking action courageously, and producing results long before a truly comprehensive strategy could be voiced. Long before it became clear what strategic pathways would take one from here to there, companies had to plunge into the first steps, reap the first low-hanging fruits, develop the first new capabilities, and survive the first failures. In other words, they had to learn their way into the sustainable business.

Clearly, transformational work in the field of sustainability requires flexibility of thinking and action. That does not mean that it lacks clarity or deliberation. Experience of companies who have already ventured into this territory suggests four interdependent and interconnected lines of action to guide the journey (Laszlo and Zhexembayeva 2011; Zhexembayeva 2014):

1. *Getting the Right Start*: Mobilizing, educating, and acting around specific cross-functional projects that can generate clear win-win results for business and society within a relatively short period of time.

2. *Building the Buy-In*: Aligning the company, value chain, and all other stakeholders around the vision of embedded sustainability with the goal of creating a true ownership of the process by the entire business.

3. *Moving from Incremental to Breakthrough*: Developing clear but unorthodox goals, specific for the company and designing the strategy for capturing value through co-creation and innovation.

4. *Staying with It*: Managing organizational learning and energy while making sustainability ubiquitous in business practice.

While the above list may suggest a possible linear sequence, in reality, much of the sustainability journey is nonlinear, with some efforts starting simultaneously, while others repeated more than once. This is, indeed, at the center of the first consideration for OD professionals working in the field of sustainability: Build your transformation as a flexible, fluid, and emergent process, rather than a rigid hard-to-change action plan.

CONSIDERATION 2: HARVEST THE LOW-HANGING FRUIT

Whenever we talk about transformation, it is assumed that the product of the change process has to be big. Breakthrough. Breathtaking. Yet, the most potent and often most difficult type of change comes in small packages. This is exactly where sustainability companies start with their journey. Experimentation— packaged in small portions, focused on quick wins and low-hanging fruit—is what allows you to make a lot of mistakes (safely!), train your eye to be able to notice the hidden value, and build the managerial muscles needed for this demanding transformation. This is something that international retailer Walmart started with.*

From Walmart's humble beginnings in 1962 to its present state as an international superpower, Walmart rightly claims the position of being one of the most renowned businesses worldwide. One might think that for a corporate superpower of such unlimited resources, innovation should be a natural aspect of daily life, whereby every possible discovery for a better business performance is made and implemented at the speed of light. Indeed, the company is well known for its outstanding practices in supply-chain and inventory management, where it has invented like no other. Yet, one of its most recent waves of innovation came from the place least anticipated for an international giant.

In 2005, facing the pressures of declining resources and increasing demands, all fueled by increasing transparency, Walmart made its first official sustainability commitment by setting three specific goals:

1. To be supplied 100 percent by renewable energy

2. To create zero waste

3. To sell products that sustain resources and the environment

---

*Special Note: The data for Walmart stories came from a DVD I purchased from Walmart in 2006. It was produced by Walmart and titled *Sustainability 101*, and it has been a great addition to my executive education classes ever since. On January 13, 2014, I was able to access it online in full at http://greenenergytv.com/watch.php?v = 367.

Corresponding short-term goals were set in each category, such as "fleet 25 percent more efficient in three years" for the energy category and "25 percent reduction in solid waste in three years" for the waste category—all driving significant innovation wrapped in small packages. So, how did the transformation work, exactly? With the goals set, it was time to experiment—searching for new ways of doing business that would allow for achievement of the tightly set requirements. One of Walmart's first experiments in the domain of zero waste was an effort to "right-size" the packaging for a private-label line of children's toys. For years, the cost-cutting champion followed the lead of its suppliers when selecting specific packages for the products sold in Walmart stores. The zero-waste goal created a new lens for assessing and making packaging decisions, driving a fundamental quest for reducing the packaging material. And with the new lens, it became apparent that some of Walmart's packages had room to spare; the product fit in a loose fashion, with some space left between the product and the package. Making the first step with just one of thousands of product lines, Walmart tested "right-sizing" for all 350 items in the product line. Shaving just about an inch (three to four centimeters) from each box in the line as well as master cartons, Walmart was able to save 3,425 tons of corrugated paper materials, 1,358 barrels of oil, 5,190 harvested trees, and 727 shipping containers, while creating savings of $3,540,000 in transportation costs in one year—an ultimate "aha!" moment for the accidental innovators.

It seemed to be a rather simple solution—just an inch off a box—but experiments similar to the one in the right-sizing story bring about a depth of discoveries:

- First, starting with "small" innovation trains your eyes to notice invisible risks and new opportunities.

- Second, countless examples show that even a rather timid transformation of this kind requires a significant mobilization of the company to drive changes in product design, production, packaging, supplier relations, and more. Doing it first at a relatively small scale allows you to learn from your own mistakes—in other words, to learn how to learn, faster.

- Third, a story of this kind quickly makes it through the corridors of the corporation, becoming fuel for the next wave of valuable discoveries. (As the example of Silicon Valley shows, one big success is enough to drive thousands more efforts.)

CONSIDERATION 3: DEVELOP NEW COMPETENCIES FOR NEW CHALLENGES

While traditional business skills remain vital when embedding sustainability into the DNA of a company, they must be complemented with new competencies. Four essential skills have been identified but are yet to be valued in today's corporate world: design, inquiry, appreciation, and wholeness (Laszlo and Zhexembayeva 2011). These four skills are also at the core of the OD profession.

Design is first and foremost an attitude or mode of thinking. At its core is an assumption strikingly different from the one that underlies the typical business decision. If decision-making is all about making a hard choice between easy-to-identify alternatives, design attitude assumes an easy choice between difficult-to-create alternations. Tim Brown, CEO and President of IDEO, ranked among the 10 most innovative companies in the world, illustrates this point in the following way:

> A management philosophy based only on selecting from existing strategies is likely to be overwhelmed by new developments at home and abroad. What we need are new choices—new products that balance the needs of individuals and of society as a whole; new ideas that tackle the global challenges of health, poverty, and education; new strategies that result in differences that matter and a sense of purpose that engages everyone affected by them. What we need is an approach to innovation that is powerful, effective, and broadly accessible. Design thinking ... offers just such an approach. [Brown 2009, 4]

The next two competencies—*inquiry* and *appreciation*—build respectively on what is possible and on the existing strengths present in every business system. A well-known OD methodology—Appreciative Inquiry—has, as its name implies, these two competencies at its very core (Cooperrider and Srivastva 1987, Cooperrider and Whitney 2001). Appreciative Inquiry has enabled managers at leading firms such as Hewlett-Packard, Walmart, and McKinsey to discover the best of their shared experiences and tap into the larger system's capacity for cooperation. Efforts to discover and elaborate the positive core—the past, present, and future capacities of the whole system—lead to innovations that integrate societal stakeholder issues that are often excluded from consideration in conventional approaches to decision-making.

Wholeness is the final skill needed to master the complex challenge of embedding sustainability across entire business systems. It requires an ability not only to see the big picture but also to understand the linkages within the system. Donella Meadows, the systems scientist, quotes an ancient Sufi teaching that captures this focus: "You think because you understand *one* you must understand *two*, because one and one makes two. But you must also understand *and*" (Wheatley 1994, 9). Learning systems tools such as feedback loops, life-cycle analyses, and stakeholder value maps can help managers develop solutions that are less fragmentary and contradictory than bolt-on sustainability measures developed in isolation.

Together, these competencies allow managers across functions and hierarchies to deal with the complex challenge of sustainability in business.

SUMMARY

Embedded sustainability—or the incorporation of environmental, health, and social value into the core business with no trade-off in price or quality—has become a key priority of organizations worldwide. The task of embedding sustainability requires systematic and strategic transformation effort—one that is particularly dependent on the skills and capabilities of OD professionals. However, to make meaningful contributions, OD teams need to consider that embedding sustainability into the core business strategy is a deliberate, nonlinear, and iterative process—a process in which conversations about strategy and strategic transformation and change become relevant only once the company has already harvested some low-hanging fruit and thus engaged its employees in practical day-to-day action; and in which new competencies are needed as a foundation for transitioning from incremental to deeper change.

Discussion Questions

1. What are the similarities and differences between sustainability and any other transformation challenges?

2. How does the challenge of sustainability impact the life of your organization today? What does your organization do to manage these challenges effectively?

3. What OD methods and approaches, in addition to the ones already named, might be particularly effective when addressing the challenges of sustainability in business?

Resources

The Challenge of Sustainability in Business: www.youtube.com/watch?v = FTNI_ToDISc

Overfished Ocean Strategy: Powering Up Innovation for a Resource-Deprived World: www.youtube.com/watch?v = FTNI_ToDISc

Overview of Embedded Sustainability Approach: www.europeanfinancialreview.com/? p = 2927

Innovation for Positive Sustainable Development: http://positivitystrategist.com/ innovation-positive-sustainable-development-nadya-zhexembayeva-ps018/

LinkedIn profile of the author featuring articles and podcasts on sustainability and transformation: www.linkedin.com/pub/nadya-zhexembayeva/0/627/88b/

References

Aiken, C., and S. Keller. 2009. "The Irrational Side of Change Management." *McKinsey Quarterly*. www.mckinsey.com/insights/organization/the_irrational_side_of_change_management.

Brown, T. 2009. *Change by Design*. New York: HarperCollins.

Cooperrider, D. L., and S. Srivastva. 1987. "Appreciative Inquiry in Organizational Life." In *Research in Organizational Change and Development*, edited by R. W. Woodman and W. A. Pasmore, 129–169. Stamford, CT: JAI Press.

Cooperrider, D. L., and D. Whitney. 2001. "A Positive Revolution in Change." In *Appreciative Inquiry: An Emerging Direction for Organization Development*, edited by D. L. Cooperrider, P. Sorenson, D. Whitney, and T. Yeager, 9–29. Champaign, IL: Stipes.

Kotter, J. P. 1996. *Leading Change*. Boston: Harvard Business School Press.

Laszlo, C., and N. Zhexembayeva. 2011. *Embedded Sustainability: The Next Big Competitive Advantage*. Stanford, CA: Stanford University Press.

Martin, R. L. 2010. "The Execution Trap." *Harvard Business Review*. https://hbr.org/2010/07/the-execution-trap.

Wheatley, M. J. 1994. *Leadership and the New Science: Learning about Organization from an Orderly Universe*. San Francisco: Berrett-Koehler.

Zhexembayeva, N. 2014. *Overfished Ocean Strategy: Powering Up Innovation for a Resource-Deprived World*. Stanford, CA: Berrett-Koehler.

CHAPTER TWENTY

Organization Design that Transforms

Amy Kates

A foundational understanding of organization design frameworks and methods should be in the toolkit of any organization development (OD) and human resource (HR) professional. Many business leaders understand that the design of an organization is just as much a source of competitive advantage as strategy or talent. While not all OD practitioners and HR generalists will engage in the design of whole new organizations, most will be asked to help *activate* these changes—to bring to life the assumptions that business leaders have made about how strategy should be executed, where the power and resources lie, how decisions are made, and the behaviors that are essential to that organization's culture.

To make the right choices about what interventions and support to provide, the OD practitioner must understand how the organization has been designed if brought in after the fact, and be ready to guide leaders in making sound choices when given the opportunity. This chapter discusses the relationship between organization design and OD, highlights key frameworks and methods in the field, and suggests some of the competencies needed for those who wish to pursue a deeper practice in organization design.

THE RELATIONSHIP OF ORGANIZATION DESIGN TO ORGANIZATION DEVELOPMENT

Organization design is a decision science for selecting among competing alternatives to match the optimal organizational model to the strategy (Boudreau and Ramstad 2007). Making good design choices is not enough to successfully carry out a strategy. OD can be thought of as the discipline of implementing these design choices. Organization design is then the link between business strategy and execution.

Without organization design, there is no framework within which to determine what OD activities will have the most impact and when they should be carried out. Understanding organization design concepts and options and analyzing existing designs and anticipating the predictable consequences of various choices will aid practitioners in making better decisions regarding what OD interventions will be most effective and how best to implement them. Many experienced OD practitioners are seeking to learn about organization design because it moves them up the value chain in their discussions with their business clients. Participating in the discussion places them closer to strategic decisions and in a position to more fully influence their organization development work.

One can also define organization design by its relationship to talent. An analogy is that of architecture to city planning. Architecture focuses on individual buildings and their relationship to one another. City planning is about urban systems; it not only deals with the built environment, but with political, social, economic, and transportation networks. In the same way, organization design is about complex, interconnected systems that create the conditions in which individuals and teams—that is, "talent"—can succeed. Organization and talent work together, but organizational choices must be first understood to avoid designing around people (Worren 2012).

KEY CONCEPTS IN ORGANIZATION DESIGN

The essential model in organization design is the Star Model, which was developed by Jay Galbraith in the 1970s and is shown in Figure 20.1 (Galbraith 2014). There are many versions of the Star Model in use such as McKinsey's "Seven S," but they all incorporate a holistic view and emphasize the importance of understanding that organizations are systems. A change to one element will require a change to other elements to create alignment. Many companies, including P&G, GlaxoSmithKline, BASF, Intel, and MetLife use the Star Model as the core of their

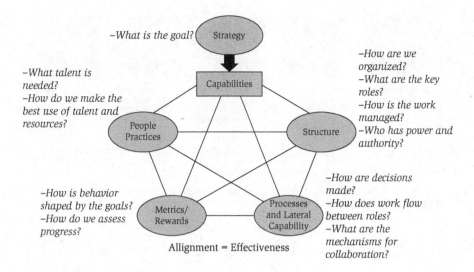

-What is the goal?

-What talent is needed?
-How do we make the best use of talent and resources?

-How are we organized?
-What are the key roles?
-How is the work managed?
-Who has power and authority?

-How is behavior shaped by the goals?
-How do we assess progress?

Allignment = Effectiveness

-How are decisions made?
-How does work flow between roles?
-What are the mechanisms for collaboration?

Figure 20.1. The Star Model

organization design methodology and find that line managers appreciate that it is both comprehensive and practical.

The Star Model includes the basic elements that must be considered in organization design: strategy, capabilities, structure, process, metrics, and people. Only those elements a leader has direct influence over are included in the model. Therefore, although culture is an essential part of an organization, it is not an explicit part of the model. A leader cannot design culture directly. Culture is a product of the cumulative design decisions made in the past and of the leadership and management behaviors that result from those decisions.

Besides the "what" of organization design summarized by the Star Model, there is also a "how to" that is emerging as a core design methodology in the field. Figure 20.2 summarizes the five-milestone organization design process (Kesler and Kates 2011).

This chapter cannot cover the many decision frameworks and methods that one can use to guide choices about structure, matrix relationships, levels and layers, management processes, decision rights, matching talent to roles, and reward systems. Rather, what are emphasized are the two steps that come before any solutions are generated or evaluated. The core elements of the first milestone in the organization design process—business case and discovery—are the assessment and design criteria development. The experienced OD practitioner will find both steps consistent with any good problem-solving process.

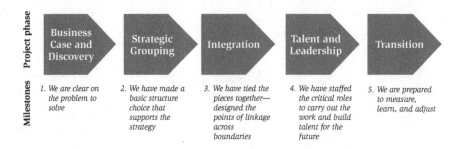

Figure 20.2. The Organization Design Process

From Greg Kesler and Amy Kates, *Leading Organization Design* (San Francisco: Jossey-Bass, 2011), 10. With permission from John Wiley & Sons.

THE ASSESSMENT

Organization design starts with a clear identification of the problem to solve. Failure to do this leads to wasted effort and sometimes the wrong fix—which is why multiple organization changes are often made with no change in business results. A presenting problem is usually articulated by the top executive at the beginning of the discovery process. Listen closely to what executives say because they capture frustrations as well as aspirations for the future. But smart leaders do not want their internal or external OD practitioners buying in to the presenting problem too quickly.

The current-state assessment must do more than report back what people in the organization are thinking. The assessment must deliver an articulated problem statement. This requires that a fact-based, diagnostic point of view be reached. An effective problem statement should be written in specific, concise language that can be supported by the data and captured in five to seven statements. Typically the problem statement is crafted through several iterations of dialogue with the key executives. This is time well spent. Table 20.1 shows an example of a problem statement for a medical device company. The division president had articulated the initial presenting problem as, "We need to tie the front and back of the business together, get everyone on the same team; and we need to learn how to do integrated solutions selling and marketing." Note how the analysis evolved.

We call this a "problem statement," but the case for change may be a gap, a response to a new opportunity, or an anticipated change in the external environment. The problem statement provides the focus for the next design steps. When design teams lose their bearings, they can refocus by asking, "What problem are we trying to solve?"

Table 20.1. Sample Problem Statement

- There are major disconnects between the customer—represented today exclusively by the sales organizations—and center-led product, product development, and marketing.
- New product development is widely regarded as the single greatest gap in capability today, leading to a commodity versus solutions view, lack of momentum in new products, and USA-centric deliverables.
- Product management is distributed across functions (and geographies) with fragmented and undisciplined roles and process (lacking a life-cycle view), low customer connectivity for development organization, and poorly defined product specs for software development.
- Marketing lacks effective role focus and vertical market specialization; alignment with the field is not strong, and processes do not bring the voice of the customer into product groups.
- Sales teams' roles and skills need to transition from legacy-product sales to systems and solution selling. The current sales structure, sales role definitions, metrics, and rewards systems work against longer-cycle, systems selling.
- Sales and service (front-end) organizational models and performance vary widely by region (and within regions) relative to vertical market specialization, key account coverage, and linkage between sales and service management.

DESIGN CRITERIA

The organization design process is a series of choices and decisions. In any decision-making process, clear criteria serve the purpose of allowing alternatives to be evaluated against agreed-upon standards. The criteria that should be used to make organization design decisions are the organizational capabilities that will differentiate the organization and help it execute its strategy. Different strategies require different capabilities. Different capabilities lead to different design choices. The terms *organizational capabilities* and *design criteria* can be used interchangeably.

For the medical device company discussed above, one important needed capability uncovered by the assessment is to bring the voice of the customer into the new product development process. If the company was a consumer packaged goods company used to feeding robust consumer insights into the R&D process, this may be easy and obvious and not even worth mentioning. For this company, connecting the front-end sales and customer-sensing part of the company with the engineers focused on pushing out the latest technological advances is quite new and difficult but important to the company strategy. Therefore, it is a capability worth developing for them.

As part of a set of design criteria, this capability might be written as: "We need to design an organization that is able to bring the voice of the customer into the new product development process." Building this capability may be accomplished through structure and role, new processes, incentives, or some combination of changes. The diagnostic and the design criteria do not jump to solutions. They provide the benchmark against which alternatives can be tested.

The organization development practitioner can play a critical role to ensure these two steps are taken before line managers jump to developing possible answers. One does not have to be an expert in organization design to use these tools. And just by ensuring a disciplined thought process that starts with a robust diagnostic and a clear set of criteria, the quality of design decisions will be improved.

What Makes a Good Organization Designer?

As OD practitioners seek to add organization design to their service portfolios, it is worth reflecting on what defines a skilled organization designer. As in any field, knowledge is not enough. Organization design requires a particular set of competencies and skills.

Diagnostic and Analytic Skills. The organization designer must ask the right questions and make sense of the answers. Like a physician who sorts through symptoms that may have many causes and determines the correct underlying disease, the organization designer must be able to determine the root causes of performance issues in the system. As important, the designer also must be able to recognize internal best practices to leverage and strengths that can be sustained over time (Heath and Heath 2011). The designer then analyzes what changes will have the most impact with the greatest likelihood of success in this context.

Deep Curiosity about Organizations as Systems. Effective organization designers are fascinated by the complexity of business and organizational life. They like to solve multifaceted problems and do not stop at easy answers or one-dimensional solutions. One needs to be able see an organization as more than a collection of individuals and to discern the interconnected political, social, and information networks that have formed. Transforming a system requires curiosity about how the pieces interact.

Design Mindset. Designers—whether of organizations, buildings, information technology systems, or functional objects—share a common ability to conceive of and articulate how their designs will work. They take problems and frame them so the right questions are asked, a wide range of options is generated, and the best solutions are chosen. They know that the process is rarely linear but rather iterative and enhanced by contributions from different perspectives. Designers are often ambidextrous thinkers, comfortable with solving for both the possible and the practical (Mootee 2013).

Pattern Recognition. Organization design is not for the neophyte. One must have enough hands-on, personal experience working with a variety of organizations to build the expertise to recognize and sort patterns. While one can become familiar with frameworks from training programs and reading, pattern recognition cannot come from a book. Each designer must have his or her library of experiences and examples to draw upon. This is where collaborating with OD and HR colleagues in the work can be beneficial to test assumptions and share insights.

Consulting and Enabling Skills. Successful organization design requires a high level of confidence and competence to guide leadership teams through a design process. All of the core consulting skills—contracting, assessment, facilitation, written communication, and presentation abilities—are used in the organization design process. Handing down expert answers from on high does not work in design. The leader and leadership team must discover and own the solution themselves; the designer is there to educate the team about the realities and possibilities, to provide them the language and tools to decide, and to challenge and guide them to implementable solutions.

SUMMARY

Organization design will continue to grow as a topic of importance for business leaders as they transform their organizations to pursue new strategies. The OD practitioner that understands the core models, frameworks, and design skills will be well positioned to influence and guide this important work.

Discussion Questions

1. Does our organization use assessments and diagnostics to help make data-based organizational decisions? If not, how can I build an appreciation among clients of the importance of understanding the problem to solve before generating options?

2. What capabilities does my client organization(s) need? What differentiates them strategically from their competitors? How might the use of capabilities (stated as design criteria) help them make better decisions?

3. What design frameworks do my clients use when they make organizational changes? Where could they benefit from a more disciplined and comprehensive approach and process?

4. Do we have an organization design capability in our HR team? Where do we need to invest—conceptual understanding, common tools and methodology, and/or consulting skills?

5. How do generalists and specialists on our HR team work together to deliver organization design solutions to our clients? What do we need to do to improve how we deliver complex consulting seamlessly?

6. How would I rate myself against the competencies of a good organization designer? What development activities could I do to build on my strengths? Who can I partner with to develop areas where I have less experience?

Resources

Design blog and articles from Kates Kesler: www.kateskesler.com

Organization Design Community (global academic association producing a journal, webinars, and annual conference): www.orgdesigncomm.com

Organization Design Forum (U.S. and Europe-based professional association for practitioners): www.organizationdesignforum.org

Organization re-Design Blog: www.organizationdesign.net

References

Boudreau, J. W., and P. M. Ramstad. 2007. *Beyond HR: The New Science of Human Capital.* Boston: Harvard Business School Press.

Galbraith, J. R. 2014. *Designing Organizations: Strategy, Structure, and Process at the Business Unit and Enterprise Levels.* 3rd ed. San Francisco: Jossey-Bass.

Heath, C., and D. Heath. 2011. *Switch: How to Change Things When Change Is Hard.* New York: Crown.

Kesler, G., and A. Kates. 2011. *Leading Organization Design: How to Make Organization Design Decisions to Drive the Results You Want.* San Francisco: Jossey-Bass.

Mootee, I. 2013. *Design Thinking for Strategic Innovation: What They Can't Teach You at Business or Design School.* San Francisco: John Wiley & Sons.

Worren, N. 2012. *Organization Design: Re-defining Complex Systems.* Essex, England: Pearson.

CHAPTER TWENTY-ONE

Mergers and Acquisitions

Still Crazy After All These Years

Mitchell Lee Marks and Philip H. Mirvis

Mergers and acquisitions (M&A) are a way for organizations to maintain their competitiveness and generate transformational change in an increasingly global market place (Faulkner, Teerikangas, and Joseph 2012). They are used to achieve economies of scale, diversification, and economic growth (Giessner, Ullrich, and van Dick 2012). In the 2010 edition of this handbook, we anticipated that the easing of the global economic crisis would stimulate an increase in M&A activity worldwide (Marks and Mirvis 2010b). We got it right: M&A activity is growing at a pace not seen since 2007, and the number of global deals is up 53 percent from 2013 to 2014 (Mattioli 2014).

A variety of trends are fueling the M&A boom. Some are financial. Interest rates are low, many firms have large stockpiles of cash, and some companies, particularly in health care, are making overseas acquisitions to take advantage of lower tax rates. Psychological factors also are contributing to the wave of M&A activity. Major deals spawn "copy-cat" combinations as CEOs want to eat before being eaten. In the telecom and media sector, A&T's $50 billion acquisition of DirectTV was followed by Charter's $55 billion offer to take over Time Warner Cable. And some deals are done for strategic reasons. Tech firms like Google and Facebook use acquisitions as a proxy for internal R&D efforts.

Despite this flurry of M&A activity, one thing has not changed since we wrote about the organization development (OD) role in M&A five years ago: the dismal track record of mergers and acquisitions results. Fewer than half of all corporate combinations achieve their financial or strategic objectives (Das and Kapil

2012; Gomes, Angwin, Weber, and Tarba 2013). Many factors account for the high M&A failure rate: buying the wrong company, paying the wrong price, or combining at the wrong time. However, based on insights from our experiences in over 100 cases of mergers and acquisitions—as well as our review of the literature on the human, cultural, and organizational aspects of M&A—the primary reason why most combinations fail is *the process through which the partner companies are integrated* (Marks and Mirvis 2014).

In this chapter, we briefly review the M&A process and highlight the success factors and common problem areas in each of the three phases of a deal. Then, we present recent developments in M&A practice, with a focus on how OD practitioners can assist early on as the deal is being conceived and planned.

THE M&A PROCESS

Our 30-year research program on M&A highlights important differences between the "typical" cases and "successful" ones that achieve their financial and strategic objectives (Marks and Mirvis 2010b). These differences are observed over the three phases of a deal:

1. The *Precombination Phase*, when a deal is conceived and negotiated by executives and then legally approved by shareholders and regulators.

2. The *Combination Phase*, when planning ensues and integration decisions are made.

3. The *Postcombination Phase*, when implementation occurs and people settle into the new roles.

The Precombination Phase

As the deal is conceived and negotiated by executives and then legally approved by shareholders and regulators in the Precombination Phase, much of the emphasis in the typical case is on financial matters. Buyers concentrate on the numbers: what the target is worth, what price premium to pay if any, what the tax implications may be, and how to structure the transaction. The decision to do a deal is thus framed in terms of the combined balance sheet of the companies, projected cash flows, and return on investment.

Two interrelated human factors add to this financial bias. First, in most instances members of the "buy team" come from financial positions or backgrounds. They bring a financial mindset to the study of a partner, and their judgments about synergies are informed by financial models and ratios. They often lack expertise in engineering, manufacturing, or marketing and do not bring an experienced eye to assessing a partner's capabilities in these regards. Second, there is a tendency for "hard" criteria to drive out "soft" matters in these cases: If the numbers look good, any doubts about, say, organizational or cultural fit tend to be scoffed at and dismissed.

In successful cases, by contrast, buyers bring a strategic mindset to the deal. But there is more to this than an overarching aim and intent. Successful buyers also have a clear definition of the specific synergies they seek in a combination and concentrate on testing them well before momentum builds. They also incorporate human factors in conducting a "diligent" due diligence.

The Combination Phase

As the two sides come together, politics typically predominate. Oftentimes, it is power politics: The buyer decides how to put the two organizations together. But even when a buyer seeks to combine on the basis of operational synergies, politics can intrude. Corporate staffers bring in their charts of accounts, reporting cycles, planning methods, and the like, and impose them on subsidiaries. It does not matter that these systems seldom enhance growth and often prove unworkable for the needs and business cycles of the acquired firm.

Meanwhile, individuals jockey for power and position, and management teams fend off overtures for control from the other side by hiding information or playing dumb. In the typical situation, transition teams are convened to recommend integration options, but personal empire building and conflictual group dynamics block efforts to seek out and capture true synergy. Meanwhile, culture clash rears up as people focus on differences between the partners and fixate on which side wins what battles rather than join together to build a united team going forward.

In successful combinations, there are still politicking and gambits for self-preservation, but much of the energy typically directed into gamesmanship is more positively channeled into combination planning. Leadership clarifies the critical success factors to guide decision making and oversees the integration process to ensure that sources of synergy are realized. Managers and employees come together to discuss and debate combination options; if the process is well managed, high-quality combination decisions result.

The Postcombination Phase

We have received calls 18 months after a combination from executives bemoaning that their best talent has bailed out, productivity has gone to hell in a handbag, and culture clash remains thick. Often this is because the executives grew impatient with planning and hurried implementation, to the extent that their two companies failed to integrate and serious declines resulted in everything from employee morale to customer satisfaction. Much can be done in this damage-control situation, but it is obviously better to preclude the need for damage control by following the successful path from the onset.

In successful combinations, managers and staff from both sides embrace the strategic logic and understand their roles and responsibilities in making the combination work. To facilitate this transition, we have seen combining companies engage thousands of their employees in integration planning and, later, implementation efforts that they have helped to shape. This phase sees successful companies intentionally go through the work of organization and team building in combined units and functions and forge a common culture. And, reflecting the complexity of joining previously independent organizations, we find that most successful combinations have major mid-course corrections and turn a potential disaster into a winning combination.

RECENT DEVELOPMENTS IN M&A PRACTICE

In recent years, the most striking changes in M&A practice have occurred during the *Precombination Phase*—the period when the deal is conceived and negotiated by executives and then legally approved by shareholders and regulators. The actions taken in this phase have a critical impact on employee sense-making and other responses to a deal's announcement (Monin, Noorderhaven, Vaara, and Kroon 2013). Given that employee identification with the combined organization is an important element in M&A success, research finds that companies are wise to pay closer attention to human factors prior to the legal closing of the deal (Giessner et al. 2012). Four key developments in the M&A process during the Precombination Phase are particularly relevant to OD practice: conducting behavioral and cultural due diligence, establishing a vision for the combined organization, initiating the integration planning process, and establishing integration principles and priorities.

Behavioral and Cultural Due Diligence

It is important that the lead company delve into its candidate to understand what is being purchased, how well it might fit with the lead company's current businesses, and what potential pitfalls may lie ahead. Without a close look at the capabilities and characteristics of a partner, it is easy to overestimate revenue gains and cost savings and to underestimate the resource requirements and headaches involved in integrating businesses (Marks and Mirvis 2010a).

To offset these tendencies, we recommend that companies broaden the perspective of the deal-making team. HR professionals, operations managers, marketers, and other nonfinancial personnel are better equipped than M&A staff to compare the two companies' business practices, organization structures, and corporate cultures and determine what these could mean for the combination. The inclusion of line management in the search-and-selection builds understanding of and buy-in to the acquisition strategy among the people who will be running the acquired business.

Where does OD fit in? Traditional OD practices—such as collecting valid data and helping clients to use the findings to develop insights and plan actions—certainly apply here. More specifically, OD specialists can help companies to preview human, organizational, and cultural issues likely to emerge in a combination. This provides potential buyers with a "reality check" on wishful thinking and gives them a head start on addressing issues that are likely to impact the integration process after the deal receives legal approval. OD and operational inputs can also influence the valuation and purchase price, the pace through which integration occurs, and the placement of personnel. Moreover, an OD-based assessment of an acquired leadership team (of their skills and desire to stay on after the sale) can help a buyer understand the extent to which people from the lead company need to be more or less hands-on in running a new acquisition (Marks, Mirvis, and Ashkenas 2013).

Diligent due diligence pays off: A study of large combinations found that successful acquirers were 40 percent more likely to conduct thorough human and cultural due diligence than unsuccessful buyers (Anslinger and Copeland 1996). Paying attention to human dynamics in the Precombination Phase has the added benefit of signaling to to-be-acquired employees that the lead company is sensitive to this subject, which, in turn, breeds confidence that the buyer will manage the integration process well.

Vision for the Combined Organization

Authoritative studies emphasize that the most successful companies operate with a strong and clear sense of purpose (Collins and Porras 2002). This sense of purpose comes from a guiding vision (what we hope to accomplish), a defining mission (what we do), and deep understanding of markets served, strategies, competencies, and such that add granularity and distinctiveness to the vision and mission. The value of a clear vision is quite relevant to the M&A situation—the sooner employees on both sides of the deal have a sense of the combined organization, the more likely they are to transfer their identity and commitment to it (Venus 2013).

Leaders need to be active agents of change by providing a clear vision with a purpose. But, when we stress the importance of a vision to hard-nosed executives, their first reaction is that it sounds "soft." For them, it is all about strategy. We do not disagree with the emphasis on strategy. But what a vision does is make a connection between strategy and larger goals: the purpose for combining and what can be accomplished together. We also get some push-back from executives that it is "too soon" to discuss a vision. ("What if the deal doesn't go through?" "What if market conditions change in the months it may take to gain approval for the deal?") We acknowledge these concerns, but also point out that the Precombination Phase is the right time to craft a compelling vision statement—a message used to strengthen employee commitment to the combined entity just as a business case is used to attract investors to it—before things get too busy in the Combination Phase when people have to run a business while managing a transition. This is also a good time for OD practitioners to develop a post-close process for conveying the vision and assessing the extent to which employees understand and buy into it.

Integration Planning Process

Since 2009, buyers have increasingly used the Precombination Phase to get a head start on integration planning. Since government regulation prevents the exchange of sensitive information before the deal receives legal approval, buyers have to be exceedingly careful not to jeopardize their pending combination or to engage in illegal activity. In the past few years, two models of early integration planning have been used to accelerate the process while staying within legal constraints. One approach uses independent third parties— a "clean team" of experts from consulting firms—that have legal clearance to view data from both sides in advance of the merger's close. The team collects information from each organization to prepare baseline data on business and functional cost structures in the two companies to be used by in-house transition teams later in the Combination Phase. They also prepare pro-forma pictures of synergies that might emerge in various integration and consolidation scenarios. The second approach is to have "separate but equal" integration planning teams in each organization coordinated by external consultants in a process akin to "shuttle diplomacy."

We have observed both models of early integration planning being greatly enhanced by the involvement of OD practitioners. In the "clean team" approach, OD practitioners can liaison between external consultants and internal managers. In the "separate but equal" approach, OD practitioners can directly facilitate the work of the internal teams and coordinate the two sets of data. They can also clarify inconsistencies between the partners (in everything from language to styles) that inevitably arise as previously separate entities begin the integration process.

As the third party steps away, executives and staffs from the two partners must learn to "play well" together. However, people from both sides may be more concerned with looking back at what they are losing rather than looking ahead to what they may be gaining in the combination. So, OD practitioners play the added role of coaching leaders and managers on cross-company interactions as well as facilitating early meetings in the transition from the Precombination Phase to Combination Phase. Studies find that these early cross-company meetings are important in "setting a tone" for the combination and send signals to both organizations about how to (and how not to) work together (Chreim and Tafaghod 2012; Jacobs, Oliver, and Heracleaous 2013).

Integration Principles and Priorities

We find that successful integration planning teams (i.e., those that succeed in identifying and bringing to life the true strategic and financial synergies in a deal) benefit from a senior leader who shapes the process with principles and begins impressing upon people the priorities for the transition period (Marks and Mirvis 2010a). Efforts to clarify principles and priorities early on clear a path for the complex and high stakes work of combination planning. They do so by making explicit to all involved "what matters" as they make the journey toward attaining the vision. However, this comes more naturally to some executives than others. So, OD practitioners can add tremendous value in the Precombination Phase by impressing upon CEO or business unit leader clients the need for integration principles and priorities, assisting in articulating and communicating them through the ranks, and assessing the extent to which they are being followed in the planning process.

SUMMARY

Given the seemingly contradictory realities that M&As are frequently occurring events yet only a minority achieve their desired strategic or financial objectives, there is a tremendous potential for OD practitioners to add value to the M&A process. Much more than simply move people and organizations through the process, OD interventions early on in the Precombination Phase can set the stage to help leaders use M&A to transform workplaces, achieve globalization, and respect and sustain human capital.

Discussion Questions

1. How can OD practices and professionals be used in a transformational merger or acquisition?
2. How can OD practitioners gain access to organizations planning or engaged in M&A?
3. In what ways can OD enhance the M&A success rate?
4. What are the latest developments in using OD to make mergers and acquisitions work?

Resource

YouTube Video on "Success Factors in Making Mergers and Acquisitions Work": www
.youtube.com/watch?v = riYzM7IH8F8

References

Anslinger, P. L., and T. E. Copeland. 1996. "Growth through Acquisitions: A Fresh Look." *Harvard Business Review* 74 (1): 126–135.

Chreim, S., and M. Tafaghod. 2012. "Contradiction and Sensemaking in Acquisition Integration." *The Journal of Applied Behavioral Science* 48 (1): 5–32.

Collins, J. C., and J. I. Porras. 2002. *Built to Last: Successful Habits of Visionary Companies*. New York: Harper.

Das, A., and S. Kapil. 2012. "Explaining M&A Performance: A Review of Empirical Research." *Journal of Strategy and Management* 5 (3): 284–330.

Faulkner, D., S. Teerikangas, and R. Joseph. 2012. "Introduction." In *Handbook of Mergers & Acquisitions*, edited by D. Faulkner, S. Teerikangas, and R. Joseph, 1–14. Oxford, UK: Oxford University Press.

Giessner, S. R., J. Ullrich, and R. van Dick. 2012. "A Social Identity Analysis of Mergers & Acquisitions." In *Handbook of Mergers & Acquisitions*, edited by D. Faulkner, S. Teerikangas, and R. Joseph, 474–494. Oxford, UK: Oxford University Press.

Gomes, E., D. N. Angwin, Y. Weber, and S. Y. Tarba. 2013. "Critical Success Factors through the Mergers and Acquisitions Process: Revealing Pre- and Post-M&A Connections for Improved Performance." *Thunderbird International Business Review* 55 (1): 13–55.

Jacobs, C. D., D. Oliver, and L. Heracleaous. 2013. "Diagnosing Organizational Identity Beliefs by Eliciting Complex Multimodal Metaphors." *The Journal of Applied Behavioral Science* 49 (4): 485–507.

Marks, M. L., and P. H. Mirvis. 2010a. *Joining Forces: Making One Plus One Equal Three in Mergers, Acquisitions and Alliances*. San Francisco: Jossey-Bass.

Marks, M. L., and P. H. Mirvis. 2010b. The OD Role in Making Mergers & Acquisitions Work. In *Practicing Organization Development: A Guide for Managing and Leading Change*, 3rd ed., edited by W. Rothwell, J. Stavros, and R. Sullivan, 457–464. San Francisco: John Wiley & Sons.

Marks, M. L., and P. H. Mirvis. 2014. *The Employee Handbook for Navigating Mergers and Acquisitions: A Guide for Preparation, Patience, and Perseverance*. Dallas, TX: M&A Leadership Council.

Marks, M. L., P. H. Mirvis, and R. A. Ashkenas. 2013. "Making the Most of Culture Clash in M&A." *Leader to Leader* (Winter): 45–53.

Mattioli, D. 2014. "Competition, Stock Surge Fuel Boom in Mergers." *Wall Street Journal*, July 19, 1.

Monin, P., N. Noorderhaven, E. Vaara, and D. Kroon. 2013. "Giving Sense to and Making Sense of Justice in Post-Merger Integration." *Academy of Management Journal* 56 (1): 256–284.

Venus, M. 2013. *Demystifying Visionary Leadership: In Search of the Essences of Effective Vision Communication.* ERIM PhD Series Research in Management. Rotterdam: Eramus Research Institute of Management.

CHAPTER TWENTY-TWO

Exploring the Relationship between Organization Development and Change Management

Tim Creasey, David W. Jamieson, William J. Rothwell, and Gail Severini

In the past decade, change management has emerged and grown significantly. We all recognize the acceleration of continuous change, increased need for change implementation help, and generally poor results across many change approaches. However, why change management? This chapter explores the dynamics between the two fields of organization development (OD) and change management (CM).

As often happens with many emergent groups, they tend to create new identities, highlight their differentiation, create separate associations, and find fault with closely related fields. CM advocates often describe OD as:

- Too high-level, conceptual, soft, and touchy feely
- Not pragmatic enough
- Does not pay enough attention to on-the-ground implementation
- Too disconnected from delivering real traction/ROI

While OD advocates often describe CM as:

- Just a rebranding of what we have been doing and on the more critical side
- Too mechanical and too focused on tools
- Too structured and "one size fits all"
- Too focused on the project and not enough on the people and the system

We came together to explore the differences and similarities in the two fields. We began by acknowledging that our unique perspectives, as shaped by our deep individual experiences and scholarship, probably led us into biases. This realization liberated us to speak more freely and candidly—to really probe the potential overlap and differences.

We have consequentially approached our chapter on the premise that aligning on common goals and recognizing the different levels of delivery and foci of interventions is the key to optimizing them in concert. Further, we recognized that, given that the changing nature of change is only accelerating and becoming more complex, the onus is on us to raise our game. This leads us to the need for multidisciplinary perspectives inclusive of CM and OD.

Our intents in the chapter are: to bring clarity to the fields, their overlaps and differentiated contributions, and to conclude with some suggestions on how to optimize the benefits of CM and OD.

WHAT IS ORGANIZATION DEVELOPMENT?

OD is best known as a process of planned intervention(s) utilizing behavioral and organizational science principles to change a system and improve its effectiveness, conducted in accordance with values of humanism, participation, choice, and development so the organization and its members learn and develop (Jamieson 2014). The focus of OD work is:

- Series of planned and emergent actions that intervene in organization structures, systems, processes, and relationships
- Using theory, principles, and practices from the behavioral (psychology, sociology, anthropology, and economics) and organization (organization theory, organization design, systems theory, management theory) sciences
- Understanding an organization system and its present behaviors and taking actions to improve its effectiveness in achieving its mission, strategy, or desired outcomes (process and content, mission and results, social and technical), and its workplace health
- Conducting in accord with certain values, guiding both processes and outcomes, that are represented by: humanism (authenticity, openness, honesty, fairness, justice, equality, diversity, respect); participation (involvement, participation, voice, responsibility, opportunity, collaboration, democratic principles and practices); choice (options, rights, accountability); development (personal growth, reaching potential, learning, self-actualization)
- Having the organization and its members learn and grow in capacity, capability, and achievement of potential

OD is concerned with whole organization systems at different levels and scale. Because systems are regularly nested in larger systems, it is important to begin with the organization's context (environment, societal, sector, and cultural influences) and clear desired outcomes (what is effectiveness and health for this system). Next, one must know the relevant stakeholders that make up and influence this system (Who cares? Who counts? How influential are they?). Finally, an understanding of the presenting situation (changes, events, trends, successes, failures, markets, products/services, etc.) is needed. One is then prepared to plan change and draw on relevant theory and methods to apply. Each situation has differences, so little is prepackaged but the process is developed along the way from current data, experiences, and drivers. As one author often stated, "If you know step two, you're probably not doing OD."

WHAT IS CHANGE MANAGEMENT?

A regional utilities firm is undergoing a strategic transformation to become more customer-focused. A global manufacturer is implementing the next iteration of its enterprise resource planning (ERP) application to improve end-to-end data flows. A local health care system is installing electronic medical records to become compliant and improve access to information. A food and beverage firm is introducing an open office concept. A management consulting firm is moving from desktop applications to web-based applications.

While each of these efforts is varied in motivation, impact, scope, and strategic importance, there is a single common denominator for achieving the desired results and outcomes of these initiatives. Each impacts how individual employees do their jobs (for example, their processes, workflows, systems, tools, critical behaviors, and mindsets, to name a few). CM is the emergent discipline focused on individuals affected by change and catalyzing their adoption and proficient usage of the changes affecting how they do their jobs. When successful, CM contributes to achieving the initiative's targeted results.

CM is a relatively young discipline drawing on diverse bodies of knowledge including psychology, behavioral science, social science, OD, project management, process management, and neuroscience. During the 1990s, "change management" entered the lexicon of organizations with major works from contributors like Daryl Conner (1992), Todd Jick (1993), Jeanenne LaMarsh (1995), John Kotter (1996), and Spencer Johnson (1998). Each highlighted the importance of the people side of change on initiative results. Since 2000, the discipline of CM has been marked by continued formalization of processes, tools, job roles, organizational functions, and even industry associations. In leading organizations, CM has gained a regular "seat at the table" and is recognized as a key contributor to successful change.

We use Prosci's definition of CM to start the conversation: "The application of processes and tools to manage the people side of change from a current state to a new future state so that the desired results of the change are achieved" (Hiatt and Creasey 2012, 9).

The definition contains three essential components, which we will address in reverse order:

- "To achieve a desired result"—CM's goal is to drive and capture the portion of benefits that depend on employee adoption and usage. Organizations are experiencing tremendous amounts and types of change, including developmental, transitional, and transformational (to draw on Ackerman-Anderson and Anderson 2011). Many are technology changes, process changes, and strategic changes. Each has a desired outcome, and CM's purpose is to enable the realization of those expected benefits.

- "The people side of change"—At the macro level, change involves numerous moving parts and systems. At the most foundational and fundamental level, organizational change impacts and depends upon employees changing the way they work. The scope of CM is supporting those individual transitions and, as defined below, the steps needed to catalyze individual adoption and usage. CM considers the organizational systems and cultures, and the initiative level actions necessary, but these are addressed in their impact on individual change journeys.

- "The application of processes and tools"—While change ultimately depends on and requires individual transitions, successful change does not happen by chance. With an understanding of how individuals experience their own change process, the targeted use of organizational and project levers can support and catalyze those necessary individual changes.

CM is most often applied to a defined project or initiative. The scope of CM does not extend into identifying opportunities or issues to address or into designing the actual solution for the change initiative (although it can provide valuable input and direction). CM's focus is on applying a structured approach to enable individual employees to successfully adopt and proficiently use the new processes, systems, or behaviors required by the change initiative, so the organization's change achieves its intended results.

THE RELATIONSHIP OF ORGANIZATION DEVELOPMENT AND CHANGE MANAGEMENT

The relationship between OD and CM is interesting and complex. This chapter began by clarifying the purpose and intent of the two separately and distinctly. This section introduces three dimensions of difference and three significant

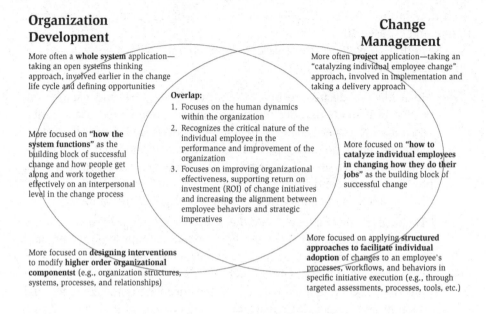

Organization Development

More often a **whole system** application—taking an open systems thinking approach, involved earlier in the change life cycle and defining opportunities

More focused on **"how the system functions"** as the building block of successful change and how people get along and work together effectively on an interpersonal level in the change process

More focused on **designing interventions** to modify **higher order organizational componentst** (e.g., organization structures, systems, processes, and relationships)

Change Management

More often **project** application—taking an "catalyzing individual employee change" approach, involved in implementation and taking a delivery approach

More focused on **"how to catalyze individual employees in changing how they do their jobs"** as the building block of successful change

More focused on applying **structured approaches to facilitate individual adoption** of changes to an employee's processes, workflows, and behaviors in specific initiative execution (e.g., through targeted assessments, processes, tools, etc.)

Overlap:
1. Focuses on the human dynamics within the organization
2. Recognizes the critical nature of the individual employee in the performance and improvement of the organization
3. Focuses on improving organizational effectiveness, supporting return on investment (ROI) of change initiatives and increasing the alignment between employee behaviors and strategic imperatives

Figure 22.1. OD and CM: Overlap and Dimensions of Difference

overlaps that provide the foundation for convergence and collaboration in the disciplines. While examining the divergence of the two provides insights into their unique contributions and applications, the success of organizational change—and the disciplines—can be improved if the shared values and overlaps are leveraged. The Venn diagram in Figure 22.1 presents the three dimensions of difference and the overlap of OD and CM.

Three primary dimensions of difference are identified: scope of application, focus of effort, and level of engagement.

Scope of Application

At a high level, the scope of application provides insight into which situations within an organization might lean more heavily on OD and which might lean more heavily on CM. For OD, application is often a whole system application while remaining sensitive to interpersonal relationships and group dynamics. For CM, application is more often a specific project or initiative with specified results and outcomes that require changes in individual behaviors.

Focus of Effort

The focus of effort dimension reflects the fundamental building blocks the discipline hopes to impact in application. For OD, the focus of the effort is "how the system functions" while the focus of effort in CM is "how to catalyze individual employees in changing how they do their jobs." These are not mutually exclusive—how the system functions impacts how employees react in times of change, and how employees adopt the new way of doing their jobs impacts the system.

Level of Engagement

The level of engagement dimension identifies the targeted approach taken by practitioners in the discipline. For OD, the focus is on designing interventions to modify higher-order organizational components, those that inform the functioning of the system. CM focuses on structured and repeatable approaches to facilitate individual adoption and usage, leveraging assessments, processes, and tools that can aid an employee in making a successful personal transition required by an organizational change.

Overlap

While the scope of application, focus of effort, and level of engagement are different, the disciplines of OD and CM have shared values that provide groundwork for convergence and collaboration. The three overlaps identified next can and should be leveraged by thought leaders and practitioners.

First, each focuses on the human dynamics within the organization—even though the starting points are different (system versus individual), both OD and CM acknowledge, appreciate, and focus on the human dynamics within an organization and the important contribution, especially in times of change, of those human dynamics.

Second, each recognizes the critical nature of the individual employee in the performance and improvement of the organization—in OD, this emerges through the focus on self, while in CM this manifests in the unique contribution of individual adoption and usage to initiative results and outcomes. In both cases, the employees that make up an organization are viewed as crucial to any successful change.

Third, each focuses on improving organizational effectiveness, supporting return on investment (ROI) of change initiatives, and increasing the alignment between employee behaviors and strategic imperatives. This final overlap is essential to build credibility and buy-in for both disciplines with executives and leaders. The value of both OD and CM is driving more successful change and enabling organizations to achieve their intended results.

EXAMPLE: A MERGER

A merger of two organizations presents an entry point to explore the unique opportunities for both OD and CM to contribute to successful change. A merger creates numerous changes within an organization, including: strategy, leadership, organization design, culture, human resources, information technology and financial systems, reporting relationships, roles, and operations. OD's perspective on supporting a successful merger would focus on the larger, systematic changes including outlining impacts on all aspects of organization systems such as strategy, mission, charters, structure, culture, systems, processes, and people's behaviors. OD would address team dissolutions, formations, integrations, and development. When the implications of the organizational changes reach the granular level of impact on specific jobs and behaviors, CM provides guidance and direction to catalyze those individual transitions. For example, employees using a newly integrated ERP application must adopt and use new systems and workflows. Operational changes would require new job roles, mindsets, and behaviors that would be supported by CM execution. For the merger to succeed, both OD and CM are required, and both uniquely contribute to organizational performance.

SUMMARY

The wall between OD and CM may not be as high as purported by some or even still being constructed by others. In today's world of ever-increasing change, there is a marked need for approaches and disciplines to improve change effectiveness. Both OD and CM provide necessary and crucial support to successful change.

This chapter presented the disciplines side-by-side, attempting to add clarity by delineating them and then drive convergence by showing the differences and overlaps. Through the examination, there emerged a common set of shared values and perspectives that should serve to unify the disciplines rather than promote divergence, namely the critically important contribution of individual employees to the overall health and success of organizations in times of change.

The key takeaway should be that both OD and CM support successful change, and the question is not "OD or CM?" but rather "When OD and/or CM?" With a better understanding and foundation of each discipline, practitioners can better identify when each provides the greatest value and addresses the issues they are facing at a given point in time. As Gail commented during one conversation, "I cannot do my work without both. I can no longer think about them as one or the other."

Change is not slowing down, and the importance of individuals within the systems of the organization will only increase with new values and relationships emerging. The question for you, and for those hoping to advance the disciplines in academia and elsewhere, is not "which" but, "when and for what purpose?" To conclude the chapter, we will leave you with some questions to ponder as you evaluate your role and approach in bringing more successful change outcomes to your organization.

Discussion Questions

1. What do you see as the similarities and differences between OD and CM?
2. What strengths do you see each discipline bringing to the conversation?
3. How can each be leveraged to advance change success?
4. When and where do OD and CM add unique value?

Resources

Association of Change Management Professionals (ACMP) Global: www.acmpglobal.org

Change Management Institute (CMI): www.change-management-institute.com

Change Management Learning Center tutorial index: www.change-management.com/tutorials.htm

Organization Development Network (ODN): www.odnetwork.org

Institute of Organization Development (IOD): www.instituteod.com

References

Ackerman-Anderson, L., and D. Anderson, 2011. *The Change Leader's Roadmap*. San Francisco: Pfeiffer, an Imprint of John Wiley & Sons.

Conner, D. 1992. *Managing at the Speed of Change*. New York: Random House.

Hiatt, J., and J. Creasey. 2012. *Change Management: The People Side of Change*. Loveland, CO: Prosci Learning Center.

Jamieson, D. 2014. "Panorama of OD (Introductory Course for Doctoral Program)." Unpublished presentation. Minneapolis: University of St. Thomas.

Jick, T. 1993. *Managing Change: Cases and Concepts*. Boston: Irwin McGraw-Hill.

Johnson, S. 1998. *Who Moved My Cheese?* New York: G.P. Putnam's Sons.

Kotter, J. 1996. *Leading Change*. Boston: Harvard Business School Press.

LaMarsh, J. 1995. *Changing the Way We Change*. Reading, MA: Addison-Wesley.

CHAPTER TWENTY-THREE

Positive Organizational Change

What the Field of Positive Organizational Scholarship Offers
to Organization Development Practitioners

Kim Cameron and Jon McNaughtan

On September 11, 2001, two hijacked planes were used by terrorists to attack the World Trade Center towers, a third plane was flown into the Pentagon, and a fourth plane crashed on a field in Shanksville, Pennsylvania. In total, 2,996 people were killed and over 6,000 were injured. The effects of that tragic day were far reaching, of course, but no industry was hit harder than the U.S. airline industry. Not only did national governments worldwide prohibit airline flights for the next several days, but passengers were fearful that this industry, in particular, was the primary target of terrorists. Fear was rampant, and passengers were reticent to return to the air.

In particular, the short-haul carriers—the two companies most heavily dependent on short flights—were abnormally affected. Passengers chose trains, buses, or automobile travel instead of airline flights for relatively short distance travel. US Airways and Southwest Airlines were the two firms hurt the worst financially, although virtually every airline lost millions of dollars daily (Sharkey 2004). Reductions in flights averaged 20 percent, and the average number of layoffs was 16 percent across the industry.

Not all airlines handled this crisis the same way and an analysis of the 10 airline companies' response to the tragedy uncovered an important finding. A strong correlation exists between the way an airline company handled the adversity and the company's financial recovery (see Gittell, Cameron, Lim, and Rivas 2006).

Specifically, airlines that engaged in positive practices experienced significantly higher financial return than those that did not. Positive practices included prioritizing human capital over financial capital, providing protection for employees' jobs, and ensuring compassionate support for employees' families. As paradoxical as it may seem, the airlines that did not engage in typical cost-saving measures, such as layoffs, during the crisis experienced the fastest recovery to their stock price and more productivity during the years after the crisis.

Southwest Airlines was the quintessential example of using a crisis to turn challenges into opportunities, strengthen relationships with employees, and reinforce a culture of compassion that resulted in positive outcomes. Southwest CEO Jim Parker stated, "We are willing to suffer some damage, even to our stock price, to protect the jobs of our people" (Conlin 2001, 42). This unique approach to crisis and adversity provides one example of how positive organizational scholarship (POS) offers a positive lens for the practice of OD.

This chapter describes the emerging field of POS and its connection to organization development (OD). The case of the airline industry following September 11, 2001, provides an illustration of positively deviant organizational performance, a key focus of POS research. A framework for POS is described as a way to differentiate between "abundance" versus "deficit" approaches to OD. The chapter concludes with an overview of POS findings.

POSITIVE ORGANIZATIONAL SCHOLARSHIP

Analyzing positive practices in the U.S. airline industry after September 11 provides an example of the research interests of scholars in the field of POS. This approach to scholarship originated in 2001 at the University of Michigan as an alternative to the dominant scholarly paradigm at the time (Cameron and McNaughtan 2014). POS is distinct from traditional organizational studies in that it seeks to understand what represents and approaches the best of the human condition. The concept of *positive* refers to (1) positive deviance (such as explaining extraordinary positive outcomes and the processes that produce them), (2) an affirmative orientation (such as focusing on strengths rather than weaknesses or on flourishing relationships rather than problematic relationships), and (3) virtuousness and elevating processes (such as doing good in addition to doing well). *Organization* is this context in which these positive phenomena occur; the dynamics of the workplace are centrally important. And *scholarship* describes the intention of grounding all findings and prescriptions in rigorous, theoretical and empirically based research in order to understand what makes these kinds of positive dynamics and organizational breakthroughs possible (Cameron, Dutton, and Quinn 2003).

Although not without critics (Fineman 2006; George 2004), POS scholars have helped develop an understanding of organizations that nurtures flourishing (Fredrickson and Losada 2005), thriving (Spreitzer et al. 2005), optimal functioning (Keyes 2002), capacity-building (Dutton and Glynn 2007), and general excellence in the human condition (Cameron 2003). POS scholars focus on understanding enablers and motivators, as well as "the outcomes or effects associated with positive phenomenon" (Cameron, Dutton, & Quinn 2003, 3).

A POSITIVE ORGANIZATIONAL SCHOLARSHIP FRAMEWORK

The need for scholarship that focuses on the positive can be illustrated by using Figure 23.1. This figure illustrates how the dynamics associated with helping people and organizations flourish are likely to be different than the dynamics of helping a person or organization reach effective functioning.

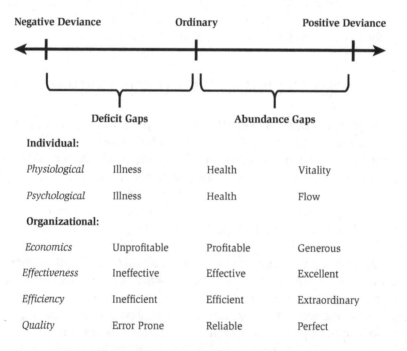

	Negative Deviance	Ordinary	Positive Deviance
	Deficit Gaps	Abundance Gaps	
Individual:			
Physiological	Illness	Health	Vitality
Psychological	Illness	Health	Flow
Organizational:			
Economics	Unprofitable	Profitable	Generous
Effectiveness	Ineffective	Effective	Excellent
Efficiency	Inefficient	Efficient	Extraordinary
Quality	Error Prone	Reliable	Perfect

Figure 23.1. The Positive Deviance Continuum

Source: Adapted from Kim. S. Cameron, "Organizational Virtuousness and Performance," in *Positive Organizational Scholarship: Foundations of a New Discipline*, edited by K. S. Cameron, J. E. Dutton, and R. E. Quinn (San Francisco: Berrett-Koehler, 2003), 53.

Loosely speaking, we can think of people and organizations in terms of three states: negative deviance, normal performance, and positive deviance. At the extreme left end of the continuum is negative deviance, or the dysfunctional state. In this state, people experience illness, and organizations are unprofitable, ineffective, and inefficient. Quality is problematic and errors in production are customary. Unethical behaviors may be evident. Interpersonal relationships between people are often toxic. Metaphorically, this condition might be characterized by individuals or organizations in need of a hospital.

At the right end of the continuum is positive deviance or an extraordinarily high-performing condition. Individuals in this condition might be characterized by vitality, flow, and flourishing in their work (Csikszentmihalyi 1990). Organizations might be characterized by thriving and contributing extraordinary value. They achieve not merely effectiveness but excellence. Virtuousness characterizes organizational practices. Quality is error-free, people honor one another, and flourishing occurs by "achieving the best of the human condition" (Cameron 2012, 11). Metaphorically, this condition might be characterized by individuals or organizations functioning like an Olympic athlete or OD practitioners who transform visions of possibilities.

The experience of these airline companies exemplifies both extremes. Following the crisis, these companies were clearly in a negatively deviant, highly dysfunctional condition. By 2005, the airlines that utilized positive practices had become positively deviant, extraordinarily performing organizations. In fact, the correlation between financial return and the implementation of positive practices was p = .86 (Cameron 2013).

A POSITIVE ORGANIZATIONAL SCHOLARSHIP LENS IN THE PRACTICE OF ORGANIZATION DEVELOPMENT

The POS approach to change provides a framework for identifying the two fundamental motivations for change. Specifically, the question might be asked: "Is the change intended to fix a dysfunctional aspect of the organization (closing deficit gaps), or is the change intended to extend or elevate the strengths in the organization (closing abundance gaps)?"

With respect to the first motive, the resolution of deficit gaps, OD practitioners are typically brought into an organization when dysfunction exists (Burke 2002). The OD professional functions much like a physician in diagnosing the issues, prescribing solutions, and working to heal the organization from its ills. The organization's starting point for change is a state of negative deviance. The intention of a change intervention is to solve problems. OD practitioners address deficit gaps while reinforcing expected norms and routines.

Many change experts, for instance, advocate the need to create urgency for change (Kotter 2008) or the importance of diagnosing issues (Cummings and Worley 2009), tacitly acknowledging the normative power of identifying a common concern and the motivating potential that may come in the process of overcoming such challenges (Cameron 2008).

The second motive for change is a transformation beyond a normal, expected state to an extraordinary, positively deviant state. This means changing from normal performance to extraordinary performance—unleashing the latent positive energy in a system so that thriving and flourishing can occur (Spreitzer et al. 2005). As illustrated in Figure 23.1, tremendous resistance exists in organizations anytime they move away from the center of the continuum—in both negative and positive directions. A great deal of momentum exists to remain at the center of the continuum. Just as an Olympic athlete immediately experiences decline toward the normal state if he or she ceases training at the highest level, extraordinary organizations also quickly slip into a pattern of ordinariness that is consistent with expected, average performance. Extraordinary performance is always dynamic and difficult to sustain.

THE APPLICATION OF POSITIVE ORGANIZATIONAL SCHOLARSHIP IN ORGANIZATION DEVELOPMENT

Positive organizational change has emerged in the last decade as an attempt to rebalance organizational change research and to examine previously ignored relationships in the discipline of POS. Because the importance and credibility of any new approach depends, at least partly, on verified relationships with successful performance and change, a sampling of what has been uncovered to date about successful positive organizational change is provided. Of course, no summary can capture the breadth and core themes of all the work being done, but an examination of the empirical literature has uncovered a set of themes that describe several of the main thrusts.

One irony in many of these findings is that, by definition, positive practices do not need to produce traditionally pursued organizational outcomes in order to be of worth. Nevertheless, studies have shown that organizations in several industries (including financial services, health care, manufacturing, education, pharmaceuticals, and government) that implemented and improved their positive practices over time also increased their performance in desired outcomes such as profitability, productivity, quality, customer satisfaction, and employee retention (Cameron and Lavine 2006).

Organizational Virtuousness. A number of studies have examined virtuousness as a source of positive organizational change. For example, one study conducted on 14 Portuguese businesses found that organizational virtuous-ness led to higher organizational citizenship and employee well-being (Rego, Ribeiro, and Cunha 2010). O'Donohoe and Turley's (2006) interview study of newspaper staff dealing with bereaved clients found the staff engaged in "phi-lanthropic emotion management"—in which they made personal sacrifices for the sake of grieving clients—even though these sacrifices were neither required nor rewarded by the organization.

Several studies also link virtuousness to performance. One study within a health care network showed how units that were supportive of their members' spirituality produced higher levels of customer satisfaction (Duchon and Plow-man 2005). Stephens and colleagues (2013) found that virtuous relationships with coworkers who were willing to share both positive and negative feelings correlated with resilience to adversity.

Leadership. Several investigations of the role of leadership and positive change have been conducted. Bono and Ilies (2006) described a series of studies showing that leaders who express more positive emotions engender the same emotions in followers, who then perceive that leader as more charismatic and effective. Similarly, Army leaders who expressed more vision and love for their troops satisfied their followers' needs for the same, fostering greater well-being, commitment, and productivity among followers (Fry, Vitucci, and Cedillo 2005).

In the fast-food industry, leader hope has been linked to follower satisfaction and retention (Peterson and Luthans 2003). Similarly, Cameron (2011) argued that responsible leadership and virtuous leadership are synonymous and both lead to amplification of employees' performance and strong positive outcomes.

Positive Relationships and Performance. Interpersonal relationships serve as another important source of performance benefits investigated in the posi-tive change literature. For example, the work of Dutton (2003) on high-quality connections is compelling. High-quality connections are temporary encounters with another individual, in contrast to an ongoing relationship. These con-nections can be life-giving and enhancing or deenergizing and diminishing. Dutton's extensive research indicates that forming high-quality connections produces higher amounts of learning, resilience, cooperation, job satisfaction, involvement, commitment, and physical health in individuals. And, it produces increased cooperation, attachment of employees, suppliers, and customers, as well as more adaptability in organizations (Dutton and Ragins 2007).

Energy. Owens, Baker, and Cameron (2014) investigated the positive energy displayed by unit leaders in a variety of business units. Several forms of energy exist, such as physical energy, emotional energy, and psychological energy. With each of these forms of energy, their use diminishes energy and requires rest and recuperation for renewal. People become exhausted after expending physical energy (e.g., running a marathon), emotional energy (e.g., cheering for the home team in a finals game), or psychological energy (e.g., studying for an exam).

This study assessed relational energy, defined as the uplifting, motivational, and life-giving influence leaders have on employees as a result of interactions. Only with relational energy does expending lead to renewal (e.g., people do not tire of being cared for and loved). The results showed that positively energizing leaders have a significant, positive impact on individuals—including their performance, engagement, well-being, satisfaction, and even family life—as well as on the organization's performance, teamwork, innovation, and learning orientation.

In studies of energy networks—that is, the position of individuals in a network in which giving and receiving relational energy was assessed—an individual's position in that network was found to be significant. Those who energized others performed substantially higher than even those who were assessed as powerful or central in the information network. Energy trumped power and information in predicting improvements in performance (Baker, Cross, and Parker 2004; Baker, Cross, and Wooten 2003). Moreover, individuals who provided positive energy to others were four times more likely to succeed than individuals who were at the center of information or influence networks.

SUMMARY

This chapter introduces the concept of positive organizational change which has emerged from the field of POS. The research suggests that what is currently known about dysfunctional organization (deficit gaps) is vastly greater than what is known about extraordinary organization functionality (abundance gaps). POS attempts to address this imbalance, not to the exclusion of problem-based scholarship and practice, but as a complementary extension. Implications for expanding the practice of OD through POS are numerous, and we have focused in this chapter on briefly reviewing research that can lead to positive change interventions. Both positive and negative factors may perpetuate positive change, but when both are present, the negative tends to dominate. Therefore positive factors must be emphasized in order for positive change to be stimulated.

This helps explain why a historical bias exists in OD toward deficit-oriented more than abundance-oriented change (Cameron 2012). Baumeister and colleagues (2001) even went as far as to state that "Bad is stronger than good" in capturing our attention and motivating a response. Positive climate, positive energy, and high-quality relationships, however, unleash the heliotropic effect in individuals and organizations, and this, in turn, produces extraordinary performance. Learning to detect and emphasize what is positive, in addition to what is negative, is an important prescription for OD in the future.

Discussion Questions

1. In what ways can the positive deviance continuum be a helpful framework to your own work?

2. How can you ensure virtuous performance in your own work and within your organization?

3. How can you become a positive energizer to those around you?

4. Have you seen heliotropism in your own work? If so, how can you take advantage of it?

5. How can positive organizational scholarship provide a new approach for leading organizational change?

Resources

The Center for Positive Organizations (this center is run out of the University of Michigan and has current research and information for those who wish to research POS or enhance their practice): http://positiveorgs.bus.umich.edu/

TED[X] Beacon Street talk on Leading Positive Change is a talk by Rosabeth Moss Kanter who discusses six steps to leading positive change: www.tedxbeaconstreet.com/rosabeth-moss-kanter/

References

Baker, W., R. Cross, and A. Parker. 2004. "What Creates Energy in Organizations?" *Sloan Management Review* 44: 51–56.

Baker, W., R. Cross, and L. Wooten. 2003. "Positive Organizational Network Analysis and Energizing Relationships." In *Positive Organizational Scholarship: Foundations of a New Discipline*, edited by K. S. Cameron, J. E. Dutton, and R. E. Quinn, 328–342. San Francisco: Berrett-Koehler.

Baumeister, R. F., E. Bratslavsky, C. Finkenauer, and K. D. Vohs. 2001. "Bad Is Stronger Than Good." *Review of General Psychology* 5: 323–370.

Bono, J. E., and R. Ilies. 2006. "Charisma, Positive Emotion and Mood Contagion." *Leadership Quarterly* 17: 317–334.

Burke, W. W. 2002. *Organization Change: Theory and Practice*. Thousand Oaks, CA: Sage.

Cameron, K. S. 2003. "Organizational Virtuousness and Performance." In *Positive Organizational Scholarship: Foundations of a New Discipline*, edited by K. S. Cameron, J. E. Dutton, and R. E. Quinn, 48–65. San Francisco: Berrett-Koehler.

Cameron, K. S. 2008. "A Process for Changing Organizational Culture." In *Handbook of Organization Development*, edited by T. G. Cummings, 429–445. Thousand Oaks, CA: Sage.

Cameron, K. S. 2011. "Responsible Leadership as Virtuous Leadership." *Journal of Business Ethics* 98 (1): 25–35.

Cameron, K. S. 2012. *Positive Leadership: Strategies for Extraordinary Performance*. San Francisco: Berrett-Koehler.

Cameron, K. S. 2013. *Practicing Positive Leadership: Tools and Techniques That Create Extraordinary Results*. San Francisco: Berrett-Koehler.

Cameron, K. S., J. E. Dutton, and R. E. Quinn. 2003. "Foundations of Positive Organizational Scholarship." In *Positive Organizational Scholarship: Foundations of a New Discipline*, edited by K. S. Cameron, J. E. Dutton, and R. E. Quinn, 3–13. San Francisco: Berrett-Koehler.

Cameron, K.S., and M. Lavine. 2006. *Making the Impossible Possible: Leading Extraordinary Performance—The Rocky Flats Story*. San Francisco: Berrett-Koehler.

Cameron, K. S., and J. McNaughtan. 2014. "Positive Organizational Change." *The Journal of Applied Behavioral Science* 50 (4): 445–462.

Conlin, M. 2001. "Where Layoffs Are a Last Resort." *BusinessWeek*, October 8, 42.

Csikszentmihalyi, M. 1990. *Flow: The Psychology of Optimal Experience*. 1st ed. New York: Harper & Row.

Cummings, T. G., and C. G. Worley. 2009. *Organization Development and Change*. Mason, OH: South-Western Cengage Learning.

Duchon, D., and D. A. Plowman. 2005. "Nurturing the Spirit at Work: Impact on Work Unit Performance." *Leadership Quarterly* 16: 807–833.

Dutton, J. E. 2003. *Energizing Your Workplace: Building and Sustaining High Quality Relationships at Work*. San Francisco: Jossey-Bass.

Dutton, J. E., and M.A. Glynn. 2007. "Positive Organizational Scholarship." In *Handbook of Organizational Behavior*, edited by C. Cooper and J. Barling, 693–711. Thousand Oaks, CA: Sage.

Dutton, J. E., and B. R. Ragins. 2007. *Exploring Positive Relationships at Work: Building a Theoretical and Research Foundation*. Mahwah, NJ: Lawrence Erlbaum.

Fineman, S. 2006. "On Being Positive: Concerns and Counterpoints." *Academy of Management Review* 31 (2): 270–291.

Fredrickson, B. L., and M. Losada. 2005. "Positive Affect and the Complex Dynamics of Human Flourishing." *American Psychologist* 60 (7): 678–686.

Fry, L. W., S. Vitucci, and M. Cedillo. 2005. "Spiritual Leadership and Army Transformation: Theory, Measurement, and Establishing a Baseline." *Leadership Quarterly* 16: 835–862.

George, J. M. 2004. "Positive Organizational Scholarship: Foundations of a New Discipline." *Administrative Science Quarterly* 49 (2): 325–330.

Gittell, J. H., K. S. Cameron, S. Lim, and V. Rivas. 2006. "Relationships, Layoffs, and Organizational Resilience: Airline Industry Responses to September 11." *The Journal of Applied Behavioral Science* 42 (3): 300–328.

Keyes, C. L. M. 2002. "The Mental Health Continuum: From Languishing to Flourishing in Life." *Journal of Health and Social Behavior* 43 (2): 207–222.

Kotter, J. P. 2008. *Sense of Urgency*. Cambridge, MA: Harvard Business School Press.

O'Donohoe, S., and D. Turley. 2006. "Compassion at the Counter: Service Providers and Bereaved Consumers. *Human Relations* 59 (10): 1429–1448.

Owens, B., W. Baker, and K. S. Cameron. 2014. "Relational Energy at Work: Establishing Construct, Nomological, and Predictive Validity." Working paper, Ross School of Business, University of Michigan.

Peterson, S. J., and F. Luthans. 2003. "The Positive Impact and Development of Hopeful Leaders." *Leadership and Organization Development Journal* 24 (1): 26–31.

Rego, A., N. Ribeiro, and M. P. Cunha. 2010. "Perceptions of Organizational Virtuousness and Happiness as Predictors of Organizational Citizenship Behaviors." *Journal of Business Ethics* 93 (2): 215–235.

Sharkey, J. 2004. "Fewer Are Flying on Short Routes." *New York Times*, February 17, C9.

Spreitzer, G., K. Sutcliffe, J. Dutton, S. Sonenshein, and A. M. Grant. 2005. "A Socially Embedded Model of Thriving at Work." *Organization Science* 16 (5): 537–549.

Stephens, J. P., E. D. Heaphy, A. Carmeli, G. M. Spreitzer, and J. E. Dutton. 2013. "Relationship Quality and Virtuousness: Emotional Carrying Capacity as a Source of Individual and Team Resilience." *The Journal of Applied Behavioral Science* 49 (1): 13–41.

CHAPTER TWENTY-FOUR

Positive Organizational Ethics

Adult Moral Development in the Workplace

Leslie E. Sekerka

The word *ethics* comes from both Latin and Greek meaning *character* (Oxford English Dictionary 2013; see www.oed.com/). Broadly speaking, ethics refers to the philosophy of human conduct, which is the determination of right and wrong behavior. When ethics is applied to an organization, it relates to its principles and values and the choices derived from them, applied to successfully achieving operational performance. Until recently, organizations were considered ethical so long as they were law abiding. With ongoing demonstrative evidence that malfeasance occurs with regulatory controls in place, many realize that prevention of moral ineptitude does not ensure ethical behavior. This is especially the case when business operates without a strong moral foundation. When motives are not backed by socially responsible performance, organizational ethics is unreliable. When organization development (OD) is used to help firms build moral strength, people work together to enhance productivity, learning, and core competencies that can benefit the company and its broader community (McLean 2006). Because OD professionals commit to promoting justice and serving the well-being of all living beings, it is assumed that those working in this field are interested in advancing moral responsibility in business enterprise (see www.theodinstitute.org/; www.iodanet.org/).

An initial challenge in organization ethical development is to consider the level of moral responsibility that a firm *must* or *should* adopt. Prescriptive demands and normative declarations are not realizable unless there is a willingness to go beyond the moral minimum imposed by externally driven legal standards. The strength of a firm's ethics calls for an internally driven moral awareness, with decisions and actions directed to the pursuit of ethical performance. While the firm's values represent elements of identity, ethical character begins with the underlying management philosophy.

This chapter provides foundational information regarding the use of OD to build ethical strength within a firm. Challenges and opportunities are presented, along with a technique to advance adult moral development in the workplace. Key lessons and discussion questions are offered for reflective consideration.

PRINCIPLED PERFORMANCE

Studies in the general area of positive psychology (PP), positive organizational scholarship (POS), and positive organizational behavior (POB) have put a spotlight on the best aspects of our organizational systems at both individual and collective levels. Research in this area seeks to enhance organizational effectiveness in a way that goes beyond promoting the basic survival of the firm, seeking instead to uncover what contributes to personal and collective thriving in workplace task action. The idea or expectation that organizations protect people and the planet as they earn profits for investors is not guaranteed by external mandates.

Principled performance embraces an ethics of care, manifested by a firm's self-directed concern for corporate citizenship, corporate social responsibility, and/or environmental sustainability. Driving the organization's ethical character are decisions made by top management, which are then implemented by employees at every level. When ethics are based on governance to address legal mandates, organizational ethics programs are unlikely to be designed to promote, develop, or endorse a deep and abiding sense of moral responsibility. A more broadly defined sense of duty within the organization's identity is required, advancing both the breadth and depth of ethics *en route* to performance. OD experts are encouraged to consider the domain of positive organizational ethics (POE) to advance their understanding of strengths-based approaches to business ethics. As an emerging field, POE is a home for those interested in going beyond compliance to encourage systemic change, educating leaders, managers, and employees to use character strengths to activate the ethical core of their organization (Sekerka, Comer, and Godwin 2014).

The philosophy that drives corporate decision making is often visible by its time horizon for how success is measured. Stakeholder concerns typically require short- and long-term considerations, whereas shareholder concerns center on meeting quarterly and annual targets (Wagner 2011; see http://dowelldogood.net/; www.businessdictionary.com/). Regardless of value statements and rule-based behaviors, when an organization focuses largely on its own self-interest, its ethics are often less durable than those also interested in the concerns of others (Sekerka and Stimel 2011). Organizations that fully embrace moral responsibility make ethics central to their purpose, and reflect this with the use of triple-bottom line (TBL) accounting. A proactive approach to ethics requires a genuine respect and care for others, not only striving to do no harm, but actually working to do "good."

When management is ready, OD experts can help members co-create a broader ethical identity, and help with the design of performance metrics that track, measure, and reward people on how to achieve objectives in a morally responsible manner. Practitioners can assist planners in aligning strategic operations to inculcate a range of stakeholder concerns, and foster the creation of operational processes and strategic alignment that connect success with environmental and socially responsible goals. Processes driven by OD professionals can enable the identification of opportunities, restrictions, threats, and incentives that will help build ethical strength within a firm's business strategy (Schaltegger and Synnestvedt 2002), ensuring objectives and goals are defined with specific implementation plans that are supported with concrete actions.

A challenge for OD is to help organizations balance their commitment to social goals when competitive demands call for economic results. Ontological differences may exist regarding the role of OD to increase efficiency and effectiveness toward economic performance or to advance organizational learning, helping firms to become better corporate citizens. Experts in OD can play a pivotal role here, advancing moral responsibility as a capacity-building endeavor, one that offers beneficial economic implications as well as promoting the growth and empowerment of organizational members. Going beyond

Illegal Action	Compliance	Virtuous Action
Does Harm	Does no Harm	Reduces Harm
Nonadherence to Regulation	Adherence to Regulation	Supersedes Regulation
Avoidance Orientation	Prevention Orientation	Promotion Orientation
Disobedience/Punishment	Obedience/Control	Empowerment/Developmen

← Closed/Control Open/Discovery →

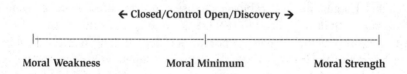

| Moral Weakness | Moral Minimum | Moral Strength |

Figure 24.1. Compliance as the Moral Minimum

Source: From L. E. Sekerka, "Compliance as a Subtle Precursor to Ethical Corrosion: A Strength-Based Approach as a Way Forward," *Wyoming Law Review* 12, no. 2 (2012): 286.

compliance means people are encouraged to engage in virtuous action, to do more than what is required as a way of conducting the firm's business to ensure its ethicality. (See Figure 24.1.)

ETHICS AS A PRACTICE

While the ethical framework is cast by management, at the heart of organizational ethics is the individual character strength of each organizational member. While policies and procedures must be upheld, ethics is demonstrated by employees in their everyday workplace routines. Social norms that support ethics are created through reward systems and complemented by management role-modeling and open and transparent communication. But moral competency (Sekerka, McCarthy, and Bagozzi 2011) and moral intelligence (Wickham and O'Donohue 2012) is built and affirmed by the way business is conducted on a daily basis. Ethical awareness and personal governance that support the ability to engage in moral action are important, especially when values compete for supremacy (Bagozzi, Sekerka, Hill, and Seguera 2013), when rules conflict, or when situations are complex and answers are not clear cut.

Being ethical is both a cognitive and affective process, where responsibility is driven by norms, shaped by culture, beliefs, principles, and values. Because living one's values requires self-awareness, a desire to act morally, and a decision to engage in moral action, ethics is a very personal experience. Relationships and interactions with others provide the motive and motivation to act ethically, or to do otherwise. Therefore, OD efforts to help people come together and work through their salient ethical challenges, fostering collaborative reflection and dialogue in the workplace, is critical. People need skills and supportive contexts to foster their ability and willingness to achieve business goals in a morally responsible manner.

This calls for self-directed governance, enabling members to learn how to manage their temptations, fears, and desires, deterrents that can intervene and distract movement toward moral action. Ethics is supported by people thinking through their values, principles, and objectives, and then determining appropriate choices, given the particular circumstances. Learning to seek out ethical concerns and to discuss them with others is very different from reacting to ethical problems as they emerge. Experts in OD can help organizations co-create a proactive ethical culture, contexts where identifying ethical risks and bringing forward uncertainties becomes the expected norm. Efforts that support such openness and transparency around ethical concerns are a means to develop trust, which can bolster organizational commitment.

Given the complexity of views, perspectives, and traditions, the reality is that most ethical issues are a mix of black, white, and gray. Ethical issues may not even be perceived similarly, given the cultural lens that is applied (Marar Yacobian and Sekerka 2014). Even when mandates declare the rightness (or wrongness) of an action, determining the best "right" in circumstances can be difficult, depending upon the person, situation, and context (Treviño 1986). People see things differently and are not necessarily consistent in applying their own views and values. Despite training and code of conduct directives, issues are rarely crystal clear. Dealing with ethical ambiguities means people learn how to discuss sensitive concerns that might become problematic before they become full-blown issues. Making sense of matters calls for collaboration; people need to work together to build a shared ideology for how to conduct morally responsible actions, given their area of expertise. Practitioners in OD can be a conduit for advancing this sort of development by creating "safe spaces" and helping people conduct difficult conversations (e.g., speaking truth to power). Scientists explain that moral judgment is a function of our cognitive and intuitive-emotional systems, involving both rational and affective components that drive ethical thinking, feeling, and behavior. This underscores why employees need to learn how character strength comes from within, learning to balance internal competing values and emotions with external pressures.

Personal governance is driven by a willingness to maintain personal and organizational integrity, underwriting the motivation to address tough ethical concerns. This means learning how to address fears that can derail moral intent. If a firm is truly committed to principled performance, a prevention/promotion orientation is needed, teaching and encouraging members how to work together to thwart ethical risk and leverage ethical strength. Organizational ethics means employees work to sustain their desire and ability to do the right thing in their daily workplace routines. This suggests that employees need to establish a shared goal to inculcate this expectation in the meaning of work itself. Techniques that foster reflective dialogue can empower employees and build positive momentum which, in turn, can broaden capacity for moral strength. Rather than limiting ethics to values, rules, codes, and governance, facilitated OD can help employees co-create the conditions that render their ethical skills development, process creation, and organizational scripts to support the use of character strengths.

TECHNIQUES FOR ETHICAL DEVELOPMENT

Best practices in ethics education and training show that employees need to engage in face-to-face interaction to learn how to address ethical risks in the workplace (Sekerka 2009). It is important for people to be part of a learning community, working together with peers, managers, and leaders to understand what can threaten principled performance and how to address these challenges as a collective. Whatever issues employees deem relevant are an important focal point for interactive experiential learning processes. Use of the *balanced experiential inquiry* (BEI) process has been shown to increase curiosity, decrease negative emotions, and bolster managers' desire to proceed with moral action, without the need for external affirmations or praise (Sekerka, Godwin, and Charnigo 2012, 2014).

The BEI method is considered a hybrid approach linking personal learning and OD, by weaving two very different core change management techniques together (diagnostic- and appreciative-based inquiry) (Sekerka and Godwin 2010). Employees share their ethical challenges, airing both successes and times of difficulty. This provides a platform for how to conduct ongoing reflection and discovery, and to help people recognize and review how they overcame barriers to moral action or were blocked by them. Employees are guided to use their own stories to determine how their personal and organizational strengths can be leveraged, as well as how to resolve unsettled conflicts.

Initially facilitated by an OD trainer, BEI must eventually become inculcated into workplace routines to sustain its benefits. The goal is to help managers conduct BEI as a part of staff and planning meetings, as well as being integrated into personal coaching and feedback sessions. Techniques like BEI prompt a deeper level of adult learning than what is garnered from the typical static delivery of rote content material. Participants engage in reflective and critical ethical thinking, role-play decision-making processes, and begin to practice new behaviors in a "safe space." Social engagement and practice are necessary if ethical strength is to become a part of employees' expected regular performance capability. Information gleaned from BEI helps people identify where potential ethical risks reside and how people can help one another pursue moral action with personal governance. As organizational inconsistencies emerge, members in different roles, functions, and status work together to see where their assets reside and where improvements need to be exacted.

Using BEI, employees work together to draw upon strengths as they identify organizational shortcomings, practicing transparency in a social setting. People can therefore become more aware of and sensitive to their emotional signals and then self-regulate these feelings as they prepare for moral action. But it is the actions of management that ultimately serve as the cornerstone for securing the organization's ethical health. While individual contributors need to practice and exercise their moral competencies, leaders are responsible for setting a consistent example and creating a workplace that expects, supports, and nurtures employees' character strength. When employees develop daily habits of principled performance, they make it a practice to look for how and where activities may be vulnerable to ethical weakness, while also looking for where *moral potency* can be leveraged to empower moral responsibility and leadership (Hannah and Avolio 2010).

SUMMARY

This chapter sets forth an introduction to core terms and offers several core concerns and elements of conducting organizational ethical development. Key lessons from this offering include:

- OD experts are charged with advancing the moral responsibility of business and committed to promoting justice and serving the well-being of others.

- A firm is committed to principled performance by adopting a stakeholder philosophy and proactive approach to ethics, emphasizing character strength at the organizational and individual levels and expressing this commitment in prosocial performance expectations and measurement criteria.

- A challenge for OD is to help firms balance their commitment to society when competitive demands call for short-term economic results. Experts can help members strengthen their commitment to ethics, elevating prosocial duty as an important and necessary element of its stakeholder strategy.

- OD experts can help ensure a firm's values are integrated into strategic processes and implemented as elements of daily practice, helping the organization to build a more genuine and lasting form of organizational ethics.

- Face-to-face activities using experiential learning methods are essential toward supporting ongoing adult moral development and ongoing organizational learning.

In shaping principled performance, OD experts must strive to go beyond a surface approach, working to establish a more durable and proactive form of ethics. If the main thrust of programming is to convey rules, codes, regulations, policies, and reporting channels, then the value of ethics will remain dubious at best. Working with management, OD professionals must help establish ethical criteria connected to performance goals and support ongoing education that treats "right" action as an expected duty and responsibility of POE in business enterprise.

Discussion Questions

1. When discussing OD, is the topic of ethics considered an area for ongoing advancement? Why or why not?

2. If a firm is interested in pursuing organizational ethical development, does management focus largely on the prevention of unethical activity,

as compared to building ethical strength? What can OD professionals do to cultivate a more proactive approach to ethics in organizational settings?

3. When moving to align ethics with strategic planning and performance targets and their associated metrics, are moral competency development and individual ethics objectives and their associated metrics included?

4. When a firm is largely driven by a shareholder philosophy, what might attract them to a more broadly defined ethical identity?

5. How do organizations undergoing rapid expansion stay true to their ethical identity? In the case of mergers and acquisitions, how does a firm honor the character strengths of an acquired firm, while maintaining its original ethical core?

Resources

B Corporation: People Using Business as a Force for Good: www.bcorporation.net/b-the-change

The Do Well Do Good Second Annual Public Opinion Survey Report on Cause Marketing and The Do Well Do Good Second Annual Public Opinion Survey Report on Sustainability: http://dowelldogood.net/?page_id = 688

Ethics in Action Research & Education Center, Menlo College, Atherton, CA: www.sekerkaethicsinaction.com/

Ethics Resource Center—National Business Ethics Survey: www.ethics.org/nbes/

Organizational Development International—The ODI Code of Ethics: www.theodinstitute.org/od-library/code_of_ethics.htm

Santa Clara University's Markkula Center for Applied Ethics—Business and Organizational Ethics Partnership: www.scu.edu/ethics-center/programareas/businessethics/

Ethics Training in Action: An Examination of Issues, Techniques, and Development. Ethics in Practice Series. Charlotte, NC: Information Age Publishing: www.infoagepub.com/products/Ethics-Training-in-Action

References

Bagozzi, R. P., L. E. Sekerka, V. Hill, and F. Seguera. 2013. "The Role of Moral Values in Instigating Morally Responsible Behavior." *Journal of Applied Behavior Sciences* 49 (1): 69–94.

Hannah, S. T., and B. J. Avolio. 2010. "Moral Potency: Building the Capacity for Character-Based Leadership." *Consulting Psychology Journal: Practice and Research* 62 (4): 291.

Marar Yacobian, M., and L. E. Sekerka. 2014. "Business Ethics and Intercultural Management Education: A Consideration of the Middle Eastern Perspective." *Journal of Business Ethics Education* 11 (no pages assigned).

McLean, G. N. 2006. *Organizational Development: Principles, Processes, Performances.* San Francisco: Berrett-Koehler.

Schaltegger, S., and T. Synnestvedt. 2002. "The Link Between 'Green' and Economic Success: Environmental Management as the Crucial Trigger between Environmental and Economic Performance." *Journal of Environmental Management* 65: 339–346.

Sekerka, L. E. 2009. "Organizational Ethics Education and Training: A Review of Best Practices and Their Application." *International Journal of Training and Development* 13 (2): 77–95.

Sekerka, L. E. 2012. "Compliance as a Subtle Precursor to Ethical Corrosion: A Strength-Based Approach as a Way Forward." *Wyoming Law Review* 12 (2): 277–302.

Sekerka, L. E., D. Comer, and L. Godwin. 2014. "Positive Organizational Ethics: Cultivating and Sustaining Moral Performance." *Journal of Business Ethics* 119 (4): 435–444.

Sekerka, L. E., and L. Godwin. 2010. "Strengthening Professional Moral Courage: A Balanced Approach to Ethics Training." *Training & Management Development Methods* 24 (5): 63–74.

Sekerka, L. E., L. Godwin, and R. Charnigo. 2012. "Use of Balanced Experiential Inquiry to Build Ethical Strength in the Workplace." *Special Issue on Experiential Learning for the Journal of Management Development* 30 (3): 275–286.

Sekerka, L. E., L. N. Godwin, and R. Charnigo. 2014. "Motivating Managers to Develop Their Moral Curiosity." *Journal of Management Development* 33 (7): 709–722.

Sekerka, L. E., J. D. McCarthy, and R. Bagozzi. 2011. "Developing the Capacity for Professional Moral Courage: Facing Daily Ethical Challenges in Today's Military Workplace." In *Moral Courage in Organizations: Doing the Right Thing at Work*, edited by D. Comer and G. Vega, 130–141. Armonk, NY: M. E. Sharpe.

Sekerka, L. E., and D. Stimel. 2011. "How Durable Is Sustainable Enterprise? Ecological Sustainability Meets the Reality of Tough Economic Times." *Business Horizons* 54 (2): 115–124.

Treviño, L. K. 1986. "Ethical Decision Making in Organizations: A Person-Situation Interactionist Model. *Academy of Management Review* 11 (3): 601–617.

Wagner, M. 2011. "Corporate Performance Implications of Extended Stakeholder Management: New Insights on Mediation and Moderation Effects." *Ecological Economics* 70 (5): 942–950.

Wickham, M., and W. O'Donohue. 2012. "Developing an Ethical Organization: Exploring the Role of Ethical Intelligence." *Organizational Development Journal* 30 (2): 9–29.

CHAPTER TWENTY-FIVE

The Classic T-Group

Matt Minahan and Robert Crosby

"Oh, man, are we gonna sit here all day? In this silly circle? I wonder what the agenda is? Why won't they just tell us what we're going to do? If someone doesn't speak up soon, I'm gonna go nuts.... And why don't the leaders just lead?" The inner monologue of a typical T-group participant on the first day.

It seems like torture to subject people to a large circle of colleagues and peers or even strangers for several days, without an agenda, without a clear plan, and with leaders who do not seem to lead. And yet, that is exactly the fertile ground in which mountains of learning erupt that make the silence and early ambiguity worth it. This chapter describes the T-group as a form of personal and professional development including its history, growth, decline, and current applications.

T-GROUP DEFINED AND EXPLAINED

The T-group is a "type of experience-based learning environment" (Seashore 1999, 271) whose ultimate purpose is to develop and enhance the members' human relations competencies (Tannenbaum, Weschler, and Massarik 2013). The T-group helps members increase their own interpersonal skills, understand the impact of their own behavior on others, and others' behavior on them.

Experiential learning groups, such as T-groups "focus primarily on developing members' understanding of group-level processes and of their own behavior in groups" (Gillette and McCollum 1995, 3). The T-group provides participants with an "opportunity to learn about themselves, their impact on others and how to function more effectively in group and interpersonal situations. It facilitates this learning by bringing together a small group of people for the express purpose of studying their own behavior when they interact within a small group" (Gallagher 2012, 2).

Participants and one or two trainers sit in a circle in a group of 7 to 15, interacting with each other on ideas and topics that emerge from their own conversations, rather than from a preplanned agenda or curriculum. The interaction among the members as topics are suggested and pursued, or suggested and ignored, allows the participants to

- Observe the impact of their behavior on the group
- Gain insights from other participants and occasionally the trainers about how they are perceived by others
- Practice the skills of giving and receiving feedback, including the full range of emotions involved
- Improve their ability to observe interactions "in the moment," and notice the impact of others' behavior on themselves
- Experiment with different behaviors of their choosing
- See how participants react, observing the results the new behaviors might generate

In addition, interactions are happening and learning can occur at the level of the

- *Individual*, where most participants gain insights into their own thoughts, feelings, and reactions to what's going on around them
- *Interpersonal*, where most participants can assess the impact of their behavior on other people and the group. The participant can assess whether the degree to which that impact is aligned with their own conscious intentions and can monitor their own feelings
- *Group*, where cohesion, power, group maturity, climate, and structure can be affected by certain behaviors and feelings
- *Organization*, where authority, decision making, business process simplification, cross-unit conflict, communication, stereotyping, and so on, can be figural (Seashore 1999)

This includes the full range of emotions involved, and places the T-group as a precursor to the quest for emotional intelligence. John Wallen, who coauthored with Carl Rogers *Counseling with Returned Servicemen* in 1946, forged his remarkably clear distinctions between the "description" of an emotion ("I'm irritated by how you said that") and its expression ("Shut up!"). Finding that emotion and describing it became one of the key features of the T-group, especially in the Pacific Northwest of the United States where Wallen led National Training Laboratory (NTL) T-groups and other programs for years.

Also powerful was his distinction between openness (describing an emotion) and personal confession. Participants already were highly skilled in telling personal secrets, such as, "I've been divorced twice." Many assumed that openness meant more expressions and confessions. Perhaps even more critical was that few knew the distinction between being judgmental versus being descriptive of behavior, which is the bedrock "scientific" skill learned in the T-group. It is this capacity to differentiate between actual phenomena and the internal thoughts and feelings they generate that helps create a balance between the thinking and feeling parts of the brain.

KEY PRINCIPLES OF T-GROUP PARTICIPATION

Given its unique form as a learning laboratory and specialized focus, the T-group has its own principles and practices, such as learning how to learn and peers as teachers, which contribute to its success (Golembiewski 1999).

Laboratory Learning

Even though it is possible to generalize about the outcomes of a T-group, it is impossible to predict the topics or conversations that can occur. Each T-group is a laboratory in which individual participants engage in experiments of their own design. They are both the scientists in this laboratory, creating and testing hypotheses about themselves, others, and the group, and the subjects of their own experiments, doing the things designed by their inner scientist to see what happens and how they feel about it.

Learning How to Learn

Rather than being driven deductively by predetermined content, learning occurs inductively from the experiences that take shape in the group. That is true especially over time, as the first few hours and days of a T-group are often disquieting and uncomfortable, especially for those expecting a traditionally structured training course. Effective T-groups engage participants' "emotions, values, and motoric skills"—the ability to execute a new skill so effectively that it becomes tacit or unconscious—"in ways that are strikingly uncommon in a typical classroom" (Crosby 2013b, 55).

Peers as Teachers

Much of the learning in the laboratory is based on feedback received from other T-group participants; therefore, the "teachers" are other members of the T-group. It is not uncommon for a T-group trainer to begin by saying something like, "Look around this room, around this circle. These are your teachers, and it is from them you will learn much, much more than the staff can ever teach you."

Here and Now

As any mindfulness practitioner or teacher will know, keeping our consciousness in the present, in the "here and now," is difficult on a good day. When you add 6 to 14 other people to the mix, with all of the distractions and anxieties involved, it is hard work to keep the group's focus on the events they themselves are creating in the "here and now." Stories about past experiences and workplace troubles and other historical events are the currency we exchange in everyday life and conversation. But to create the laboratory in which participants can experiment, the focus must be on what the group is doing and feeling in this present moment, so that all in the circle have access to the same data in real time.

T-GROUP: CONTENT AND PROCESS

The other major concept that drives the T-group experience is the difference between the *content* of the work and the *process* by which it is done. "The easy answer is that process is not the what but the *how*" (Schein 2013, 66).

Using the iceberg as a metaphor, the content of the work occurs above the waterline ... that which we can see and hear and is happening in the open, in plain view of all. That is most of the focus of our work and daily lives, as seen in Figure 25.1.

The process of the work occurs below the waterline. The variables we are seldom trained to observe, but which generate thoughts and feelings in us about which we are often not even aware. Process variables are typically observed and noted by the leader at first, until the group itself takes over and becomes self-enforcing.

Process variables include, but are not limited to, who is in the group and how they show up, who is taking on what roles, how leadership is enacted, how decisions are made, how members deal with disagreements and conflicts, how members relate to authority, how members use "I" statements to speak for themselves and own their own perceptions, how members know of the emotionality of the group and its work, how they separate feelings from thoughts or

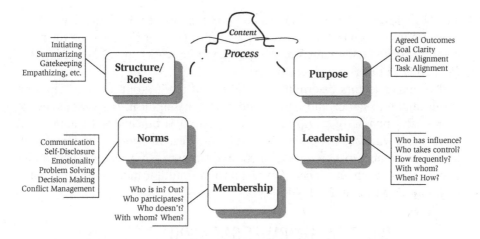

Figure 25.1. Group Dynamics

judgments, how the group develops its own emergent norms around communication, conflict management, problem solving, decision making, and so on.
Because the "real world" is driven by content, it does not train or teach how
to monitor and observe these process variables in real time. That is why the
T-group is the ideal setting for participants to focus on the process variables,
because the content of the conversation is about those dynamics below the
waterline, the "here and now" work of the group, which is where the real bal-
last of the iceberg and the power of group life live and which provides grounding
for the other dimensions of communication.

THE ROLE AND SKILLS OF THE T-GROUP TRAINER

In a traditional program, the expert management consultant or stand-up trainer
"typically intervenes on the content of the work: He or she makes recommendations about how to solve problems." However, an OD practitioner or T-group
trainer intervenes "on the variables that fall below the waterline of the iceberg,
those process variables that affect the group and how it does its work" (adapted
from Minahan 2014, 400).

The T-group leader leads no discussion of topics. Instead, she brings to consciousness dynamics about which the participants are not usually aware, the
process variables (Crosby 2013a).

The goal of the effective T-group trainer is to support the group as it develops the capacity to do its own work and to overcome its dependency on the
trainer. The T-group trainer most often intervenes early in the life of the group

almost exclusively on interpersonal and group processes. Within a day or two, most groups get what is needed, and the T-group trainer can focus on the more complex, systemic dynamics of the group and its work, often intervening less frequently as the T-group goes on.

Two major factors determine the success of the T-group leader. "The first is our ability to notice and understand what's going on in the various levels, stages, and phases of group life.... The second is our ability to notice and understand what's going on in our own inner lives; our work as an intervener, leader, or member of a group is a function of our own self-awareness and ability to communicate about the complex factors and "multiple motivations that make us human" (Minahan 2014, 404).

WHAT PARTICIPANTS SAY ABOUT T-GROUPS

It was at the Academy of Management annual conference in 2009 in Chicago that many of the past chairs of the OD Division of the Academy—including Stafford Beer, Warner Burke, Frank Friedlander, Larry Greiner, Bob Golembiewski, Craig Lundberg, and Dale Zand among others, cited their T-group experience as the moment that changed their lives for the better. These leaders in leadership, management, and OD said it was in their T-group experiences and training that they learned to notice process, to operate in the here and now, to test their observations and inferences before acting, and to empathize with others in ways that had not happened previously.

Quotations from participants acknowledge their T-group: "was a life changing experience. It has stuck with me even though I did it many years ago" (engineer). "I went through this almost 20 years ago ... and it is the only training that has ever stuck with me. I use the skills and concepts every day" (nuclear power industry). "My employee grew more in one T-group than he had in the previous 24 years I have known him" (plant manager). "I've never had such a powerful experience in my life" (accounting manager). So, despite the complaints in this chapter's first paragraph, these quotations are more typical of what people say at the end of their T-group experience.

THE PAST, PRESENT, AND FUTURE OF T-GROUPS

Soon after its creation as a social justice and racial equality intervention in the late 40s, the T-group quickly became mainstream. Thousands attended sessions. *Life Magazine*, perhaps the most prestigious publication of that time, ran a major article featuring the personal growth aspect of this new popular movement. They dubbed it "sensitivity training." While that term had been in earlier use referencing sensitivity to group processes, it was rapidly being interpreted exclusively as referring to intrapersonal/interpersonal sensitivity.

With rapid growth came the inevitable decrease of quality as trainers proliferated without training or grounding in this social-psychological phenomenon. The Wallen distinctions mentioned earlier were blurred or unknown. A decline was perhaps to be expected. Countless stories abound of groups (under names such as Encounter, Sensitivity, T-group, etc.) that became "spill your guts" sessions. One major corporation began such groups with practices so foreign to the original intent that participants were even encouraged to drink before evening sessions to help them be more "open." A decade later, one of the authors of this piece (Crosby) was constantly having to ease some frightened participants in that corporation into industry-wide T-group training because of those earlier efforts. As the T-group form evolved through the 1960s and 70s, "the motoric element emerged on par with the cognitive and affective domains. This was commonplace in sports, but virtually unknown in this educative arena. 'Experimental try' of new behaviors was encouraged" (Crosby 2013a, 4).

Today, there are two basic forms of the T-group. The first form is T-groups among strangers, which are offered by NTL Institute approximately monthly on a first-come, first-served basis among participants who come together for a week and then disband. The other is T-groups conducted among people who know each other in university and organizational settings. The most popular elective course for Stanford University's MBAs is a T-group, lovingly referred to as "Touchy-Feely." Many other universities teach about T-groups and their history, and several conduct actual T-group sessions as part of the OD curricula. One of the authors (Crosby) continues to facilitate T-groups with intact work groups within organizations and in open sessions twice a year, with one major client finding statistically significant improvements in boss-employee relationships among those who have attended.

As for the future, the T-group must be grounded again in its original intent. The possibilities of this transformative training that Carl Rogers (1970) reportedly called "the most important social invention of the 20th century" (15) have yet to be realized in the political, social, and business community. Learning to adapt and market it lies ahead, as does deeper grounding and training. Energy spent inventing new interventions could be well spent digging deeper into this one, still barely known or applied even in the OD world.

Perhaps the biggest challenge for the future is the velocity of time in today's organizational world. Few organizations think they can spare key staff and managers for the full five days that the form requires to achieve its optimal results. Trainers continue to experiment with shorter forms, but have found nothing that achieves the same benefit as the five-day format of today's T-group.

SUMMARY

The T-group as a form of personal and organizational intervention is entering its eighth decade, having clearly evolved from its simple creation at a workshop on racial equality. Its use grew rapidly through the 50s and 60s, expanding into personal growth and management development, and has been applied well, and perhaps sometimes misapplied in settings and situations for which it was not ideally suited. However, when designed and facilitated well, the T-group remains among the most powerful personal, interpersonal, and organizational interventions. Participants continue to report "life-changing" insights and experiences; trainers continue to experiment with the form to make it ever more relevant to today's world; and, organizations continue to benefit from the T-group as a personal skills and organization development intervention.

Discussion Questions

1. Please reflect upon your own learning experiences. Which ones were the most powerful for you, and what made them so?

2. Did your most powerful learning experiences occur in a social setting, that is, in the presence of other people, or when you've been alone?

3. What role do you think other people play in learning lessons about yourself and your impact on others?

4. To what extent could you be comfortable in a learning environment that was mostly unstructured and unplanned, but still governed by principles supporting personal growth and managed by a trained and skilled facilitator?

Resources

NTL Institute on the origins of the T-Group methodology: www.ntl.org/?page = OriginsTGroupMethod

History of T-groups: www.youtube.com/watch?v = IdxxRYNwMG8

On the heart of T-groups by Robert Crosby: www.youtube.com/watch?v = po2yu-FCUNk

On openness in T-groups by Robert Crosby: www.youtube.com/watch?v = dsh7F3beJf4

References

Crosby, R. P. 2013a. "The Heart of the T-Group." Unpublished discussion paper.

Crosby, R. P. 2013b. "T-Group as Cutting Edge: Today? Really?" *OD Practitioner* 45 (4): 55–60.

Gallagher, R. A. 2012. "About T-Groups." Retrieved from www.congregationaldevelopment.com/storage/About%20T-groups.pdf.

Gillette, J., and M. McCollum. 1995. *Groups in Context: A New Perspective on Group Dynamics*. Lanham, MD: University Press of America.

Golembiewski, R. T. 1999. "Perspectives on the T-Group and Laboratory Learning." In *Reading Book for Human Relations*, 8th ed., edited by A.L. Cooke, M. Brazzel, A.S. Craig, and B. Greig, 183–190. Silver Spring, MD: NTL Institute.

Minahan, M. C. 2014. "Working with Groups in Organizations." In *The NTL Handbook of Organization Development and Change*, 2nd ed., edited by B. B. Jones and M. Brazzel, 385–406. Silver Spring, MD: NTL Institute.

Rogers, C. 1970. *On Encounter Groups*. New York: Harper & Row.

Rogers, C., and J. Wallen. 1946. *Counseling with Returned Servicemen*. New York: McGraw-Hill.

Schein, E. H. 2013. "Notes Toward a Better Understanding of Process: An Essay." In *Handbook for Strategic HR: Best Practices in Organization Development from the OD Network*, edited by J. Vogelsang, M. Townsend, M. Minahan, D. Jamieson, J. Vogel, C. Royal, and L. Valek, 66–70. New York: AMACOM.

Seashore, C. N. 1999. "What Is a T-Group?" In *Reading Book for Human Relations*, 8th ed., edited by A. L. Cooke, M. Brazzel, A. S. Craig, and B. Greig, 271–272. Silver Spring, MD: NTL Institute.

Tannenbaum, R. J., I. R. Weschler, and F. Massarik. 2013. *Leadership and Organization: A Behavioral Science Approach*. New York: Routledge.

CHAPTER TWENTY-SIX

Leveraging Diversity and Inclusion for Performance

Judith H. Katz and Frederick A. Miller

The opportunity inherent in global diversity and inclusion comes with the challenge of eliminating miscommunication and misunderstandings—in short, the waste in interactions—that often comes with interacting across differences (Legas and Sims 2012; Mor Barak and Travis 2010). This speaks to the need for a set of common mindsets and behaviors to enhance interactions, expressed in a common language that everyone readily understands and uses. *Diversity* can be defined as "The collective mixture of differences and similarities that includes ... individual and organizational characteristics, values, beliefs, experiences, backgrounds, preferences, and behaviors" (Society for Human Resource Management, n.d.). We have defined *inclusion* as a feeling of belonging and respect as each person is seen for whom he or she is, an individual in a collective group where the work can best be done (Katz and Miller 2012).

In this chapter, we discuss two foundational elements for leveraging diversity: a mindset of *joining* rather than *judging* others; and, the use of the 4 Keys to create a common language that people can readily use and understand. The language of the 4 Keys—*lean into discomfort, listen as an ally, state your intent and intensity, and share your street corner*—founded on the basic choice to join rather than judge, paves the way for faster, more inclusive collaboration, better decision making, and the elimination of waste in interactions. In achieving these results—by providing a simple, practical way to live out the basic principles of inclusion—the 4 Keys provide an intervention to enhance effectiveness that lies at the heart of organization development (OD).

THE ESSENTIAL CHOICE IN EVERY INTERACTION: TO JUDGE OR TO JOIN?

Most people have learned to approach interactions and differences from a standpoint of judging. In judging mode, we evaluate people (pass/fail, up/down, okay/not okay), compare them, withhold benefit of the doubt, fail to start from a place of positive intent, and engage with them cautiously, if at all. Often, the more different people are from us, the more easily we judge them. Judging places distance between us and others, and it puts the person being judged in a box (Bloom and Bloom 2014). When we feel judged by others, we often tend to judge them back, creating a lose-lose situation.

The effect on organizational performance can be substantial. Judging limits productivity, the ability to solve problems quickly, and progress toward the team's or organization's goals (Katz and Miller 2013a). In addition, when people feel judged, they do not trust one another, leading to miscommunication and potentially lower productivity and motivation (Blake n.d.). Moreover, a judging mode creates waste in two ways: we waste substantial time and energy in the process of ranking others, and because judging places limits on the person being judged, we lose the ability to draw fully on her or his contributions. Figure 26.1 identifies the many ways in which judging and joining impact contribution.

Figure 26.1. The Judging versus Joining Continuum

From J. H. Katz and F. A. Miller, "Judging Others Has Not Worked … So Let's Join Them," *Leader to Leader* (2013): 51–57.

Rather than judge, we can engage in interactions by using *joining* behaviors as illustrated in Figure 26.1 (Katz and Miller 2013a). In joining mode, we approach differences from a stance of openness and support rather than caution and defensiveness. We begin with the assumption that each of us has something to offer the other. The goal of joining is to learn and to assume that you will partner with the other person. In joining, we extend trust, assume positive intent, give people the benefit of the doubt, and, most importantly, invest in the interaction.

Nowhere is this more important than in working across differences. *Joining* in this context means that we approach the other person (or team) from a stance of curiosity. We are willing to invest the time in developing the relationship necessary to build trust. We are willing to slow down in our interactions, providing time for others who may need to translate a question from English to their language (and then translate their response back to English), so they can fully contribute. We test our assumptions versus acting on them without complete information. We see ourselves truly in partnership with others, working and aligned to the same goals.

This makes a marked difference in interactions. In joining, people seek out areas of agreement, find ways to link to the perspective of others, and foster collaboration. We work through conflicts with an understanding that we are working for the best interests of the team and organization. We see ourselves on the same side of the table, not in opposition. When people feel joined, they are likely to be more open and willing to join.

ENHANCING INTERACTIONS WITH THE 4 KEYS

The joining mode is necessary but not sufficient to enhance interactions. The 4 Keys (see Figure 26.2) provide a concrete way to demonstrate and live a joining mindset through a common language that changes the interactions and the results and leads to people being included and more fully able to do their best work.

Key 1: Lean into Discomfort

Trust is fundamental to our most productive interactions and critical for working across differences (Covey 2006). Unfortunately, trust generally takes time to develop—time that many people believe they cannot afford. Building trust becomes even more challenging as individuals work virtually across time zones, geographies, and cultures.

Leaning into discomfort creates an environment in which trust can grow quickly. It involves making the choice to step outside our comfort zones and take a risk during an interaction. When we lean into discomfort, we make

- **Lean into Discomfort**
  Be willing to challenge self and others. Speak up—bring your voice and street corner.
- **Listen as an Ally**
  Listen, listen, listen, and engage. Be a partner.
- **State Your Intent and Intensity**
  Clarify intent at outset: State Notions, Stakes, Boulders, and Tombstones. Say what you mean and how much you mean it.
- **Share Street Corners**
  Accept others' thoughts and experiences as true for them. Hear others' differences as additive.

Figure 26.2. 4 Keys that Change EVERYTHING

ourselves open to change to try something new. And we inspire others to respond in kind, both bridging differences and leveraging the different perspectives we bring. An environment evolves in which everyone feels safe enough to speak up, offer new ideas, take worthwhile risks, raise difficult issues, co-create solutions, and collaborate freely.

The best time to lean into discomfort, in general, is as soon as we begin to sense discomfort. Saying "I am going to lean into discomfort" signals to others that we are reaching out, making ourselves vulnerable, and extending an invitation to reciprocate. When working across differences, the language of leaning into discomfort provides people with a shared "code" of understanding. It gives people the permission and the safety to speak up and share their perspective. This becomes even more important as we work across differences in cultures where bringing another point of view could be seen as inappropriate or too aggressive.

Key 2: Listen as an Ally

Many organizations operate with little sense of solidarity. Expanding our sense of "we" involves becoming an ally—learning from and reaching across differences in order to collaborate—and the first step toward becoming an ally is listening (and challenging) as an ally.

In listening as an ally, we listen deeply and with full attention, viewing others as partners on the same side of the table. We look for value in the speakers' perspectives and build on what they say. We slow down to truly hear others and engage with them in the conviction that we are all in this together. As a result, people feel that they have been heard and valued, and that their contribution matters. Listening as an ally opens the door for collaboration to take place and for breakthroughs to arise. When individuals work across differences, the need to listen as an ally is critical, particularly when language challenges or cultural differences may provide nuances that must be heard for real collaboration to exist.

Moreover, listening as an ally does not mean you always agree; one can also challenge as an ally. The result of challenging as an ally is that the other person hears a different "street corner" (see Key 4), but it is shared from a perspective of joining and strengthening the team, not breaking it down and finding fault.

Key 3: State Intent and Intensity

When we clearly state what we mean and how committed we are to the idea, it enables others to fully understand our meaning and expectations. In today's global workplace, a common language for stating intent and intensity eliminates miscommunication across language and culture—and the waste in interactions that results from it. Figure 26.3 is a model for stating intent and intensity (Katz and Miller 2013b) that provides people with this common language.

Notions are statements that require no action from others; notions are offered simply as an invitation for further discussion. By positioning a statement as a notion, we open the door to exploring an idea and seeing where it will take the group, if others find it of value.

Stakes, like tent stakes, establish a place for a discussion to start, with the knowledge that the initial place can be moved. When we put our stake in the ground and demonstrate that we are willing and able to move it, we are saying that others may have insights and information that might reveal a better position for the stake.

Boulders offer much less latitude. They imply a strong investment in seeing the idea addressed in the way we have framed it. If you are going to change a boulder, it is best to come with a lot of data and a lot of friends.

Tombstones leave no room for negotiation. When we label a statement as a tombstone, it indicates total commitment to the idea or issue—so much so that we may be willing to quit our jobs over it, or ask others to quit their jobs if they cannot abide by the tombstone. Tombstones usually are about values, safety, legal requirements, ethics, or policy issues that are nonnegotiable. When faced with a tombstone, it is best to focus on how you might implement rather than discussing the issue at hand.

To illustrate how this might work, imagine a new product strategy meeting in which the chief marketing officer announces, "We should introduce the product to the market by year-end." That could be interpreted as a "go do," whether or not the leader wanted to hear from others about the timing. Now consider the scenario if the leader said, "I have a stake about introducing the new product by year-end." Suddenly the direction of the ensuing conversation is obvious—the

Initiator has:	Intent	Intensity of Commitment	Desired Response
Notions	Discussion Possible	• Low investment • Testing if idea makes sense to others and/or hoping others will build upon the idea • Individual is willing to let go of the idea • Totally open to influence	Discuss if interested/ willing to explore; Action optional
Stakes	Discussion Initiation	• Some investment • State a position • Wants to hear others' Street Corners • Willing to be influenced	Discuss, to be considered or explored in depth; Acted upon if parties agree after discussion
Boulders	Discussion for Understanding	• Strong investment • Firmly entrenched in position • Wants it to happen • Difficult to influence This level of acting on an idea or making a decision should not be used frequently.	Action expected; Substantive objections somewhat okay
Tombstones	Discussion, if any, under Duress	• Total investment • Worth quitting over • No ability to influence This level should not be used more than twice a year, if that frequently.	Act now, or else

Figure 26.3. Guide to Notions, Stakes, Boulders, and Tombstones

From J. H. Katz and F. A. Miller, *Opening Doors to Teamwork and Collaboration: 4 Keys that Change EVERYTHING* (San Francisco: Berrett-Koehler, 2013b), 72–73.

leader has a strong opinion about action, but is seeking conversation about that opinion. It is an invitation for others to offer alternatives (such as a different timeline); even if they think the original idea is reasonable. People on the team are clear about how they can add value to the thought process.

Key 4: Share Your Street Corner

One of the great benefits of collaboration is that it enables organizations to bring together people with many different perspectives, or "street corners" (as in "the view from my street corner"; Miller and Katz 2012). Ensuring that all street corners are represented—and encouraging people to share them freely—yields as close to a 360-degree view as possible, which in turn leads to more effective solutions and better decisions.

In many organizations, it is difficult to speak up and share another point of view (Bang 2012). The greater the differences among individuals, the more challenging this becomes. The language of "sharing my street corner" or "wanting to hear your street corner" lets people know it is not only safe to have a different opinion, but other ideas or opinions are in fact sought after in order to solve problems more effectively and have the best possible decisions. As a result of inviting different street corners, people bring their best thinking to the problem or opportunity.

Using the language of street corners to work across differences leads to a different set of questions and interactions. Asking for all street corners invites people to share their different perspectives without being seen as a devil's advocate. People begin to ask questions that *seek out* differences. Do we have the right people with the right information included? Are there street corners we are missing? Moreover, inviting in others' street corners means that each person must truly listen as an ally—hearing and learning from others' perspectives while leveraging those differences, leading to greater collaboration and breakthroughs.

THREE STRATEGIES FOR CREATING THE CHANGE

The 4 Keys have transformed interactions throughout the world. Yet how does one introduce them into a system so that they "take hold"? We have found several strategies to be particularly effective.

Executive Feedback Pods

The mindsets and behaviors of senior leaders set the tone for any organization. To create a breakthrough in these areas, leaders can benefit from a supportive environment in which to grow, learn, and hear honest feedback about how they are incorporating a joining mindset and the 4 Keys into their interactions. The executive feedback pod creates precisely this environment (Katz 2011).

To start an executive feedback pod, each leader selects a small group of people (typically six to eight) to provide feedback on her or his behavior over the course of a year. Pod members are people who interact with the leader on a regular basis and reflect a diversity of backgrounds, functions, levels, and regions. All pod members must be willing to provide *honest* feedback about the leader's behavior, so the leader can continue to make progress toward living and modeling the 4 Keys.

Internal Change Agents

The role of internal change agents is to accelerate application of the 4 Keys via peer-to-peer leadership and accountability (Davis-Howard 2014). After participating in an intensive education program, internal change agents adopt the new language and create an inclusive, collaborative workplace by changing their day-to-day interactions with peers and colleagues. In addition to joining with others and using the language of the 4 Keys, each internal change agent brings together a group of three to five individuals whose role is to support the internal change agent and model the new language with others. The effect is to spread the 4 Keys faster through peer-to-peer interaction than traditional top-down initiatives typically would.

Embedded Consulting

Embedded consultants "live" in the organization or team with which they work, modeling joining and the 4 Keys and providing real-time coaching (DaRos and Pfeffer 2011). Embedded consultants attend work meetings, observe, assess leadership actions and group processes, and evaluate effectiveness. The real-time aspect of their feedback is invaluable for individuals and groups as they problem-solve work issues in progress. Embedded consultants help to slow down interactions so leaders and others can recognize opportunities to apply joining and the 4 Keys. With this kind of support and guidance, improvement in interactions becomes normative over a short period of time, resulting in higher levels of performance more quickly than many other approaches (e.g., exclusive use of classroom training) can achieve.

SUMMARY

Differences *can* make a difference for a team or organization—if they are leveraged and valued. Sharing common language and mindsets are critical to leveraging the vast richness of skills, talents, abilities, and differences of all team members across the globe. The mindset of joining others and the common language of the 4 Keys pave the way for an environment of inclusion in which greater trust and collaboration, making problems visible, and faster decision making, are evident—all of which eliminate waste and create the environment that enables breakthroughs. In this way, the 4 Keys are a powerful contributor to two commitments at the heart of organization development: a respect for the dignity and contributions of *all* people, and a drive to optimize the performance of organizations.

Discussion Questions

1. Are there individuals or groups in your organization that get *joined* more? *Judged* more? What actions are you taking to help others feel joined?
2. How can practitioners and leaders provide the sense of safety necessary for people to speak up, make problems visible, and lean into discomfort?
3. How might listening as an ally facilitate your efforts to create a sense of "we" in the teams with which you work?
4. How might the language of notions, stakes, boulders, and tombstones clarify intent and facilitate decision making in your team?
5. In the next meeting you attend, imagine all the street corners that could be of value to the topic at hand. Then look around the room. Who should be at the meeting but is absent? Who is in attendance that should not be?
6. How might you and others listen as an ally and leverage different street corners to create breakthroughs?

Resources

Remarkable Leadership interview with Judith Katz and Frederick Miller (Podcast) by Kevin Eikenberry: http://members.remarkable-leadership.com/files/teles/guest/katz-miller-aug13-audio.mp3

Opening Doors to Teamwork and Collaboration by Judith Katz and Frederick Miller (Video): www.kjcg.com

The WOW Club interview with Judith Katz and Frederick Miller (Video): www.kjcg.com/video

References

Bang, H. 2012. "What Prevents Senior Executives from Commenting upon Miscommunication in Top Management Team Meetings?" *Qualitative Research in Organizations and Management: An International Journal* 7 (2): 189–208.

Blake, I. A. n.d. "How to Overcome Mistrust and Tension in the Workplace." *The Houston Chronicle.* http://work.chron.com/overcome-mistrust-tension-workplace-6594.html.

Bloom, L., and C. Bloom. 2014. "Are You Using Your Judgment or Just Being Judgmental?" *Psychology Today* blog, January 17. www.psychologytoday.com/blog/stronger-the-broken-places/201401/are-you-using-your-judgment-or-just-being-judgmental.

Covey, S. M. 2006. *The Speed of Trust: The One Thing That Changes Everything*. New York: Free Press.

DaRos, D. J., and C. A. Pfeffer. 2011. "Presence Consulting Creates Lasting Change." *ASTD Links*, June 25. www.astd.org/Publications/Newsletters/ASTD-Links/ASTD-Links-Articles/2011/06/Presence-Consulting-Creates-Lasting-Change?mktcops = c.learning-and-development&mktcois = c.beginner-level-content ~ c .change-management ~ c.coaching.

Davis-Howard, V. 2014. "Unleash Change Through a Peer-to-Peer Approach." *TD: Training & Development*, July 20, 76–77.

Katz, J. H. 2011. "Grow Yourself, Grow Your Team, Grow Your Business: The Challenge for Today's Leaders." *Practicing Social Change: NTL Institute for Applied Behavioral Science* 4: 17–20.

Katz, J. H., and F. A. Miller. 2012. "Inclusion: The How for the Next Organizational Breakthrough." *Practising Social Change: NTL Institute for Applied Behavioral Science* 5: 16–22.

Katz, J. H., and F. A. Miller. 2013a. "Judging Others Has Not Worked … So Let's Join Them." *Leader to Leader* 70: 51–57.

Katz, J. H., and F. A. Miller. 2013b. *Opening Doors to Teamwork and Collaboration: 4 Keys that Change EVERYTHING*. San Francisco: Berrett-Koehler.

Legas, M., and C. Sims. 2012. "Leveraging Generational Diversity in Today's Workplace." *Online Journal for Workforce Education and Development* 5 (3): 1–9.

Miller, F. A., and J. H. Katz. 2012. *"The Four Corners Breakthrough: A Game Changer"*. Unpublished manuscript. The Kaleel Jamison Consulting Group, Troy, NY.

Mor Barak, M. E., and D. J. Travis. 2010. "Diversity and Organizational Performance." In *Human Services as Complex Organizations*, 2nd ed., edited by Y. Hasenfeld, 341–378. Thousand Oaks, CA: Sage.

Society for Human Resource Management. n.d. "SHRM's Diversity and Inclusion Initiative (PowerPoint)." www.shrm.org/Communities/VolunteerResources/Documents/Diversity_CLA_Definitions_of_Diversity_Inclusion.ppt.

CHAPTER TWENTY-SEVEN

The Global Organization Development* Professional

Therese F. Yaeger and Peter F. Sorensen

A special issue confronting the field of organization development (OD) today is the phenomenon of globalization, as reflected in world markets in which corporations strategize, produce, and market across national boundaries. Countries that once seemed absent on the global stage now have a growing presence in the world of business. African countries and Southeast Asian countries now represent new ways the world does business (Sulamoyo 2012; Yeh 2011). But it is not just globalization in terms of business that is changing rapidly—the world is also changing in beliefs and ideologies, creating implications for peace or conflict. The increased globalization activities provide the needed and expanding role of OD.

Global OD is much broader than in-country OD, where it is often a process in a single local organization to improve organizational effectiveness. *Global* refers to being cognizant there may be different political, economic, legal, and cultural factors that may influence a change initiative or may alter the OD approach. What a wonderful time to be an OD professional, to be a member of a field dedicated to the implementation of effective change within a set of uncompromising human values when we see changes occurring at an ever-accelerating rate.

---

*In this chapter, we use global OD and international OD interchangeably.

In this chapter, we present some important issues for professionals who work globally. We begin and conclude with overarching questions and an overview of the critical issues and questions the global OD professional must ask, and then summarize critical issues and how these issues can influence the work of the OD professional. Then, we address the skills and abilities required of the OD professional in the complex, global world.

National culture values and OD continue to represent fundamental questions for the OD professional:

- To what extent am I, as an OD professional, committed to the core OD values?
- To what extent are national cultural values compatible with the core values of OD?
- What is my role as an OD professional in working within cultures with national cultural values opposed to the values of OD?

CRITICAL ISSUES AND THEIR INFLUENCE ON GLOBAL ORGANIZATION DEVELOPMENT

Many would be surprised at the success rate of OD both in the United States and internationally. The best-documented OD work on success is by Golembiewski and Luo (1994), who report success rates for OD at approximately 90 percent, with relatively comparable success rates for OD in developing countries and Southeast Asia. Their work is supported by more recent experts in countries such as Denmark and Japan (Kjar 2007; Kongsbak 2010). What are the issues and questions to ask in successful international OD? One critical issue in the success of global OD consulting is understanding the national cultural values.

Culture

Knowledge of cross-cultural dimensions can assist in addressing OD's fit in other nations. The work of Geert Hofstede (2001; Hofstede and Hofstede 2004) and his concepts regarding societal orientation in terms of power, uncertainty, masculinity, and individualism are essential tools when practicing OD internationally.

- *Power distance* is the extent to which a society accepts that power in institutions and organizations is distributed unequally.
- *Uncertainty avoidance* is the extent to which a society feels threatened by uncertain and ambiguous situations.

- *Individualism* is a loosely knit social framework in which people should take care of themselves and their immediate families only, while collectivism is characterized by a tight social framework in which people distinguish between in-groups (relatives, clan, organizations) to look after them.

- *Masculinity* is the extent to which the society is assertive and aggressive rather than contemplative (indicative of a feminine culture).

Culture has important implications for the global OD professionals as national cultural values play a major role in terms of differences in resistance to change, the nature of leadership roles, organizational structure, and the application of OD techniques such as team building, survey feedback, job redesign, and large group methods.

Economic Development

Although Golembiewski reports high levels of success in developing countries, there are several critical questions for the OD professional. A country's level of economic development places constraints on applying OD in terms of technology and information systems, employee and management skill levels, project planning and organizing, and motivational and reward systems, among others (Cummings and Worley 2015).

These include:

- What is the economy's base: agricultural, manufacturing, service, or diversified?
- What is the skill level of the labor force?
- What are the labor costs (wages, benefits, social programs)?
- What is the general quality of life? Quality of work life?
- What is the native managerial skill level?

Legal Issues

Probably one area that has not received sufficient attention but which is critical for the practice of global OD is issues of legality. Some of the questions we feel the OD professional must ask include:

- What are the national laws that the client must follow?
- Which laws are enforced by the government and which are not?
- What are the national laws the consultant must obey?
- Is the OD professional prepared to deal with ethical dilemmas that might occur?

On a more personal level, questions that the OD professional may want to ask include:

- Is it possible to enter the country on a regular visitor's visa, or is a special business visa required?
- Will my copyrights be valid and actively protected?
- Will I encounter any problems in being compensated for my services?
- Will I have access to the information I require to make good decisions?

Answers to these questions can help the OD professional when undertaking work in other countries.

THE ROLE OF CULTURE IN GLOBAL ORGANIZATION DEVELOPMENT

Culture exists at multiple levels, such as national cultures and corporate cultures. Culture shapes the other elements of legal and economic development. Lack of cross-cultural knowledge is often at the root of failed global OD work (Kudonoo 2013; Lu, Yaeger, and Sorensen 2011). Culture makes a difference in how we practice OD globally. There are three answers: yes, no, and maybe.

There has been considerable work on matching national cultural values to the core values of OD. The basic question is not "Can OD be successful in different countries with different values?" That has been answered by the work of Golembiewski, cited earlier. The "yes, it works," "no it does not," and the "maybe" answer are more complex. The maybe answer deals with changing national cultural values and the question: "Do we have OD approaches which transcend national cultural values?"

Matching Organization Development Practices with Cultural Values

The matching approach to global OD is based on work by Jaeger (1986), who compared the national cultural values established by Hofstede, defined as low power, collectivism, feminine, and low on uncertainty avoidance, with the core humanistic values of OD, such as trust, respect, and collaboration. How compatible national cultural values are with the values of OD has important implications.

Those countries with values most compatible with OD were identified as Denmark, Sweden, and Norway. Countries with values moderately different from those of OD included Australia, France, Germany, Great Britain, India,

Singapore, South Africa, Turkey, and the United States. Countries that differ the most were identified as Argentina, Belgium, Greece, Hong Kong, Italy, Japan, Mexico, Pakistan, Taiwan, and Thailand.

Matching values has important implications for the global OD professional. The Scandinavian countries are characterized by values compatible with, and reinforcing, OD values. These countries have a long history of OD-related activities, including early work on industrial democracy in Norway, the Saab-Scania/Volvo work on work redesign. In these countries, resistance to change would be expected to be low, so a full range of OD interventions would be appropriate, ranging from job redesign to sociotechnical change and large-group interventions.

Countries with values moderately consistent with OD also provide a favorable environment for the global OD professional. Many have a rich history of contributions to the field where a wide range of OD interventions are appropriate. Team building should be more explicitly task-focused and autonomous work groups would require more attention to development and implementation. Data to support the need for teamwork are evidenced by Schroeder, Sorensen, and Yaeger (2014) finding that the true test of whether a team is global is not in its structure or espoused values, but in the way the team works together and how its attitude about being global manifests in team interactions. Also, transition and change to a more organic organization require greater time, effort, and preparation.

In countries with values least consistent with the values of OD, greater attention must be given to the choice of interventions, the method of implementation, and the role of the global OD professional. In these countries, the acceptance of the OD professional is based on a demonstration of "expert" knowledge. Here, the OD professional will be challenged and may need to find innovative and creative ways of resolving value dilemmas. Implementing any change may well be more directive and less inclusive and participatory. Interventions may have to be more task-oriented and structured, such as job enrichment and job redesign, management by objectives, and survey feedback.

Cultures in Transition

Due to the recent increases in technology and rapid development of global business enterprises, some nations have experienced unprecedented growth and change that have led to rapid and large-scale movement in their cultural values. African countries and Southeast Asian countries undergoing significant political and economic change represent significant opportunities for the OD professionals. One example of a country going through rapid transition is China. For an elaboration of change and a country's social responsibility beyond China, which includes three regions of Eastern Asia, Southeast Asia, and Asia Pacific, see the work of Thanetsunthorn (2014). Although countries in transition are an important topic, relatively little is known about the practice of OD in countries characterized by rapid transition. This rapid transition can have impacts far beyond one particular country's borders, as seen with immigrants and refugees predominantly from East Asian countries (Rao 2014). In this case, exploring the employee's openness to change and how openness, through appreciative discourse, can be cultivated with multicultural groups proved beneficial for both the diverse staff of employees and the refugee clients they served.

While little is known regarding cultures in transition, some indication exists that approaches in OD, specifically Appreciative Inquiry (AI), have applications in countries undergoing rapid transition. See, for example, the concept of Ubuntu and AI in the country of Malawi (Sulamoyo 2012).

What Other Professionals Have to Say

In this last section, we would like to present the results of interviews we held with over 100 experienced OD professionals, including past chairs and presidents of NTL, primary architects of AI, primary architects of the Managerial Grid, Peace Corp members; not-for-profit executives, and Fortune 50 executives. These results continue to be dramatically reinforced and reiterated through recent conferences and schools including the OD Network conferences, the Academy of Management, the International Society of OD, and in continuing work at the Copenhagen Business School, Benedictine University, and the University of Lyon-ISEOR in France.

Here are some of their thoughts:

1. The humanistic values of OD are at the forefront of successful global OD consulting.
2. The discerning ability to encounter and overcome cross-culture complexities while accomplishing successful global OD work exists with the global OD professional.
3. Divergence continues in cross-cultural consulting, but convergence in the future is the preferred future state. These consultants paradoxically recognize divergence and believe that geographical boundaries are becoming less important.

Global OD professionals possess a powerful set of values that allow for successful global work. These consultants are the future "value-setters." Their attraction to OD work is often a result of their strong OD values base, similar to that of Lewin who accepted the unknown not as a mystery, but as a frontier against which all scientists must strive to push back if they are to achieve a better understanding of the social world about which science still knows so little (Marrow 1969).

SUMMARY

The competencies for the global OD practitioner are considerably more complex than for the traditional "in-country" practitioner. International OD work is not the place for amateurs. Competencies for traditional nonglobal OD exist as highlighted in Chapter Seven in this handbook.

What specifically must global OD professionals do to practice successfully? First, the OD professional must know of success rates of OD across national cultural boundaries. For the best source of information on success rates, see the work of Robert Golembiewski (2002). Second, the international OD practitioner must maintain a network of professional colleagues from such associations as the ODC Division of the Academy of Management, ISOD, and ODN, as these colleagues may assist in becoming networked and familiar with the continuously developing literature related to global OD. Third, the OD professional must know of the client's dominant cultural values and how these values might affect the nature of one's work. A helpful framework for understanding the role of national culture is Hofstede's value typology. Finally, it is critical that professionals know their personal value orientations, the value orientation of OD, and how these need to be combined in doing effective OD work. The combination of these values will determine both the process and selection of interventions and will determine the extent to which the overall process and interventions must be modified consistent with the cultural values of the client.

Discussion Questions

The following questions represent a significant source of debate within the profession. They can serve as a guide to the practice of global OD:

1. How is OD perceived in the host nation? How will I be perceived, and what is expected of me? Are the clients expecting a facilitator, or an expert? Does the client know of OD?

2. How am I to be perceived by the client as an OD consultant?

3. What are the client organization's values as reflected in a particular country's culture? Are they compatible with my OD values?

4. What is the nature of the political system?

5. What is the appropriate OD process? What interventions are appropriate and what needs to be modified?

Resource

The OD International Registry of OD Professionals, 22nd International Code of OD Ethics: www.theodinstitute.org/od-library/code_of_ethics.htm

References

Cummings, T., and C. Worley. 2015. *Organization Development and Change*. 10th ed. Cincinnati, OH: Cengage.

Golembiewski, R. T. 2002. *Ironies in Organization Development: Revised and Expanded*. Vol. 100. Boca Raton, FL: CRC Press.

Golembiewski, R. T., and H. Luo. 1994. "OD Applications in Developmental Settings: An Addendum About Success Rates." *International Journal of Organization Analysis* 2 (3): 295–308.

Hofstede, G. 2001. *Culture Consequences: Comparing Values, Behaviors, Institutions, and Organizations Across Nations*. 2nd ed. Thousand Oaks, CA: Sage.

Hofstede, G., and G. J. Hofstede. 2004. *Culture and Organizations: Software of the Mind*. 2nd ed. New York: McGraw-Hill.

Jaeger, A. 1986. "Organization Development and National Culture: Where's the Fit?" *Academy of Management Review* 11: 178–190.

Kjar, R. 2007. "A Time of Transition: Lessons in Global OD from a Successful Japanese Firm." *OD Journal* 25 (3): 11–16.

Kongsbak, H. 2010. "From Crisis to Global Competitiveness: Learning from a Spectacular Journey." *AI Practitioner* 12 (3): 10–14.

Kudonoo, E. C. 2013. *Success Rates of OD and Change Initiatives in Anglophone West Africa: A Case Meta-Analytic Review*. Benedictine University, ProQuest, UMI Dissertations Publishing. 3536442.

Lu, L., T. Yaeger, and P. Sorensen. 2011. "Appreciative Inquiry International: Extending the AI Concept to Chinese Executives." In *Global and International Organization Development*, 5th ed., edited by P. Sorensen, T. Head, T. Yaeger, and D. Cooperrider, 525–526. Champaign, IL: Stipes.

Marrow, A. J. 1969. *The Practical Theorist*. New York: Basic Books.

Rao, M. 2014. "Cultivating Openness to Change in Multicultural Organizations." *Organization Development Journal* 2 (3): 75–88.

Schroeder, K. A., P. F. Sorensen, and T. Yaeger. 2014. "Accelerating Global Hybrid Team Effectiveness." *Research in Organizational Change and Development* 22: 335–364.

Sulamoyo, D. 2012. *Creating Opportunities for Change and Organization Development in Southern Africa*. Charlotte: NC: Information Age.

Thanetsunthorn, N. 2014. "Ethical Organization: The Effects of National Culture on CSR." *Organization Development Journal* 32 (3): 89–109.

Yeh, C. W. 2011. *Soft Total Quality Management and Organization Sustainability: National Culture Implications*. Benedictine University, ProQuest, UMI Dissertations Publishing. 3471402.

CHAPTER TWENTY-EIGHT

The Convergence of Organization Development and Human Resource Management

David W. Jamieson and William J. Rothwell

According to human resource (HR) professor David Ulrich, human resource management can play the role of change agent in organizational settings (Ulrich, Younger, Brockbank, and Ulrich 2012). Ulrich's perspective is important, since it is possible to get an MBA degree from a leading U.S. school and never hear a word about how to bring about change in organizational settings. And, maybe, the leading skill of business leaders will be to initiate and manage change. More professionals in organization "helping roles" are being called on to assist with change, and human resource management (HRM) is at the center of that effort in most organizations. One value of organization development (OD) is to bring a mindset, theories, methods, and skills to change planning and execution.

This chapter examines recent changes and trends in both HRM and in OD; provides a brief history of the relationships of these two fields of practice; presents conceptual overviews of HRM and OD; describes similarities and differences of HRM and OD; and describes present and future challenges in the relationship between HRM and OD, centering on mindsets, skills, acceptance of new roles by client managers, and the design of organization units and departments.

THE GROWING CONVERGENCE OF HUMAN RESOURCE MANAGEMENT AND ORGANIZATION DEVELOPMENT

For the past 50 years, HRM and OD have operated more apart than together. They have been housed both together and separately. There have been clashes resulting from differences in status, pay, and mindsets (where OD often pursued change while HRM often pursued stability). There have also been tensions between the HRM compliance drivers and OD's need for creative solutions to organizational issues.

More recently (last 15 years), that has been changing, mostly driven by organization leaders needing new expertise to solve unprecedented problems, change the "what" and "how" of their organizations and create new workplaces and workforces to meet twenty-first-century challenges. Organization leaders must attract and keep the people they require strategically, comply with requisite laws to manage risk and manage continuous change, simultaneously. Organizations are being challenged strategically and operationally to create new work, workplaces, and workforces to engage successfully with rapid, continuous, and disruptive changes. The knowledge and skills from HRM and change resources (OD and CM) are both needed. While some of the legacy and baggage remain, the convergence has begun and, in most sectors, both disciplines are collaborating, housed together, more integrated, or have segmented and coordinated by level and scale of change work, where large-scale, enterprise-wide, transformational change is handled by special OD-type units and regular, smaller-scale, incremental changes are embedded in internal consulting/HR roles serving organizational segments or units.

In discussing the relationship, convergence, and challenges between HRM and OD, it is helpful to share a conceptual grounding for the work of each field. This helps to see the similarities and differences and options for integrating and segregating the different work.

A CONCEPTUAL VIEW OF HUMAN RESOURCE MANAGEMENT

Historically, HR was the personnel department that cared for finding employees, managing their paperwork, supporting them with benefits, training them in job skills and required information, managing the organization's compliance with employment law, managing labor relations (in union contracts), and problem-solving employee relations issues (Rothwell 2012). The work of these departments was support, service, and compliance. Even as the names changed from HR to HRM, the functions stayed the same. As the environment became more volatile and talent (in many forms) became more central strategically, HRM was pushed for more strategic results while still maintaining all the operational services needed by employees. Dave Ulrich's series of publications in the 1990s and 2000s (Ulrich 1997; Ulrich et al. 2009; Ulrich et al. 2012) and other thought leaders (Rothwell, Prescott, and Taylor 2008; Lawler 2008; Christenson 2006, Boudreau and Ramstad 2007) encouraged and supported the transition of HRM into more strategic arenas of the organization. Central in Ulrich's work has been the research, updated a few times, on the roles that HRM must play in the organization. The latest version outlines (Ulrich et. al. 2012):

- Strategic positioner
- Credible activist
- Capacity builder
- HR innovator and integrator
- Change champion
- Technology proponent

These roles outline a comprehensive view of what HRM must accomplish to add value in today's organizational world. The HRM innovator and technology proponent are critical to creating efficient, accessible services for employees. The rest of the roles lean more toward adding strategic value through connecting HRM with business strategy, advocating human capital implications for strategy, developing and retaining needed talent, building organization capacity to execute new strategies, dealing with changing environments and creating change-ready and change-capable organizations.

In addition, the practice worlds of HRM, HRD, and OD and the academicians converged, as the knowledge and skills of each came to bear on faster changes and new challenges for organizations (Ruona and Gibson 2004). Today, we can add change management (CM) and some of the process improvement work using Lean and Six Sigma. In subsequent years, boundaries have been loosening among these areas of practice, roles are combining tasks and skills across these areas, and organization structures for HRM, OE, and L&D are shifting into a wide range of configurations.

The dilemma today involves:

- Growing need for interdisciplinary perspectives on organizational challenges (for example, business, HRM, OD, learning and development)

- Increasing demand for the operational support and well-being services of human resources
- Rising attention to compliance and risk management issues in a litigious society

It is hard to find people that are fluent or skilled across such diverse areas, or people who can lead the interdisciplinary combinations. There are a set of operational HRM functions that need efficiency, accessibility, and effectiveness, and there are a growing set of strategic HRM (and business) roles involving connecting strategies, people, technology, and change. The centrality of talent issues in strategy execution and the equalization of many other resources (financial, technological, material resources, etc.) has raised the bar for strategic HRM roles at the enterprise leadership table. These functions involve such things as talent planning, acquisition, development, succession, and retention; culture development in alignment with strategies; organization design for new internal and external relationships; engagement and productivity of the workforce; continuous organization learning in changing times; and rewards that align with motivations and strategic behavior. As HRM moves from operational ("do for me") tasks to more strategic ("partner with me") roles, the abilities of OD in such areas as collaborating, consulting to, and joining with organization leaders become more critical.

A CONCEPTUAL VIEW OF ORGANIZATION DEVELOPMENT

OD operates mostly at the whole organization systems level (including subunits of larger wholes). It pursues organization effectiveness by working on all parts of the socio-technical system that makes up any organization. It was always best known for its focus on the human element, but that is not all that is important. In the early days of the field, the human element was the least considered when management control, financial issues, and engineering were dominant mindsets during the industrial revolutions and the early information age. However, the whole organization contains numerous elements important to the functioning of whole systems—including environmental interfaces, strategy, structure, culture, systems and processes, and relationships and human dynamics within and across groups.

A recent definition of OD helps to capture the essence of the work of OD (Jamieson 2014), and is a modification of one developed earlier by Jamieson and Worley (2008): "OD is a process of planned intervention(s) utilizing behavioral and organizational science principles to change a system and improve its effectiveness, conducted under values of humanism, participation, choice, and development so the organization and its members learn and develop" (Jamieson 2014, 104). The *key ingredients* in this definition and the *focus of the work in OD* are:

- Series of planned and emergent actions that intervene in organization structures, systems, processes, and relationships
- Using theory, principles, and practices from the behavioral (psychology, sociology, anthropology, and economics) and organization sciences (organization theory, organization design, systems theory, management theory)
- To understand an organization system and its present behaviors and take actions to improve its effectiveness in achieving its mission, strategy, or desired outcomes (process and content, mission and results, social and technical), and its workplace health
- Conducted in accord with certain values, guiding both processes and outcomes, that are represented by: humanism (authenticity, openness, honesty, fairness, justice, equality, diversity, respect); participation (involvement, participation, voice, responsibility, opportunity, collaboration, democratic principles, and practices); choice (options, rights, accountability); and development (personal growth, reaching potential, learning, self-actualization)
- For the organization and its members to learn and grow in capacity, capability, and achievement of potential

So *critical elements* to pay attention to *in the practice of OD* include an understanding of:

- The present state of a system (diagnosis or discovery)
- The desired future state and evidence used to assess (planning, visioning, metrics)
- Who is involved and their roles (stakeholders)
- Change theories and processes (alternatives for organization change)
- Strategies for intervention (and their selection) for change in sociotechnical systems (change methods and tools)
- The operationalization of core values in practice (being authentic)
- Creation of system and individual learning (sustaining change and building capacity)
- How the elements of an organization system operate interdependently (systems theory)

- Establishing cycles of understanding, action, and reflection, leading to new understanding, action, and reflection, because in complex systems there is continuous change in numerous variables creating dynamic interactions (action research)

ORGANIZATION DEVELOPMENT AND HUMAN RESOURCE MANAGEMENT: SIMILARITIES AND DIFFERENCES

How is HRM similar to, and different from, OD? Consider several points of agreement and difference.

First, there are points of agreement. Both HRM and OD focus on the human side of the enterprise. Both HRM and OD can—but do not always—regard themselves as "people advocates," spokespersons for human capital's strategic role and high ethical standards. Both HRM and OD can emphasize the human element in organizational change and in strategic planning. Both bring the talent perspective and well-being of the human resources into planning and decision-making and humanistic values into balance with financial, technical, and managerial values.

Now for some points of possible difference. HRM has historically been conflicted, with one half focused on organizational compliance with government laws, rules, regulations, organizational policies and procedures, and collective bargaining agreements where they may exist. That half, the yin of HRM, is defensive (as in sports) in the sense of preventing loss and minimizing risks. The other half of HRM, the yang, is offensive (also as in sports) and should maximize productivity, human performance, creativity, and innovation.

OD is more in alignment with the yang part, such that OD is an offensive issue. OD creates and sustains organizational cultures in which the human spirit can flourish, creative and innovative thought can be maximized, and human productivity can be enhanced. That is accomplished by divorcing the value of ideas from the status of those who present those ideas, since OD practitioners assume that everyone (and not just senior executives) has valuable ideas that may be worth hearing. OD is interested in bringing together diverse voices and perspectives to engage people in ownership of solutions and changes.

Parts of HRM must process and serve many micro-tasks in an operational manner and in high volume. Most OD practitioners must think strategically first and plan changes through the more operational implementation stages. Each of these task characteristics requires different mind and skill sets.

PRESENT AND FUTURE CHALLENGES IN HUMAN RESOURCE MANAGEMENT AND ORGANIZATION DEVELOPMENT

As the two fields move closer together, a few challenges will need innovation and solutions.

- Integration of some tasks and roles into new blended strategic partner positions
- Separation of some aspects of the work to match mind and skill sets to the nature of the work
- Designing HRM (with OD) into new delivery models and functions

Strategic Partnering Roles

Some of the work will require a combination of strategic HRM understanding and change capability. The strategic business partner role (Jamieson, Eklund, and Meekin 2012) is one such role. These people must partner with business leaders across many functions and understand their business; how to operate as an equal partner; and have foundational knowledge of HRM and OD to assist with planning, decision making, and change. Other similar roles could involve integrated talent management or combinations of talent management and organization effectiveness.

Operational/Transactional Tasks

Much HRM work involves repeatable, transactional tasks that support employment, compensation, benefits, well-being, and ER issues. These need to be efficient, high volume, consistent, and easily accessed. Using technology to make more self-administered and use people for whom routine is enjoyable work are both ways to make this area work. These tasks take up most of the time of many HRM generalists today and overwhelm many roles asked to do these plus be strategic with business leaders.

Human Resource Management Organization Design

Today, most organizations are experimenting with new structures (organizing schemes) of how to design their functions into manageable units that provide the needed support for the organization and add value. One common approach is to separate operational and strategic tasks. Centers of excellence and shared service units are one model. Yet these need to be pulled together around strategic issues as well and need to be coordinated for speed, access, and delivery to users. Some organizations are moving more toward integrated roles requiring special selection and/or training to develop the right skills. Some create different roles to oversee and integrate across functions, such as organization effectiveness covering all L&D, OD, and some talent management. Where organization design and culture work get located is also an important choice.

SUMMARY

This OD and HRM convergence has been underway for about 15 years and still seems in process.

- Deep understanding of what the organization needs in talent and change is a critical first step. These will differ across organizations, sectors and industries.
- Getting past the old legacies and tensions must occur for the professionals to become colleagues and the clients to understand and expect different behaviors.
- Cross training will help to create useful integrated roles.
- Finding ways for talent and change practitioners to know the business needs will greatly help the transition.
- Helping leaders to see how different disciplines can serve the strategic needs of the organization, including HRM, OD, L&D, CM, and PM, when integrated or coordinated.

The changing environment is a strong driver for continued innovation in both what the organization does and how the organization and its workforce are designed, developed, and operate.

Discussion Questions

1. In what ways are HRM and OD different?
2. In what ways are HRM and OD similar?
3. What is the justification for believing that HRM and OD are converging?

Resources

OD—Past, present, future: www.employment-studies.co.uk/pdflibrary/wp22.pdf

This article describes the history of OD and discusses possible reasons for the convergence of HRM and OD: http://organisationdevelopment.org/history-of-od/od-hrm/
The article explains why OD and HRM are converging.

References

Boudreau, J., and P. Ramstad. 2007. *Beyond HR: The New Science of Human Capital*. Boston: Harvard Business School.

Christenson, R. 2006. *Roadmap to Strategic HR: Turning a Great Idea into a Business Reality*. New York: AMACOM.

Jamieson, D. 2014. "Panorama of OD." Unpublished presentation. Minneapolis: University of St. Thomas.

Jamieson, D., S. Eklund, and B. Meekin. 2012. "Strategic Business Partner Role: Definition, Knowledge, Skills & Operating Tensions." In *The Encyclopedia of Human Resource Management: Volume III: Topical Essays*, edited by W. Rothwell and G. Benscoter, 112–128. San Francisco: Pfeiffer/Jossey-Bass.

Jamieson, D., and C. Worley. 2008. "The Practice of OD." In *The Handbook of Organization Development*, edited by T. Cummings, 99–122. Thousand Oaks, CA: Sage Publications.

Lawler, E. 2008. *Talent: Making People Your Competitive Advantage*. San Francisco, CA: Jossey-Bass.

Rothwell, W., ed. 2012. *Encyclopedia of Human Resource Management*. 3 Vols. San Francisco: Pfeiffer.

Rothwell, W., R. Prescott, and M. Taylor. 2008. *HR Transformation: Demonstrating Strategic Leadership in the Face of Future Trends*. Boston: Nicholas Brealey.

Ruona, W., and S. Gibson. 2004. "The Making of 21st Century HR: An Analysis of the Convergence of HRM, HRD, and OD." *Human Resource Management* 43 (1): 49–66.

Ulrich, D. 1997. *HR Champions: The Next Agenda for Adding Values and Delivering Results*. Boston: Harvard Business School.

Ulrich, D., J. Allen, W. Brockbank, J. Younger, and M. Nyman. 2009. *HR Transformation: Building Human Resources from the Outside In*. New York: McGraw-Hill.

Ulrich, D., J. Younger, W. Brockbank, and M. Ulrich. 2012. *HR from the Outside In: Six Competencies for the Future of Human Resources*. New York: McGraw-Hill.

CHAPTER TWENTY-NINE

Constructive Use of Power for Organization Development Practitioners

L. Mee-Yan Cheung-Judge

I n organization development (OD), context is everything. Organization context provides a reference point for our diagnostic work, the design of our intervention, and helps clients and ourselves to decide upon the best way to support the organization.

Most Western organizations—and/or those whose parent company is from the West—operate from both a political and a pluralist model. A pluralistic organization comprises different interest groups, each asked to pursue individual functional or specialist interests legitimately. In a political organization, decisions are made through coalitions, partnership, jockeying for dominance, influence, or resource control, based on preserving the interest of one's part of the organization. In such organizations, *power* is an inherent feature. When each subsystem is charged to pursue its own agenda, power often becomes the intervening variable between desired outcomes and actual results. Conflict is also inherent and a way of getting things done; hence, political behavior is part and parcel of the daily work in organizations.

OD practitioners charged to support this organization in change will be ill-equipped if they do not understand power. In this chapter, the following is covered:

1. What is power and politics?

2. Why power relates to OD?

3. The concept of power bases and power strategies.

4. How to increase power and influence to achieve greater impact?

393

WHAT IS POWER AND POLITICS?

Here are definitions of power by OD writers:

- "Power is the potential for influence ... the potential must be acted upon" (Burke 1982, 149).

- "A capacity that A has to influence the behavior of B, so that B does something he or she would not otherwise do" (Brooks 2008, 237).

- "The potential ability to influence behavior" (Pfeffer 1992, 30).

- "The capacity of an individual or group to affect the outcome of any situation so that access is achieved to whatever resources are scarce and desired within a society or a part of the society" (Watson 2011, 140).

- "Power is defined as the capacity to effect (or affect) organizational outcomes" (Mintzberg 1983, 4).

These definitions show us three things about power: First, power is about creating the outcome one wants or what the situation requires—for example, getting people to amend the way they view the change. Second, exercising power happens in the social arena in the "in between" zone among people. Third, power use is always "potential" as the effectiveness of power use depends on what we have (power bases) channeling through activities and behaviors (power strategies) to achieve the change goals. This last point defines the word "politic," which are the processes, actions, and behaviors one uses to achieve the influence one desires. Organizational politics is "power-in-action"—getting things done that otherwise one would not have accomplished.

WHY POWER RELATES TO ORGANIZATION DEVELOPMENT

Two OD leaders have articulated why power relates to OD. The first is "Organization development signifies change, and for change to occur in an organization, power must be exercised. For OD, therefore, the consultant must understand the nature of power, from both a personal and an organization perspective, and be able to determine, within an organization, who has power, how power is exercised, and where the leverages for change (exercising power) are likely to be" (Burke 1982, 127). The second is "Power and politics, indisputable facts of organizational life, must be understood if one is to be effective in organization ... the OD practitioner needs both knowledge and skill in the arenas of organizational power and politics," (French and Bell 1999, 282).

Should the use of power among OD practitioners be different? Greiner and Schein (1988) point out that, "The effective combination of OD and power represents, for us, taking the high road to organization improvement" (7). What is this high road? It is when OD practitioners, through the way we work, and our presence

- teach and encourage people to collaborate in decisions that affect their own destiny;
- show people how to deploy power strategies that are open and aboveboard and prove more creative and efficient than political bargaining;
- assist the power structure to confront and transform itself so change can be more lasting; and
- uphold the concerns and interests of those with less power affected by these changes.

Sticking to this high road should build power users into powerful role models for better ways to wield power for the good of the entire organization—and that is the heart of OD values.

THE CONCEPT OF POWER BASES AND POWER STRATEGIES

Power bases are composed of unique resources over which we have control. Power bases will determine the power strategies for influencing others. Power bases, which are dynamic means, can be developed, expanded, or eroded depending on our circumstances and actions taken.

French and Raven (1959) explained that power is used by those who, in Richard Emerson's (1962) terms, have control of desired commodities by accumulating various bases of power, and then use it to do things. He defined five classic power bases. Another writer, Michael Beer (1980), identified similar power bases. These are summarized and listed in Table 29.1.

If OD practitioners want to be effective in supporting a client system through change, they need to know of and own a variety of power bases, intentionally build on them, and develop a strategy to expand and update them to increase the impact in the change work undertaken. This may include teaching clients how to use power in a constructive way within their organizations.

POWER STRATEGIES

Power strategies are used by power holders (actions, activities, behaviors) to achieve work-related objectives. There are many types of power strategies—the main ones are summarized in Table 29.2.

Table 29.1. Power Bases

French and Raven (1959)	Michael Beer (1980)
Reward power—The ability of the power holder to do or give something valued by another.	*Competence*—Demonstrating competence in delivering the jobs that we are commissioned to carry out.
Coercive power—The potential ability of the power holder to punish another.	*Political access and sensitivity*—Cultivating and nurturing multiple sources of support by offering our services to support the overall organizational agenda.
Legitimate power—Power comes from having legitimate right to exert influence, and those around him/her have a legitimate obligation to comply.	*Sponsorship*—Having multiple senior leaders giving sponsorship to the value of OD role in supporting changes.
Expert power—Power based on the person possessing expert knowledge, information, or important facts that are needed by another.	*Stature and credibility*—Having early success on any OD initiatives will lead to the building of credibility and stature.
Personal referent power—The highest form of power base—by being "who" the person is, they attract others as people around them "refer to" or "identify" with them.	*Resource management*—Power accrues to those who control resources—in this case, the resources of OD expertise and ability to help organizations will strengthen our power base.

Table 29.2. Power Strategies

- Form alliances and coalitions
- Surround oneself with competent colleagues
- Trade favors
- Focus on needs of the target groups
- Work around road blocks
- Use data to convince others
- Present a persuasive viewpoint
- Be persistent
- Increase relationship traction
- Use contacts for information
- Deal directly with key decision makers
- Deal with others socially
- Use threats
- Use organizational rules
- Give guarantees

The list of power strategies can be endless depending on who we are, what type of power bases we have, and the context in which we operate. Remember, whatever we do, we are there to promote the use of positive power and role model an alternative set of power behaviors.

HOW TO INCREASE POWER AND INFLUENCE
TO ACHIEVE IMPACT

Since power can evolve, maintain, erode, and expand, OD practitioners must be vigilant to keep power in an increasing measure in their work. Many appropriate approaches can be used.

1. **Become a "desired commodity."** Professionally, to be a desired commodity means to have in possession competence, stature, and credibility in dealing with the range of relevant organization issues, and be well versed in applied behavioral science, people matters, organization, and change. Such expertise is a rare and valuable commodity within the leadership community.

2. **Make change approach work.** OD principles of change put people at the center in a development way. Encourage people to have information for choice, to have a voice, and to participate in creating what matters to those whom the change will affect. As a default methodology, make co-construction a norm and encourage others to work collaboratively to facilitate their change work. This approach will work, and success will accrue more power.

3. **Get involved in strategic change work.** Make sure one of the top priorities is to get involved in *strategic change initiatives*. OD is a twin to strategy. When OD initiatives are aligned to the organization's strategic change priorities, it demonstrates the value of OD.

4. **Making relationships work.** In the world of complex change, it is not a formula or a mechanistic approach but authentic relationships that will gain the trust of people to help navigate their change journey. By turning advocacy into inquiry, judgement into curiosity, conflict into shared inquiry, defensiveness into self-reflection (phrases from Glenda Eoyang, HSDP Certification Workshop), you become the person that others want to relate to and spend time with. Developing this power base will require a "deeper" work with ourselves as part of the continuous development of self as an instrument.

SUMMARY

Change is to alter or make a situation different or to pass from one state to another. It is all about movement, transformation, and transition. The question that bothers people-centric leaders is, "Do I/we have the right to ask people to move from a state of comfortable mastery to one of psychological disorientation?" This, coupled with the awareness that they know little about how to effect change, makes them turn to OD practitioners for help.

To do effective change work, especially when we have no formal power, power bases must be built to earn trust and credibility to ensure people will allow us to walk alongside them and support their self-organized change work. In the "complexity and chaos" work situation, every individual change agent within the system will act in a semiautonomous way to impact on the change outcome anyway. In this context, the power bases crucial for practitioners are: personal referent power—using it to increase our relationship traction; act as a container for the change team by using our expert and competence power to offer a safe space for them to experiment; using our political access to help people to build a sense of alliance and a network of hope to work in a collaborative way; doing favors for people by supporting them to succeed; and using our stature and credibility to pass change capability to people so they can continue to do their own change work. To accept that reliance on a dominant change expert power base will no longer work in the complex adaptive system context; hence, there is a need to rethink how to exercise influence in different ways as part of personal change work.

What will ground us will always be our primary sources of power—our expertise in applied behavioral science, our love for people, and our ability to observe how power dynamics work between different agents and subsystems. Our personal referent power, driven by value and calling from our deep self, will always keep us strong and credible.

Finally, in the continuously changing world of work, our job is to continue to deploy our power bases and power strategies to facilitate our clients to achieve their change work and help them to experiment with ways to deliver change marked by positive use of power within an ethical base. That is the dual goal OD practitioners always ambitiously aim for.

Discussion Questions

1. Do you have a clear idea of what your power bases are—operating either as an internal or an external OD practitioner? Name them.

2. How deliberate have you been in channeling your power bases into power strategies to accomplish what you set out to do for the client system? Share a story.

3. In your diagnostic work, how often do you diagnose the power terrain of the client system? Once you have the data, what do you use them for in your change work?

4. As an interventionist, how conscious and intentional have you been in designing interventions that will minimize the power differential and encouraging cross-rank and cross-border collaboration? Recall cases so you can teach others.

5. On a continuum of 0 to 10, where 0 means you never deliberately use power and politics to support change work and 10 means you deliberately use power and politics all the time in change work, where would you position yourself? What action steps would you take to climb a notch or two on the continuum?

6. If you gave a short introductory workshop for OD novices on power and politics, what key points would you include in your workshop outline?

Resources

"As a Leader, Political Savvy Is NOT About Being Political," by Robert Denker: www .rdpusa.com/political-savvy-not-about-being-political

"Women and Political Savvy: How to Build and Embrace a Fundamental Leadership Skill." A Whitepaper by W. Gentry and J. L. Brittain: www.ccl.org/leadership/pdf/ research/WomenPoliticalSavvy.pdf

Mind Tools, French and Raven's Five Forms of Power: Understanding Where Power Comes from in the Workplace: www.mindtools.com/pages/article/newLDR_56.htm

"Power: How to Get It, Use It and Keep It," by Jeffrey Pfeffer: www.youtube.com/watch? v = jk4m-S73Ijc

References

Beer, M. 1980. *Organization Change and Development: A Systems View.* Santa Monica, CA: Goodyear.

Brooks, I. 2008. *Organizational Behaviour: Individuals, Groups and Organization.* 4th ed. Harlow, England: Financial Times/Prentice Hall.

Burke, W. 1982. *Organization Development: Principles and Practice.* Boston, MA: Little Brown.

Emerson, R. 1962. "Power Dependence Relations." *American Sociological Review* 27: 31–40.

French, J., and B. Raven. 1959. "The Bases of Social Power. In *Studies in Social Power*, edited by D. Cartwright, 160–167. Ann Arbor, MI: University of Michigan.

French, W., and C. Bell. 1999. *Organization Development: Behavioral Science Interventions for Organization Improvement.* 6th ed. Englewood Cliffs, NJ: Prentice Hall.

Greiner, L., and V. Schein. 1988. "A Revisionist Looks at Power and OD." *The Industrial-Organizational Psychologist* 25 (2): 59–61.

Mintzberg, H. 1983. *Power In and Around Organizations.* Englewood Cliffs, NJ: Prentice Hall.

Pfeffer, J. 1992. *Managing with Power: Politics and Influence in Organizations.* Boston: Harvard Business School Press.

Watson, T. 2011. *Sociology, Work, and Organization.* 6th ed. Abingdon, UK and New York: Routledge.

CHAPTER THIRTY

Beyond Social Networks

The Über Connection

Karen Stephenson

A conventional organizational classification schema should be expanded to include heterarchy, in addition to networks (Powell 1990), markets, and hierarchy (Williamson 1976). Heterarchy is a precise amalgamation of networks and hierarchies (Stephenson 2009). This organizational structure challenges more traditional forms of governance and organizational change and therefore presents an opportunity for organization development (OD) research in the twenty-first century.

We are on the cusp of a tipping point in twenty-first-century governance. With the addition of network science in OD and the general, albeit young, practice of social network analysis, academics are researching and recording the successes and failures of singular hierarchical governance in diverse cultures in global society. Social network analysis is best defined as the practice of mapping and measuring a network of social relationships. A network is depicted as a set of nodes, representing individual actors, and edges, representing the relationships between the individuals and usually drawn as lines connecting the nodes to each other. A network diagram can represent friendship, kinship, market relations, and organizational behavior.

Singular hierarchical governance, meaning a chain of command, worked well when the world was large and flat. That was before the advent of the digital domain that has made our world small and über connected (meaning superiorly connected and derived from Nietzsche's 1883 coinage of the term "Übermensch" to describe a higher state of man). It is suggested that this digital landscape will rival anything the Serengeti plains offered our hominid ancestors. In fact, we need not look back millennia but only 100 years to read Durkheim's vision of the world as a vast interconnected network of institutions (Durkheim 1933). He was correct. Organizations have morphed beyond singular entities into vast networks or conglomerates. Networks of organizations—or so-called heterarchies (McCulloch 1945)—come with an innovative form of governance. Capitalizing on this organizational structure may require a rethinking of governance models and institutional change in future OD research.

Heterarchy is an organizational structure comprising a network that links three or more different organizations (hierarchies) to each other, where no single organization is privileged over the other (Stephenson 2014). Networked together, these hierarchies share in the collective governance of the whole to achieve a greater good that no single organization could achieve on its own. This requires participating organizations to suppress their competitive drive in lieu of a collaborative ethos that benefits the whole network (Coase 1937). We know something about larger heterarchies because of their spectacular failures. For example, the 2010 Deepwater Horizon oil spill was a man-made collision of special interests, which resulted in a natural disaster of epic proportions. Specifically, multiple organizations such as Halliburton, British Petroleum, and several insurers were locked in contractual relationships when an explosion struck and eleven lives were lost. In a maelstrom of publicly abdicating responsibility, organizations passed the blame while the deep sea rig bled oil into the Gulf of Mexico destroying marine and wildlife habitats, and fishing and tourism industries in what was to become the largest oil spill in the history of the petroleum industry.

Heterarchies are not dysfunctional by nature; they *become* dysfunctional when a leader of a single hierarchy naively privileges his or her own interests over the whole. Said differently, leaders mistakenly assume that their special interests are the only things that matter. This is largely due to how leaders learn their tradecraft by practicing as serial CEOs or directors of singular hierarchies. Alternatively, they may have been educated in business schools that are grounded in nineteenth-century norms of leadership. Either way, leaders are generally unprepared to manage the social networks embedded in heterarchies.

SEGMENTARY SYSTEMS

Heterarchies require much more than a coalition of the willing; they demand a well-designed and coordinated network to ensure the alignment of tasks across multiple and (at times) competing organizations. Not recognizing the primacy of this network structure in heterarchies is precisely why the most well intentioned leader will be derailed by segmentary politics. For example, teams or departments are created not from the ground up, but from subunits of existing segments, mimicking cellular division. As smaller "chiefdoms" proliferate, they compete against one another, calling a truce only when a larger chiefdom threatens their mutual existence (Sahlins 1961). For example, consider a government division where one team jockeys for position with another, one department attacks another to protect its budget, and the overarching division as a whole fights other divisions to defend its turf. In these systems there is no internal structure or infrastructure to join up the system as whole; it is simply a collection of hierarchies or vertically "integrated" silos. As such, segmentary systems are never more (and often much less) than the sum of their parts, calculating power by comparing and contrasting their stock, status or budgets with other segments. If push comes to shove, they will cannibalize other parts of the organization in order to preserve their part (Douglas 1986). This ruthless survival tableau describes segmentary politics. If leaders could step back and see the whole network of interacting organizations instead of only their portion, then no one would have to die, pay amends, or bear any of the blame.

An example of segmentary politics in health care happened in 2014, when the U.S. military health care system experienced an alarmingly high number of "never events" (fatalities which are potentially preventable). The system is organized as a coalition of the willing and comprised of four major players: Army, Navy, Air Force, and the Department of Defense (DoD). When certain "never events" were revealed in a *New York Times* exposé, each leader of the member hierarchy blamed the others, when in fact, forensic analysis revealed that refusal to share patient data across the heterarchy is what led to the fatalities. As a former Army policy officer said, "Why should the Army safety system want to play with DoD? Because then I have less control over my data, less control over my *kingdom* (emphasis mine), and potentially DoD is going to tell me what to do" (LaFraniere and Lehren 2014, 32). His words were taken straight from a page in the playbook of segmentary politics (Sahlins 1963).

Heterarchies are an entirely different species altogether. Member hierarchies within the heterarchy will suppress the killer instinct in lieu of collaboration with others because they understand that if the higher objective is achieved, then they all stand to benefit, and not at the cost of a peer. By leveraging crosscutting collaboration to solve crosscutting problems, greater systemic benefits can be achieved. An example of a successful health care heterarchy is summarized in Sobczak (2013). Wisconsin hospital administrators recognized that "coalitions of the willing" in managing readmissions would break down once collaboration clashed with the individual hierarchical chains of command in participating organizations. So they designed a sustainable heterarchy by (1) rewriting policy to account for institutional integration and collaboration, (2) designing the collaborative network that would sustain the heterarchical structure, and (3) building in individual incentives specifically targeting lateral collaborative behaviors that were a regular part of individual performance measures. Space constraints prohibit further elaboration of case studies, but the reader is referred to the reference material for additional supporting examples (Stephenson 2008).

SUMMARY

Twenty-first-century organizational governance must address a structural "deficit' in theory and practice that only heterarchy can fill (Stephenson 2011). Blueprints of the industrial complex—conventional hierarchical governance— are still needed and well researched. But, there is a new class of blueprint that is required and addresses the social networks *between* organizations, and not just at the board level, but at *all* levels. Heterarchical governance is deeply rooted in social network theory and practice. I suggest it may require a broadening of what problems we choose to research in OD going forward.

Discussion Questions

1. Network connections are generally trust-based; hierarchical connections are generally authority-based. How would you use this framework to construct a research design for the study of heterarchies?

2. Can you identify historical geopolitical conflicts and deconstruct their outcome in terms of heterarchical governance or the lack thereof?

3. What industries are most likely to organize themselves as heterarchies and why?

4. Have you observed heterarchical structure in your own work or research? If so, can you describe specific examples of the management or mismanagement of heterarchy?

5. How can the concept of heterarchy provide insight and new directions for OD practitioners?

Resources

For a practical case study of organizational heterarchy applied to hospital readmissions, read "Wisconsin Hospitals Tackle Readmissions with Inside/Outside, Macro/Micro Strategy" by Stephanie Sobczak: www.wha.org/pdf/Readmissions0614Sobczak.pdf

"Social Network Analysis on Unique Characteristics of Organizational Heterarchies" by Karen Stephenson: http://web.archive.org/web/20130729204859id_/http://itc.conversationsnetwork.org/shows/detail1080.html

References

Coase, R. 1937. "The Nature of the Firm." *Economica* 4 (16): 386–405

Douglas, M. 1986. *How Institutions Think.* New York: Syracuse University Press.

Durkheim, E. 1933. *The Division of Labor in Society.* New York: The Free Press.

LaFraniere, S., and A. Lehren. 2014. "In Military Care: Pattern of Errors but Not Scrutiny." *New York Times*, June 28, 32.

McCulloch, W. 1945. "A Heterarchy of Values Determined by the Topology of Nervous Nets." *Bulletin of Mathematical Biophysics* 7 (2): 89–93.

Powell, W. 1990. "Neither Market nor Hierarchy: Network Forms of Organization." *Organizational Behavior* 12: 295–336.

Sahlins, M. 1961. "The Segmentary Lineage: An Organization for Predatory Expansion." *American Anthropologist* 63: 322–345.

Sahlins, M. 1963. "Poor Man, Rich Man, Big Man, Chief: Political Types in Melanesia and Polynesia." *Comparative Studies in Society and History* 5 (3): 285–303.

Sobczak, S. 2013. "Wisconsin Hospitals Tackle Readmissions with Inside/Outside, Macro/Micro Strategy." Readmission News, Health Policy Publishing LLC. www.wha.org/pdf/Readmissions0614Sobczak.pdf.

Stephenson, K. 2008. "Rethinking Governance: Conceptualizing Networks and Their Implications for New Mechanisms of Governance Based on Reciprocity." In *The Handbook of Knowledge-Based Policing: Current Conceptions and Future Directions*, edited by T. Williamson, 323–340. San Francisco: John Wiley & Sons.

Stephenson, K. 2009. "Neither Hierarchy nor Network: An Argument for Heterarchy." *People and Strategy* 31: 4–13.

Stephenson, K. 2011. "From Tiananmen to Tahrir: Knowing One's Place in the 21st Century." *Organizational Dynamics* 40 (4): 281–291.

Stephenson, K. 2014. "Essay: Hierarchy and Heterarchy." *ESB Dossier Ecosystemen* 99: 72–77.

Williamson, O. 1976. *Markets and Hierarchies.* New York: The Free Press.

PART FIVE

THE FUTURE OF ORGANIZATION DEVELOPMENT: EMBRACING TRANSFORMATION AND NEW DIRECTIONS FOR CHANGE

CHAPTER THIRTY-ONE

The Dialogic Organization Development Approach to Transformation and Change

Gervase R. Bushe and Robert J. Marshak

I n the past 30 years, the postmodern orientation in the social sciences, and the
discoveries in nonlinear and complexity natural sciences, have been influential in altering ideas about change and change practices. These ideas and
change practices have led to a variety of methods (see Table 31.1) that devi-
ate from key tenets of the diagnostic forms of organization development (OD)
created during the 1960s and 1970s. We have labeled these ideas and practices
Dialogic OD (Bushe and Marshak 2009) and have been studying their common
philosophical basis, and how they actually create change in practice (Bushe
and Marshak 2014a). Overall, we've concluded that simply having "good dialogues" is not enough to create change, but that Dialogic OD approaches can
help leaders and organizations meet adaptive challenges (Heifetz 1998) and
create transformational change (Bushe and Marshak 2015a). In this chapter,
we identify eight key premises of a Dialogic OD mindset and contrast these
with a *Diagnostic OD Mindset*. We also identify the three core change processes
that, whether practitioners are aware of it or not, are the source of change in
Dialogic OD efforts. Based on our research we believe that Dialogic OD practices are now widely used, but under a variety of names and without a clear
understanding of their shared premises nor their similarities and differences
with foundational OD. Furthermore, dialogic methods seem to be especially
effective when dealing with two types of contemporary issues. One is when
the prevailing ways of thinking, talking about, and addressing organizational

Table 31.1. Examples of Dialogic OD Methods

Appreciative Inquiry (Cooperrider)	Preferred Futuring (Lippitt)
Art of Convening (Neal and Neal)	REAL model (Wasserman and Gallegos)
Art of Hosting (artofhosting.org)	Real Time Strategic Change (Jacobs)
Charrettes (Lennertz)	Re-Description (Storch)
Community Learning (Fulton)	Reflexive Inquiry (Oliver)
Complex Responsive Processes of Relating (Shaw)	Search Conference (Emery and Emery)
	Six Conversations (Block)
Conference Model (Axelrod)	SOAR (Stavros)
Coordinated Management of Meaning (Pearce & Cronen)	Social Labs (Hassan)
	Solution Focused Dialogue (Jackson and McKergow)
Cycle of Resolution (Levine)	
Dynamic Facilitation (Rough)	Sustained Dialogue (Saunders)
Engaging Emergence (Holman)	Syntegration (Beer)
Future Search (Weisbord)	Systemic Sustainability (Amodeo and Cox)
Intergroup Dialogue (Nagada, Gurin)	
Moments of Impact (Ertel & Solomon)	Talking Stick (preindustrial)
Narrative Mediation (Winslade and Monk)	Technology of Participation (Spencer)
Open Space Technology (Owen)	Theory U (Scharmer)
Organizational Learning Conversations (Bushe)	Visual Explorer (Palus and Horth)
	Whole Scale Change (Dannemiller)
Participative Design (M. Emery)	Work Out (Ashkenas)
PeerSpirit Circles (Baldwin)	World Café (Brown and Issacs)
Polarity Management (Johnson)	

From: G. R. Bushe and R. J. Marshak, "Introduction to the Dialogic Organization Development Mindset," in *Dialogic Organization Development: The Theory and Practice of Transformational Change*, edited by G. R Bushe and R. J. Marshak (Oakland, CA: Berrett-Koehler, 2015).

dilemmas traps an organization and its leaders in repetitive but futile responses. The other is when facing wicked problems, paradoxical issues, and adaptive challenges, where there is little agreement about what's happening and where there are no known solutions or remedies available to address the situation. Dialogic approaches work by fostering generativity to develop new possibilities rather than problem-solving, altering the prevailing narratives and stories that limit new thinking, and working with the self-organizing, emergent properties of complex systems. Dialogic OD offers a viable alternative to create a vision, plan a path to it, and implement through action teams the practice of organizational change, and is better able to meet some of the challenging complexities of twenty-first-century organizing.

EIGHT KEY PREMISES OF DIALOGIC ORGANIZATION DEVELOPMENT

Dialogic OD is still an evolving convergence of newer premises, principles, and resulting practices that lead practitioners to approach situations with a different way of thinking and acting. We hope to speed up this convergence by giving it its own name and identity—Dialogic OD—and inviting OD practitioners into a conversation about its underlying premises and practices, both now and going forward.

Based on our review of the range of methods listed in Table 31.1 and an in-depth analysis of six major theories of Dialogic OD practice (Bushe and Marshak 2014b; 2015b), we have identified eight key premises that we believe shape the Dialogic OD Mindset, a set of fundamental beliefs about organizations and change that differ in important ways from the thinking found in Diagnostic OD.

1. *Reality and relationships are socially constructed.* The Dialogic OD Mindset believes that organizations are socially constructed realities. It is how we socially define and describe objective and subjective "facts" that influence what people think and do. In every conversation, this reality is being created, maintained, and/or changed. Furthermore, there is no single objective social reality. Instead, there are many different "truths" about any organization, some dominant and some peripheral.

2. *Organizations are meaning-making systems.* The Dialogic OD Mindset thinks of organizations not just as open systems interacting with an environment, but as dialogic systems in which people are continuously sense-making and meaning-making, individually and in groups. What happens in organizations is influenced more by how people interact and make meaning than how presumably objective external factors and forces impact the system.

3. *Language, broadly defined, matters.* The Dialogic OD Mindset believes that words (and other forms of communication) do more than convey information, they create meaning. Thinking is powerfully influenced by written and verbal communications and the underlying narratives, stories, and metaphors people use when engaging with each other. Change is created and sustained by changing what words mean and by changing the words, stories, and narratives that are used in groups and organizations.

4. *Creating change requires changing conversations.* The social construction of reality occurs through the conversations people have, everyday.

Change requires changing the conversations that normally take place. This can occur from changing who is in conversation with whom (e.g., increasing diversity, including marginalized voices), what is being talked about, how those conversations take place, increasing conversational skills, and by asking what is being created from the content and process of current conversations.

5. *Groups and organizations are inherently self-organizing.* The Dialogic OD Mindset believes that organizations are self-organizing, emergent systems where social reality is being constructed every day. The Dialogic OD Mindset finds it more useful to think of organizations as continuous flows, rather than stable entities, where different processes, structures, and ideas vary in how quickly they are changing. OD practitioners may nudge, accelerate, deflect, punctuate, or disrupt these normal processes, but they do not unfreeze and refreeze them. Stakeholders who care about the state of the system, who are able to develop rich enough information networks, and are not constrained by any one group's power, will frequently find ways to respond to challenges that are too complex for leaders to successfully address through planning and controlling approaches. Instead, the leader's job in Dialogic OD approaches is to create spaces where useful changes can emerge, and then support and amplify those changes.

6. *Increase differentiation in participative inquiry and engagement before seeking coherence.* In foundational OD, organizational system members are involved at various times in diagnosing themselves and making action choices to address identified issues. The Dialogic OD Mindset reflects a much broader conception of engagement that is based on methods of inquiry intended to discover new and transformational possibilities. The resulting processes of participative inquiry (rather than diagnosis), engagement, and reflection are designed to: (a) maximize diversity, (b) encourage stakeholders to voice their unique perspectives, concerns, and aspirations, and (c) surface the variety of perspectives and motivations in the system, without privileging anyone, before seeking new convergences and coherence.

7. *Transformational change is more emergent than planned.* Transformational change cannot be planned toward some predetermined future state. Rather, transformation requires holding an intention while moving into the unknown. Disrupting current patterns in a way that engages people in uncovering collective intentions and shared motivations is required. As a result, change processes are more opportunistic and heterarchichal, where change can and does come from anywhere in the organization, more than planned, hierarchical, and top-down.

8. *Consultants are a part of the process, not apart from the process.* OD practitioners cannot stand outside the social construction of reality, acting as
independent facilitators of social interaction. Their mere presence is part
of the discursive context that influences the meaning making taking place.
OD practitioners need to be aware of their own immersion in the organization and reflexively consider what meanings they are creating and what
narratives their actions are privileging and marginalizing.

As shown in Figure 31.1, these premises lead to different ways of thinking about the basic building blocks of organization transformation and change,
even as practitioners may on the surface seem to engage in similar steps as
in Diagnostic OD. For example, one can use AI methods diagnostically: collect and analyze stories during Discovery, identify preferred outcomes during
Dream, propose alternative actions during Design, and choose and implement
changes during Destiny. Yet when decisions and actions follow from a Dialogic
OD Mindset, the choices made and actions taken will be very different (Bushe
2012). As Shaw (2002) notes in discussing foundational OD, "Above all I want
to propose that if organizing is understood essentially as a conversational process, an inescapably self-organizing process of participating in the spontaneous

Diagnostic OD		Dialogic OD
	Ontology	
Positivism Objective Reality		Interpretive, Constructionist Social Reality
	Organizations are	
Open Systems		Dialogic Networks
	Emphasis on	
Behavior and Results		Discourse and Generativity
	Change is	
Planned Episodic More Developmental		Emergent Continuous and Iterative More Transformational
	Consultants	
Stay Apart at the Margins Partner with		Are Immersed with Part of
	Change processes	
Hierarchical Start at Top, Work Down		Heterarchical Start Anywhere, Spread Out

Figure 31.1. Contrasting Polar Ideal Types: Diagnostic and Dialogic Mindsets

Source: From G. R. Bushe and R. J. Marshak, "The Dialogic Mindset in Organization Development,"
Research in Organizational Change and Development 22 (2014): 86.

emergence of continuity and change, then we need a rather different way of thinking about any kind of organizational practice that focuses on change" (11).

THE CORE PROCESSES OF TRANSFORMATIONAL CHANGE IN DIALOGIC ORGANIZATION DEVELOPMENT

Simply having good "dialogues," creating spaces where people are willing and able to speak their minds and listen carefully to one another, is not sufficient for transformational change to occur. We propose that three underlying change processes, singly or in combination, are essential to the successful use of any of the Dialogic OD methods listed in Table 31.1 (Bushe and Marshak 2015a). Said another way, we believe that failures of any Dialogic OD method to stimulate transformational change is a result of none of the following three transformational processes having happened.

Transformational Process 1: Emergence

Transformational Process 1 is when a disruption in the ongoing social construction of reality is stimulated or engaged in a way that leads to a more complex reorganization. This disruption occurs when the previous order or pattern of social relations falls apart, and there is little chance of going back to the way things were. Disruptions can be planned or unplanned, and the group or organization may be able to self-organize around them without much conscious leadership. From a Dialogic OD perspective, however, transformation is unlikely to take place without disruption of the "established" meaning-making processes (Holman 2015; Stacey 2005; 2015).

A variety of Dialogic OD methods can be used to create containers for productive conversations to take place that support reorganizing at higher levels of complexity despite the anxiety that disruptive endings can create. However, once disrupted, it is impossible to plan or control what might then happen; the options range from complete dissolution to reorganization at a higher level of complexity (Prigogine and Stengers 1984). Practitioners operating from a dialogic Mindset tend to encourage leaders to confront and push the system close to chaos while expanding and enriching the networks among stakeholders, rather than pursuing diagnostically induced planned change from a current to a desired future state. It is at the close to chaos boundary that self-organizing changes can emerge (Kauffman 1995; Pascale, Milleman, and Gioja 2001). Dialogic OD practitioners assume that fully engaging organizational members in such self-organization will lead to more impactful changes, more quickly, than attempts to plan and implement prescribed changes.

Transformational Process 2: Narrative

Transformational Process 2 is when there is a change to one or more core narratives. Core narratives are the storylines people use to explain and bring coherence to their organizational lives by making sense of ongoing "facts" and events. Changing what people think or their social agreements—for example, about the role of women in organizations, or about hierarchical structures, or even about how change happens in organizations—requires changing the common, prevailing storylines endorsed by those presently and/or historically in power (Marshak and Grant 2008). Stories are a way of managing change, particularly culture change, and transformational change is often constituted by transformations in the narratives that participants author (e.g., Brown and Humphreys 2003; Buchanan and Dawson 2007). A variety of the methods listed in Table 31.1 can be used as a conscious intervention into the narratives and story-making processes of an organization (Storch 2015; Swart 2015).

Transformational Process 3: Generativity

The third transformation process happens when a generative image is introduced or surfaces that provides new and compelling alternatives for thinking and acting. A generative image is one or more words, pictures, or other symbols that provide new ways of thinking about social and organizational reality. They, in effect, allow people to imagine alternative decisions and actions that could not be imagined before the generative image surfaced. "Sustainable development" is one iconic example of a generative image. Even though it cannot be defined (one quality of truly generative images) it continues to spin off innovations more than 25 years after it was first coined. A second property of generative images is that they are compelling; people want to act on the new opportunities the generative image evokes. A variety of the methods listed in Table 31.1 are often supported by using generative images as the initiating themes or questions for inquiry (Bushe 2013b) or by evoking new generative images in the process of dialogue and inquiry (Storch and Ziethen 2013). Bushe's research has found that generative images are central to successful applications of AI (Bushe 1998, 2010, 2013a; Bushe and Kassam 2005), and we propose that they are also central to Dialogic OD approaches more broadly defined (Bushe and Storch 2015).

WHAT DO DIALOGIC ORGANIZATION DEVELOPMENT PRACTITIONERS DO?

Dialogic OD practice differs along a continuum from episodic change practices to continuous change practices (Bushe and Marshak 2014a). An episodic change practice focuses on one or more events intended to help a group or organization transform from one semistable state to another. A continuous change practice is based on a stream of ongoing interactions intended to make small alterations to the ongoing patterns of interaction or self-organization that, over time, accumulate into a transformed state of being.

Those sponsoring Dialogic OD usually do not know exactly what changes are needed, wanted, or how to achieve them. The complexity of the issues and dynamics that leaders and organizations face in the twenty-first-century world of work means that application of "best practices" or preexisting knowledge to identify and then implement change is unlikely to be successful. This has been described by Heifetz (1998) as the difference between technical problems and adaptive challenges, and by Snowden and Boone (2007) as the difference between complicated and complex decision situations. Dialogic OD practitioners believe that dialogic processes are the most effective way to deal with adaptive, complex challenges. During the entry process, the Dialogic OD practitioner will work with the sponsors to identify, in general, their intentions and the range of potentially affected stakeholders who need to be engaged in the Dialogic OD process. They may or may not decide it is important to create a "planning" or "hosting" group that in some way represents those stakeholders to help architect the change effort. This is usually more important when the change involves a complex issue, for example: transportation in the region, where there's a need to engage a large or very large group of stakeholders and when operating from a more episodic change mindset. It's critical at this stage for the OD practitioner and the sponsor to agree on the desired directions of the change effort and for the sponsor to be able and willing to make the necessary resources, particularly time, money, and personal commitment, available for the project.

Some Dialogic OD methods involve participants in becoming explicitly aware of the stories, narratives, and patterns of discourse they are embedded in while others do not. In either case, all assume that personal and/or organizational change will require a change in those narratives. Some focus primarily on changing the discourse while others focus on both discourse and the changes in decisions and action that emerge from it. Like Diagnostic OD, Dialogic OD involves both structured interventions (like action research) and experiential interventions (like process consultation). In the following we briefly summarize both types of Dialogic OD practice.

Structured Dialogic Organization Development

Structured Dialogic OD involves one or more events. These events are designed so that relationships and communications are enhanced to enable more creativity and engagement. Practitioners create a "container" (Corrigan 2015) within which new conversations can take place, new relationships forged, and ideas for change emerge. Much of the difference in Dialogic OD methods concerns ways of orchestrating (rather than facilitating) what happens in these containers. In all cases, when successful, participants make personal, voluntary commitments to new behaviors and projects. An emergent or improvisational, as opposed to a planned implementation, approach to the action phase is generally used. Events are intended to generate and support self-organizing groups with ideas for change to take action, without knowing which of these will actually be successful. Practitioners work with leaders to watch and learn, cultivate the ideas that lead the organization in the desired direction, amplify their impact, and embed them into the organization's fabric (Roehrig, Schwendenwein, and Bushe 2015).

Unstructured Dialogic Organization Development

We refer to less-structured approaches to Dialogic OD as "dialogic process consultation." In these approaches, a practitioner will bring a dialogic mindset to one-on-one and small-group interactions. In some approaches to dialogic process consultation, the OD practitioner helps individuals become aware of and take more control over the prevailing images, metaphors, and narratives that are shaping how people think and act (Marshak 2013). They may focus attention to the ways in which conversations that differ from the prevailing wisdom are restricted or encouraged, for example the degree to which a diversity of participants and perspectives are included or excluded in key organizational decisions. They may invite consideration of processes of generativity; especially how to foster new images that will influence the ongoing construction and reconstruction of social reality (Storch and Ziethen 2013).

The most provocative approaches to dialogic process consultation are based on concepts of complexity, meaning making, emergence, and self-organization. These dialogic process activities assume relationships and organizations are continuously recreating themselves through the ongoing conversations that occur at all levels and parts of an organization (Shaw 2002; Stacey 2015). Any shifts in the nature of these conversations, for example, their participants, emphases, or patterns, will encourage incremental shifts that lead groups to self-organize in new and different ways without the need to bring anything to awareness. There is no use of specially structured events to shift from a current state to a more desired future state (Goppelt and Ray 2015; Ray and Goppelt 2013). Instead the OD practitioner enters into a team or organization that is assumed to be in the continuous process of becoming, participates fully in the ongoing life of the system while seeking to draw attention to, or modify, any ongoing dialogic patterns that may be blocking or limiting the organization's ability to evolve, and/or by accentuating differences that might encourage new patterns to emerge.

SUMMARY

Dialogic and Diagnostic OD are not two different things—they are different ways of thinking. We believe they both exist, more or less, in the mental maps of individual OD practitioners. Like yin and yang, they can combine in a myriad of ways to affect an OD practitioner's choices and actions. We advocate avoiding either/or arguments and, instead, inquiry into the opportunities for change each mindset provides separately and in combination.

It is unclear to us, at this time, whether dialogic transformational change requires all or most all of the eight premises, and more than one of the three core transformational processes to be successful. To us and other Dialogic OD practitioners, they do seem related, either explicitly or implicitly. It is difficult to imagine, for example, a change in a core narrative that did not also involve a disruption to the prevailing social construction of reality. But changes in core narratives do occur over time, which do not necessarily involve an abrupt disruption. In a world of constant change, however, "disruption" is mainly a matter of temporal perspective. Our current proposition is that transformational change from Dialogic OD results from some combination of the three change processes as supported by the eight key premises. Hopefully, Dialogic OD, and the narrative advanced in this chapter, serves as a generative image evoking new insights into the potential for OD practices to transform organizations and realize more effective organizing.

Discussion Questions

1. What aspects of the Dialogic Mindset are consistent with or contrast with your current ways of thinking about organizations and change?

2. When might it be more, or less, appropriate to use Dialogic OD methods? Or, perhaps to combine Dialogic with Diagnostic OD approaches?

3. Based on reading this chapter, what ideas would you like to learn more about? How might you do that?

Resources

Go to www.dialogicod.net for articles, resources, and a list of readings for all the approaches presented in Table 31.1. This website includes links to videos, presentations, and useful information on Dialogic OD.

References

Brown, A. D., and M. Humphreys. 2003. "Epic and Tragic Tales: Making Sense of Change." *Journal of Applied Behavioral Science* 39 (2): 121–144.

Buchanan, D., and P. Dawson. 2007. "Discourse and Audience: Organizational Change as Multi-Story Process." *Journal of Management Studies* 44 (5): 669–686.

Bushe, G. R. 1998. "Appreciative Inquiry in Teams." *Organization Development Journal* 16 (3): 41–50.

Bushe, G. R. 2010. "A Comparative Case Study of Appreciative Inquiries in One Organization: Implications for Practice." *Review of Research and Social Intervention* 29: 7–24.

Bushe, G. R. 2012. "Appreciative Inquiry: Theory and Critique." In *The Routledge Companion to Organizational Change*, edited by D. Boje, B. Burnes, and J. Hassard, 87–103. Oxford, UK: Routledge.

Bushe, G. R. 2013a. "Generative Process, Generative Outcome: The Transformational Potential of Appreciative Inquiry." In *Organizational Generativity: Advances in Appreciative Inquiry*, vol. 4, edited by D. L. Cooperrider, D. P. Zandee, L. Godwin, M. Avital, and B. Boland, 89–122. Bingley, UK: Emerald Press.

Bushe, G. R. 2013b. "Dialogic OD: A Theory of Practice." *OD Practitioner* 45 (1): 10–16.

Bushe, G. R., and A. Kassam. 2005. "When Is Appreciative Inquiry Transformational? A Meta-Case Analysis." *Journal of Applied Behavioral Science* 41 (2): 161–181.

Bushe, G. R., and R. J. Marshak. 2009. "Revisioning Organization Development: Diagnostic and Dialogic Premises and Patterns of Practice." *Journal of Applied Behavioral Science* 45 (3): 348–368.

Bushe, G. R., and R. J. Marshak. 2014a. "Dialogic Organization Development." In *The NTL Handbook of Organization Development and Change*, 2nd ed., edited by B. B. Jones and M. Brazzel, 193–211. San Francisco: John Wiley & Sons.

Bushe, G. R., and R. J. Marshak. 2014b. "The Dialogic Mindset in Organization Development." *Research in Organizational Change and Development* 22: 55–97.

Bushe, G. R., and R. J. Marshak, eds. 2015a. *Dialogic Organization Development: The Theory and Practice of Transformational Change*. Oakland, CA: Berrett-Koehler.

Bushe, G. R., and R. J. Marshak. 2015b. "Introduction to the Dialogic Organization Development Mindset." In *Dialogic Organization Development*, edited by G. R. Bushe and R. J. Marshak, 11–32. Oakland, CA: Berrett-Koehler.

Bushe, G. R., and J. Storch. 2015. "Generative Image: Sourcing Novelty." In *Dialogic Organization Development*, edited by G. R. Bushe and R. J. Marshak, 101–122. Oakland, CA: Berrett-Koehler.

Corrigan, C. 2015. "Hosting and Holding Containers." In *Dialogic Organization Development*, edited by G. R. Bushe and R. J. Marshak, 291–304. Oakland, CA: Berrett-Koehler.

Goppelt, J., and K. W. Ray. 2015. "Dialogic Process Consultation: Working Live." In *Dialogic Organization Development*, edited by G. R. Bushe and R. J. Marshak, 371–399. Oakland, CA: Berrett-Koehler.

Heifetz, R. 1998. *Leadership Without Easy Answers*. Cambridge, MA: Harvard.

Holman, P. 2015. "Complexity, Self-Organization and Emergence." In *Dialogic Organization Development*, edited by G. R. Bushe and R. J. Marshak, 123–149. Oakland, CA: Berrett-Koehler.

Kauffman, S. 1995. *At Home in the Universe: The Search for the Laws of Self-Organization and Complexity*. New York: Oxford University Press.

Marshak, R. J. 2013. "Leveraging Language for Change." *OD Practitioner* 45 (2): 49–55.

Marshak, R. J., and D. Grant. 2008. "Organizational Discourse and New Organization Development Practices." *British Journal of Management* 19: S7–S19.

Pascale, R., M. Milleman, and L. Gioja. 2001. *Surfing the Edge of Chaos*. NY: Crown Business.

Prigogine, I., and I. Stengers. 1984. *Order Out of Chaos*. Boulder, CO: Shambhala.

Ray, K. W., and J. Goppelt. 2013. "From Special to Ordinary: Dialogic OD in Day-to-Day Complexity." *OD Practitioner* 45 (1): 41–46.

Roehrig, M., J. Schwendenwein, and G. R. Bushe. 2015. "Amplifying Change: A 3-Phase Approach to Model, Nurture and Embed Ideas for Change." In *Dialogic Organization Development*, edited by G. R. Bushe and R. J. Marshak, 325–348. Oakland, CA: Berrett-Koehler.

Shaw, P. 2002. *Changing Conversations in Organizations: A Complexity Approach to Change*. London, UK: Routledge.

Snowden, D. J., and M. E. Boone. 2007. "A Leader's Framework for Decision-Making." *Harvard Business Review* 85 (11): 69–76.

Stacey, R., ed. 2005. *Experiencing Emergence in Organizations*. London: Routledge.

Stacey, R. 2015. "Understanding Organizations as Complex Responsive Processes of Relating." In *Dialogic Organization Development*, edited by G. R. Bushe and R. J. Marshak, 151–175. Oakland, CA: Berrett-Koehler.

Storch, J. 2015. Enabling Change: The Skills of Dialogic OD. In *Dialogic Organization Development*, edited by G. R. Bushe and R. J. Marshak, 197–218. Oakland, CA: Berrett-Koehler.

Storch, J., and M. Ziethen. 2013. "Re-Description: A Source of Generativity in Dialogic Organization Development." *OD Practitioner* 45 (1): 25–29.

Swart, C. 2015. "Coaching from a Dialogic OD Paradigm." In *Dialogic Organization Development*, edited by G. R. Bushe and R. J. Marshak, 349–370. Oakland, CA: Berrett-Koehler.

CHAPTER THIRTY-TWO

The Future of Organization Development, Transformation, and Change

Allan H. Church, Amanda C. Shull, and W. Warner Burke

What is the future of organization development (OD)? What factors and trends are influencing and will influence the evolution of the field for the next 10 to 20 years? As scientist-practitioners, we intend to look to the data. One of the most fundamental principles and differentiators of OD is its emphasis on using data through action research as a catalyst for individual and large-scale change. Whether data are at the individual (micro), group (meso), or organization (macro) level, the basic premise is the same. Although the paradigm continues to evolve with the concept of dialogic OD in the prior chapter (e.g., Bushe and Marshak 2009), at its core, OD is about using data to (a) create a felt need for change through self-awareness and facilitated learning, (b) develop a collaborative diagnosis of the prevailing and underlying issues, and (c) determine and enact an intervention set with full organizational engagement intended to achieve a desired future state (Burke 2011; Shani and Coghlan 2014; Waclawski and Church 2002).

This chapter applies this same logic to the future of the field. Specifically, we will highlight five key themes which have both immediate and long-term implications for the science and practice of OD. These themes are based on several sources including data from a 2012 survey collected with over 400 OD practitioners (Shull, Church, and Burke 2013; 2014), and another study conducted in 2013 with the heads of talent management from 84 "top development" companies (Church and Rotolo 2013). The chapter concludes with discussion questions for further consideration.

THE FIVE EMERGING TRENDS

Listed below are five observations and trends for the field based on data and insights gleaned from various sources. These trends coupled with a review of emerging practice areas suggest that the field is once again experiencing significant growing pains. Influences occur at the cultural, systems, and individual levels (see Table 32.1).

Organization Development Values Are Here to Stay

As many researchers and practitioners have discussed since the origins of the field, OD is grounded in the normative and humanistic values of helping individuals in organizations develop, grow, and achieve their potential. While this emphasis is understandable given OD is rooted in the 1960s social context, over the years there has been considerable debate and consternation that the values were waning or had been lost in favor of organizational effectiveness and the bottom line. Data from practitioner studies in the 1990s supported this dichotomy and raised concerns that the future would see the end of the field.

More recently, data from both OD practitioners and heads of talent management in top development companies indicate this is not the case. In these studies, practitioners rate the importance of focusing their efforts on enhancing empowerment, welfare, and development at least equally, and sometimes ahead of, pure business outcomes. The vast majority of feedback and assessment tools in use today are targeted at individual development efforts. However, decision-making is becoming increasingly a second priority when talent management and succession planning goals are involved (Church 2013, 2014). Despite perceptions over the weakening of traditional values, the field of OD has settled nicely into owning the tension between an emphasis on helping people and improving performance. We would argue that the field has come to terms with and embraced its inherent conflict—even to the point that Worley (2014) has called for us to move on from the debate entirely.

Organization Development Practitioners Lack the Data Skills Needed for the Future

Just because our values are stable does not mean the field should stop evolving. As new concepts and areas of practice emerge, practitioners must continue to enhance their skills to stay relevant. One of the key areas we see trending in research and practice is the use of data. While the field has long been grounded in action-research and data-driven methods (e.g., Burke 2011; Waclawski and Church 2002), the game has changed. With the rise of talent management, individual assessments (e.g., psychological, cognitive, and 360-degree feedback),

Table 32.1. Sample Emerging Practice Areas Influencing the Future of OD

Practice Area	Emphasis
Diversity and Inclusion	• Valuing differences in background, orientation, cultures, styles, and preferences including a focus on culture and behavior change through measurement, training, and other interventions
	• Encouraging people to bring their whole selves to work to promote diverse thinking and perspectives
Sustainability	• Applying efforts to focus on the triple bottom line that includes: people, planet, and profit
	• Broader definition may include emphasis on designing self-monitoring, self-regulating, and self-sustaining systems, continuous improvement, and learning
Employee Engagement	• Measuring employee and manager behaviors and attitudes including satisfaction, pride, commitment, and discretionary effort, which have been empirically linked to organizational outcomes
	• Focusing on data-based insights and action-planning efforts targeting key drivers of attraction and retention, culture and behavior change, as well as individual and organizational performance
Talent Management	• Designing and implementing an integrated set of processes, programs, and cultural norms to attract, develop, deploy, and retain talent in order to achieve strategic business objectives
	• Differentiating on the "few" select populations including high-potentials, key talent segments, pivotal roles, and/or C-suite successors that are deemed most critical for the future success of the business, rather than broad-based development of the "many"
Individual Assessment	• Promoting individual growth and development through the use of data-based tools and feedback applications (e.g., 360s, personality, simulations, cognitive, judgment, values) for enhancing self-awareness
	• Making administrative decisions for hiring, performance management, team composition, or advancement through the use of validated criteria and measurement of psychological constructs, behaviors, and abilities
Coaching	• Enhancing self-awareness and creating behavior change through individualized development with a focus on building on strengths and/or addressing opportunities to support individual and organizational goals
	• Placing emphasis on areas such as leadership orientation, on-boarding, fix-it, executive presence, management skills, presentation style, nonverbal cures, process consultation, group dynamics, etc.

(continued)

Table 32.1. (*Continued*)

Practice Area	Emphasis
Big Data	• Integrating, analyzing, and telling a compelling story based on massive amounts of information that can be used to inform and advance strategic business decisions
	• Emphasizing four areas: volume, velocity, variety and veracity of data, all of which impact quality and validity of results; however, currently there are no values considerations being applied to Big Data applications

and particularly the implications of Big Data for the field (Church and Dutta 2013), OD professionals are becoming woefully ill-equipped to remain current. While some authors argue against the overreliance on measurement methods for driving change, research indicates that using these tools is increasing particularly at the most senior levels in the organization (Church and Rotolo 2013). Unfortunately, OD practitioners are just beginning to understand this trend, evidenced by a ranking of these practices of 30 among 64 possible interventions in the most recent practitioner survey by Shull et al. (2014). Further, Big Data is not even on the radar yet. An examination of various OD textbooks (e.g., Cummings and Worley 2015) yields a similar issue with no mention of these newer data methodologies.

While it was acceptable in the early days of OD to be facile with tools such as the Myers-Briggs Type Indicator and others for individual and team interventions, and these remain tools for leadership development and coaching (e.g., Burke and Noumair 2002; Church 2014), organizations have become increasingly sophisticated in their need for and use of empirically valid and behaviorally grounded information about their talent. If we ignore these areas and lack the skills to integrate data from multiple methodologies, we will continue to fall short of our full potential as change agents. It is time for OD professionals to up their game in data analytics and actionable insights.

The Organization Development Field Needs to Build a Differentiated Coaching Model

Coaching is hardly a new concept to the field of OD. Practitioners have been coaching their clients in some form since the inception of the field. However, the emphasis and playing field for individual and executive coaching today has changed dramatically. Hiring an executive coach is no longer an outgrowth of the process consultation model but now targets a wide range of goals such as coaching for individual development, on-boarding, "culture fit," leadership succession, executive presence, management skills, and health and stress management (Hernez-Broome and Boyce 2011). Coaches come in all shapes and sizes including formally trained I-O and counseling psychologists, certified coaching professionals, former athletes and retired executives, motivational speakers, and even school teachers. While coaching is on the rise as a practice area (as indicated by 47 percent of practitioners from the 2012 study), the field is so cluttered with models and methods it is difficult to differentiate an OD approach from others.

What is needed is a defined and articulated means for OD practitioners to offer something unique to the process. Given our strong humanistic values and core tool suite, this should not be that difficult, but it is desperately needed if OD is to have a lasting impact in organizations with this intervention. If we couple our observation with the one regarding data, particularly around assessment and development in a talent management and succession planning context (Church 2013, 2014), OD practitioners should define our unique niche going forward.

Organization Development Practice Appears to Be Moving Away from Large-Scale Change

One of the consequences of the shift to focusing on the individual in OD (e.g., an emphasis on individual feedback and coaching) is what appears to be a trend away from interventions targeting large-scale organizational change. Data from the 2012 OD practitioner survey indicate that interventions have declined considerably over the last 20 years since a prior survey of the field (as first reported by Church, Burke, and Van Eynde 1994). Similarly, while practitioners have written about the link between OD and other organizational change domains such as diversity and inclusion (e.g., Church, Rotolo, Shull, and Tuller 2014), and sustainability (e.g., Laszlo and Laszlo 2011), these types of boundary-spanning examples are not as common as they were in the 1960–1980s. Data from the 2012 study showed that culture change efforts focused on diversity and inclusion, global mindset, and sustainability, were not ranked particularly highly on the values or interventions lists, nor were these areas among the top most important. This trend is troubling.

While OD has always operated at multiple levels of intervention, one of the hallmarks historically has been a focus on large-scale change (e.g., Burke and Litwin 1992). If we lose this aspect of the field with an overemphasis on individual relationships, collaborative discovery, and learning, we risk becoming less relevant for long-term impact from a total systems perspective. This is even more important when we consider the potential future role and impact of Big Data on organizational processes, policies, and decisions, which exist by definition at the broadest and most complex levels of analysis.

Optimism in Organization Development Is High but Commitment in Organization Development Is Low

Overall, we were encouraged to note that 79 percent of respondents to the 2012 survey were optimistic about the future of OD despite some of the issues and challenges raised (Shull et al. 2014). The values remain strong and grounded in the dual purpose of helping employees grow while improving organization effectiveness, and practitioners are engaging in a variety of interventions. These are all signs the field is healthy and continuing to evolve. What may trouble practitioners are some of the other external indicators, namely professional membership and the perceived level of practitioner engagement in the field today. This seems paradoxical.

In the beginning, there were no formal programs in OD. Practitioners came from many other disciplines including social psychology, management science, organizational behavior, and clinical psychology (Burke 2014). Today, while we have many formal academic and professional programs and certification processes in place, OD professional groups appear to be stagnant while other professional organizations are growing. Why is this? Is it that belief in the field is high in principle but low in commitment and/or as an affiliation of practice?

One answer, which has its roots in past debates, may be the lack of a unified definition of the field and single governing professional body (Church 2001). Another may be that OD embraces the value of inclusion of practice so openly that it has diluted its core of everything but the values themselves (per above). However, this reflects some of the emerging practice trends cited earlier.

First, many organizations today have moved away from having formal OD functions. They instead have blended their subfunctions with more current and trendy content practice areas as talent management, organizational learning, leadership development, or culture and transformation. While this comingling of domains internally is not new, the segmentation and deep specialization externally in the HR realm is new and driving challenges in the profession. Specifically, although OD internally might be integrated with the talent management or organizational learning teams, the outcome is a targeting of types of *external participation* to build knowledge and networks versus identifying with the OD profession. Visible engagement with OD broadly is affected with practitioners attending conferences on more targeted topics such as coaching, performance management, or talent management instead. To combat this issue, our professional associations must seek feedback and become more nimble and adaptive to meet the needs of the field.

Second, OD may not be as appealing as a label as it once was, and that was questionable even in the early days of the field (Burke 1982). As many organizations move to follow influential thinking regarding HR as a strategic business partner (e.g., Boudreau 2010; Ulrich 1997), much of the classic OD work is being transferred to the HR generalist. Specifically, these models focus on the role of HR as stewards of the culture, externally oriented or "outside-in," and data-driven in their approach. The 2012 practitioner survey provides support for this trend. Based on a group of 50 HR professionals responding, 41 percent were using survey feedback, 34 percent were engaged in team building, 32 percent were focused on changing the culture, and 29 percent were doing leadership development. It's as if the HR community is transforming to be more effective OD practitioners than many of the traditionally trained OD people in the field today.

SUMMARY

A field is defined by its values, practices, vibrancy, and impact. When all four are strong and evolving in a positive direction, the field benefits and grows. Based on the data, we see evidence of positive growth, some signs of stall, and some potential declines as well across these four indicators. While OD values remain at the core of the profession, and we agree it is time to stop the debate, the practices and capabilities required of practitioners must continue to change to support the new realities.

The data indicate that practitioners must build skills and define their perspectives in the areas of coaching, talent management, and assessment, Big Data/analytics, global thinking, and diversity and inclusion. We also need to ensure a continued emphasis on large-scale systemic organizational change, and data or evidence-based methods for evaluating that change, to ensure long-term impact. Finally, we need to better bridge the gap between classic OD and the new and more relevant HR practice areas on which senior leaders are focused.

While we are not advocating for a change in the name or discipline of OD (that has been tried before with change management and others and was unsuccessful), practitioners should embrace the boundary-spanning and systems thinking tenets of the past. OD should be the focal point or hub to connect between other areas and disciplines such as I-O and consulting psychology, talent management, human resources, diversity and inclusion, learning, and other related areas. Although this idea has been advocated before (e.g., Church 2001), the supporting evidence for this recommendation is becoming increasingly clear. OD should remain at the center of the organizational change nexus and assist in integrating all the parts of the process together. Sounds like we should go back to our roots, doesn't it?

Finally, to drive our main point home regarding values, practices, and integration across disciplines, let us consider an analogy from the writings of James O'Toole (1995) regarding leadership. He is a strong critic of contingency and situational theories of leadership stating these theories suggest that people in positions of leadership can behave in any manner they may wish and justify their actions. These theories have a core set of values and ethics that never change. Total flexibility is the order of the day. O'Toole contends that effective leadership is based on a core set of beliefs and values that never change regardless of situation (torture is out of the question). Effective leaders can modify their behavior depending on context but these changes in behavior never violate nor contradict one's core values. Let it be so for the future of competent OD practitioners. The effective practice of OD should be to leverage a variety of interventions in their work (with sufficient knowledge and skill) to help organizations across a wide range of content domains while still holding true to basic core values of the field.

Variety in use does not contradict the core humanistic values of OD such as respect for individual differences, involving employees in decisions that directly affect them, and avoiding arbitrary uses of power. Nor should it overemphasize the importance of focusing on individual decision making and organizational performance. OD should be about balance and being at the nexus of positive change.

Discussion Questions

1. Where are you on the humanistic versus organizational effectiveness values continuum?

2. How strong are your measurement and data analytic skills? Do you understand linkage research and how to connect information across different levels of analysis?

3. How would you design an individual feedback framework for assessment and development? What tools would you select and why?

4. How would you describe your approach to coaching? What types of coaching engagements do you prefer and why?

5. Which professional associations and conferences are you engaged in and why? How many are focused on OD versus content or practice domain specific?

Resources

Links to the full studies of OD values by Shull, Church, and Burke (2014) and assessment practices of top development companies by Church and Rotolo (2013): http://c.ymcdn.com/sites/www.odnetwork.org/resource/resmgr/Center_for _Professional_Development/ODP-V46No4-Shull_Church_Burk.pdf www.apa .org/pubs/journals/features/cpb-a0034381.pdf

OD and Big Data: www.linkedin.com/in/allanchurch

References

Boudreau, J. W. 2010. *Retooling HR: Using Proven Business Tools to Make Better Decisions About Talent*. Boston: Harvard Business Press.

Burke, W. W. 1982. *Organization Development: Principles and Practices*. Boston: Little Brown.

Burke, W. W. 2011. *Organization Change: Theory and Practice*. 3rd ed. Thousand Oaks, CA: Sage.

Burke, W. W. 2014. "On the State of the Field: OD in 2014." *OD Practitioner* 46 (4): 8–11.

Burke, W. W., and G. H. Litwin. 1992. "A Causal Model of Organizational Performance and Change." *Journal of Management* 18: 523–545.

Burke, W. W., and D. A. Noumair. 2002. "The Role of Personality Assessment in Organization Development." In *Organization Development: A Data-Driven Approach to Organizational Change*, edited by J. Waclawski and A. H. Church, 55–77. San Francisco: Jossey-Bass.

Bushe, G. R., and R. J. Marshak. 2009. "Revisioning Organization Development: Diagnostic and Dialogic Premises and Patterns of Practice." *Journal of Applied Behavioral Science* 45: 348–368.

Church, A. H. 2001. "The Professionalization of Organization Development: The Next Step in an Evolving Field." In *Research in Organizational Change and Development, Vol. 13*, edited by R. W. Woodman and W. A. Pasmore, 1–42. Greenwich CT: JAI Press.

Church, A. H. 2013. "Engagement Is in the Eye of the Beholder: Understanding Differences in the OD vs. Talent Management Mindset." *OD Practitioner* 45 (2): 42–48.

Church, A. H. 2014. "What Do We Know About Developing Leadership Potential? The Role of OD in Strategic Talent Management." *OD Practitioner* 46 (3): 52–61.

Church, A. H., W. W. Burke, and D. F. Van Eynde. 1994. "Values, Motives, and Interventions of Organization Development Practitioners." *Group & Organization Management* 19 (1): 5–50.

Church, A. H., and S. Dutta. 2013. "The Promise of Big Data for OD: Old Wine in New Bottles or the Next Generation of Data-Driven Methods for Change?" *OD Practitioner* 45 (4): 23–31.

Church, A. H., and C. T. Rotolo. 2013. "How Are Top Companies Assessing Their High-Potentials and Senior Executives? A Talent Management Benchmark Study." *Consulting Psychology Journal: Practice & Research* 65 (3): 199–223.

Church, A. H., C. T. Rotolo, A. C. Shull, and M. D. Tuller. 2014. "Inclusive Organization Development: An Integration of Two Disciplines." In *Diversity at Work: The Practice of Inclusion*, edited by B. M. Ferdman and B. R. Deane, 260–295. San Francisco: Jossey-Bass.

Cummings, T. G., and C. G. Worley. 2015. *Organization Development & Change*. 10th ed. Stamford, CT: Cengage Learning.

Hernez-Broome, G., and L. A. Boyce, eds. 2011. *Advancing Executive Coaching: Setting the Course for Successful Leadership Coaching*. San Francisco: Wiley.

Laszlo, A., and K. C. Laszlo. 2011. "Systemic Sustainability in OD Practice: Bottom Line and Top Line Reasoning." *OD Practitioner* 43 (4): 10–16.

O'Toole, J. 1995. *Leading Change*. San Francisco: Jossey-Bass.

Shani, A. B., and D. Coghlan. 2014. "Action and Collaboration Between Scholarship and Practice: Core Values of OD Research." *OD Practitioner* 46 (4): 35–38.

Shull, A. C., A. H. Church, and W. W. Burke. 2013. "Attitudes About the Field of Organization Development 20 Years Later: The More Things Change, the More They Stay the Same." In *Research in Organizational Change and Development*, vol. 21, edited by A. B. Shani, W. A. Pasmore, R. W. Woodman, and D. A. Noumair, 1–28. Bingley, UK: Emerald Group.

Shull, A. C., A. H. Church, and W. W. Burke. 2014. "Something Old, Something New: Research Findings on the Practice and Values of OD." *OD Practitioner* 46 (4): 23–30.

Ulrich, D. 1997. *Human Resource Champions: The Next Agenda for Adding Value and Delivering Results*. Boston: Harvard Business School Press.

Waclawski, J., and A. H. Church, eds. 2002. *Organization Development: A Data-Driven Approach to Organizational Change*. San Francisco: Jossey-Bass.

Worley, C. G. 2014. "OD Values and Pitches in the Dirt." *OD Practitioner* 46 (4): 68–71.

CHAPTER THIRTY-THREE

Authors' Insights on Important Organization Development Issues

D. D. Warrick

For each new edition of the *Practicing Organization Development* book, I survey the contributing authors in the book to find out what they think about important issues in organization development (OD). The process generates valuable information for those interested in OD. The issues addressed in this edition are:

1. The relevancy and future of OD as compared with the 2010 survey
2. The most important OD concepts that should be taught to leaders and students
3. The keys to successful OD
4. The most important competencies OD practitioners should have
5. Favorite tasks for generating important information
6. Lessons learned in practicing global OD
7. The greatest challenges OD practitioners face in practicing OD

Each issue will be addressed with an overall perspective of the authors' comments followed by a summary of the major themes presented by the authors.

THE RELEVANCY AND FUTURE
OF ORGANIZATION DEVELOPMENT

You will see in Table 33.1 the results of how the current authors rated questions on the relevancy and future of OD as compared with ratings from the authors of the 2010 edition. The current authors are more optimistic about the relevance of OD and slightly less optimistic about the future of OD.

Summary of Major Themes: The Relevancy of Organization Development

- We live in a world of constant, unrelenting change, and OD is a discipline devoted to understanding and implementing effective change.

- How organizations manage OD and change will be critical to their present and future success.

- OD is a field where leaders and organizations should be familiar if they hope to succeed in a world of dynamic change and intense competition.

- Skills in managing change and building organizations capable of succeeding in today's times have become a major source of competitive advantage and OD specializes in these important areas.

- The speed and velocity of change in organizations and increased need to build organizations capable of succeeding in a complex, high-tech, global organization world, makes the help of skilled OD practitioners increasingly important.

- OD is one of the greatest methodologies for dealing with many of today's organization challenges and building healthy, high-performance organizations and managing change will be essential to the future success of organizations.

Summary of Major Themes: The Future of Organization Development

- The issues that OD addresses, such as change and transformation, will only increase in importance, and the future looks bright.

Table 33.1. The Relevance and Future of OD

How Relevant Is OD for Today's Organizations?			*How Bright Is the Future of OD?*		
Responses of Authors	*2010 Edition*	*2015 Edition*	*Responses of Authors*	*2010 Edition*	*2015 Edition*
Very relevant	75%	89%	Very bright	53%	41%
Somewhat relevant	18%	11%	Somewhat bright	35%	41%
Somewhat irrelevant	0%	0%	Not very bright	10%	18%
Very irrelevant	7%	0%	Definitely not bright	2%	0%

- There will be a growing need for knowledge and research in OD and especially in creating new models and knowledge on managing change.

- OD is continuing to evolve methods and applications such as being more global and focusing on large-scale change.

- More top-level leaders realize they need help with dealing with change, managing change, and building organizations for success.

- The challenge will be to advocate the need for OD while overcoming a mindset of economic rewards at any cost and doing everything faster and cheaper.

- There are concerns that OD has not been effective at: (1) making known what it can do; (2) becoming a field like HR that has name recognition; and (3) not screening and certifying those who practice OD to avoid being identified with poorly educated and trained practitioners who practice under the name of OD.

- OD is often presented under other labels, such as change management or organization transformation in practitioner books, textbooks, articles, and training sessions, which causes OD to lose its unique identity.

- There is a need for new champions and researchers in the field capable of promoting new theory, practice, research, and breakthrough paradigms in the field.

THE MOST IMPORTANT OD CONCEPTS THAT SHOULD BE TAUGHT TO LEADERS AND STUDENTS

The responses to listing the most important OD concepts that should be taught to leaders and students make you proud to be in OD. The field of OD has produced valuable concepts not just important to OD professionals. You could make a strong case that many OD concepts should be standard required knowledge for leaders and for preparing students in several majors for future success.

Summary of Major Themes: Important Concepts That Should Be Taught to Leaders and Students

- The purpose of OD according to Richard Beckard is to increase organizational effectiveness and health.

- OD models and theories for understanding, developing, and changing organizations.

- The importance and payoffs of pursuing both organizational effectiveness and health.

- The importance of self-awareness and feedback and organizational awareness and feedback.

- Action research and systems thinking as ways of approaching OD issues and change.
- How to design and implement changes.
- The importance of leader involvement and support in making changes.
- Interventions for improving the performance and effectiveness of individuals, teams, and organizations.
- Understanding the differences in healthy and unhealthy organizations.
- The importance of knowing reality before treating reality (using assessment methods to discover what is going on before designing solutions and processes).
- The importance of collaboration and involving the right stakeholders in identifying, planning, and implementing changes (whole system change).
- The importance of understanding process and content (how you do things is as important as what you do).
- How to build high-performance teams and understand the differences and purposes of action-oriented and experiential-oriented team-building methods.
- Understanding, building, and changing organization culture.
- How to transform organizations.
- The normative values underlying the field and the importance of values-based practices.
- How to change complex, global, virtual organizations.
- How to apply Appreciative Inquiry (AI).

THE KEYS TO SUCCESSFUL ORGANIZATION DEVELOPMENT

The next responses contain insightful information on the keys to successful OD. The most mentioned key was having a competent OD practitioner. This was closely followed by strong leader commitment and involvement.

Summary of Major Themes: Keys to Successful Organization Development

- Competent OD practitioner(s) who can build a trusting relationship with the client.
- Present models of what best-run organizations are like and data regarding the potential payoffs of building healthy, effective organizations and costs when you don't.

- Deliver a good contract for change with a clear understanding of the process, and realistic expectations and objectives aligned with the organization strategy.
- Engage with a willing client and strong leader buy-in and sponsorship.
- Building the top leadership team into an effective team committed to championing the change.
- Encourage full engagement of those who can best contribute to the success of the change.
- Prepare a useful assessment and agreed upon plan for feeding back and utilizing the data.
- Design a flexible change plan that keeps people engaged and achieves quick, convincing short-term and long-term results.
- Use a holistic and open frame of mind to meet the client where they are.
- Have a willingness to do what is right for the client including challenging present processes and practices.
- Use a positive approach to address issues and implement changes.
- Help others identify and solve their own challenges rather than playing the expert role.
- Educate managers and involve employees on theories and practices needed to build successful organizations and make changes successful.
- Frequent monitoring to know what is working and not working and what needs to be changed.
- Planned evaluation of the process and follow-through to assure that the changes are sustained.

THE MOST IMPORTANT COMPETENCIES OD PRACTITIONERS SHOULD HAVE

Being an effective OD practitioner, as in any profession, requires knowledge, practice, continuous learning, and growing. The responses from the authors identified several important competencies that OD practitioners should have.

Summary of Major Themes: Most Important Competencies OD Practitioners Should Have

- Knowledge of OD (purpose, history, values, concepts, interventions, past and present practices and skills, what makes organizations successful, the critical role of leadership).
- Interpersonal skills (passion for what you do, genuine concern for others, high self-awareness and willingness to learn, grow, and model what you

teach, ability to build trust, uplifting and humble attitude that promotes the success of others).

- Sound philosophical and ethical basis for practicing OD.
- Conceptual skills (ability to see things from a big picture, systems perspective and to conceptualize and design the interventions and change process that fit the needs of clients).
- Consultation skills (skills in gaining entry, proposal writing, contracting for change, teaching and communicating ideas, diagnosing what is going on, data collection, analysis, and feedback, implementing changes, accomplishing goals, learning from the process).
- Training and development skills and particularly skills in educating people on the importance of OD, change, and transformation.
- Skills in listening, facilitating, interviewing, conflict resolution, coaching, overcoming resistance to change, and giving candid, straightforward, helpful feedback.
- Understand business fundamentals.

FAVORITE TASKS FOR GENERATING IMPORTANT INFORMATION

Most OD practitioners facilitate groups to generate important information. The responses below provide a wide variety of approaches that can be used.

Summary of Major Themes: Favorite Tasks for Generating Information

- Create a safe environment for participants to speak freely (agree on protocol, prepare leaders to set the tone, plan proven processes for exploring ideas, visualizing the desired future, and addressing issues. etc.).
- Complete SWOT analysis (strengths, weaknesses, opportunities, threats).
- Engage in SOAR dialogue (strengths, opportunities, aspirations, results).
- Present and discuss best practices by the best organizations and benchmark how the organization is doing on key measures and what it could do to improve.
- Evaluate research regarding best practices such as what the best regarded organizations do to get the best results and have the best places to work do.
- Evaluate helpful information prepared from surveys, interviews, and other relevant sources.

- Develop a shared view of skilled leadership, high-performance teams, high-performance organizations, and a vision for the future and how to get there.
- Use Lewin's force-field analysis process to identify enablers and inhibitors of the desired state.
- Use Appreciative Inquiry (AI), Future Search, Open Space, large-group or whole system approaches, and other known methods.
- Have a well-chosen design team identify conversations, issues, or survey or interview questions that must be asked prior to a meeting of the people, and structure the meeting around their recommendations.

LESSONS LEARNED IN PRACTICING GLOBAL ORGANIZATION DEVELOPMENT

Even domestic organizations are not the same and practitioners must know and understand the organizations and culture they are working with, whether domestic or international. People and organizations around the globe have more similarities than differences and the OD principles used and the principles for personal and organizational success are likely to apply globally but need to be adapted to each unique organization. While differences in cultures are important, the differences and stereotypes are not universal even within cultures. Sometimes, there is too much of a focus on differences and too little focus on what the best organizations do around the world.

The following are lessons learned in practicing global OD:

Summary of Major Themes: Lessons Learned in Practicing Global Organization Development

- Make sure that senior leaders understand, embrace, and support what is being done.
- Partner with internal professionals who have a good understanding of the organization and culture.
- Work with the team or teams to plan processes and changes.
- Adapt to different cultures or organizations, which may mean using different methods such as a greater emphasis on anonymous and written activities rather than oral activities.
- Global OD practitioners must have the humility to learn, grow, and adapt to situations they may not be accustomed to.

THE GREATEST CHALLENGES OD PRACTITIONERS FACE

OD is a field for the times, as there is a great need for what OD studies, teaches, researches, and practices, and organizations are in need of what OD practitioners can provide. However, the authors are also realistic in their responses regarding the challenges in practicing OD. The responses are instructive about what OD practitioners must be prepared for.

Summary of Major Themes: Greatest Challenges in Practicing Organization Development

- Communicate the value and documented payoffs of OD.
- Know the difference between OD and change management.
- The short-term, cost-cutting, performance-at-any-cost mentality that leaders are often rewarded for that discourages engaging in OD thinking and processes.
- Developing faster, accelerated OD methods better adapted to changing times that accomplish more in less time.
- Make OD more technology savvy, especially in diagnosing organizations, building teams, working with virtual and international teams, and using social media to communicate and effect change.
- Lack of quality control over those practicing OD who may be well intended but are not well trained in OD.
- Understand the complexities of organizational change in today's rapidly changing and complex organization world.
- Greater experience and knowledge in applying OD to global environments.
- Encourage education in OD in academic and professional leadership training curriculums.

SUMMARY

The responses to the questions for this edition of *Practicing Organization Development* have provided a wealth of information for OD practitioners. There are reasons to be hopeful about the practice of OD as fully 100 percent of the respondents rated the relevancy of OD very relevant (89 percent) or somewhat relevant (11 percent). What could be more relevant for today's times than a field devoted to understanding how to build healthy, high-performance organizations and manage change? However, there are also legitimate concerns about the future of OD and the challenges in practicing OD. This would likely be true of almost any field in times of dynamic change, so let us hope that the champions in the field will rise to the challenge and continue to practice OD; teach OD; provide valuable books, articles, and research on OD; and keep the field relevant and a valuable contributor to the success of organizations.

Discussion Questions

1. Discuss each of the items in the chapter by commenting on what the author has said and then adding any additional insights.

2. Take time to review what chapters in the book can best help you address the issues, challenges, and suggested learning to be a most effective OD practitioner.

ABOUT THE EDITORS

William J. Rothwell, PhD, SPHR, CPLP Fellow (wjr9@psu.edu), is president of Rothwell & Associates, Inc. and Rothwell & Associates, LLC (see www.rothwellandassociates.com). He is professor in the Workforce Education and Development program and Department of Learning and Performance Systems at the Pennsylvania State University, University Park campus. He has authored, coauthored, edited, or coedited 300 books, book chapters, and articles—including over 90 books. He directs an online Master's degree program in Organization Development and Change at Penn State.

Before arriving at Penn State in 1993, he had 20 years of work experience as a training director and HR professional in government and business. He has also worked as a consultant for over 40 multinational corporations—including Motorola China, General Motors, Ford, and many others. In 2012, he earned ASTD's prestigious Distinguished Contribution to Workplace Learning and Performance Award, and in 2013 ASTD honored him by naming him as a Certified Professional in Learning and Performance (CPLP) Fellow. In 2014, he was given the Asia-Pacific International Personality Brandlaureate Award (www.thebrandlaureate.com/awards/ibp_bpa.php).

His recent books include *Beyond Training and Development*, 3rd ed. (HRD Press, 2015), *Career Planning and Succession Management*, 2nd ed. (Praeger, 2015), *Organization Development Fundamentals: Managing Strategic Change* (ATD Press, 2015), *The Competency Toolkit*, Second Edition (HRD Press, 2015), *Creating Engaged Employees: It's Worth the Investment* (ATD Press, 2014),

The Leader's Daily Role in Talent Management (Institute for Training and Development [Malaysia], 2014), *Optimizing Talent in the Federal Workforce* (Management Concepts, 2014), *Performance Consulting* (Wiley, 2014), the *ASTD Competency Study: The Training and Development Profession Redefined* (ASTD, 2013), *Becoming An Effective Mentoring Leader: Proven Strategies for Building Excellence in Your Organization* (McGraw-Hill, 2013), *Talent Management: A Step-by-Step Action-Oriented Approach Based on Best Practice* (HRD Press, 2012), the edited three-volume *Encyclopedia of Human Resource Management* (Wiley, 2012), *Lean But Agile: Rethink Workforce Planning and Gain a True Competitive Advantage* (Amacom, 2012), *Invaluable Knowledge: Securing Your Company's Technical Expertise-Recruiting and Retaining Top Talent, Transferring Technical Knowledge, Engaging High Performers* (Amacom, 2011), and *Competency-Based Training Basics* (ASTD Press, 2010).

Jacqueline M. Stavros (Jackie), DM (jstavros@ltu.edu), has 25 years of international experience in the fields of leadership, strategy, strategic planning, organization development and change, and marketing. Jackie is professor for the College of Management, Lawrence Technological University. She teaches leading change, strategic management, organization development, qualitative research design, creating sustainable business value, principles of management, and leadership. She integrates strengths-based, whole system, and sustainability concepts and practices such as Appreciative Inquiry (AI) and SOAR (www.soar-strategy.com) into her research, teaching, training, and consulting work.

She has coauthored five books, 16 book chapters, and 30 articles. Coauthored books include: *Practicing Organization Development: A Guide for Leading Change* (third edition), *Thin Book of SOAR: Building Strengths-Based Strategy*, *The First Appreciative Inquiry Handbook: For Leaders of Change*, and *Dynamic Relationships: Unleashing the Power of Appreciative Inquiry in Daily Living*.

She helps organizations identify and articulate their values, vision and mission statements, strategy, and strategic initiatives and build collaborative teams and communities for inspired action that centers on the positive strategic core. Clients include ACCI Business System, BAE Systems, Covenant Community Care, Fasteners, Inc., General Motors of Mexico, Jefferson Wells, Tendercare Healthcare Centers, PriceWaterhouseCoopers (PwC) Advisory University, Girl Scouts, National Education Association, Orbseal Technologies, and several automotive suppliers, nonprofit organizations, and higher education institutions. She has worked in 17 countries. She has done over 150 presentations on OD & Change, AI, Creating Sustainable Value, Positive Organizational Scholarship (POS), and SOAR at Australian Management Institute, Business Links, Cengage Learning (Asia/Pacific Rim), Hewlett-Packard, American Dietetic Association, PricewaterhouseCoopers, gedas USA, National City Bank, National Multiple Sclerosis

Society, Oakland Leadership, Linkage's National OD Conference, National Training Labs (NTL), and many national OD and management conferences.

She earned her doctorate in management at Weatherhead School of Management at Case Western Reserve University. Her dissertation title was *Capacity Building Using an Appreciative Approach: A Relational Process of Building Your Organization's Future.*

R**oland L. Sullivan** (R@rolandsullivan.com) learned directly from Lewin-led founders of the organization development profession at National Training Laboratories starting in 1962. He has led transformation efforts in over 1,000 organizations in 44 countries. He coined the phrase "Whole System Transformation"© (WST) in 1974. He has taught organization transformation around the world at 22 universities including Pepperdine (the most recognized international organization development program worldwide). He has received numerous national and international awards, especially for achieving transformative results, leading participative research on competencies for change agents and large group team-building summits in the context of enterprise-wide change.

There is a great deal of talk about transformation today. Roland is known for actually leading effective organization transformation efforts. His focus is on positive organization-wide change sustainment via the transference of change competency to an internal change agent. Many of Sullivan's cases leading change and transformation have been published. A recent client just became the "CIO of the Year" for Germany because of his ability to engage his organization via WST toward extraordinary client service. Roland's current professional competence development is to integrate intuitive yoga meditation practice, Whole Brain Literacy, and neuroleadership science research into his work. His greatest joy is to see his daughter, Arielle, following in his professional footsteps.

ABOUT THE CONTRIBUTORS

Billie Alban, MFA (albanb@aol.com), is President of Alban & Williams, Ltd. She teaches in executive development programs at Columbia, and other universities. She has served on the board of the Organization Development Network and the Board of Advisors of the Yale Divinity School. She has consulted in Latin America, Europe, the UK, and New Zealand. Billie speaks fluent Spanish.

Linda Ackerman Anderson, EdD (lindasaa@beingfirst.com), is co-founder and Vice-President of Being First, Inc., a training and consulting firm specializing in leading conscious transformation in Fortune 1000 companies, military, government, and large nonprofits. She helped define the field of organization transformation and speaks globally about transformation. She coauthored *The Change Leader's Roadmap: How to Navigate Your Organization's Transformation* and *Beyond Change Management: How to Achieve Breakthrough Results from Conscious Change Leadership*, and spearheaded the Change Leader's Roadmap Methodology. She coaches senior leaders on enterprise change strategies. Her clients include Pacific Gas and Electric, Lockheed Martin, Loblaw, PeaceHealth, Canadian Government, Shell, Intel, The Nature Conservancy, and Wachovia.

Warner Burke, Ph.D. (wwb3@columbia.edu), is the Edward Lee Thorndike Professor of Psychology and Education, founder of the .graduate programs in social-organizational psychology at Teachers College, Columbia University since 1979. He has consulted with a variety of organizations: corporate, nonprofits, educational institutions, and federal government agencies. Warner teaches leadership and organization change. Warner also co-directs the Eisenhower Leadership Development Program at the United States Military Academy, West Point. Warner's publications include 16 books and over 150 articles and book chapters. Warner was the original executive director of the OD Network and later was honored with the OD Network's Lifetime Achievement Award.

Gervase R. Bushe, Ph.D. (bushe@sfu.ca), is the Professor of Leadership and Organization Development at the Beedie School of Business, Simon Fraser University, Vancouver, Canada. He has published over 80 articles and books and won numerous awards for his research, including the McGregor Award twice. His book, *Clear Leadership*, has been translated into six languages. Gervase's research is supported by an active consulting and leadership development practice, and his Clear Leadership course is licensed by over 100 certified instructors, worldwide. With Bob Marshak, he has been defining the theory and practice of Dialogic Organization Development.

Steve H. Cady, Ph.D. (scady@bgsu.edu), is a professor, author, speaker, and consultant. As a graduate faculty member at BGSU, he serves as director of the Institute for Organizational Effectiveness. He has also served as director of the Master of OD Program and chief editor for the *OD Journal*. Steve's area of focus is on organizational behavior and psychology, change management, and OD. Prior to receiving his PhD in organizational behavior with a support area in research methods and psychology from Florida State University, Steve studied at the University of Central Florida where he obtained an MBA and a BSBA in finance.

Kim Cameron, Ph.D. (cameronk@bus.mich.edu), is a William Russell Kelly Professor of Management and Organizations in the Ross School of Business. He currently serves as associate dean of executive education in the Ross School. His research on organizational virtuousness, downsizing, effectiveness, corporate quality culture, and the development of leadership excellence has been published in more than 120 academic articles and 15 scholarly books. He is one of the co-founders of the Center for Positive Organizations at the University of Michigan and has served as dean at the Weatherhead School of Management at Case Western Reserve University.

L Mee-Yan Cheung-Judge, Ph.D. (lmycj@quality-equality.com), began her career as an academic and then in 1987 founded Quality and Equality Ltd. She is primarily an OD practitioner working with organizations on complex change issues. She combines consultancy work with speaking, writing, and delivering OD capability development programs across the world. She was voted one of the most influential thinkers in the United Kingdom by *HR Magazine* in 2008, 2012, and 2013. In 2013, she was presented with OD's highest award in the international field—the OD Network's Lifetime Achievement Award—in recognition of her outstanding contribution to the field of OD globally.

A llan H. Church, Ph.D. (allanhc@aol.com), is the vice president of OD Global Groups and Functions, and Executive Assessment at PepsiCo. Previously, he was a consultant with Warner Burke Associates and worked at IBM. He has served as an adjunct professor at Columbia University, a visiting scholar at Benedictine University, and past chair of the Mayflower Group. He has written over 150 articles and book chapters. Church received his PhD in organizational psychology from Columbia University. He is a fellow of the Society for Industrial-Organizational Psychology, the American Psychological Association, and the Association for Psychological Science.

D avid L. Cooperrider, Ph.D. (dlc6@case.edu), holds the Fairmont David L. Cooperrider Professorship in Appreciative Inquiry at the Weatherhead School of Management, Case Western Reserve University. He also is the honorary chair for the David L. Cooperrider Center for Appreciative Inquiry in the Stiller School of Business, Champlain College. As the co-creator and creative thought leader for Appreciative Inquiry, he has served as an advisor to senior executives around the world, including projects with five presidents and Nobel laureates, the UN, McKinsey, Boeing, and the U.S. Navy. He has published over 15 books and 50 articles.

T im Creasey (tcreasey@prosci.com) is a presenter, researcher, and thought leader on managing the people side of projects and initiatives to deliver results and outcomes. His work forms the foundation of change management body of knowledge. Through conference presentation, webinars, tutorials, and tools, he has advanced the discipline of change management, moving it toward a structured, rigorous approach for driving change success. Tim coauthored the book *Change Management: The People Side of Change* and led Prosci's last six benchmarking studies. He was instrumental in the development of Prosci's integrated approach and has worked to support leading organizations in building change agility and capability as a core competency.

Robert Crosby (rcrosby1909@hotmail.com) experienced his first T-Group at Boston University in 1953. In charge of the Methodist T-Group movement in the 1960s, he was elected an NTL Associate. In 1969, he founded Leadership Institute of Spokane/Seattle (LIOS). He started the first master of arts in the applied behavioral sciences in 1973. For 15 years, he led an Alcoa LIOS MA program with managers and steelworkers. Alcoa's Davenport plant was visited by President Obama to celebrate their productivity. They had 1,300 T-group participants over an eight-year period. He continues working with sons Gilmore and Chris in their business adaptation of the T-group, called Tough Stuff.

Thomas G. Cummings, Ph.D. (TCummings@marshall.usc.edu), is professor and chair of the Department of Management and Organization in the Marshall School of Business, University of Southern California. His research and teaching interests are strategic change and designing high-performance organizations. He has published 23 books, 83 journal articles, was founding editor of the *Journal of Management Inquiry*, and is a fellow of the Academy of Management. He was formerly president of the Western Academy of Management, Chair of the Organization Development and Change Division of the Academy of Management, and president of the Academy of Management.

Wesley E. Donahue, Ph.D., PE, PMP, (wdonahue@psu.edu), is associate professor and coordinator of Penn State's online Master of Professional Studies in Organization Development and Change program. Formerly, he was director of Penn State Management Development, a self-supporting provider of education and training services to business and industry clients around the world. Before joining Penn State, he was regional sales vice president for Mar-Kay Plastics in Kansas City, Missouri; co-founder and executive vice president of Leffler Systems of New Jersey, a manufacturing company; and manager of corporate development and international manager of technology for a Fortune 500 company, Brockway Inc.

Jeffrey H. Dyer, Ph.D. (jdyer@byu.edu), is the Horace Beesley Professor of Strategy at Brigham Young University. Jeff has published five times in both *Strategic Management Journal* and *Harvard Business Review*. His Harvard Press books, *The Innovator's DNA* and *The Innovator's Method* are best-sellers and his research has been featured in publications such as *Forbes*, *The Economist*, *Fortune*, *Businessweek*, *Wired*, *Entrepreneur*, and the *Wall Street Journal*.

W Gibb Dyer, Ph.D. (W_dyer@byu.edu), is the O. Leslie Stone Professor of Entrepreneurship and the academic director of the Center for Economic Self-Reliance in the Marriott School of Management at Brigham

Young University. He has served as a visiting professor at IESE in Barcelona, Spain, and was a visiting scholar at the University of Bath in England. He is currently an associate editor of the *Family Business Review*. He received his BS and MBA degrees from Brigham Young University and PhD in management philosophy from the Massachusetts Institute of Technology.

Ann E. Feyerherm, Ph.D. (Ann.Feyerherm@pepperdine.edu), is a department chair and professor of organization theory and management at Pepperdine's Graziadio School of Business and Management. Before earning her doctorate at USC, Ann spent 11 years in management at Procter & Gamble, where she was involved in organization design and manufacturing operations. She researches the role of leadership in interorganizational collaborations. Her work has been published in the *Leadership Quarterly, Journal of Applied Behavioral Science, The Graziadio Business Report, Organization Dynamics*, and the *OD Practitioner*. Dr. Feyerherm is a past chair of the Organization Development and Change Division of the Academy of Management.

Jane Galloway Seiling, MOD, Ph.D. (janeseiling@aol.com), is a retired consultant and educator, writer, editor, and support for PhD students writing their dissertations. She enjoys coauthoring with other academic scholars. Seiling's consulting was based on "the principles of membership" that underlie the responsibility of all members to contribute to the welfare of their organizations. She wrote *The Membership Organization: Achieving Top Performance in the New Workplace Community*, which won the 1998 SHRM Book of the Year Award, *The Meaning and Role of Organizational Advocacy: Responsibility and Accountability in the Workplace* (2001), and is currently coauthoring *Change Capacity: Leading Change and Capacity Building in Nonprofits*.

Lindsey N. Godwin, Ph.D. (godwin@champlain.edu), is an associate professor of management in the Robert P. Stiller School of Business at Champlain College, where she serves as the academic director of the David L. Cooperrider Center for Appreciative Inquiry. As an active positive OD scholar, she recently guest edited a special issue on positive organizational ethics for the *Journal of Business Ethics*, as well as a special issue on advances in the AI Summit for the *AI Practitioner Journal*. As an active positive OD practitioner, she has consulted with organizations around the world using Appreciative Inquiry to help organizations create positive change.

Marshall Goldsmith, Ph.D. (Marshall@marshallgoldsmith.com), was recognized as one the Top Ten Most Influential Business Thinkers in the World—and top-rated executive coach at the 2013 biennial Thinkers 50 Ceremony in London. His 34 books have sold over two million copies. He has written two *New York Times* bestsellers, *MOJO* and *What Got You Here*

Won't Get You There—a *Wall Street Journal* #1 business book and winner of the Harold Longman Award for Business Book of the Year. Marshall has produced 50 short videos with Thinkers50, from nearly four decades of experience with top executives. He earned a Ph.D. from UCLA Anderson School of Management in Los Angeles, California.

David W. Jamieson, Ph.D. (djamieson@stthomas.edu), is professor and department chair, Organization Learning & Development at the University of St. Thomas. He is also president of the Jamieson Consulting Group, Inc., and practicum director for the MS in Organization Development Program at American University. He has 40 years of experience consulting to organizations on leadership, change, strategy, design, and human resource issues. He currently serves as convener for the OD Education Association. He has published five books, 14 chapters, and numerous articles in journals and newsletters, and serves on three editorial review boards.

Amy Kates (amy@kateskesler.com) is a managing partner in the firm Kates Kesler Organization Consulting. She works with leaders around the world and across industries to shape effective organizations. She teaches organization design in the executive MBA program at the Danish Business School in Copenhagen, at Ashridge University in London, and Cornell University in New York. She is a board member of the Organization Design Community. Amy is the coauthor, with Greg Kesler, of *Leading Organization Design* (Jossey-Bass, 2011) and, with Jay Galbraith, of *Designing Your Organization* (Jossey-Bass, 2007) among other books. Amy has a master's degree from Cornell University.

Judith H. Katz (judithkatz@kjcg.com) brings more than 30 years of experience to her consulting work in strategic culture change. Judith has consulted with many organizations, including Allstate, Cisco Systems, Dun and Bradstreet, E. I. du Pont de Nemours and Company, Eileen Fisher, Singapore Telecommunications Ltd., Toyota Motor Sales, and United Airlines. In 1985, she joined The Kaleel Jamison Consulting Group, Inc., and serves as executive vice president. She is the coauthor with Frederick Miller of *Be BIG: Step Up, Step Out, Be Bold* (2008) and *The Inclusion Breakthrough: Unleashing the Real Power of Diversity* (2002). In 2007, she was recognized for her work by *Profiles in Diversity Journal*.

Taesung Kim, Ph.D. (tzk5085@psu.edu), earned his Ph.D. in the Workforce Education and Development (WFED) Program with an emphasis in HRD/OD at The Pennsylvania State University. He received both his BA in education and MEd. in HRD at Yonsei University in South Korea. He has over 10 years of extensive experience in the HRD/OD field as an internal manager and an external consultant, and most recently worked for KPMG Korea as a senior manager in the Learning and Development Center. He is currently working as a faculty curriculum assistant in WFED and a faculty member in human resources and employment relations at Penn State.

Patricia **Malone**, DBA (pritzlermalone@yahoo.com), is presently senior director of business process transformation at SunEdison, Inc. She holds an MBA from Ohio State University and a DBA from Lawrence Technological University. Patricia has extensive experience in leading transformational change, Lean Six Sigma Methodologies, business excellence, and finance. Her research interests include strategy, building strategic capacity, SOAR, positive organizational scholarship, and organization development.

Mitchell **Lee Marks,** Ph.D. (marks@sfsu.edu), is professor of leadership in the College of Business at San Francisco State University and president of the consulting firm JoiningForces.org. His research and consulting focuses on teambuilding, strategic direction, corporate culture, and the planning and implementation of mergers and acquisitions, restructurings, leadership succession, and other workplace transitions. He has authored eight books, including *Charging Back up the Hill: Workplace Recovery after Mergers, Acquisitions and Downsizings*, and scores of articles in academic and practitioner journals. His Ph.D. in organizational psychology is from the University of Michigan.

Robert **J. Marshak**, Ph.D. (bobmarshak@aol.com), is distinguished scholar in residence for OD programs at American University, Washington, DC, and has been an organizational consultant for more than 40 years. He has published three books and more than 85 articles and book chapters on organizational consulting and change, served on the board of directors of NTL Institute and the OD Network, and was the acting editor of the *Journal of Applied Behavioral Science*. His current interests include defining, with Gervase Bushe, the theory and practice of Dialogic Organization Development. Bob is a recipient of the OD Network's Lifetime Achievement Award.

Jon **McNaughtan** (jonmcnau@umich.edu) is a doctoral student at the University of Michigan, where his research interests focus on the intersection of employee well-being, sense of purpose, and how those constructs affect turnover. Before attending the University of Michigan, he served as the President's Council fellow at Southern Utah University where he worked on the executive leadership team to transform the university from a regional comprehensive institution to the state-designated liberal arts and sciences institution. In addition to his role as the fellow, he served as the associate director of the Michael O. Leavitt Center for Politics and Public Service.

Frederick A. Miller (familler@kjcg.com) is the CEO of The Kaleel Jamison Consulting Group, Inc. He has 30 years of experience developing and implementing strategies that increase engagement, team and individual performance, and culture alignment with organizations. He is the coauthor with Judith Katz of *Be BIG: Step Up, Step Out, Be Bold* (2008) and *The Inclusion Breakthrough: Unleashing the Real Power of Diversity* (2002). Frederick was recognized for his work and named one of 40 Pioneers of Diversity by *Profiles in Diversity Journal* (2007). He was also noted as one of the forerunners of corporate change in *The Age of Heretics* (Currency Doubleday, 1996).

Sheryl A. Milz, Ph.D. (sheryl.milz@utoledo.edu), is the chair and associate professor in the Department of Public Health and Preventive Medicine in the College of Medicine and Life Sciences at the University of Toledo. She is also a co-director of the Northwest Ohio Consortium for Public Health. She is a graduate student in the Master of Organization Development program at Bowling Green State University.

Matt Minahan, Ph.D. (matthew@minahangroup.com), has over 30 years experience in strategic planning, organization design and development, executive coaching, and leadership development. His consulting practice focuses on those who are planning strategic change programs. He is a volunteer and former board member of NTL Institute, where he is a dean and staff member of both its Human Interaction Laboratory and Interpersonal Skills for Leadership Success T-group. He holds an adjunct faculty appointment in the School of Public Affairs at American University and is a visiting professor in several doctoral programs. He is the 2015 chair of the Board of Trustees of the Organization Development Network.

Philip H. Mirvis, Ph.D. (Pmirv@aol.com), is an organizational psychologist whose studies and private practice concern large-scale organizational change, characteristics of the workforce and workplace, and business leadership in society. An advisor to companies and NGOs on five continents, he has authored 12 books including, with Mitchell Marks, *Joining Forces: Making One plus One Equal Three in Mergers, Acquisitions, and Alliances*. Mirvis was recognized as Distinguished Scholar-Practitioner by the Academy of Management and teaches in executive education programs in business schools around the world. His PhD in organizational psychology is from the University of Michigan.

Rachael L. Narel, CISA (rlnarel@hotmail.com), is engagement manager at an IT consulting company leading their Business Intelligence practice area. Rachael has spent over 13 years in various leadership, product development, customer development, marketing, and operational roles at a controls and analytics software company working closely with customers and team members on several of their product lines. She is pursuing a Ph.D. in organization development at Benedictine University where she also earned her master of science in management and organization behavior. She has a bachelor of science degree in psychology and biology from Saint Xavier University and is a certified technical trainer.

Jong Gyu Park (pvj5055@psu.edu) is a Ph.D. candidate in the Workforce Education and Development program, with an emphasis on human resource development and organization development, at Pennsylvania State University. He is also a PhD candidate in business administration, with an emphasis on management, at Sungkyunkwan University School of Business in Seoul, South Korea. Before studying at Penn State, he was a management consultant at Deloitte and Towers Watson.

D Scott Ross (sross@Prosci.com) is a master instructor for Prosci, Inc. He is also president of Cue 7 Consortium, Inc., a change management consulting firm in Minneapolis-St. Paul, Minnesota. He has broad experience managing change involving large-scale systems and processes, regulatory and compliance, and product development in the United States, Europe, and Asia. His industry experience includes medical devices, computers and electronics, software, wholesaling, manufacturing, financial services, education, and non-profits. Prior to consulting, he was employed by Amdura (formerly known as American Hoist & Derrick), serving as corporate vice president, responsible for strategic planning, communications, and special projects.

Edgar Schein, Ph.D. (scheine@comcast.net), received his doctorate in social psychology from Harvard in 1952, worked at the Walter Reed Institute of Research and then joined MIT in 1956. He has published extensively. He continues to consult and recently has published a book on the general theory and practice of giving and receiving help, *Helping* (2009), as well as *Humble Inquiry* (2013), which won the 2013 business book of the year award from the International Leadership Association. He is the 2009 recipient of the Distinguished Scholar-Practitioner Award of the Academy of Management, the 2012 recipient of the Lifetime Achievement Award from the International Leadership Association, and has an honorary doctorate from the IEDC Bled School of Management in Slovenia.

John J. Scherer, Ph.D. (john@scherercenter.com), is an international respected consultant, speaker, writer, and change facilitator with organizations and their leaders, including Boeing, GTE, the government of Canada,

Unilever, DHL, Netia, Aetna and many others. Leaders from 28 countries have graduated from his Executive/Leadership Development Intensives (EDI/LDI). Honored by *Executive Excellence* magazine as one of America's Top 100 Thought Leaders in Personal/Leadership Development, since 2008 he has been writing, speaking, consulting, and producing videos from his base in Krakow, Poland. John is also co-creator of the LIOS MA-ABS program, and currently co-director of Scherer Leadership International and creator of WiserAtWork .com.

L eslie E. Sekerka, Ph.D. (lsekerka@menlo.edu), focuses on research in areas of character strength in personal and organizational growth, ethical decision-making, and moral courage in the workplace. Her book, *Ethics Training in Action*, highlights best practices in organizational ethics training. As founder/director of the Ethics in Action Research and Education Center, she works with Silicon Valley business leaders on ethical issues. She is an academic partner at Santa Clara University's Markkula Center for Applied Ethics. She is known globally as a business ethics specialist, providing workshops and seminars to help advance employees' moral competencies and build organizational ethical strength. She received her Ph.D. in organizational behavior from Case Western Reserve University.

G ail Severini (gailseverini@symphini.com) has partnered with business leaders executing global strategies such as product development, operational excellence, business model innovation, customer centricity and health care reform for over 20 years. She has a visceral understanding of the real challenges of transformation. Clients have included: Manulife Financial, Royal Bank of Canada, Trillium Health Centre, Canadian Blood Services, Highmark Blue Cross Blue Shield, and HSBC. Gail publishes on her blog, *Change Whisperer*, and speaks often on strategy execution. She leads Symphini Change Management, Inc., and is an associate with Conner Partners.

Z achary D. Shoup (zacshoup@gmail.com) has 10 years' expertise from varied angles including the behavioral sciences and management. He obtained a master of organization development from Bowling Green State University. Zac's area of focus includes organizational change, leadership development, and innovation.

A manda C. Shull, Ph.D. (amanda_shull@glic.com), is senior manager of talent and organization capability at Guardian Life. She leads enterprise-wide talent management, with responsibility for design and delivery of all core talent processes. Prior to joining Guardian, Amanda was manager of organization and management development at PepsiCo. Amanda completed her Ph.D. in social-organizational psychology at Teachers College, Columbia

University. She is an author of several book chapters and peer-reviewed journal articles and is an active research contributor and presenter at professional conferences.

Peter F. Sorensen, Ph.D. (psorensen@ben.edu), is professor and director of the Ph.D. program in organization development, and the MS program in management and organizational behavior at Benedictine University. He has authored more than 300 articles, papers, and books, including a number of best paper selections. His work has appeared in the *Academy of Management Journal, Group and Organization Studies, Leadership and Organization Development Journal, Journal of Management Studies*, and *Organization and Administrative Science*, among others. He has been chair of the ODC Division of Academy of Management, and serves on editorial boards for *OD Journal*, the *OD Practitioner*, and the French journal *RSDG* (*Revue Sciences de Gestion*).

Karen Stephenson, Ph.D. (karenor182@gmail.com), began as a quantum chemist and ended as a classically trained Harvard anthropologist. In 2013, she was appointed the H. Smith Richardson Fellow by the Center for Creative Leadership. She was the first Katherine Houghton Hepburn Fellow for her groundbreaking work in the social sciences. She was noted in Business 2.0 as "The Organization Woman" and distinguished in Random House's *Guide to the Management Gurus*. She was featured in *The New Yorker* by Malcolm Gladwell for her research on the workplace and corporate office. She has taught at UCLA and Harvard, and she now lectures at Yale University as well as Erasmus University in the Netherlands.

Ann M. Van Eron, Ph.D. (avaneron@potentials.com), is principal of Potentials, a global coaching and organization development consulting firm. She has coached leaders, teams, and organizations for over 30 years. Ann provides leadership development and teaches leaders how to be effective in coaching their teams. She assists teams and organizations in creating cultures of respect with mindful conversations for results using proven OASIS Moves®. Clients include Fortune 100 corporations, government and nongovernmental organizations, health care, nonprofit, and privately held companies. Ann is a faculty member and certifies executive coaches as a master coach for the International Coach Federation. She earned her Ph.D. from Columbia University.

DD. Warrick, Ph.D. (DDWarrick@aol.com), is an educator, author, and consultant. He is a professor of management and organization change at the University of Colorado, Colorado Springs, where he received the Chancellor's Award and holds the lifetime title of President's Teaching Scholar. He is the author/coauthor of eight books and over 90 articles, book chapters, and professional papers. He has received many awards, including the Outstanding Organization Development Practitioner of the Year, the Outstanding Human Resources Professional of the Year, and the Best Professor in Organizational Development. He received his BBA and MBA from the University of Oklahoma and doctorate from University of Southern California.

Marvin Weisbord, Ph.D. (mweisbord@futuresearch.net), was for 50 years a manager, teacher, researcher, writer, and consultant to companies and communities worldwide. His book, *Productive Workplaces* (third edition) was named Best Business Book on Organizational Culture by *strategy+business* in 2012. He also authored *Organizational Diagnosis* and *Discovering Common Ground*. He was a partner in the consulting firm Block Petrella Weisbord, a member of NTL Institute, the European Institute for Transnational Studies, and the World Academy of Productivity Science. He co-founded Future Search Network with Sandra Janoff. They are coauthors of *Future Search* and *Don't Just Do Something, Stand There!*

Alan Weiss (www.summitconsulting.com) has been honored as a Fellow of the Institute of Management Consultants and inducted into the Hall of Fame of the National Speakers Association. He is the only nonjournalist in history to receive the Lifetime Achievement Award from the American Press Institute. He has written 55 books appearing in 12 languages. His client list has included organizations such as IBM, Mercedes, Merck, HP, Toyota, JPMorgan Chase, and the Federal Reserve, among hundreds of others. His best-selling *Million Dollar Consulting* (McGraw-Hill) has been on the shelves through four editions and over 20 years.

Therese F. Yaeger, Ph.D. (Tyaeger@ben.edu), is professor at Benedictine University in the Ph.D. OD and MS management and organizational behavior programs. Managerial and consulting roles during her 25-year professional career have included manufacturing, small business, government, and military organizations. Publications include *Critical Issues in Organization Development: Case Studies for Analysis and Discussion* with Sorensen and Johnson (2013), *Global Organization Development: Managing Unprecedented Change* with Sorensen and Head (2006), and *Appreciative Inquiry: Foundations in Positive Organization Development* with Cooperrider, Sorensen, and Whitney (2005). Yaeger was Chair of Management Consulting Division of Academy of Management. She is former president of the Midwest Academy of Management.

Nadya Zhexembayeva, Ph.D. (nadya.zhexembayeva@gmail.com), is a business owner, author, and educator working in innovation, leadership, and sustainable growth. Her client engagements include Coca-Cola Company, ERG (formerly ENRC PLC), Erste Bank, Henkel, Knauf Insulation, and Vienna Insurance Group. Nadya also served as the Coca-Cola Chaired Professor of Sustainable Development at IEDC-Bled School of Management, an executive education center based in Slovene Alps, where she continues to teach courses in leadership strategy, change management, and sustainability. She coauthored with Chris Laszlo (2011), *Embedded Sustainability: The Next Big Competitive Advantage* and then wrote *Overfished Ocean Strategy: Powering Up Innovation for a Resource-Deprived World* (2014).

INDEX

Page references followed by *fig* indicate an illustrated figure; followed by *t* indicate a table; followed by *e* indicate an exhibit.

Self-awareness: as component of transformational leadership, 80; creating, 83–84; know thyself for, 84–85; self-directed ethics and, 351–352

Self-managed work teams, 30–31

Self-management competency, 118–119

Seligman, M. E., 82, 100, 110, 111

Semeijn, J. H., 119

Senge, P. M., 76, 163, 275

Separation: OD competencies for, 129t; perpetual and instantaneous positive change model phase of, 52

September 11, 2001, 338

Sethi, D., 92

Severini, G., 330

Shani, A. B., 275, 419

"Sharing street corners," 369fig, 372

Sharkey, J., 338

Shaw, P., 411, 415

Shechtman, D., 160

Shepard, H., 29, 33, 36, 158, 235

Shepard, K., 127

Sherwood, J., 37

Shevat, A., 37

Shoup, Z. D., 117

Shull, A. C., 419, 422, 424

Sims, C., 366

Simultaneity principle, 102

The Six Box Model, 175

Sminia, H., 78

Smith, C., 15

Smith, J., 249, 250–254

Smither, R., 164, 165, 168

Smollan, R. K., 54

Snowden, D. J., 414

Snyderman, B., 32

SOAR framework: aligning and magnifying strengths using, 111; applications in different types of

organizations, 288t–289; description of, 287–288; the 5-I approach to using the, 289fig–291; historical perspective on, 286; for launching transformation, 72; linking strategy and OD, 286–287; overview of, 285–286; personal care division (PCD) team transformation using, 291–299; SOAR dialogue for generating information, 434

Sobczak, S., 402

Social constructionism, 96, 97

Social media marketing tools, 146

The Social Psychology of Organizations (Katz and Kahn), 38

Society for Human Resource Management (SHRM), 126–127; competency framework developed by, 124; increased membership of, 2

Society for Industrial and Organizational Psychology (SIOP), 120, 124–125

Socio-technical consulting, 30–31

Solga, M., 79

Sorensen, P. F., 101, 376, 379, 380

Southwest Airlines, 261

Spalding, J., 197

Speaking engagements, 146–147

Sponsors: definition of, 19; identifying the client and, 156–157

Spreitzer, G. M., 111, 340, 342

Srivastva, S., 35, 44, 96, 99, 100, 101, 310

Staats, B., 224

Stacey, R., 412, 415

Stakeholder engagement: in action planning, 184, 185e, 191; during change implementation, 189e; for successful transformation, 73